PRIVATE PROFITS VERSUS PUBLIC POLICY

The Pharmaceutical Industry and the Canadian State

The widespread condemnation of drastic price increases on life-saving drugs highlights our growing dependency on and vulnerability to international pharmaceutical conglomerates. However, aren't the interests of the public supposed to supersede the pursuit of private profit?

In his new work, *Private Profits versus Public Policy*, Joel Lexchin addresses this question as he examines how public policy with respect to the pharmaceutical industry has evolved in Canada over the past half century. Although the Canadian government is supposed to regulate the industry to serve the needs of public health, waves of deregulatory reforms and intellectual property rights legislation have shifted the balance of power in favour of these companies' quest for profit. Joel Lexchin offers a series of recommendations to tip the scale back in the public's favour. This enlightening work is the first book that deals exclusively with the pharmaceutical industry in Canada in over thirty years.

JOEL LEXCHIN is a Fellow of the Canadian Academy of Health Sciences. He is a professor in the School of Health Policy and Management at York University and works as an emergency physician at the University Health Network.

JOEL LEXCHIN

Private Profits versus Public Policy

The Pharmaceutical Industry and the Canadian State

UNIVERSITY OF TORONTO PRESS
Toronto Buffalo London

Toronto Buffalo London
www.utppublishing.com
Printed and bound by CPI Group (UK) Ltd, Croydon, CR0 4YY

ISBN 978-1-4426-4917-0 (cloth) ISBN 978-1-4426-2659-1 (paper)

Library and Archives Canada Cataloguing in Publication

Lexchin, Joel, 1948–, author
Private profits versus public policy : the pharmaceutical industry and the Canadian state / Joel Lexchin.

Includes bibliographical references and index.
ISBN 978-1-4426-4917-0 (cloth). ISBN 978-1-4426-2659-1 (paper)

1. Pharmaceutical industry – Government policy – Canada. 2. Drug development – Government policy – Canada. 3. Prescription pricing – Government policy – Canada. 4. Profit – Government policy – Canada. I. Title.

HD9670.C22L48546 2016 338.4'761510971 C2016-902984-0

This book has been published with the help of a grant from the Federation for the Humanities and Social Sciences, through the Awards to Scholarly Publications Program, using funds provided by the Social Sciences and Humanities Research Council of Canada.

University of Toronto Press acknowledges the financial assistance to its publishing program of the Canada Council for the Arts and the Ontario Arts Council, an agency of the government of Ontario.

Canada Council for the Arts Conseil des Arts du Canada

Funded by the Government of Canada Financé par le gouvernement du Canada

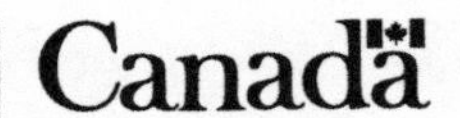

Contents

List of boxes, figures, and tables

Boxes

Figures

Tables

Preface

This excellent, thoroughly researched book, *Private Profits versus Public Policy: The Pharmaceutical Industry and the Canadian State,* examines the nature and causes of a serious, health-threatening problem hardly unique to Canada, the United States, or anywhere else. Readers from around the world will find extensive evidence of the well-documented imbalance between the powerful pharmaceutical industry and the more subservient government entities tasked with regulating it. The predictable outcomes are public policies tilted more towards the economic well-being of the industry and its investors than to the health needs of the public. Using publicly available documents and other information, mostly from Canada but frighteningly familiar and often applicable to the United States and most other countries, Lexchin concludes with a discussion of specific remedies that could benefit much of the world.

The book's two major topics of critical analyses are, first, inadequate government regulation over the processes of determining efficacy and safety, approvability, transparency of drug testing data, and controls on promotion of pharmaceuticals. The second includes problems with intellectual property rights, domestic price controls, and national governments' responsibility to help people in developing countries – called the Global South – to obtain drugs at lower prices by advocating for compulsory licensing.

For the past two decades, in both Canada and the United States, the drug industry has formally been the major client of their respective drug agencies, Health Canada and the Food and Drug Administration (FDA). Although the main client of a government drug regulatory agency should be the public – with public funding and public health foremost in its priorities – massive, direct drug industry funding of these two agencies, which started in the 1990s, has further shifted the balance of power towards what is best for the industry. In 2015, via the US Prescription Drug User Fee Act (PDUFA), more than US$750 million of drug industry money went to the FDA, and an estimated one-half of Health Canada's budget for drugs came from that industry.

A report authored by a major auditing company and cited in this book states that user fees are "a means of transferring some or all of the costs of a government activity from the general taxpayer to those who more directly benefit from or who 'trigger' that special activity." And from inside Health Canada, an official advised staff that "the client is the direct recipient of your services. In many cases this is the person or company who pays for the service."

In a 1998 survey by Public Citizen of FDA physicians who review drugs (medical officers), by which time the PDUFA effect had clearly sunk in, many of the 53 respondents expressed concern that drugs they thought should not have been approved had been approved, despite negative safety conclusions, with many saying that standards of safety and efficacy had been weakened since the 1992 passage of the law. Nineteen medical officers stated they thought that 27 of the approved new drugs they had reviewed in the previous three years should not have been approved. Twelve medical officers identified 25 new drugs that they had reviewed in the past three years that in their opinion had been approved too fast.

Drug industry influence over government regulation is not limited to its direct impact on the drug regulatory agencies themselves, via user fees, influence on advisory committees, and the selection of industry-favouring officials to run the agencies. Equally dangerous are the drug industry's impacts on the legislative process, getting more favourable laws written through massive lobbying efforts and cash donations to members of the legislature. All this adds to the imbalance of power, with government goals more and more closely aligned with those of the industry.

The book's discussion of the myriad serious problems in evaluating and regulating the safety of drugs shows that they are closely related to the lack of government adherence to the precautionary principle. Paraphrased, in the context of drug safety, this principle should mean that if a drug has no unique benefit, in comparison with other drugs for the same disease, but has a clear or strongly suspected unique risk that is known before approval, it should not be allowed on the market. If the risk is discovered only after the drug is on the market, it should be promptly withdrawn. To do less is to dangerously transform a precautionary, preventive public safety principle into one of "managing" risks that should not be tolerated. This default of managing risks is one that is frequently accompanied by inadequate, industry-friendly government determinations of the benefit-risk ratio of drugs, either before or after approval.

In the United States, the FDA has regulatory authority over prescription drug advertising, but it has recently been required to go through a series of bureaucratic delays before concluding a violation has occurred, significantly reducing the timeliness and volume of government advertising regulation. In Canada, the voluntary, independent Pharmaceutical Advertising Advisory Board (PAAB) is financed by drug companies paying to have their advertisements reviewed. As further evidence that this important government function has been weakened, PAAB decisions are neither legally binding nor enforceable. Poor enforcement of drug advertising results in doctors being misled into thinking some drugs are safer and more effective than they are, to the detriment of their patients' health.

Lexchin includes an excellent analysis of how drug prices bear little if any relationship to the actual costs of their research and development but are linked to what the market will bear, that is, to achieving the largest profit possible. But once this is determined for the first drug in a therapeutic class, the Canadian government allows subsequent entrants to that class to charge the same price, even without evidence that the second or third drug has any benefit in efficacy or safety compared with the first. Such indefensibly high prices inflict a toll on many patients: in Canada, people with lower household incomes, under $20,000 a year, are only one-tenth as likely as those with incomes greater than $80,000 to be able to afford the drugs they are prescribed, creating what is described as *cost-related non-adherence.*

The editors at the International Society of Drug Bulletins (ISDB) have articulated three separate concepts that are accepted as drug innovation:

- The commercial concept: any *newly marketed* me-too product, new substances, new indications, new formulations, and new treatment methods.
- The technology concept: any *industrial innovation,* such as the use of biotechnology, or the introduction of a new substance delivery system (patch, spray, etc.), or selection of an isomer or a metabolite.
- The *therapeutic advance* concept: a new treatment that benefits patients when compared with previously existing options.

In the absence of this *therapeutic advance,* the first two kinds of "innovative" products are too often created entirely for the financial interests of drug companies. But *therapeutic advance*, a drug with a benefit-risk ratio superior to its predecessors, clearly benefits patients and the innovative company that developed the therapeutically advanced drug. However, the industry domination of the drug approval and pricing processes weighs heavily against therapeutic advances for the large number of diseases for which drugs are available. First, the government approval standard does not include a requirement for testing against the best approved drug for the disease, thus usually precluding the possibility of finding the new drug to be superior. Second, as mentioned above, the Canadian government will allow the same high price for subsequent drugs as long as they are treatments in the same therapeutic class, despite a lack of superiority.

Regulatory authorities that frequently allow the first two kinds of innovation, devoid of the third, are doing a much better job of serving the interests of their client, the drug industry, than of advancing public health.

Despite the implicit despair embodied in this analysis of the powerful drug industry, Lexchin ends the book with a chapter of optimism, beginning with the words of one of Canada's most brilliant and successful political figures, Tommy Douglas, a social democrat and the father of Canada's single-payer health system, who said, "Courage, my friends; 'tis not too late to build a better world."

As was the case with Douglas, whose accomplishments were heavily dependent on a groundswell of strong public participation and action, Lexchin points to the need for the same strong-willed leadership supported by the public to build a better world in which the pharmaceutical industry would be doing much more to provide affordable products that are more effective and safer than those currently used.

The comprehensive list of 48 specific recommended changes at the end of the book, many of which are applicable to many countries, includes a variety of ways that this dangerous imbalance between pharmaceutical industry goals and public needs throughout the world can be safely reduced, with rejuvenated governments moving back to the more legitimate role of a partner with the public rather than with the industry.

In case this preface or the book sounds rhetorical in terms of the currently mismatched power of the pharmaceutical industry, Lexchin recalls the advice of Milton Friedman, a Nobel Prize–winning free-market economist: "Few trends could so thoroughly undermine the foundation of our free society as the acceptance by corporation officials of a social responsibility other than to make as much money for their shareholders as possible." Friedman's faith in market solutions to most problems would probably have precluded him from even imagining that important parts of the business model of making as much money as possible are massive pharmaceutical industry criminal and civil penalties for violating US laws concerning their products, violations that typically have yielded more profits than penalties paid and thus continue. Public Citizen's database of such violations, from 1991 through 2015, has documented more than US$35 billion in such government penalties.

Social responsibility? Undermining the foundation of our free society? Is this how the free market functions?

Sidney M. Wolfe, MD
Founder and Senior Advisor, Public Citizen's
Health Research Group and WorstPills.org

Abbreviations

ACTA	Anti-Counterfeiting Trade Agreement
ADR	adverse drug reaction
AE	adverse event
AG	auditor general
ARR	absolute risk reduction
ASC	Advertising Standards Canada
AZT	zidovudine
BGTD	Biologics and Genetic Therapies Directorate
BMS	Bristol-Meyers-Squibb
BTS	Business Transformation Strategy
CAMR	Canada's Access to Medicines Regime
CBC	Canadian Broadcasting Corporation
CDA	Canadian Diabetes Association
CDR	Common Drug Review
CETA	Comprehensive Economic and Trade Agreement
CGPA	Canadian Generic Pharmaceutical Association
CIHR	Canadian Institutes of Health Research
CMAJ	Canadian Medical Association Journal
COI	conflict of interest
CPMA	Canadian Pharmaceutical Manufacturers Association
CRO	Contract Research Organization
DES	diethylstilbestrol
DFAIT	Department of Foreign Affairs and International Trade
DIN	drug identification number
DSEN	Drug Safety and Effectiveness Network
DTCA	direct-to-consumer advertising
EAC	Expert Advisory Committee

EMA	European Medicines Agency
EU	European Union
FDA	Food and Drug Administration
F&DAct	Food and Drugs Act
FDD	Food and Drug Directorate
FTE	full time equivalent
FTA	Free Trade Agreement
GD-R	Government Directive on Regulating
GMP	Good Manufacturing Practices
HPB	Health Protection Branch
ICH	International Conference on Harmonization of Technical Requirements for Registration of Pharmaceuticals for Human Use
IND	Investigational New Drug
IPR	intellectual property right
IPRC	Industry Practices Review Committee
ISDB	International Society of Drug Bulletins
ISDS	investor state dispute settlement
LDC	least developed country
MEDEC	Canada's Medical Technology Companies
MHPD	Marketed Health Products Directorate
MRC	Medical Research Council
NAFTA	North American Free Trade Agreement
NAICS	North American Industry Classification System
NAS	new active substance
NCD	non-communicable disease
NCEHR	National Council on Ethics in Human Research
NDP	New Democratic Party
NGO	non-governmental organization
NICE	National Institute for Health and Care Excellence
NOA	Notice of Allegation
NOC	Notice of Compliance
NOC/c	Notice of Compliance with conditions
NPS	National Pharmaceuticals Strategy
NNT	number needed to treat
OECD	Organisation for Economic Co-operation and Development
OTC	over the counter
PAAB	Pharmaceutical Advertising Advisory Board
PCPA	Pan-Canadian Pharmaceutical Alliance

PEM	Prescription Event Monitoring
PhRMA	Pharmaceutical Research and Manufacturers of America
PM	product monograph
PMA	Pharmaceutical Manufacturers Association
PMAC	Pharmaceutical Manufacturers Association of Canada
PMPRB	Patented Medicine Prices Review Board
R&D	research and development
REB	Research Ethics Board
RRR	relative risk reduction
Rx&D	Canada's Research-Based Pharmaceutical Companies
SBD	Summary Basis of Decision
SMON	subacute myelo-optic neuropathy
TB	tuberculosis
TDF	tenofovir disoproxil fumarate
TPD	Therapeutic Products Directorate
TPP	Therapeutic Products Programme
TRIPS	Trade-Related Aspects of Intellectual Property Rights
WHO	World Health Organization
WTO	World Trade Organization

PRIVATE PROFITS VERSUS PUBLIC POLICY

The Pharmaceutical Industry and the Canadian State

Introduction: Why do we care about the pharmaceutical industry in Canada?

Over 30 years ago, my first book, *The Real Pushers: A Critical Analysis of the Canadian Drug Industry*, started with the question "Why write a book about the Canadian prescription drug industry?" My answer was then, and remains, that people's health is so intimately intertwined with medicines and the companies that manufacture them that the significance of the pharmaceutical industry extends far beyond the size of the companies and how much money they earn or how much money we spend on medicines.

Given the central role that medicines play in keeping us healthy, it is essential that we understand the policy environment that governs drug development, from the initial basic research to the sale of the manufactured products to the patients who use them. Although the Canadian market is the eighth largest in the world (1), Canada tends to get short shrift in books about the pharmaceutical industry, meriting only a few lines or a footnote to the analyses about the US Food and Drug Administration (FDA) or the European Medicines Agency (EMA). There are few book-length examinations of the Canadian situation. The two exceptions are *The Push to Prescribe,* a groundbreaking book focusing on women's issues (2), and *Death by Prescription,* Terence Young's personal story about how his daughter died from a drug she was prescribed but shouldn't have been taking (3). The few other book-length examinations of the Canadian situation all are now dated (4–6).

What happens in Canada may resemble, in many respects, what goes on in other markets, but Canada is not merely a small-scale replica of the United States or Europe. The Canadian pharmaceutical industry developed in these dominant markets' shadows but evolved its own unique characteristics. The US-dominated industry did not understand the economic, historical, and political differences between Canada and the United States, and that led to the US industry's defeat in the 1960s in the battle over allowing early entry of generic drugs into the Canadian market.

To understand how important context is, it is instructive to examine the very different outcomes of the United Kingdom and Canadian battles between government and industry during the 1950s and 1960s (4). In the United Kingdom, the pharmaceutical industry was not nationalized nor were its products subject to aggressive price regulation by the then Labour government. This situation occurred largely because the United Kingdom had a strong national industry that had worked closely with the government and thus had a strong economic presence that the UK government was unwilling to disturb. In contrast, in Canada by the mid-1960s, the last of the major Canadian-owned companies had passed into non-Canadian hands, leaving the country with a branch plant industry that was "content to portray itself as a foreign dominated sector of the market place" (4 p294). When the intellectual property rights (IPRs) that the industry relied – and still relies – on were threatened, the Pharmaceutical Manufacturers Association of Canada (PMAC), the organization representing the multinational brand-name companies, found itself shunned by government departments, including the Department of Industry, which should have been its strongest governmental supporter. The Canadian industry's domination by US companies, and especially its overriding concern with the possibility of US price regulation, in the light of the ongoing US Kefauver hearings into drug prices, meant that Canada received little attention in the early days of the debate. When the Canadian subsidiaries realized that they needed to act, they didn't understand what type of action was appropriate in the Canadian environment: "The Canadian association's policy of 'seeking out and talking to anyone who may be influential,' resembled more the US style of lobbying than a parliamentary one" (4 p296). The social fabric that the industry existed in mattered in the 1960s, and it matters still.

This is a book about Canada and how public policy with respect to the pharmaceutical industry has evolved in this country over the past half century (with occasional forays into the more distant past). It is about pharmaceutical politics in the last half of the twentieth century and the first 15 years of the twenty-first, and how the interplay between the federal government, both Liberal and Conservative, and the industry has led to the current situation. The pharmaceutical industry has become a topic of intense debate, and stories appear in the press almost daily:

there are frequent hearings on pharmaceutical issues before committees of the House of Commons and the Senate; drug costs now make up the second-largest proportion of health care expenditure (7); and pharmaceutical interests drive our dealings with IPRs both domestically and in international trade deals.

I am no fan of either the brand-name pharmaceutical industry or the federal government, particularly Health Canada. At the same time, I believe many good people work in both areas, people whose primary goal is to help ensure that patients live healthier and longer lives. As a doctor working in an emergency department, I write prescriptions every time I work, and I believe that these prescriptions help my patients. I have a great respect for the value of medications when they are affordable and used properly. I am not a conspiracy theorist. I do not believe that drug companies are keeping secret cures locked in their basements or that cabals of government bureaucrats and industry executives meet to plot strategies. In fact, there were times when the interests of industry and governments were not aligned. The battle in the 1960s over IPRs, referred to above, is one example where government responded to concerns about drug prices and affordability. Another is the continued ban on direct-to-consumer advertising of prescription drugs, half-hearted though that ban is (8). However, I do think that government and industry have come to share far too many of the same goals, for reasons described in this book.

My reason for writing this book is to focus on the systemic issues that have led to our current situation. I explain how and why we reward drug companies for the products that they develop, and I explore the ideological basis behind the way that government (mostly federal but occasionally provincial and territorial) deal with the industry. Taking the lead from the recent and highly influential book by Davis and Abraham (9), I adopt an empirical, realist, interests-based approach. I start from the position that we should not be under any illusion about why pharmaceutical companies exist. Like any other corporations, they have an obligation to make profits for shareholders and investors. They should, therefore, do whatever is legal to advance this objective. This is not a cynical statement but a realistic one, and it would be naive to think otherwise.

However, the companies' economic aims often seem to conflict with their declared goal of improving health, as acknowledged by Davis and Abraham (9). The point that they make is that society has a dual expectation from the pharmaceutical industry. On the one hand, companies should make profits for shareholders and investors, while on the other, the products that they produce should also provide a health benefit. From the viewpoint of the industry, that is exactly what it has been doing, and its economic success is a mirror of the success that it has had in creating products and innovations needed by patients. Governments also recognize the dual nature of the industry and are not naive enough to accept that the pharmaceutical industry's commercial motives will always deliver new drug products in the best interests of patients. As a result, government drug regulatory agencies exercise a check on drug companies' claims both before and after products are marketed. Davis and Abraham further explain that "there is a paradox at the heart of pharmaceutical regulation in the neo-liberal era. On the one hand, state regulation has been introduced and maintained on the assumption that the interests of the pharmaceutical industry and public health do not always converge. On the other hand, the last 30 years has seen a raft of deregulatory reforms, ostensibly to promote pharmaceutical innovation deemed to be simultaneously in the commercial interests of industry and the health interests of patients" (9 p2–3). The question that I attempt to answer is, whose interests are being served in the way that the state is regulating the industry?

When it comes to economic and industrial policy, the best interests of the pharmaceutical companies do not necessarily coincide with what is best for the entire country and for public health writ large. Here again, we assume that government balances these interests when it makes decisions about IPRs, how much drugs should cost, how best to encourage research that advances public health, and how to ensure that people in the Global South have the kind of access to essential medicines enjoyed by most Canadians. Whether our expectations are being met is explored in the second half of this book.

As with any book about a complex subject, there are limits to what can be covered. There are many actors when it comes to pharmaceuticals: the companies; the federal, provincial, and territorial governments; supranational organizations, such as the World Health Organization and the World Trade Organization; the medical and pharmacy professions, and to a lesser extent other health care professions; patient and consumer groups; various think tanks on the left and right; and of course the patients themselves. They are the ones on the receiving end of all this effort, the ones for whom everyone else is – at least theoretically – acting.

Because this is a book about public policy, I focus on the pharmaceutical industry and the federal government, because in Canada the federal government has the power to approve drugs, regulates their promotion, monitors their safety, and sets the economic and industrial policies that the industry exists under. Other groups are mentioned only as they interact with these two primary players. Therefore, I extensively examine the regulation of promotion but do not detail the long and intimate relationship between the industry and the medical profession. Funding for health care in Canada is complex. The federal government provides about 25% of the money that pays for hospitals and doctors' services, with the provincial and territorial governments providing the rest. But when it comes to public payment for prescription drugs, there are no federal dollars; provincial governments carry the entire cost. Therefore, provincial governments are mentioned to the extent that they are trying to make price-setting policy for brand-name drugs. I discuss the plans that they have put in place to subsidize the cost of prescription drugs to various sectors of their populations and how industry reacted to these programs and tried to influence them. There is a growing literature about patient groups in Canada and how they relate to both the pharmaceutical industry and the federal and provincial governments (see, for example the chapter by Sharon Batt in *The Push to Prescribe* (10)), but this is another topic that I have not been able to cover in this book. A national, publicly funded pharmacare program is critical in ensuring that people can access the medicines that they need, but industry has largely stayed silent on this issue and therefore is referred to only in passing in relation to why Canada does not have a pharmacare plan and how that affects how much Canada spends on drugs. I mention the important international battles about drug access in Chapter 9, but as this is a book about Canada, I limit the discussion to what Canada has or has not done to help (or hinder) the Global South in its struggles to provide medicines for their populations. Again because this is a Canadian book, I have kept material from other countries to a minimum, not because it is irrelevant to the issues being discussed, but because it is important to examine what takes place here and not to infer our situation from the US or European experience. Consequently, where I have used information from other countries, it is primarily to contrast what is happening there with the Canadian situation.

The contents of this book are drawn from the extensive documentary collection I have accumulated in the form of reports, books, articles, and newspaper and magazine stories. Virtually everything in this book is based on publicly accessible material; there are no secret documents. In writing about public policy, I believe that it is important for readers to be able to check sources themselves. Where these documents are not easily accessible, I will commit to providing them to interested readers. Over the years, a variety of names have been attached to the parts of the federal government that deal with drugs: Food and Drug Directorate, Drugs Directorate, Therapeutic Products Programme, Therapeutic Products Directorate, Biologics and Genetic Therapies Directorate, Marketed Health Products Directorate, Health Protection Branch, Health Products and Food Branch – just to mention the most common ones. To keep it easy for readers, I mainly use the terms *Health Canada* and *agencies within Health Canada*. Similarly, the organization representing the major brand-name companies has gone through a succession of name changes, starting with the Canadian Pharmaceutical Manufacturers Association, moving to the Pharmaceutical Manufacturers Association of Canada, and then to Canada's Research-Based Pharmaceutical Companies (Rx&D). (At the start of 2016, the organization underwent yet another name change, this time to Innovative Medicines.) In this case, the name the association used at the point in history will be the one used in this book.

This book documents a range of public policies that industry has supported and advocated. Table 0.1 is based on a series of reports and documents that the industry has produced and publicized. It lays out the range of major industry demands in the twenty-first century. Not surprisingly, what industry has asked for each time is remarkably consistent and reflects its self-interest: stronger intellectual property rights, faster drug review times, higher prices, quicker access to provincial and territorial markets, a wider definition of what counts as spending on research, restrictions on how quickly generics can enter the market, and an expanded definition of innovation.

To deal with all these issues in a thematically coherent manner, this book is divided into two sections. The first, Chapters 1–5, deals with the relationship between the pharmaceutical industry and Health Canada, the regulatory agency set up to protect our health. The term "regulatory science" is often found in Health Canada documents (11–13), implying that what the organization does is based on objective evidence and that subjective judgments do not enter into decisions. The false concept that regulation is purely objective is beneficial to both industry and government. Both can point to data generated from research, clinical trials, and postmarket monitoring to shield themselves from charges of bias and, in the case of government, of being influenced by the values of industry. Sheila Jasanoff, who brought the term regulatory science into widespread use, points out how this perception of regulation is

Table 0.1 Major pharmaceutical industry policy recommendations, 2002–2010

Document	• *Improving health through innovation: a new deal for Canadians*	• *Information guide, 2nd ed.*	• *Towards increasing research and development in Canada: a new innovative pharmaceutical strategy*	• *Rx&D response to* Sharpening Canada's Competitive Edge *from Competition Policy Review Panel*	• *Review of federal support to research and development: expert panel submission*
Date	• September 2002	• May 2003	• October 2004	• 11 January 2008	• 18 February 2010
Intellectual property rights (IPR) and data protection	• Create a patent term restoration system that closes the IPR competitiveness gap with other nations • Effectively enforce a competitive data protection provision for drug submissions	• Maintain and improve mechanisms for patent protection and ensure their effective enforcement • Bring effective patent life in line with other countries, like the United States and member countries of the European Union	• Provide better protection of intellectual property	• Create a best-in-class intellectual property regime	• Strengthen the intellectual property system in Canada to make our country competitive globally
Drug review standards	• Establish and meet drug review performance standards that are consistent with those of the European Medicines Agency and the US Food and Drug Administration, and link cost recovery fees to the attainment of revised internationally competitive performance standards	• Shorten the time it takes to review and approve new medicines federally	• Improve drug review and approval times	• Foster an efficient and harmonized regulatory environment	• Improve Health Canada's regulatory review performance

(Continued)

Table 0.1 (Continued)

Availability of new medicines	• Work cooperatively with the provincial and territorial authorities to reduce the time taken between the granting of the market authorization by Health Canada and the listing of those new drugs on the various drug benefit formularies – with a view to seeking greater uniformity between jurisdictions • Work cooperatively with the provincial and territorial authorities to ensure that the products of innovative pharmaceutical research, new medicines, are broadly available to Canadian patients	• Work with the provinces and territories to expand access to innovative medicines and reduce the time it takes to have them listed on provincial/territorial drug benefit plans	• Provide better access to medicines across provinces and territories	• Provide patient access to medicines	• Target higher public reimbursement rates for innovative medicines and vaccines
Definition of *research and development (R&D)* and *taxation*	• Broaden the definition of R&D in the Income Tax Act and harmonize it with the OECD [Organisation for Economic Co-operation and Development] definition	• Broaden the definition of R&D in the Income Tax Act and harmonize it with the Organisation for Economic Co-operation and Development (OECD) definition	• Improve taxation legislation	• Make corporate taxes competitive	
Patented Medicine Prices Review Board (PMPRB)	• Recognize that price restrictions impede innovation and ensures that the policies of the PMPRB encourage – not further deter – pharmaceutical R&D investment in Canada	• Recognize that the Patented Medicine Prices Review Board may in fact have exceeded its mandate and ensure that its policies encourage pharmaceutical R&D investment in Canada	• Use a model at the PMRPB that reflects innovation		

Notice of Compliance (NOC) linkage regulations	• Maintain the NOC linkage regulations and ensure their effective enforcement				
Cross-border trade in pharmaceuticals				• Implement effective Government of Canada action on cross-border trade of pharmaceuticals	
Research capacity					• Increase access to talent and public sector research capacity

Sources: Rx&D. Improving health through innovation: a new deal for Canadians. Ottawa: Rx&D; 2003; Rx&D. Information guide. 2nd ed. Ottawa: Rx&D; 2003; Rx&D. Towards increasing research and development in Canada: a new innovative pharmaceutical strategy. Ottawa: Rx&D; 2004; Rx&D. Rx&D response to sharpening Canada's competitive edge. Ottawa: Rx&D; 2008; Rx&D. Review of federal support to research and development expert panel submission. Ottawa: Rx&D; 2010.

fundamentally incorrect: "When knowledge is uncertain or ambiguous, as is often the case in science bearing on policy, facts alone are inadequate to compel a choice. Any selection inevitably blends scientific with policy considerations, and policymakers accordingly are forced to look beyond science to legitimate their preferred reading of the evidence" (14) (p. 29–30).

Chapter 1 challenges this idea of an objective regulatory environment free of subjective biases, laying out examples of the interactions between industry and government from the 1930s to the present. It shows how the interactions evolved through a model known as clientele pluralism, situated within corporate bias theory, in which industry assumes some of the roles of government with the consent of government, and a strong proactive government intervenes on behalf of industry (15). With Chapter 1 having established the relationship between the two, Chapters 2 to 5 deal with regulation as it applies to clinical trials, the drug review and approval system, how promotion is governed, and how Health Canada deals with drug safety after products are on the market.

The second thematic section of the book, covered in Chapters 6–9, focuses on economic and industrial policies as they relate to the pharmaceutical industry. Chapter 6 examines the paramount importance that the industry places on IPRs, the patents and other "rights" that give drug companies a temporary monopoly on the drugs that they produce and make some drugs immensely profitable. Chapter 6 also looks at the economic costs and benefits from stronger IPRs and finds that the former outnumber the latter. The final three chapters in this section then look specifically at the effects of the emphasis on stronger IPRs on drug prices and overall drug expenditures, drug research from an economic perspective, and whether Canadian actions in the Global South have aligned with public health values or with the commercial values of the pharmaceutical industry.

The final chapter puts the conclusions about regulatory failure and the industry bias in economic and industrial policy into the context of the neo-liberal agenda as it pertains to deregulation and the prioritization of private IPRs over public values.

This is a book written both in despair and in hope: in despair over the present situation in which public values are subordinated to private profit and in which patients are not getting the therapy that they deserve, and in the hope that with strong public action combined with political willpower, this situation can be reversed.

1 (De)regulation through cooperation

Although drug regulatory systems in Western countries have many similarities, each one maintains a unique system that arose from its own historical context. Daemmrich refers to therapeutic cultures as "the historical evolution of a distinctive set of institutionalized relationships among the state, industry, physicians, and disease-based organizations" (1 p4). Similarly, regulatory culture is the product of many factors, including the dominant political ideology in the country; the economic and political strength of the pharmaceutical industry; the relationship between the medical profession and the industry; high-profile drug disasters, such as thalidomide (2); and the resources available to the state to regulate. This chapter explores the historical relationship between the Canadian state, as represented primarily by the federal government, the regulatory agencies that it has established, and the pharmaceutical industry.

Clientele pluralism and the government-industry relationship

The relationship between the Canadian government and the brand-name multinational pharmaceutical industry, as represented by its national organization, Canada's Research-Based Pharmaceutical Companies (Rx&D), has developed through a path termed *clientele pluralism.* As Atkinson and Coleman described it (3, 4), in such a system, the state concentrates power in a single agency – in the case of drug regulation that agency is Health Canada – that either does not possess the ability or lacks interest in developing the capacity to ensure safe and effective medications on its own. From the very start of drug regulation in Canada, the predecessors to Health Canada had limited staffing and had to rely heavily on the industry for self-regulation (5). Therefore, some authority must be voluntarily relinquished to the drug manufacturers to pursue objectives with which officials are in broad agreement. This low degree of autonomy on the part of Health Canada may partly exist because of a lack of expertise in the agency to address drug regulation, but primarily it is due to the political orientation of the state. In other words, the state sees many of its interests as synonymous with those of the industries that it is charged to regulate. For its part, the brand-name pharmaceutical industry is not interested in just assuming regulatory functions. Rx&D is also highly mobilized to be able to assume a role in the making and implementing of drug policy through an elaborate committee structure, the ability to act on behalf of its members, and the capacity to bind member firms to agreements. Clientele pluralism explains how drug regulation has evolved in Canada and why the weaknesses that we see today exist.

Clientele pluralism is "located in a broader political context" (6 p11) as one expression of corporate bias theory. This theory "allows for the possibility of a relatively strong, pro-active state, which may encourage pro-business (de)regulation in collaboration with industry" (6 p12). It contends that industry can drive regulation by influencing not just the regulatory agencies, in this case Health Canada, but also the broader government directly through lobbying and donations and through other activities, such as direct participation by having representatives appointed to task forces that help form overall government policy. The ultimate result is that the state actively supports the broad regulatory goals of industry.

Although no systematic look at the tactics that the pharmaceutical industry has used to influence public policy has occurred, anecdotal evidence abounds. For example, estimates suggest that the brand-name industry spent tens of millions of dollars between 1984 and 1986 ensuring that the weakening of compulsory licensing was a key feature of the Canada-United States Free Trade Agreement (see Chapter 6) (7). Similarly, in his abortive run for the leadership of the federal Liberal Party in 2003, John Manley received tens of thousands of dollars in donations from a group of six pharmaceutical companies and Rx&D (8). According to another Liberal parliamentarian, Manley was a key backer of the brand-name pharmaceutical industry's interests in cabinet discussions and was "part of the Praetorian Guard of status quo on high drug prices" (8 pA8). At the federal level, non-pharmaceutical industry corporate executives were heavily represented on the government's external advisory committee on smart regulation (9). (See Chapter 3 for a discussion on smart regulation.)

The close working relationship between industry and the regulator that evolved because of clientele pluralism was duly recognized by the director general of the Food and Drug Directorate (FDD). He acknowledged that it was the responsibility of the manufacturer to ensure the safety and efficacy of a drug and the job of the FDD to ensure that drugs on the Canadian market meet all the requirements of the Food and Drugs Act and Regulations (10). According to him, "quality control is the responsibility of the manufacturer firstly, positively and very strongly" (5 p9).

Industry, in return, sees itself as a partner with government. The chair of the Canadian Pharmaceutical Manufacturers Association (CPMA), later the Pharmaceutical Manufacturers Association of Canada (PMAC), and then Rx&D believed that responsible citizenship required wholehearted cooperation with government: "In this spirit, our scientists and technical people have collaborated with the FDD in the elaboration of many regulations bearing on standards for both manufacturers and particular products. We have consistently supported the strengthening of the Directorate" (11 p122).

Once Canada embarked on a regulatory system defined by clientele pluralism, it seldom strayed from this approach. This is an example of path dependence, whereby the set of decisions that are faced for any given set of circumstance is limited by the decisions that have been made in the past. Boothe's description of path dependence in explaining the failure of Canada to develop a program of universal pharmacare is equally applicable when looking at drug regulatory policy. In both cases political elites, primarily policymakers at the federal level, "adapt[ed] their expectations regarding a policy based on what has happened in the past, and these adaptive expectations influence their preferences and choices" (12 p423). Their ideas of what is and is not possible in terms of drug regulation limit the choices and actions they are willing to take in the future. Finally, in the past 30 years, the corporate bias established through clientele pluralism has been reinforced and strengthened through the deregulation brought about by neo-liberalism.

This chapter is not a systematic historical investigation into the way that Health Canada and its predecessor (Department of National Health and Welfare) interacted with the pharmaceutical industry. What follows is episodic and not the complete history that waits to be written, but it is intended to show that the available information points to the federal government accepting significant limitations in its willingness and ability to regulate the pharmaceutical industry. This is not an unbroken string of submissiveness on the part of the federal government, but the overall pattern of cooperation was reiterated over the years by various ministers of health, reflecting the clientele pluralism relationship between government and industry. Speaking to the House of Commons in 1940, Ian McKenzie explained what he considered the general approach to the administration of the Food and Drugs Act: "The statute ... is not entirely punitive. Much of the control is exercised by preventing action in which the industry and trade co-operate." Six years later, another minister of health explained that "we try to secure enforcement through co-operation, first with the representatives of the various trade associations and, second with the people in business." Again in 1953, a third minister commented, "I cannot speak too highly of the co-operation we have had from industry generally in the administration of this [Food and Drugs] Act" (5 p9). The underlying approach is perhaps best summed up in the 1975 quote from Dr A.B. Morrison, the assistant deputy minister of the Health Protection Branch (the branch that at the time was in charge of drug regulation), of the Department of National Health and Welfare: "We prefer to work co-operatively with responsible manufacturers and to encourage voluntary compliance by industry. We try to avoid unnecessary confrontation and adversary proceedings insofar as possible" (13 p642).

Canadian drug legislation: Cooperation not confrontation

The first federal legislation dealing with drugs along with food and drink dates back to an act implemented in 1875 to impose licence duties and to prevent adulteration of these products (14). At a celebration of the implementation of that act 75 years later, the minister of national health and welfare expressed the department's appreciation to the industries affected by the Food and Drugs Act (F&DAct, the successor to the 1875 legislation) for their support in making the act successful. His remarks were reciprocated by the president of the CPMA, who reinforced the industry's willingness to cooperate with the department. The publication celebrating the event had a cartoon of two men, representing the F&DAct and industry, using a crosscut saw to cut through a piece of wood with the heading "75 years of successful industry-gov't co-operation" (15).

The first substantive involvement of the nascent pharmaceutical industry, as opposed to pharmacists, apothecaries, and small local manufacturers, in drug legislation appears to relate to the 1927 amendment to the F&DAct that made it a crime to misbrand or falsely represent drugs. After the statute went through the legislative process, it was necessary to craft the regulations to put the act into practice; a draft was reviewed by a group of manufacturers and other stakeholders and then finalized (16).

In 1939, the industry, through the CPMA, endorsed another amendment to the F&DAct that strengthened the section dealing with advertising (17). However, in the same year, industry demonstrated its negative influence on public policy. Before 1939, provincial pharmacy acts placed restrictions on which drugs were available without a prescription but without consistency in the list of such drugs across provinces. The Dominion Council of Health, formed in 1919, as an advisory body to the federal minister of health on public health matters, recommended that some action be taken under the F&DAct to deal with the problem. As a result, in 1939, under an amendment to the act, the government was given the authority to make regulations defining the conditions of sale of any drug likely to be injurious to health. One measure that was proposed was the placement of a cautionary statement on the label of drugs that required a prescription. This approach was discussed with representatives of the CPMA. The organization wanted to modify the proposed cautionary statement; "however as it was considered the one recommended by the Association would nullify the intention of the original suggestion, the matter was dropped at that time" (16 p412). Again, in 1941, the industry (and pharmacists) initially objected to an Order in Council prohibiting the sale to the public of a number of potent drugs without a prescription from a doctor (10). However, this measure was implemented despite these objections.

The relationship between the government and industry (and other stakeholders) was formalized in 1942 with the formation of the Canadian Committee on Pharmacopoeial Standards, that among other functions, had the mandate to advise the Department of Health on regulations with respect to drugs (17). Shortly after, in 1948, the Department of Health instituted a mechanism, Information Letters, to give industry and others the ability to comment on regulations before they were implemented. Senior bureaucrats in the department felt that Information Letters "often result[ed] in changes to the proposed regulations to bring them into line with what is practically possible to achieve ... sav[ing] us [the department] the difficulty, as well as the embarrassment, of having to change them after they have been passed" (13 p640). Herder describes a further instance of industry-government cooperation in 1951 wherein the two jointly developed a "guide" regarding labelling and advertising of foods and drugs, which manufacturers reportedly found "very useful." That same year, the Food and Drug Regulations were amended to require manufacturers to submit information regarding the safety of a drug before marketing it (18).

The Senate hearings on the 1953 revisions to the F&DAct provide further evidence of the attitude of deference that the Department of National Health and Welfare took towards the industry. In giving testimony before the Senate, one of the department's lawyers explained why no specific clause in the bill protected the information that manufacturers had to provide to the department. His point was that such a clause was unnecessary since every member of the department took an oath of secrecy (19). The clear implication is that the government regarded the information about the medications as proprietary and as such should not be publicly disclosed. As we will see in Chapter 3, the government still maintains that position, to the detriment of drug safety. The same official, in a subsequent volume on Canadian food and drugs law, also explained why the penalties in the F&DAct seemed trivial compared with those imposed by the US Food, Drug and Cosmetic Act. In his words, "with reputable firms it is not considered that a heavy fine is substantially a greater deterrent to violate the law than is a light fine" (20 p201).

Cooperation in the inspection of manufacturing facilities

The revised F&DAct provided the legal basis for the inspection of manufacturing facilities and control of drug manufacturers. The subsequent inspection program was one of the first documented instances of clientele pluralism in action as representatives of PMAC worked with government in devising the standards for manufacturing, and a number of PMAC member companies helped to train the inspectors who applied them (21). The point here is not to criticize the implementation of the inspection system, because its impact seems to have been positive: a number of Canadian manufacturers remodelled their plants and revised their quality control systems, leading to an improvement in the quality and safety of drugs sold in Canada (16). Rather, the issue is the abrogation of state power to a private interest with the active collusion of the state.

As a further refinement in regulating manufacturing practices, a joint industry and government committee was struck that led to the development of Good Manufacturing Practices (GMPs), which came into effect in 1981. After that, the companies continued to have a regular opportunity for input into refinements of GMP regulations at an annual meeting between Health Canada officials and PMAC. Other interested parties, such as workers in pharmaceutical plants and consumers, were notably excluded from participation in such meetings.

Thalidomide and the birth of modern drug regulation

Besides precipitating a major revision in the F&DAct, thalidomide also provides an illustration of how closely aligned drug regulatory officials were with the pharmaceutical industry. Thalidomide was a medication that caused children to be born missing limbs and was removed from the Canadian market in March 1962, albeit four months after it had been withdrawn in Germany. After the manufacturers were ordered to stop selling thalidomide, a number of doctors wrote to the government protesting the move. In reply to one such letter, Dr C.A. Morrell, head of the FDD, responded on 27 April 1962: "I think if the medical profession would take a stand ... that there is every possibility that thalidomide could indeed be reinstated on the Canadian market and to this end I would encourage you to urge strongly your colleagues to express themselves to us on this question" (2 p143).

Subsequently, in 1964, when Morrell testified before the Harley Committee looking into the issue of drug prices, he did not mention his defence of thalidomide and seemed to place the safety problems on the users of the drug: "I think the hazard is the inability to control the user of thalidomide after it is on the market. I am referring now to the medicine cabinet at home; you do not know who will take a pill today. Everyone wants to take pills" (22 p26). During the same hearing, he also defended the practice of choosing brand-name products over generics, aligning himself with the position taken by PMAC (11). After Morrell left the Department of National Health and Welfare in 1965, he joined the board of Ciba-Geigy (now part of Novartis), a major multinational Swiss drug company.

The post-thalidomide revisions to the F&DAct required companies to actually prove that their drugs were effective before they could be approved for marketing. In introducing these amendments, the minister was careful to emphasize that they were not intended "to affect the right of a manufacturer to inform a physician of a new product or to deny him the right to make a new product available by way of sample. This would be an unwarranted interference with the professions and with the industry" (23 p977). Manufacturers were critical of the amendments to the F&DAct that allowed Health Canada to refuse to approve new drugs and asked for an appeal mechanism. The government granted them one in the form of a New Drug Committee, a three-person panel comprising a nominee from the manufacturer and one from the minister, both of whom then appointed a chair. Although decisions of the committee were not binding on the minister, it had to be formed at the request of the manufacturer (24). There is no record of whether the committee actually ever met. The amendments also required a written request from a doctor before a company could leave behind drug samples, a measure that the companies regarded as an indirect way of controlling drug prices (24).

Thalidomide also led to major changes in US legislation. Companies were required to submit substantial evidence of effectiveness to review panels from the National Research Council for all 2820 drugs approved between 1938 and 1962. The review concluded that 7% of the drugs reviewed were completely ineffective for every claim they made, and a further 50% were only effective for some of the claims made for them (25). Health Canada did not elect to even undertake such a review. Therefore, some 1500 drugs marketed in Canada before 1963 never had to undergo testing to prove that they were effective. As late as 1982, Canadian authorities suspected that about 450 products still on the market were either completely worthless, lacked meaningful medical benefits, or were potentially dangerous (26). The attitude of Guy Beauchemin from PMAC was that the continued use of possibly inferior drugs was the result of fierce competition among drug companies (26). Although Beauchemin did not develop this idea further, possibly he was referring to competition generating advertising of less effective drugs in an attempt to retain market share.

A revised Food and Drugs Act but the same entrenched government-industry relationship

As health minister, Judy LaMarsh delivered the welcoming address at the 1964 Fifth Annual General Meeting of PMAC and warmly applauded the government-industry relationship. During her speech she noted that the "task [of the director of the FDD] would be immeasurably more difficult if he did not have access to the combined knowledge of the industry and receive its support." She went on to say, "the role of a responsible trade association, in my view, is the advice and assistance it can offer to the government in carrying out its responsibility to the Canadian people ... In the past [we have received from you] valuable help and assistance in the development and administration of our drug regulations ... In the formulation of our present Act, committees of your Association met with officers of the Department and worked out matters which are now reflected in the provisions of the law itself" (27 p298). As Anderson notes (27), the speech clearly indicates that PMAC and bureaucrats in the department were well known to each other and reveals the degree of influence that the industry had on policymaking.

The close interaction between Health Canada and the industry, illustrated by the quote from Judy LaMarsh, continued into the early 1980s, when officials from the industry and Health Canada met about every six weeks in joint committees to work on regulatory changes and their accompanying guidelines. For example, at a meeting of the Bureau of Human Prescription Drugs/PMAC Medical R&D Section Liaison Committee in the fall of 1983, the need for guidelines on filing an Investigational New Drug (IND) submission (a submission to begin testing a possible new drug) was discussed, primarily at PMAC's initiative (28). In addition, senior officials in the Health Protection Branch (HPB), the successor to the FDD, including the assistant deputy minister, met with the PMAC board of directors at PMAC's annual and semi-annual meetings (3). At these events the HPB informed the industry of its plans for the following year. The informal nature of these discussions was highlighted by the lack of any minutes (3).

However, the interaction between industry and government over the IND guidelines also emphasizes that while the dependence on industry was the ongoing operating principle, in some instances the government was not completely willing to give up its ability to act independently. The first draft of these guidelines was, according to PMAC, unexpectedly tabled at an October 23/84 Liaison Committee meeting for detailed discussion at the next committee meeting scheduled for early January 1985. However, at a November meeting between HPB officials and the PMAC board, the HPB announced that it was moving forward with the draft to the formal Information Letter stage without further preliminary informal discussion and input via the Liaison Committee. PMAC was very upset by this move and strongly requested that the document be given thorough study and review through the informal Liaison Committee mechanism before any further action was undertaken (3).

A series of articles on prescription drug regulation in the *Montreal Gazette* in 1982 showed that the Health Canada officials' attitude toward drug companies continued basically unchanged into the 1980s. Officials repeatedly told the newspaper that they had opted for a cooperative and "open door policy" with Canadian drug company officials instead of a tough adversarial stance. They were also proud of how friendly their relations were with representatives of Canadian drug subsidiaries of US companies: "We try to work things out together," said one Canadian official (29 pA6). Monique Bégin, the health minister, said that she did not believe that Canada needed detailed regulations to control the drug approval process. In her view, "the players" involved in getting a drug onto the market – federal officials, drug manufacturers and physicians conducting clinical trials – should "be forced to continue to use their heads and judgment" in carrying out the guidelines. Nor did Bégin see the need to review pre-1963 drugs for safety and effectiveness (30). The pharmaceutical industry, as represented by PMAC, was in agreement with Bégin. According to Beauchemin, representing PMAC, "some companies are strongly opposed to a review of drugs, for economic reasons ... A hell of a lot of products would drop out" (29).

The same friendly cooperative attitude continued into the late 1990s when Dr George Paterson, director general of Health Canada's Food Directorate, was interviewed in the *Globe and Mail*. He espoused "the 'trust-industry' philosophy prevalent among senior managers and bureaucrats. The pharmaceutical industry and the health-protection branch [a part of Health Canada] have a 'shared purpose' to ensure no harmful products make it to market, he said. 'In terms of good business savvy, they don't want to be in any situation where their integrity and their competitiveness would be compromised by a scare'" (31 p5).

One of the most illustrative examples of industry-regulator cooperation and how that cooperation could lead to an abrogation of public safety on the part of Health Canada comes from an analysis of how its veterinary division dealt with Revalor-H (trenbolone and estradiol), a growth hormone given to cattle. Dr Donald Landry, acting chief of the Veterinary Drugs Bureau, outlined a promise to Dr Murray Jelinski, manager of product development with Hoechst Canada Inc, to "make up for the rough time he's had with Revalor-H when we review his next submission" (32 pA1). The "rough time" referred to concerns raised by reviewers in the department about possible negative effects on humans who consumed beef from cattle treated with the drug. According to documents obtained by the *Globe and Mail*, one reviewer "'strongly' recommended that the human-safety division review the results of the animal studies on the drug" (31 pA10). Jelinski went over the head of the reviewer and directly asked both Landry and Dr George Paterson, director general of

Health Canada's Food Directorate, to intervene as the delay in getting the drug to the market cost Hoechst more than $1 million: "Scribbled on Dr. Landry's memo is a chatty, handwritten note signed by Dr. Paterson, director-general of Health Canada's food directorate branch. 'Don – Thanks for resolving the issue. Hope you didn't 'promise him the moon though.' Cheers, George." But "the moon" seems to be what Landry did offer in the form of "maybe a more expedient review of it [Hoechst's next submission] or something like that" (31 pA10).

From government to industry

Capture theory is often invoked to account for the failure of regulatory agencies to take action against the industry or corporation they are charged with regulating. Capture theory posits that initially regulatory agencies tend to be adversarial towards corporate interests "but eventually they are progressively 'captured' by, and come to share the perspectives of, the industries they are supposed to regulate" (32 p873). Abraham challenges this theory as being too narrow because in his view regulatory agencies and reforms often were not initiated solely or even predominantly in response to public campaigns for better drug regulation. Instead he favours corporate bias theory (32). While I am in agreement with him in his preference for corporate bias theory, I believe that it is still relevant to note the movement of officials between the industry and government as another illustration of the atmosphere of cooperation between the two. Crossovers are not unexpected, as people in both sectors share the same professional and class background and may have the same world view on the role of drugs in the health care system. We have already seen how Morrell left his position as head of the FDD for a spot on the board of directors of Ciba-Geigy. When Judy Erola left politics in 1984 after serving as the federal minister of consumer and corporate affairs, she went on to become the president of PMAC. However, in 1991, this intermingling of officials was taken one step further. The hiring committee for a new head of the Bureau of Non-Prescription Drugs consisted of a staffing officer in the Public Service Commission, the director general of the Drugs Directorate, and Judy Erola. The official position from Health Canada was that PMAC deals mostly with prescription drugs and as the person being hired oversaw the body dealing with non-prescription drugs, there was no conflict of interest. This explanation conveniently overlooked the fact that some companies manufacture both types of drugs (33).

Prioritizing the industry in reviewing and renewing health legislation and ignoring public input

The framing of perceived deficiencies in Canada's drug laws, described in a series of five reports dealing with the regulatory system undertaken in the 1980s and early 1990s (34–38), highlighted the priority that Health Canada gave to the industry's interests versus those of the public in the policymaking arena. All the reports conveyed a sense of urgency about the length of the drug review process, but none had any significant public input. For example, of the seven members of the Working Group on Drug Submission Review struck in the mid-1980s, six came from either government or industry. The sole other member, presumably representing the public and health professionals, came from the Canadian Public Health Association (38). In having one "outside" member the Working Group was more representative than any of the other four review teams. Although some of these reviews were entirely "in house," such as the ones from the Task Force on Program Review (37) and the auditor general (34), the ethos that underlies these reports was strongly influenced by the clientele pluralist relationship between the government and the multinational pharmaceutical industry.

The absence of significant critical public input was evident in the last of these reports (36), which was incorporated into a general review of the Canadian drug approval system. The team that produced the report had no representatives from the pharmaceutical industry, but it was still narrowly based, drawing its membership from academia and government. In the foreword to his report, the lead, Dr Denis Gagnon, implied that because of the limited time frame – the report was to be completed in six months – he felt that it was impossible to conduct a full program of public hearings. Instead, he decided to "proceed with an extensive consultation of Canadian stakeholders and various organizations" (36 pxiii). Although the review team consulted with academics, researchers, physicians, pharmacists, government departments, and pharmaceutical manufacturers, there were some notable omissions. Women's groups had been instrumental in forcing the government to rethink its position on the approval of the injectable contraceptive Depo-Provera (depot medroxyprogesterone acetate) (39), but no discussions were held with any women's health group. Similarly, AIDS activist groups that were critical of the current approval system were also left out of the consultation process. (Some AIDS groups did submit briefs to the review.)

Another Health Canada effort to modernize Canada's health protection legislation began in 1998. This attempt illustrates how Health Canada essentially ignored wide swathes of public opinion and manipulated the language of safety to its own ends. The reasons offered for this initiative included that "Some laws are obsolete and no longer reflect real world conditions ... The legislation has become fragmented and inconsistent ... Governments need to be able to respond faster to new and emerging hazards ... The present patchwork of laws provides a poor basis for policy making ... The legislation does not reflect current thinking about health and health protection" (40 p8–10). The document that initiated this proposed reform gave a variety of examples where the laws no longer reflected the current situation, for example, human organs were treated as "medical devices" under the F&DAct, legislation was not equipped to address the potential health risks and ethical questions raised by bioengineering, and penalties for violating the drug provisions of the Food and Drugs Act were capped at $5000 (40). The goal was "to update and integrate the federal health protection legislation into a coherent, comprehensive and flexible system that [would be] more responsive to present-day global, technological, social and cultural realities, and that provides the necessary tools to address the challenges of the future" (40 p11).

The document introducing this initiative called for a public consultation that would result in "The Health Protection Act" (40). While eventually the broad sweep of the initiative was abandoned in favour of piecemeal changes, the proposal provides an insight into how the federal government viewed its priorities and its relationship to what it termed its "stakeholders." Stakeholders were an agglomeration of the health community; industry; professional associations; Aboriginal organizations; universities and laboratories; consumer, environmental, religious, ethnic, and other public interest groups; other federal departments; and provincial and territorial governments and their agencies. Any eventual legislation should "favour cooperation among all stakeholders" (40 p22). Cooperation is a desirable goal, but it is also very difficult to achieve when one side has vastly superior resources than the other: witness differences between environmental groups and logging/mining companies. This difference in access to resources likely interfered with the ability of groups to make presentations around this document. The apolitical nature of this document was demonstrated in its ignoring of the fundamental differences between industry and public health and the power imbalances among the "stakeholders" (40). The document also failed to recognize areas of serious disagreement in how information or legislation should be interpreted. The section on risk management presented this process as an exact science, but in fact decisions are often made based on limited information and biases, both stated and unstated.

Accompanying the broad discussion paper was a second one that focused on identifying, assessing, and managing health risks (41). (The version of the paper that is in my possession is a draft with the heading "Draft for Discussion ... Does Not Represent Health Canada." A final version of this paper, if it exists, is nowhere to be found.) This paper used the term "precautionary principle," but not in the context that it should be the primary way of dealing with safety but in terms of making the "decision as to whether to apply a precautionary approach" (41 p8). In its true form, the philosophy behind the precautionary principle is that health regulations should be framed and enforced to emphasize safety rather than risk when present day scientific knowledge alone cannot provide clear answers (42). This was not a one-sided document; it did recognize that "interested and affected parties, including ... the public ... can play a key role in issue identification, risk assessment and risk management ... and should be involved as early as possible" (41 p13), but it also failed to acknowledge that risk management is also a political activity laden with values.

Following the first round of consultations on a new health protection act, Health Canada's Legislative Renewal staff prepared a background document on confidential commercial information. The document discussed the viewpoints that had been presented on this issue, highlighting the different values that many members of the public held versus those that the industry viewed as important: "During the Canada-wide public consultations held in the Fall of 1998 ... one of the consistent and strong messages heard was that the lack of public confidence in Health Canada cannot be fully addressed until the activities of the Department are made more transparent and the public and the interested parties can play a more significant role in the decision making process ... The Therapeutics Product Programme has conducted a consultation on the issue of improving the transparency in the drug approval process ... [Industry] strongly opposed the disclosure of submission filing dates, since they consider it would put the companies at a competitive disadvantage" (43 p3).

After having heard both sides of the argument about transparency, the Legislative Renewal staff released a second document for the next round in legislative renewal that was unwilling to adopt the position of enhanced transparency and instead asked neutral questions, such as whether the proposed act should provide authority to make public such basic information as the status of pending submissions for market approval, a summary of data presented by industry on safety and effectiveness of the new product, and Health Canada's evaluation of this industry data (44). While Health Canada did not shut the door on more transparency, neither was it willing to alienate the industry by definitively siding with the public calls for more openness. Compared with the position it took on transparency, the document's statement about risk was unambiguous: "The assessment of risk shall be based solely on science and objective observation" (44 p11), thereby, once again, failing to recognize that the same set of facts can be interpreted differently depending on the paradigm under which one is operating.

The Canadian Health Coalition, a public advocacy organization dedicated to the preservation and improvement of medicare, pointed out that "the proposal in the document to adopt a 'General Safety Requirement' in a new Act ... [was] designed to shift the burden of proof off industry onto the public. The General Safety Requirement (GSR) does not require evidence of safety. Instead, the public is required to demonstrate evidence of harm" (45 p8). Women and Health Protection, a coalition of community groups, researchers, journalists, and activists concerned about the safety of pharmaceutical drugs, saw the document as reflecting a profound shift away from an ethic of public health and health protection to one of industrial competitiveness (46).

The final round in the attempt to produce a sweeping change in Canadian health protection legislation took place over 2006–07 with the release of *Blueprint for Renewal* (2006) (47); and *Blueprint for Renewal II* (2007) (48). Women and Health Protection came "away from reading this document [*Blueprint for Renewal*] with a sense that the essence of the precautionary principle for drug and device regulation has been lost, only to be replaced by notions of 'managing risk.' With a legacy of problems that have arisen because precaution was not exercised (DES [diethylstilbestrol], HRT [hormone replacement therapy], Vioxx, etc.), it is distressing to see this ethic not being more wholeheartedly embraced by our regulators ... all safety and efficacy data submitted as part of the regulatory approval process are still considered commercially confidential and will not be released without permission of the company" (49).

Clientele pluralism, the neo-liberal state, and deregulation

Broadly speaking, the core philosophy behind neo-liberalism is the belief in the superiority of unregulated markets (50). Neo-liberal theory claims that a largely unregulated capitalist system, a free-market economy, achieves optimum economic performance with respect to efficiency, economic growth, technical progress, and distributional justice. Applying these basic tenets to the concept of government regulation, the conclusion is that corporate self-regulation is superior to government regulation and that, to the extent possible, governments should set out broad regulatory objectives but leave the actual regulation to corporations. Or to use a rowboat metaphor, government should steer and not row. As neo-liberalism gained momentum in the mid-1980s, the notion that government regulation was a hindrance to free markets began to be reflected in the relationship between Health Canada and the pharmaceutical industry. The deregulatory trend deepened the relationship that had evolved between Health Canada and the pharmaceutical industry through clientele pluralism. One of the first examples of a transfer of authority from government to industry occurred when Health Canada began considering user fees from industry in 1989 as a funding source for some of its drug-related activities (see Chapter 3). Although it took until 1994 to actually implement this initiative, the belief that the source of revenue was neutral was accepted, thereby dismissing the concept that the public and private sectors might have competing goals when it came to financing drug regulation.

Further evidence of the deregulatory environment was the 1994 introduction of Bill C-62, the Regulatory Efficiency Act, which would have allowed companies to cut individual deals with government departments and completely bypass environmental, health, and safety legislation (51). Although Bill C-62 was withdrawn in the face of strong pressure from environmental, labour, and health organizations, the philosophy underlying it persisted and reappeared in other government policies. The 1996 launch by the Treasury Board Secretariat of the Standards and Regulatory Reform Program both epitomized and fuelled the deregulatory philosophy as it encouraged all government departments to participate in developing standards-based regulatory regimes. Traditionally, regulation had been done by using a prescriptive approach whereby regulations contained detailed standards that were written into the regulations themselves, and government was under no obligation to seek the agreement of interested parties, although it often did consult them. Under the new approach, standards development organizations were the ones that developed standards. The government could also take part but only as one of several stakeholders comprising relevant industry representatives, professional bodies, technical experts, and other interested parties. Once the standards were approved and published, regulatory authorities were not obliged to incorporate them into the regulations but could refer to them in the regulations. In this situation, any subsequent changes to the standards were made by the standards development organization and not by the government agency. The government could take part in the review of the standards as an interested stakeholder, but it could not unilaterally change the organization's document. The underlying principle behind a move to standards-based regulatory regimes was supposedly to provide greater flexibility than traditional prescriptive regimes when changes to the regulations were required quickly. Proponents of standards-based regimes believed that they resulted in more acceptance and greater compliance because of reduced need for education and enforcement because the standards were usually derived from consensus of all interested parties (52). Although Health Canada shied away from a standards-based regulatory approach in most areas of drug regulation, it was already in place when it came to drug promotion, the effects of which are detailed in Chapter 4. It's also clear from subsequent events that deregulation was driving future policy directives at Health Canada, even if it was not going to manifest in standards-based regulation.

One of these manifestations occurred in mid-1997, when Health Canada alleged that budgetary restrictions were forcing it to close its pharmaceutical laboratories. (From 1993–94 to 1998 parliamentary appropriations to the section of Health Canada dealing with drugs were cut from $63 million annually to $22 million (53)). These laboratories provided the back-up research and scientific expertise for regulators assessing and approving new drugs. The plan was to contract out research projects to other Health Canada labs, universities, or commercial labs. According to Dann Michols, the director general of the Therapeutic Products Programme at Health Canada, the federal government did not have "the resources to be able to do basic or even some applied research on the pharmaceutical side. But the capacity does exist in the country. I think it's redundant for us to have that capacity" (54 pA8). Here, the issue of conflict of interest comes to the fore as a consequence of deregulation. Scientists working for the HPB highlighted this problem, charging that cuts in drug research would compromise the integrity of Ottawa's regulatory process because of a potential conflict of interest between industry and academic researchers, making it impossible for Ottawa to obtain independent scientific advice (55). In the face of severe, persistent criticism from the media, government, and other scientists and consumer organizations, the government postponed these cuts but eventually they were implemented (56).

This initial foray into deregulation was followed by the further reorientation of the regulatory process in favour of business interests through Health Canada's Business Transformation Strategy (BTS). The BTS was introduced in early 2003 and built on the commitment made by the Government of Canada to "speed up the regulatory process for drug approvals," to move forward with a smart regulations strategy to accelerate reforms in key areas to promote health and sustainability, to contribute to innovation and economic growth, and to reduce the administrative burden on business (57). One of the key phrases in the BTS was "smart regulation." Smart regulation put the emphasis on removing barriers to moving the agency to a place where it could "regulate in a way that enhances the climate for investment and trust in the markets [and] ... accelerate reforms in key areas to promote health and sustainability, to contribute to innovation and economic growth, and to reduce the administrative burden on business" (58). While health was not ignored, the emphasis was clearly on creating a business-friendly environment.

The federal External Advisory Committee on Smart Regulation explicitly stated that risk management had an essential role in building public trust and business confidence in the Canadian market and regulatory system (59). When applied to drug regulation, risk management means weighing potential negative effects against potential advantages. Potential negative effects are adverse health effects that might occur under reasonably foreseeable conditions (60). The shift from the precautionary principle to risk management is subtle but unmistakable. The precautionary principle says that if there are significant doubts about the safety of products, then they should be marketed with extreme caution, their use should be closely monitored, and their ongoing safety should be rigorously evaluated; risk management allows products on the market unless they are shown to be harmful. Realigning regulation to conform to the principles of smart regulation would not totally abandon the concept of precaution, but it seems to imply that a threat of serious or irreversible damage would have to exist before it would come into play.

According to the analysis from the Canadian Centre for Policy Alternatives, smart regulation reinforced existing federal government initiatives to ensure that corporate interests were protected through requirements that "benefits [from regulations] outweigh costs," and that "adverse impacts on the capacity of the economy to generate wealth and employment are minimized and no unnecessary regulatory burden is imposed" (61 p22). Smart regulation as part of the Government Directive on Regulating (GD-R), the government's overall proposed new regulatory policy, expanded the number of hurdles that had to be jumped for a department to pass a new regulation. The GD-R put pressure on federal departments to use non-regulatory measures wherever possible and to bring forward regulations only to the extent necessary to achieve objectives. The overall approach was generally hostile to regulation, with the onus on regulators to "demonstrate that regulation should be part of the mix of government instruments used to manage public policy issues" (61 p23). The GD-R stated that departments and agencies were expected to "limit the administrative burden and impose the least possible cost on Canadians and business that is necessary to achieve the intended policy objective" (61 p23). Although the policy was careful to say that protection would not be sacrificed, the emphasis was on cutting and streamlining regulatory processes. No mention was made of tightening regulations where necessary or expanding regulations to protect Canadians.

Industry and Health Canada versus the public

From late 2010 to early 2011, Health Canada organized a series of three public consultations to discuss the technical details of what it called *regulatory modernization,* which many saw as another manifestation of smart regulation or deregulation. For example, the session in mid-January 2011 discussed, among other things, suspending and revoking market authorization, creating information requirements in advertising, and establishing advisory committees. Many of the proposals were reasonable, but there was also an unmistakeable underlying philosophy that industry's needs should be privileged over those of the public. Where input was proposed with respect to suspending market authorization or questionable advertising, it was exclusively from company representatives. The documents were silent about consultations with other groups. Advisory committees would have industry representatives on them.

The bias in content was mirrored by a bias in the way that the meetings were structured, which reflected the nature of the relationship among Health Canada, industry, and the public (62). I was at one of these meetings. Officials from Health Canada sat at one long table facing another table with industry representatives. In the audience off to the side were people from professional organizations; consumer and patient groups, many partially funded by industry; and academics. First, Health Canada would put forward proposals, then industry would respond, and only last would the people in the audience be able to ask questions or offer comments.

Drug shortages and voluntary measures

The issue of drug shortages is one more instance that illustrates the deference to industry of Health Canada. Shortages, both in Canada and internationally, have been increasingly recognized as a serious problem creating extra stress and work for health care professionals and, more important, potentially negatively affecting the care that patients get (63). However, when Queen's University medical historian Dr Jacalyn Duffin and some of her colleagues became concerned about the situation in December 2010 and wrote to Leona Aglukkaq, the federal minister of health, it took her 16 weeks to reply. Her answer was that it was Health Canada's job to ensure the safety of drugs, but it had no role to play in their supply (64). Rx&D publicly recognized the degree of the problem and set up a voluntary website in October 2011 where companies could report shortages and, together with the Canadian Generic Pharmaceutical Association, expanded the still voluntary site in March 2012 (65). Duffin reported that compliance by companies with the initial website was poor (64). Aglukkaq accepted voluntary reporting because, according to her spokesperson, it would have taken too long to create a mandatory system. Apparently, Aglukkaq's own staff was wary of a voluntary system because there would be no way of punishing companies that failed to comply with reporting requirements (66).

The Multi-Stakeholder Steering Committee on Drug Shortages, with representation from the federal, provincial, and territorial governments; the biotechnology, brand-name, and generic companies; and health care professional associations, came up with a protocol for the notification and communication of drug shortages (67), but this protocol had serious weaknesses. Manufacturers were supposed to post comprehensive information on drug shortages as soon as an anticipated shortage was identified and were expected to provide six months' notice before voluntarily discontinuing any of their products. However, the protocol did not mention how any of these requirements would be monitored, and they were voluntary. Moreover, companies needed to post anticipated shortages only 30 days in advance, whereas in the United States it is six months (64). Twice in 2013 and again in March 2014, Health Canada sent letters to all manufacturers stating its clear expectation that every shortage should be reported on the website (68). Although the health minister who succeeded Aglukkaq was open to a mandatory reporting system (69), until February 2015 she maintained that the voluntary system was successful (70). Finally, at that point the health minister indirectly admitted that voluntary compliance was not working by announcing that henceforth the government would require companies to publicly report shortages (71).

Conclusion

This chapter shows how the Canadian state followed the model of clientele pluralism in looking to industry as its major partner in drug regulation. The matter of how the Canadian state has traditionally related to industry is of more than just historical or academic concern. When choices are made, they reflect a set of underlying values – values that can be analysed. Private values, the ones that are being prioritized, are antithetical to democracy; they speak to the need to earn a profit, not to protect public health. While the two can at times be synonymous, that happens mostly by coincidence rather than by design. Within the private sector, competition and the profit motive may be the best ways to get newer and better computers or washing detergents. However, medications are not ordinary consumer products. Government is intimately and necessarily involved with almost all aspects of medications because of their importance in health care in Canada. When government adopts the values of private industry, it is in essence telling its people that the needs and values of the private sector take precedence over their health. Democracy is not just the right to vote in an election. It is the ongoing and active participation of the citizenry in determining the policies of the government, with an expectation that government will acknowledge the views being put forward and incorporate them into its actions. The government, through its relationship with the industry, is failing to fulfil that obligation. The next four chapters will look in detail at how the government's initial adoption of an alliance with industry, an alliance that was then reinforced by deregulation, has influenced how it regulates the areas of clinical trials, the drug approval system, drug safety, promotion, and postmarket surveillance.

2 Biased testing, hidden results, and the regulation of clinical trials

Before drugs can be marketed or even considered for marketing by Health Canada, they go through a series of clinical trials. By definition, clinical trials involve humans. As there are inherent risks to the people taking part, it is essential that the trials be conducted as rigorously as possible so that the data they produce can be trusted when it comes to making decisions about whether to approve drugs. However, clinical trials have competing interests: the industry wants trials done as quickly and as inexpensively as possible, and this imperative may lead to economic values outweighing scientific ones. This chapter looks at how Health Canada balances these competing interests and how much trust we can place in what trials tell us about the value of new medicines.

Before the 1963 revisions to the Food and Drugs Act, following the experience with thalidomide (see Chapter 1), companies only had to submit data showing that their drugs were safe. It was not until after 1963 that manufacturers had to conduct clinical trials to produce "substantial evidence of the clinical effectiveness of the new drug … under the conditions of use recommended" (1). In deciding what constituted substantial evidence, Canada largely followed the lead of the US Food and Drug Administration in creating its requirements (2) and started to require a series of three sets of clinical trials (Phase I, II, and III). Phase I trials examine the pharmacological action and toxicity testing in small groups of healthy people and progress to studies in hundreds to thousands of people with the disease that the drug is designed to treat (Phase II and III) (3). (See Table 2.1) (Phase IV studies are carried out after drugs have been marketed.) The objective

Table 2.1 Pre-registration clinical trial phases

Phase	Purpose	Number of patients	Type of patients	Length of time for entire trial (years)	Risks
I	Determine pharmacological actions of the drug and side effects associated with increasing doses	20–50	Healthy	1	Drug has never been administered to humans before; safety information based on actions of drug and animal testing
II	Evaluate efficacy of the drug; determine side effects and risks	100–300	Medical condition to be treated, diagnosed, or prevented	2	Wider group of patients exposed; disease in question may alter the drug's action leading to unexpected side effects
III	Gather the additional information about efficacy and safety needed for further risk-benefit assessment of the drug	Several hundred to several thousand	Medical condition to be treated, diagnosed, or prevented	3+	Wider group of patients exposed; drug administered for longer periods of time; disease in question may alter the drug's action leading to unexpected side effects

Sources: Regulations amending the Food and Drug Regulations (1024 – clinical trials). Canada Gazette. 2000;134(4):227–60; Hawthorne F. Inside the FDA. Hoboken: John Wiley & Sons; 2005.

of the trials is to prove the efficacy of the product, that is, whether it works under ideal circumstances, and that it has an acceptable safety profile.

In addition to clinical trials being necessary to get drugs approved for marketing, they also form the basis for medical practice (4). Doctors may not read the original research, but that research is incorporated into continuing medical education talks, talks that are often commercially planned, professional clinical guidelines, Internet content, sales representative briefing materials, advertising, and review articles.

Pharmaceutical companies fund all the trials necessary to get a drug approved, but these trials also present an economic and ethical dilemma to them. The best trials address the most clinically informative questions, use rigorous methodology, study the appropriate population groups, and properly analyse the results. At the same time, companies need trials with positive results to get their drugs approved for marketing and to drive sales. Negative trials can have significant adverse effects on sales. Within one year of the publication of the Women's Health Initiative trial, a non-commercial trial funded by the US National Institutes of Health, which found that estrogen/progestin combination drugs increased the risk of cardiovascular disease and breast cancer in postmenopausal women, prescriptions for Prempro, the most widely sold estrogen/progestin combination, had declined by 66% in the United States (5). In Canada, prescriptions for estrogen replacement therapy for women 65 and over dropped by 33% in one year (6). Companies, therefore, have strong economic reasons to deviate from the ideal of conducting clinical trials to generate scientifically valid evidence, and Health Canada has an equally strong responsibility to ensure that this does not happen.

Clinical trials are a highly sought after commodity, employing the talents of researchers, bringing economic value to hospitals and universities, and enhancing the scientific prestige of the institutions and countries where they take place. In 2012, Health Canada estimated that there were about 4000 ongoing clinical trials in the country at any one time testing 700 new drugs (7). A graphic on the website of Rx&D, the organization that represents the brand-name companies in Canada, lists 4761 trials as of 2013 (8). Between 2005 and 2010, Canada ranked fifth in the world behind the US, Germany, the United Kingdom, and France in participation in new trials funded by global corporations – although the trend in the growth of new sites and newly recruited subjects fell below the global rate over that period (9). Likewise, the amount spent in Canada on applied research – research intended to improve manufacturing processes, pre-clinical trials, and clinical trials – has been shrinking recently as a reflection of a decline in total research and development spending by companies in Canada. (See Table 2.2) (See Chapter 8 for a detailed analysis about industry investment in R&D.)

Table 2.2 Spending by research-based companies on applied research, 2003–2013

Year	Total amount spent ($000,000)	Percentage spent on applied research	Amount spent on applied research ($000,000)
2003	992.9	55.2	548.1
2004	1000.8	58.3	583.5
2005	1040.1	62.4	649.0
2006	949.0	59.5	564.7
2007	1184.4	54.4	644.3
2008	1172.2	57.3	671.7
2009	1132.9	56.2	636.7
2010	1000.2	54.8	548.1
2011	901.2	55.0	495.7
2012	782.8	60.2	471.2
2013	652.0	54.0	352.1

Source: Patented Medicine Prices Review Board. Annual report 2013. Ottawa: Health Canada; 2014.

New rules for clinical trials favour pharmaceutical companies

Before any type of clinical trials on experimental drugs (drugs that have never been marketed in Canada) can proceed, they must be approved by Health Canada. (In addition, clinical trials for new indications for drugs that are already on the market must also be approved by Health Canada.) Until January 2000, the Therapeutic Products Programme (TPP), now known as the Therapeutic Products Directorate (TPD) and the Biologics and Genetic Therapies Directorate (BGTD), the branch of Health Canada dealing with prescription and non-prescription drugs, had a default time of 60 days to review applications for clinical trials. If applications had not been processed within that period, then the sponsor was free to proceed with the trial. In early 2000, Health Canada proposed to change the default time from 60 days to 48 hours for phase 1 studies. One of the main reasons offered for this change was that "the proposed option would provide the [pharmaceutical] industry with internationally competitive review times for the review of human clinical trial drug submissions" (10 p236).

In looking at changes to review times, Health Canada made it clear that it was advancing only options that would not hinder trade. Safety was definitely mentioned but seemed to take a back seat to economic considerations. What Health Canada sought to do was create conditions that would lead to increased development of the pharmaceutical industry in Canada. As a report about the benefits and costs states: “A number of firms claim to be interested in establishing facilities in Canada to conduct Phase I human clinical trials. However, it has been suggested that this can only be done if the Canadian regulatory system allows for a registration system for Phase I trials as well as reduced review times for other trials” (10 p237). While it may or may not be a reasonable objective to promote the interests of the pharmaceutical industry, this was not, and is still not, the mandate of Health Canada. The mandate of the agency was, and is, to ensure that Canadians have access to safe and effective drugs (11). But in this case, the interests of commerce, not patients, were the explicit basis of Health Canada’s policy decisions.

The initial discussion paper published by Health Canada in 2000 (10) on the proposed reduction in trial review times to 48 hours was deficient in a number of critical areas. The only mention in the entire document of how other countries regulated Phase I trials was a reference that these types of trials were not governed by legislation in the United Kingdom. The agency did not offer any evidence that other countries had changed their review times, nor that an appropriate review could be conducted in 48 hours. Dr Charles Weijer, a bioethicist then at Dalhousie University said, “this [proposed change] causes me grave concern. One has to be very careful about getting into a competition for clinical trial revenues that’s based on having the lowest ethical standards” (12 pA4).

The proposal also claimed that the changes would result in increased access to improved therapy for the Canadian population (10). This claim was a serious distortion of the nature of clinical trials. Most of these trials are randomized studies in which, by definition, half the participants receive either a placebo or the standard therapy. Moreover, the very essence of a clinical trial is that neither the patients nor the researchers know whether the new therapy is better, worse, or the same as the current standard therapy. In fact, most new therapies commonly do not offer any meaningful benefits to trial participants. Speeding up the exposure to new drugs rarely equates to better health outcomes, despite the explicit statement in the Health Canada proposal (10).

Following the release of its paper on the proposal, Health Canada held an online public consultation. Almost all of the 80 respondents objected to the 48-hour period, and in 2001, Health Canada opted for a 30-day default review time (13) for Phase I trials, which remains the standard today. In the summer of 2006, Health Canada undertook another electronic evaluation, and two-thirds of respondents strongly believed that the objective of improving safety mechanisms had been met, and three-quarters strongly believed that the objective of shortening review times had been met. (14) (The report does not document who the respondents were.) Whether Health Canada had sufficient resources to adequately evaluate clinical trial proposals was not investigated, nor has there been any published independent study of the quality of the reviews since the change to a 30-day default review. The take-home message is that commercial considerations shaped the reduction in the review period, and although most stakeholders appeared to think the revised arrangements worked well, important questions remain unanswered, particularly regarding review quality.

Research ethics boards

Before clinical trials can go ahead in Canada, they need to be approved by ethics committees known as Research Ethics Boards (REBs). All hospitals where research is conducted have REBs, as do universities. The National Council on Ethics in Human Research (NCEHR) listed 380 REBs as of May 2014 across Canada, although from the institutions where they are based, it is clear that not all are involved in approving clinical trials (15). The Food and Drug Regulations set out the minimum number of people on a REB and the range of qualifications that they need to have, but they are silent on the procedures that these boards should follow and the standards that should govern their operations (16). In addition, Canada has no accreditation or inspection system for REBs and no oversight mechanism for the way that they undertake their reviews (17); in fact, "aside from identifying information on the REB and its chair, no further information about the REB or its review is required" by the TPD (18 p405).

Members of publicly based REBs, those located in universities and hospitals, have expressed unease about the relationship that their REBs have with the pharmaceutical industry. A report on the governance of human research from the Law Commission of Canada quotes some REB members on this subject: "We have more trouble with some of the commercial protocols because we worry that their motives may be different than the motives of a cooperative study group"; "In terms of the shift to industry-sponsored research, I see the conflicts of interests that are arising at a[n] exponential rate" (19 p213). The Commission report concludes that, with industry funding such a large proportion of research, the institutions where this research is based are becoming financially beholden to companies whose primary goal is profit, not science and the generation of knowledge (19).

Perceived delays with REBs in academic institutions have led companies to move their trials out of hospitals and universities and into community settings. The 2012 report of the Standing Senate Committee on Social Affairs, Science and Technology estimated that about 70% of industry funded trials are conducted in the community setting (7), a substantial increase from about 40% 15 years earlier (20). In that setting, there are no public REBs, with the exception of Alberta where the College of Physicians and Surgeons of Alberta has set up a REB to review community-based trials (20). Elsewhere in the country, most of these trials are reviewed by for-profit REBs that are paid a fee for their work by the organization that is financing the trial, which in nearly all cases is a pharmaceutical company (21). Trudo Lemmens, who teaches at the University of Toronto Faculty of Law, believes that the credibility and integrity of the research review is compromised by the perception of a possible conflict of interest when commercial REBs approve a clinical trial. If the REB turns down too many trials or demands costly changes to the research protocol, companies may be reluctant to submit future research proposals to it. (To date, no research has been done to verify or refute this concern.) In Lemmens's opinion, the honesty of individual REB members is not enough to remedy this situation (22).

The main guideline on ethical criteria for human research in Canada, the *Tri-Council Policy Statement* (Canadian Institutes of Health Research, the Natural Sciences and Engineering Research Council of Canada, and the Social Sciences and Humanities Research Council of Canada) recognizes the potential for conflicts of interest with commercial REBs, but the document does not discuss commercial REBs any further (23). In the late 1990s, Health Canada did not even know how many such agencies were operating in the country (22) and there is no evidence that the situation has changed since then. Problems with REBs are not just confined to the for-profit sector. Academic-based REBs were described in the Law Commission report as "overburdened [and] ... stretched to the breaking point ... As the work becomes increasingly complicated with globalization, technology and commercialization, REBs are struggling to find committee chairs or even members" (19 p229).

These difficulties may help to explain serious breaches in the behaviour of academic REBs documented in a series of anecdotal reports. The University of British Columbia failed to warn patients of all the dangers and side effects of study medications for years (24). The REB at St Joseph's Healthcare Centre in Hamilton approved a study that involved distributing a questionnaire to Catholic high school girls about problems with menstruation. However, the survey consent form did not include the fact that the questionnaire was being used as a screening form to find girls who would then be asked to join a trial studying the use of Prozac (fluoxetine) for severe premenstrual syndrome (25). US investigators found that the McMaster University REB had been failing to properly review experimental pediatric cancer protocols and that consent forms "given to guardians of the children were incomplete, hard to understand, and tended to minimize the potential risks while overstating the potential benefits" (25). Although a new set of standards about the governance, membership, operations, ethics review processes, and quality management of REBs was issued by a federal government agency, the Canadian General Standards Board, in mid-2013, these are voluntary. The statement announcing their publication did not give any information about whether their uptake will be monitored (26).

Recruiting doctors and patients for trials

One of the major challenges related to clinical trials is the recruitment of patients. To get doctors to identify and enter patients into these trials, physicians may be paid anywhere from a few hundred dollars to thousands of dollars per patient. For example, in a trial instigated by Merck Frosst, the company offered $6000 per patient (27). Although doctors may claim that money is not an issue and that they are doing the research to keep on the cutting edge of therapeutics for the benefit of their patients (28), that was not the view of Dr Paul Flynne, assistant registrar of the College of Physicians and Surgeons of Alberta: "Money is an issue, I can assure you," he said (29).

Estimates of the number of Canadians taking part annually in clinical trials range from 100,000 (30) up to 1.8 million (31). On its website, the NCEHR states that up to three million people are research participants in projects conducted at Canadian universities, with an unknown number participating in trials conducted in private clinicians' offices or by non-governmental organizations, but these figures include subjects in behavioural and social science studies (32), and so not all three million are taking part in clinical trials. These wide differences in the estimates underline how little monitoring occurs of basic statistical information about clinical trials.

To be sure of observing any positive effects from the drug being tested, companies eliminate as many variables as possible. When it comes to patients, that typically means choosing those who have a certain diagnosis, whose disease is not so far advanced that therapy will not be helpful, who are not taking any other medications, who do not have any other illnesses, and who will metabolize the drug in a well understood manner, that is, they are neither children nor seniors. The result is that as few as 1 in 25 patients may meet the eligibility criteria for entry into the trial (33). Therefore, patients who are enrolled into clinical trials tend to do better than those who are excluded and they have fewer adverse events (34), thereby making the drug look more effective and safer than it may actually be. If certain groups of people are not included in clinical trials, then when doctors prescribe for them, they have little or no information to guide them (35,36).

Health Canada could dictate the composition of patients in clinical trials but has chosen not to. After the thalidomide disaster in the early 1960s, women of child-bearing age were generally systematically excluded from clinical trials. This situation did not formally change in Canada until 1997, when Allan Rock, then minister of health, announced a guideline on the inclusion of women in clinical trials. However, this guideline was voluntary and not mandatory and therefore could not be enforced (37). Despite the guideline, in the late 1990s, it still appeared that HIV-positive women were under-represented in clinical research on HIV (38). In 1999, the now defunct Women's Health Strategy of Health Canada promised to monitor compliance with the guideline on the inclusion of women in clinical trials, but no systematic mechanism was put into place to do so (39).

A new guidance document on who should be included in clinical trials was issued at the end of May 2013, and although it was an improvement on the 1997 statement, it is still only advisory. The language of the document makes it clear that Health Canada is offering only recommendations and not making mandatory requirements with words such as "encourages sponsors" and "recommend[s] that sponsors" (40). The document also includes a non-enforceable guideline regarding the inclusion of children in clinical trials (41). Health Canada says that it “reserves the right to ... define conditions not specifically described in this guidance” (40), but whether it has exercised its prerogative to demand additional conditions regarding the inclusion of children is impossible to determine. The lack of pediatric trials often means that doctors are guessing about whether drugs will be effective in children, what safety issues may arise, and what the correct dose is.

Placebos versus active controls

In the same way that the industry limits the patients who enter clinical trials to make it easier to interpret them, so too do the companies prefer placebo-controlled trials to those using an active comparator, that is, another drug that is used to treat the same condition. The logic in favour of placebo trials is simple – it’s easier to show that your drug is better than nothing than to show that it’s better than something else that works. Moreover, a trial using a placebo control requires fewer patients than one with an active control, and the lower the number of patients, the less expensive the trial is to run.

But from the viewpoint of clinicians who will be prescribing the drug once it’s marketed, placebo-controlled trials mean that they have no head-to-head trials to help them decide which drug will work best for patients. Although we have no Canadian data on the subject, in Europe and in the United States, about half of all new drugs lack comparative data, despite the existence of alternative treatment options (42,43). Besides placebos depriving prescribers of important information, patients may be harmed by the use of placebos in clinical trials. For example, 2405 patients were enrolled in 10 pivotal trials to evaluate new therapies for multiple sclerosis and received placebos. Of these patients, 2102 had relapses. About one-third of these events could have been avoided if the patients had been treated with standard therapy (44).

Health Canada’s position on the use of placebo controls is decidedly murky. According to Flood and Dyke (17), Health Canada has produced a guidance document for industry on the subject (45), but the document has no legal status as it is intended only to provide “assistance” and is not part of the Food and Drug Regulations. The guidance document is based on the International Conference on Harmonisation of Technical Requirements for Registration of Pharmaceuticals for Human Use (ICH) guidelines (46) (see Chapter 3 for a discussion of the role of the ICH in regulatory harmonization), but neither Health Canada nor the ICH is “clear about the use of appropriate comparators, although the latter does stipulate that trials should be conducted to accord with the principles of the *Declaration of Helsinki.* The *Declaration,* in turn, requires that new drugs be tested against the best current proven treatment, except where no current proven intervention exists or where there are compelling and scientifically sound methodological reasons to use a placebo control" (17 p292).

Importantly, the ICH guideline does not unambiguously state that an active control should be used in preference to placebo. Without any definitive statement from Health Canada, some REBs continue to be willing to approve clinical trials that use placebos, even if an active comparator is available (47). Health Canada's silence on this question allows industry to continue to favour placebo-controlled clinical trials, despite their negative consequences for doctors and patients.

Monitoring the conduct of clinical research

Speaking in the early 1980s, Dr Ian Henderson, former director of the Bureau of Human Prescription Drugs at Health Canada, recalled that when he was a clinical researcher, drug company monitors who came around to assess progress on a trial were mostly concerned with whether he was completing the forms properly. According to Henderson, "there are probably lots of [clinical trial] protocol violations we know nothing about ... I don't place much faith in drug-company monitoring" (48).

Asked about the lack of monitoring of drug trials, Dr Thomas Clark, who administered the University of Toronto's ethics committee in the early 1980s, said, "You're putting your finger on a weakness in the system" (48 p4). The death of a Canadian patient involved in a clinical study of a new asthma medication in the late 1980s reinforced these concerns about the ambiguities in the responsibilities of ethics committees in Canada. An investigation into the death was undertaken by a public affairs television show in 1989. On the show, Dr Gordon Johnson, the head of the Bureau of Human Prescription Drugs, stated that "they [drug trials] are constantly under the surveillance of the local ethics committee," while "the actual conduct of the trial is the responsibility of the sponsor" (49). However, according to the head of the committee that approved the trial in question, the committee did not do "as much [checking on compliance] as we would like because we don't have the resources" (49). Finally, the opinion from a representative of the drug company sponsoring the trial was that "the actual responsibility for a given circumstance is going to depend on the specific case ... It could be any one of the parties concerned, it could be all the parties or it could be none of the parties" (50).

The examples below show that there continued to be anecdotal cases that demonstrated either a lack of monitoring by Health Canada or a lack of concern about regulations being violated. Officials within Health Canada admitted that a number of trials were allowed to proceed before being approved by the organization because they had been reviewed by US authorities (49). In another example, a man with tuberculosis (TB) was included in a Phase 1 trial (a trial in healthy people) in Montreal in 2005, potentially exposing all the other trial participants and the people running the trial to TB. Even though the person in this case was apparently showing signs of the disease, SFBC Anapharm, the company running the trial, kept the person in the on-site study. It was only after this incident that Health Canada created guidelines requiring the screening of trial participants for the symptoms of this disease (51,52).

The kinds of problems raised in these anecdotal reports were noted in the 2000 report from the auditor general, which stated that Health Canada "often did not review and assess adverse reaction reports for products under clinical trials in a timely manner" (53 p26–13). In fact, before 2002 Health Canada did not routinely monitor the conduct of clinical trials. This serious gap in Health Canada's activities was underlined by the auditor general in the case of the antimalarial drug Lariam (mefloquine). Health Canada approved the protocol for a clinical trial of this product, but despite this approval, it took no steps to ensure that the trial was being conducted according to the protocol. Health Canada viewed that as the responsibility of the manufacturer as the sponsor of the study (54).

New regulations to allow for inspections came into effect in early 2002 (55), and although Health Canada aims to inspect 2% of ongoing clinical trials annually, in 2006–07 it managed to achieve only half that figure, or 40 inspections versus a targeted 80 (56), possibly because it did not allocate sufficient resources to the task (57). Another auditor general's report in 2011 documented a continuing shortfall in the number of inspections undertaken – 52 in 2009 and 50 in 2010 – largely because of a lack of resources and a reallocation of resources to other programs (58). Previously, program managers at Health Canada told the auditor general that they considered there was an insufficient level of activity at Health Canada when it came to investigating clinical trials (59).

Health Canada says that it uses "risk-based criteria" to select the trials to be inspected, but these criteria are vague and merely state that they include the number of subjects enrolled and the number of trials conducted at a specific location (60). Therefore, it is unknown whether Health Canada is actually monitoring the trials where the subjects are at the greatest risk. Moreover, "Health Canada does not regularly collect all of the information necessary to assess these factors and to make comparative risk-based decisions. Because clinical trial sponsors are not required to submit up-to-date information on clinical trial sites, inspectors must call each site directly to find out the current status of the clinical trial site and the number of participants enrolled ... Thus, inspectors have up-to-date information only for sites that they call and are unable to compare the risks posed by all sites" (58 p9). New interim risk-based criteria for trial inspections were developed and piloted by Health Canada for use during 2012–13 in conjunction with the development of a new site selection process (61), but no information has been published about these new criteria or how they are being applied.

Health Canada started publishing reports about its inspections, with the first one covering 2002 (62) and a second one, the period 2003–04 (63). After that there was a prolonged silence. As documented in Box 2.1, I wrote to Health Canada on numerous occasions between 2008 and 2011 to inquire about the delay and to find out when the next report would be released. The next report finally appeared on 28 March 2012 and covered 2004–2011 (64).

BOX 2.1 CORRESPONDENCE ABOUT REPORTS OF INSPECTIONS OF CLINICAL TRIALS

March 24, 2008

In looking at the Health Canada web site I note that there has not been any publication of reports on inspections of clinical trials since the report detailing the results of inspections from 2003 to 2004. Are these inspections still ongoing and if they are why has no report been published since December 14, 2004?

Thank you for your time.

Sincerely,
Joel Lexchin

March 26, 2008

Dear Joel:
In fact, I updated the inspection report last week. It will cover the period between April1, 2002 to March 31, 2008, so I will have to wait till a few days after March 31 to update the stats fully. The goal is to have it released by the end of April.

Good Clinical Practices Unit

2 June 2008

Towards the end of March I had some correspondence with the GCP Unit about the release of the inspection report ... At that point it was expected that the report would be released by the end of April but it is now early June and the report still has not been posted. Do you have an updated expected release date?

Sincerely,
Joel Lexchin

3 July 2008

On March 24 I wrote asking about the status of clinical trial inspection reports since the last one published was for the year 2003-04. The response I received said that an updated report was expected to be available by the end of April. On June 2 since there was no report on the web site I wrote again asking about the status of the report. I did not receive any reply to that email and so I am writing again. Could you please inform me when a new clinical trial inspection report is expected to be available.

Sincerely,
Joel Lexchin

4 July 2008

Dear Dr. Lexchin,

The Health Products and Food Branch Inspectorate is currently developing a number of documents relevant to inspections. It is our intention to post the documents on the Health Canada website in the near future.

Good Clinical Practices Unit

July 1, 2011

Food and Drugs Act Liaison Office

In the past Health Canada has published reports of inspections conducted of clinical trials. However the last report that is available covered the period 2003-04. I have had previous correspondence with Health Canada about these reports but no real satisfactory answer as to why these reports are no longer being made available. I would appreciate your help in this matter.

Sincerely,
Joel Lexchin

July 6, 2011

Good day Dr. Lexchin,
I followed-up on your inquiry and I have received a response from XXX, Acting Manager, Good Clinical Practices Unit.

I am including text from an email from Mrs. XXX for your reference: "As discussed, the GCP Compliance Unit last published a Summary Report of Inspections in 2004. An updated version to 2011 is in the final stages of development and is expected to be published in the fall of 2011." Mrs. XXX also indicated that the Good Clinical Practices Unit are looking at creating a more regular publishing cycle for these reports.

October 31, 2011

Dear YYY:
I am following up on some correspondence that we had back in early July of this year regarding the lack of any reports about clinical trial inspections since 2003-04. At that point you said that you "will follow-up with the Good Clinical Practices Unit in late August/early September to get a status update on this report and to verify if they have more precise timelines at that point. I will let you know the results of my inquiries." Could you please let me know the results of your inquiries.

Sincerely,
Joel Lexchin

Nov. 1, 2011

Good day Dr. Lexchin,
I contacted XXX in the GCP Unit, on September 13, 2011 and October 31, 2011. I received an email from Mrs. XXX on November 1, 2011 stating that they are working on this document and are currently expected to publish the report to the Health Canada website in January.

Sincerely,
YYY

When Health Canada finds problems in its inspections, there are often significant delays in dealing with these problems. The agency issued six inspection reports with non-compliance ratings in 2009 and 2010. For these six reports, "Health Canada took between 56 and 142 days to officially notify regulated parties that they were not compliant with the Food and Drug Regulations and to officially request corrective actions to address all identified deficiencies ... Health Canada also reviews the adequacy of corrective actions proposed by regulated parties, but it has not set timelines for this review, either" (58 p10).

Finally, Health Canada is much less transparent in the information it publicizes about its inspections compared with the United States. When the Food and Drug Administration finds serious problems, the results of its inspection and its warning letter to the company are posted on its website, albeit with some delay and certain information redacted (56). (Chapter 3 provides a more in-depth analysis of the lack of transparency at Health Canada.) In contrast, Health Canada provides summary statistics about its inspections but no information about individual sites, corrective actions required, the drugs involved, the names of the doctors running the trials, or the names of the companies (64,65). In 2003, the FDA investigated a pediatric clinical trial taking place at the Children's Hospital of Eastern Ontario in Ottawa and issued a warning letter about violations to the doctor running the trial. Subsequently, "Health Canada ... investigated the trial but released no information about the doctors or 7 other trial centres involved. It was later revealed that a 4-year-old boy died after being given an overdose of the cancer drug interleukin-2, at a time when the trial had not yet received Health Canada approval to proceed. Months later, that authorization was obtained and the trial continued" (56 p636).

In 2014, Health Canada told the *Toronto Star* that "'confidential and/or proprietary information is removed' from the summary reports" (66). According to the *Star*, "over the past 12 years Health Canada found at least 33 clinical trials had critical problems and were 'non-compliant.' In July [2014], the *Star* asked for details of these and other inspections, and last week [September 9] Health Canada refused, saying that providing records 'would require an exhaustive manual paper file review.' The regulator also said the release of these clinical trial inspection reports could only come after consultation with third parties, typically the doctors and drug companies. The Canadian regulator refused to say how many clinical trials it has shut down or stopped, if any" (65). Ironically, at a Biotechnology Industry Organization international meeting in San Diego in June 2008, Industry Canada handed out brochures promoting the conduct of clinical trials in Canada partly on the basis of the claim that "Canadian trial sites, are regularly monitored by Health Canada, the US FDA and industry sponsors" (56 p638).

The degree to which Phase IV studies, those done after a drug has been approved and is being marketed, are monitored is also a significant cause for concern. This type of study is typically run in a community setting and has therefore been approved by a for-profit REB. Moreover, Phase IV studies are often used by industry not to generate new scientific data but as a way to generate interest about the drug among doctors involved in the trials and get them familiar with prescribing the product (66). Previously, Health Canada's said its inspection process can be applied to these studies "as needed" (60), but what that means is not spelled out and none of the inspection reports provided information on whether any studies of this type were inspected. One older Canadian example of a Phase IV study involved Squibb (now part of Bristol-Myers Squibb) providing 2000 doctors across Canada with a computer valued at $2000 if they enrolled 10 patients into a drug trial. At the end of the trial, Squibb would retain ownership of the computers but doctors would be allowed to keep them in their offices (67).

Analysis of adverse drug reactions in clinical trials

The 2011 auditor general's report investigated the ability of Health Canada to collect and analyse adverse drug reactions (ADRs) (58). The Food and Drug Regulations require that drug companies inform the department of all serious, unexpected ADRs for drugs being tested in Canadian clinical trials, regardless of whether the adverse reaction occurred at a trial site in Canada or in another country. The report noted that Health Canada assessment officers monitored drug reaction reports from the trials that posed the highest risk, but no standard operating procedures existed to ensure that the department consistently focused on the trials that posed the greatest risk. Similarly, the department had not documented its criteria for prioritizing its assessment of potential safety issues based on the risks posed to clinical trial participants.

Health Canada responded to the auditor general's recommendation by stating that it had now implemented a process such that the safety information received for drugs in early development or being studied in high-risk populations was being evaluated first (61). The success of this process needs to be closely evaluated since it relies on reports from companies about ADRs, and documented evidence shows that some companies distort the way that they report reactions (68,69).

Contract research organizations

Although commercial interests have always played a significant role in clinical trials, commercial considerations are becoming ever more important. One manifestation of this trend is that pharmaceutical companies are turning over the management of trials to contract research organizations or CROs. CROs are for-profit organizations that, for the past two decades, have taken over nearly all aspects of the clinical trial process. Echoing a common theme about many aspects of clinical trials, observers worry there is very little oversight or information about private CROs (20,70).

The common explanation for the rise in prominence of CROs is that they can run trials more efficiently than pharmaceutical companies or hospitals and therefore save money, but the competition between CROs and academic medical centres to conduct clinical trials has negative consequences. The most egregious of these is that "as CROs and academic medical centres compete head to head for the opportunity to enroll patients in clinical trials, corporate sponsors have been able to dictate the terms of participation in the trial, terms that are not always in the best interests of academic investigators, the study participants or the advancement of science generally. Investigators may have little or no input into trial design, no access to the raw data, and limited participation in data interpretation. These terms are draconian for self-respecting scientists, but many have accepted them because they know that if they do not, the sponsor will find someone else who will" (71 p786). Moreover, the employees of CROs who do the research are not concerned about publication nor do their careers depend on the number of journal papers they produce; therefore, the likelihood is greater that information will remain unpublished. CROs are also linked to the rise in ghost authorship, whereby pharmaceutical companies pay medical writers to write up studies and then look for researchers willing to sign their names to the studies (72,73). The term "contract research organization" appears in 12 Health Canada documents based on a search of the website in September 2014, but none of these documents dealt specifically with issues unique to CROs.

Clinical trial registries: An example of inaction

In recent years, a number of high-profile scandals have led to a call for transparency in the results of clinical research. GlaxoSmithKline did not publish results that showed that Paxil (paroxetine) was ineffective for the treatment of depression in children and adolescents because, according to an internal company memo, "It would be commercially unacceptable to include a statement that efficacy had not been demonstrated, as this would undermine the profile of paroxetine" (74). The *Wall Street Journal* claimed that "internal Merck e-mails and marketing materials as well as interviews with outside scientists show that the company fought forcefully for years to keep safety concerns from destroying ... [Vioxx's] commercial prospects" (75). One result of these revelations was the strengthening of the demand that all clinical trials be registered in online, publicly accessible databases that contain key information about clinical trials. Initially, officials at Merck dismissed the idea of registries with the statement "we, like others, do not concur with calls for mandatory registration of all clinical trials at their inception to redress publication bias; rather, we commit to publish trials" (76 p482). Although Merck and other companies subsequently supported the idea of a clinical trial registry (77), compliance for industry (and non-industry funded) trials in accurately entering data into the US registry run by the National Institutes of Health needs substantial improvement, despite registration being mandatory (78). (Trials funded by industry were more than three times as likely to report results as were trials funded by the National Institutes of Health (78).)

After a series of hearings on prescription drugs in 2003, the House of Commons Standing Committee on Health recommended that Health Canada create a "public database that provides information on trials in progress, trials abandoned and trials completed" (79 p13). By the time that Health Canada first held a public workshop about a clinical trial registry in June 2005, there were already functioning registries in Australia/New Zealand (http://www.anzctr.org.au/Faq.aspx), the European Union (https://www.clinicaltrialsregister.eu/about.html), and the United States (https://clinicaltrials.gov/ct2/about-site/history). Following the workshop, an external working group met in April 2006, and in June–July 2006 the public was given the opportunity to complete an online questionnaire on the topic (80). The external working group delivered its report in December 2006 (81). According to information on the Health Canada website, after that report was published, "Health Canada will consider the results of the public consultations and the External Working Group's recommendations before making a final decision on how to proceed with the registration and disclosure of clinical trial information in Canada" (82). In its 2007 *Blueprint for Renewal II: Modernizing Canada's Regulatory System for Health Products and Food,* Health Canada committed to enhancing public access to clinical trial information (83).

Finally, after almost eight years of delay, and as part of its response to the 2011 auditor general's report (61), the federal government announced a public database of clinical drug trials authorized by Health Canada that will contain the titles of trial protocols, the medical conditions involved, the drugs and populations being studied, the enrolment status, and the dates Health Canada authorized the trials (84,85). However, the Health Canada database is mainly designed to help Canadians locate ongoing clinical trials to facilitate enrolment. In contrast to other international clinical trial registries, such as Clinicaltrials.gov in the United States, it will not list study sites, investigators and their contact information, details of trial designs, primary and secondary outcome measures, or trial results (86). That missing information is the type that allows researchers, doctors, and academics to learn about all clinical trials on new drugs, not just the trials that have been published in medical journals (85).

Conclusion

Without clinical studies, drug development would halt, and we would be left with only anecdotal data to suggest how safe and effective drugs are. No one wants this scenario, but at the same time the current situation with respect to clinical trials is not acceptable. The lack of any information on Health Canada's website about how or even whether it regulates the activities of CROs is an example of smart regulation. The case of the SFBC Anapharm trial in Montreal is an example of the triumph of risk management over the precautionary principle. If clinical trials are to serve the purpose for which they are designed, namely developing reliable and objective information about new drugs, then commercial interests expressed in smart regulation and risk management need to be explicitly rejected in favour of health interests.

The major themes that have emerged in this chapter are the influence of the profit motive in all aspects of clinical trials and the unwillingness of Health Canada to forcefully assert the public interest, including the right of patients in clinical trials to know their results. The subjugation of public interests to those of the industry in the clinical trial arena raises serious concerns about whether public health is still Health Canada's primary commitment.

3 Approving new drugs: Better or just more?

After reviewing the history and development of the Canadian regulatory system, this chapter raises concerns about how long Health Canada should take for its review, how much transparency there is in the review process, where the operational funding for the review should come from, and the push from both inside and outside Canada to harmonize Canadian regulatory requirements with those of other countries. These questions are all addressed with a particular focus on the involvement of the pharmaceutical industry in influencing the policy environment and how this involvement affects decisions about drug effectiveness and safety.

Private enterprise is responsible for developing medications, but for over 80 years, the federal government has taken a role in the process of deciding whether to allow drugs to be sold, starting with the 1921 amendments to the Food and Drugs Act of 1920. These amendments included the addition of a section providing the minister of health with the authority to license manufacturers of certain drugs (1). A further 1927 amendment made false, misleading, and deceptive advertising of drugs illegal, and in 1934, Schedule A made it an offence to advertise to the public any drug for the treatment of a list of diseases (1). (The Schedule A list of diseases was not amended until 2008, when it also became legal to publicly advertise preventive claims for certain natural health products, over-the-counter drugs, and vaccines for diseases listed in Schedule A (2). See Chapter 4 for a discussion about Schedule A in the context of direct-to-consumer advertising.)

Before 1946, the Food and Drugs Act (F&DAct) provided the authority to Health Canada's predecessor to prohibit or define the conditions of sale for drugs that might lead to health problems, but in the post–World

War II period, the limitations of the existing legislation became evident. As one example, no law prohibited the importation of new drugs from the United States, and the practice of marketing new drugs in Canada before their acceptance by US authorities became a problem. In some instances, companies had insufficient clinical experience to provide adequate directions for the safe use of the drug, and "Canada was becoming a proving ground for foreign manufacturers to test-market their new drugs" (1 p422). Because of these and other events, the Canadian government passed regulations in 1951 requiring manufacturers to file submissions with the Food and Drug Directorate (FDD) for all new drugs. These submissions included detailed reports of tests that were considered adequate and proper to establish the safety of the drug. Further, the regulations made it mandatory during the clinical trial period for the drug label to carry a statement that read "For Experimental Use by Qualified Investigators Only." The manufacturer was also required to notify the FDD when the drug was distributed for clinical trials and to keep an accurate record of where the drug was distributed (1, 3).

In the aftermath of thalidomide, the Food and Drug Regulations were further amended in 1963 to define the conditions that had to be satisfied before a drug could be allowed onto the market, or in the parlance of Health Canada, issued a Notice of Compliance (NOC). The key provisions in the amendments were that companies needed to provide Health Canada with substantial evidence not only that was the drug safe but also that it was effective, that companies had to file a preclinical submission before they could distribute a drug, and that the minister of health had the authority to suspend both a preclinical submission and a NOC, that is, the minister could stop sales of a drug (1).

To the probable surprise of most doctors and patients, the Food and Drug Regulations have never set a standard for how effective a new drug has to be. The Regulations merely say that a new drug submission has to contain "substantial evidence of the clinical effectiveness of the new drug for the purpose and under the conditions of use recommended" (4 p430). In practice, what this means is that if the manufacturer of a drug recommends its use for the treatment of, say high blood pressure, and the drug reduces blood pressure even marginally, it can potentially be approved. What Jonathan Darrow says about the US Food and Drug Administration's (FDA) criteria for approval applies equally as well to Health Canada: the perception that Health Canada's "approval guarantees substantial effectiveness can lead physicians and patients to cede responsibility for critically evaluating drug value, thus adversely affecting treatment choices" (5 p2076).

Questionable effectiveness of the 1963 amendments: The case of the benzodiazepines

Although the 1963 amendments required companies to submit substantial safety information before being issued a NOC, a case study of benzodiazepines suggests that the evidence submitted for this class of drugs was less than adequate. No documents are publicly available about the kind of clinical trials Health Canada evaluated before it approved drugs in the benzodiazepine class (sedatives and hypnotics, including Valium (diazepam) and Librium (chlordiazepoxide)), but indirect evidence strongly suggests that Health Canada approved these drugs based on poor clinical information.

In the Nordic countries in the mid-1960s, these drugs were approved based on clinical trials of poor quality; it was possible to determine the efficacy of the drugs in only about one-fifth to one-quarter of cases. Even a decade later, a drug's efficacy could be determined in only two-thirds of the applications (6). The trials that showed that benzodiazepines were effective in treating anxiety were "so poorly designed and executed as to be meaningless, the efficacy of the entire group of drugs as antianxiety agents, must be questioned" (7). Since many of the trials done to get a drug registered are used in multiple countries, the conclusions reached about the quality of trials likely apply to the trials that were considered and accepted by Health Canada.

The point about registration of drugs for unsupported indications provides another avenue to explore the adequacy of the Canadian drug review process in the mid-1960s. One of the indications for the use of diazepam in Canada was "relief of muscular disorders of central or peripheral origin" (8) or, in other words, as a muscle relaxant, a use that could not be supported by controlled studies (9). Either such studies existed but were unpublished, an unlikely event since the companies making benzodiazepines would have sought publication to increase sales, or as is more likely, Health Canada approved this indication in the absence of any good data.

Finally, there is the safety aspect of diazepam as it was initially described in the *Compendium of Pharmaceuticals and Specialties*, an annual volume from the Canadian Pharmaceutical Association that summarizes the approved information from Health Canada on products marketed in

Canada. The main side effects listed were mild ataxia (loss of balance) and a sedative effect from high doses (8). Conspicuous by its absence was any mention of the possibility of dependency. The pharmaceutical literature is littered with claims that psychoactive drugs were safe and non-addictive, but those claims have been proved wrong time after time (10). Therefore, it is hard to imagine that Health Canada did not require companies to screen psychoactive drugs, such as the benzodiazepines, for their potential for dependency, but the evidence, based on the listed side effects, is that Health Canada probably did not. This fact, of course, raises the question of why not? Was this just wilful ignorance on the part of regulators? (In this respect Canadian regulators were no better or worse than those in most other countries.) Subsequently, it became clear that dependence and withdrawal reactions were serious problems with benzodiazepines, just as they were with the drugs that preceded them (11).

Questionable effectiveness of the 1963 amendments: The case of Oraflex (benoxaprofen)

Oraflex (benoxaprofen), a non-steroidal anti-inflammatory and analgesic agent, is a second example of the problems with drugs approved through the Canadian system, specifically the absence of any requirement for manufacturers to inform Health Canada about safety problems occurring outside Canada. In 1980, this drug was marketed in Britain under the name of Opren. Shortly after the drug appeared on the shelves of British pharmacies, Eli Lilly, the maker of the drug, informed British health officials of the first of eight deaths from suspected adverse reactions. In February 1982, nine months after the first known British death, benoxaprofen was evaluated by Health Canada as safe for use in Canada. In its submission to Health Canada, the Canadian Lilly subsidiary did not mention the eight deaths in Britain or other safety data that put benoxaprofen in a negative light (12).

Although Canadian officials approved the drug for marketing in February 1982, Lilly decided to delay marketing until that September. Finally in early May, Lilly informed Health Canada about seven deaths in Britain, just before the appearance of an article in the *British Medical Journal* describing some deaths. At the same time, Lilly gave Health Canada a summary of data from a Paris symposium showing that dosages had to be modified for older patients. The combination of the two pieces of information resulted in the agency reversing its decision on the marketing of benoxaprofen in Canada. As we have seen, Canadian regulations were predicated on the assumption that companies behaved honestly and ethically, but as this example shows, that was not always the case.

Cost recovery: Paying for drug reviews

Traditionally, the money to operate the drug regulatory system has come from parliamentary appropriations, since drug regulation is seen as a service to the public. In 1985, a task force led by Deputy Prime Minister Eric Nielsen identified cost-recovery opportunities for the premarket evaluation of drugs. Cost recovery essentially means charging the users of a service, in this case charging pharmaceutical companies for reviewing their drug applications. Three years later, in 1988, the Treasury Board directed Health Canada to implement a cost-recovery program by January 1989. However, Health Canada was unable to reach an agreement with the companies for such a program (13). By 1994, the situation had changed as the government sought to eliminate the large budgetary deficit of the early 1990s. Cost recovery for the operation of the drug approval system was introduced to compensate for the reduction in direct government funding. Cost recovery was also seen as "a means of transferring some or all of the costs of a government activity from the general taxpayer to those who more directly benefit from or who 'trigger' that special activity" (14). Initially, in 1994, pharmaceutical companies paid $143,800 to have a new drug application reviewed; by 2014 that had risen to $322,056 (15). (In adopting cost recovery, Health Canada was not unique. Cost recovery is used in Australia, the European Union, the United Kingdom, and the United States (16).) As of 2015, cost recovery was expected to provide about half of the operating budget for the various drug programs of Health Canada (16).

This shift in the financing of the regulatory body has raised concerns, based on principal-agent theory, about whether Health Canada's primary commitment is to public health. Principal-agent theory proposes that a relationship exists between a principal who has a task that needs to be performed and an agent who is contracted to do the task in exchange for compensation (17). Before the introduction of user fees, the principal was the Canadian public and the agent was Health Canada. However, since 1994, a new principal has been added: the pharmaceutical industry, which is now providing a substantial fraction of the money needed to run the drug regulatory system.

One example of how cost recovery may have led to a principal-agent relationship between the industry and Health Canada was the change in how quickly drugs moved through the review process. The loudest and most influential voice calling for faster drug approvals has long been the brand-name industry. In the past, Canada's Research-Based Pharmaceutical Companies (Rx&D), the trade association representing the brand-name companies, has repeatedly complained about the excessive time it takes to get a drug approved (18, 19). Rx&D sponsored meetings in 1986 and 1987 to publicize the issue among a variety of professional and consumer groups and to put forward its message that "a supportive policy environment in terms of the regulatory review process is another factor critical to the global competitiveness of the pharmaceutical industry" (20 p16). In its 2002 report, *Improving Health Through Innovation: A New Deal for Canadians,* Rx&D explicitly linked cost-recovery fees to the "attainment of revised internationally competitive performance standards" (18).

As the table in the Introduction of this book shows, this message about shortening how long drugs spend in the review process has been repeated frequently in documents issued by Rx&D in the twenty-first century. Industry does not shy away from its commercial reasons for concern about getting drugs to market faster, but it maintains that its main interest is in the health of Canadian patients (M. McGlynn, Chairman PMAC task force on drug certification delays. Personal communication, 4 July 1986). This concern for the needs of patients might be believable if most new drugs were significant therapeutic improvements that needed to reach patients as quickly as possible but, in fact, only about 1 in 10 drugs marketed in any given year are major improvements on existing medications (21). On the other hand, companies receive a definite economic advantage in getting their products to market as fast as possible. For instance, in 2009–10, sales of Lipitor (atorvastatin) in Ontario alone were $316 million, meaning that a marketing delay of just one day would have cost Pfizer, its maker, $870,000 (22). Early marketing also allows companies to maximize the length of marketing before patent expiry.

For a number of years, documents from Health Canada have also reflected the need to satisfy the industry's desire to get drugs to the market more rapidly. One aspect of "visioning the ideal system" in a 1990 paper is "improv[ing] the business climate" while another section says that the system should not "impose a burden on the pharmaceutical manufacturer which makes it less competitive" (23 p10). Closely related to the question of the length of the review time was the "backlog," the number of new drug submissions that were waiting to enter the review queue. The longer products waited and the more products in the queue, the longer they would take to reach the drugstore shelves. According to the report of the Working Group on Drug Submission Review, which was appointed by the government in January 1987, the "backlog and delay in the submission review process has a consequence that Canadians do not have timely access to new drugs" (24 p4). The same message was echoed in the report from Denis Gagnon that looked into the entire drug approval system. This report was the result of industry pressure on the government to deal with the slowness of the Canadian approval system (25), and therefore one of its conclusions is not surprising: "Not to review the drug quickly offers the patient continued pain or possibly certain death, or both" (26 p25). Other reports in the 1980s and early 1990s also commented on the backlog in the review process, and out of six reports (24, 26–30), all but one (24) urged that major reforms be instituted to deal with this problem.

A 1991 publication from the Drugs Directorate (one of the previous names for the part of Health Canada dealing with medications) stated that "the resolution of the backlog of drug submissions remains the central focus of the Drugs Directorate's efforts" (31 p10). Following the Gagnon Report in 1992 (26), even greater priority was given to resolving the backlog and decreasing the time it took to review submissions; in response to that report, Health Canada set up the Drugs Directorate Renewal to deal with both of these issues, along with a number of others (13).

The emphasis on getting drugs to market faster continued through the 1990s, and in the middle of that decade, a working group from Health Canada looked at ways of efficiently managing its limited resources and made recommendations for moving submissions through the system more quickly. The working group report adopted language worryingly suggestive of a principal-agent relationship, admitting that "the pharmaceutical industry is looking for dramatic improvement in service" and "the implementation of the proposed changes may not result in the level of improved performance desired by our industry clients" (32). Perhaps most tellingly was a 1997 internal bulletin from the director general of the Therapeutic Products Programme (TPP), the part of Health Canada dealing with drug regulation, that discussed the question of who Health Canada's client is. In the context of cost recovery, the bulletin advised staff that "the client is the direct recipient of your services. In many cases this is the person or company who pays for the service." The one-page document focused on service to industry and relegated the public to the secondary status of "stakeholder" or "beneficiary" (33).

Figure 3.1 Relationship between the introduction of user fees and changes in positive decisions about new drugs and approval times in Canada

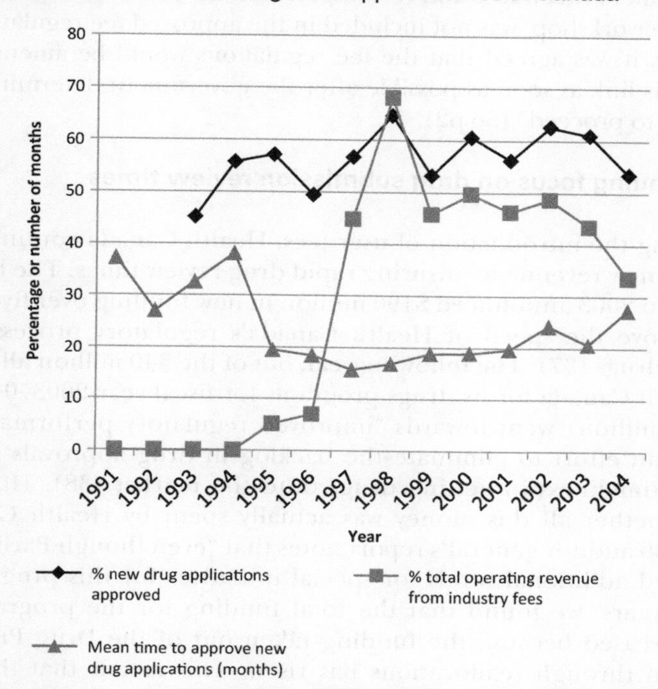

Source: Modified from Lexchin J. Relationship between pharmaceutical company user fees and drug approvals in Canada and Australia: a hypothesis-generating study. Annals of Pharmacotherapy. 2006;40:2216–22. http://dx.doi.org/10.1345/aph.1H117

The introduction of cost recovery was associated with both an increase in the percentage of new drug applications being approved and a decrease in the time drugs spent in the review process (34). (See Figure 3.1) Both these changes were favourable to the drug companies: more of their products would reach the market, and because they spent less time in the review process, the patented drugs had a longer time on the market before generics could be introduced. Importantly, these changes occurred despite there being no net increase in the resources available to Health Canada: the start of cost recovery coincided with a decrease in funding (34). Although Health Canada has explicitly denied any relationship between performance targets and user fees (35), here is a quotation from a 1998 Health Canada document about user fees: "A formal link between fees and review performance, recommended at the July 1995 workshop, was not included in the approved fee regulations ... However, it was agreed that the fee regulations would be amended to make this link as soon as possible after the government determines the best way to proceed" (36 p2).

A continuing focus on drug submission review times

Following the introduction of user fees, Health Canada continued to commit new revenue to ensuring rapid drug review times. The budget speech in 2003 announced $190 million in new funding over five years to improve the speed of Health Canada's regulatory processes for human drugs (37). The following year, out of the $40 million allocated to Health Canada for its drugs programs for fiscal year 2003–04, 78% ($31.2 million) went towards "improved regulatory performance" – mainly an effort to eliminate the backlog in drug approvals and to ensure timeliness in getting drugs onto the market (38). (It is not clear whether all this money was actually spent by Health Canada. The 2006 auditor general's report notes that "even though Parliament approved additional funds for special initiatives for this program in recent years, we found that the total funding for the program has not increased because the funding taken out of the Drug Products program through reallocations has risen. This means that the program has no additional money to deliver on its regulatory responsibilities, which continue to increase" (39 p16).) The 2006–07 *Departmental Performance Report* gave one of Health Canada's goals as having "90% of new pharmaceutical...drug submissions decisions met within internationally comparable performance targets, compared to 13% ... in 2003" (40 p40). The report briefly mentioned drug safety but no targets were set out for topics such as how quickly adverse drug reaction reports should be evaluated.

With the infusion of resources directed primarily at speeding up the drug review process, and because of the continuing pressure from the pharmaceutical industry, review times have been significantly reduced (see Table 3.1). As of 2013, Health Canada's times now are better than those of the European Medicines Agency (EMA) and just 46 days slower than the US FDA: EMA, 478 days; Health Canada, 350 days; FDA, 304 days (41).

Table 3.1 Submission review times for new active substances,* 1985–2013

Year	Median time (days)†	Median time (days) – biologics‡
1985§	654	
1986§	627	
1987§	1191	
1988§	1122	
1989§	945	
1990	1110	
1991	1135	
1992	824	
1993	991	
1994	1162	
1995	595	
1996	561	
1997	476	
1998	512	
1999	573	
2000	622	
2001	561	
2002	735	
2003‡	670	650
2004‡	719	959
2005‡	426	1005
2006‡	350	419
2007‡	386	244
2008‡	349	510
2009‡	422	372
2010‡	432	572
2011‡	349	434
2012‡	350	591
2013‡	350	458

Sources: Drugs Directorate. Annual performance report 1995. Ottawa: Drugs Directorate; 1996. Health Products and Food Branch. Annual drug submission performance report – part III: TPD & BGTD overview 2002. Ottawa: Health Canada; 2003. Health Products and Food Branch. Annual drug submission performance report – part I: Therapeutic Products Directorate (TPD) 2007. Ottawa: Health Canada; 2008. Health Products and Food Branch. Annual drug submission performance report – part II: Biologics and Genetic Therapies Directorate (BGTD) 2007. Ottawa: Health Canada; 2008; Therapeutic Products Directorate. Drug submission performance annual report fiscal year 2012–2013. Ottawa: Health Canada; 2013. Biologics and Genetic Therapies Directorate. Drug submission performance annual report fiscal year 2012–2013. Ottawa: Health Canada; 2013. Therapeutic Products Directorate. Drug submission performance annual report fiscal year 2013–2014. Ottawa: Health Canada; 2014. Biologics and Genetic Therapies Directorate. Drug submission performance annual report fiscal year 2013–2014. Ottawa: Health Canada; 2014.

* A new active substance is a molecule that has never been sold before in Canada in any form

† Times reported as medians since single outliers could distort means. From 1985 to 2002, times are for both small molecule medicines and biologics. After 2002, times are for small molecule medicines only.

‡ Times reported as medians since single outliers could distort means.

§ Times reported in months and calculated in days by multiplying number of months by 30.

Priority reviews

Shortly after cost recovery started, Health Canada introduced its priority review pathway, intended "for a serious, life-threatening or severely debilitating disease or condition for which there is substantial evidence of clinical effectiveness that the drug provides ... effective treatment, prevention or diagnosis of a disease or condition for which no drug is presently marketed in Canada; or ... a significant increase in efficacy and/or significant decrease in risk such that the overall benefit/risk profile is improved over existing therapies" (42). The company seeking approval still has to submit a complete new drug submission containing the results of Phase I–III clinical trials, but the review period is reduced from the standard 300 days to 180 days.

An analysis of how appropriately Health Canada uses the priority approval pathway shows that it is using this process for many drugs that do not offer any new significant benefits. From 1997 to 2012, 345 of the drugs approved by Health Canada had their therapeutic value assessed by one or two independent sources. Although Health Canada used a priority review in 91 cases, only 52 drugs were rated as significant therapeutic advances. The positive predictive value for Health Canada's use of priority reviews, a measure of how well it accurately judged the real value of drugs, was only 33% (43).

Notice of Compliance with conditions: Approvals but no data

Conditional approval of drug applications is used in many countries to make promising drugs available at an early stage, provided their efficacy and safety are subject to ongoing research. In Canada, provisions for conditional approval are set out in Health Canada's Notice of Compliance with conditions (NOC/c) policy. The goal of this policy is to "provide patients suffering from serious, life threatening or severely debilitating diseases or conditions with earlier access to promising new drugs" (44). In return for having their drugs approved through the NOC/c process, companies sign a Letter of Undertaking, promising to complete confirmatory clinical studies to definitively establish efficacy and submit the results to Health Canada. If these confirmatory studies do not show that the drug is efficacious, Health Canada can suspend the sale of the drug (44).

In at least one case, Health Canada allowed a drug to stay on the market despite the company not fulfilling its conditions. Iressa (gefitinib) was approved under this policy as a third-line treatment for non-small-cell lung cancer (NSCLC) on the condition that the company submit a study showing that it improved survival (45). When the study results were submitted to Health Canada, they showed no survival benefit for gefitinib compared with placebo (46). Health Canada recognized that the conditions had not been fulfilled, but rather than removing gefitinib from the market, in February 2005 it elected to allow it to continue to be sold on the rationale that "1. There is no alternative therapy available for treatment of Canadian NSCLC patients who failed two lines of therapy; 2. Iressa® shrinks tumours, which may lead to less shortness of breath, less pain and less cough; [and] 3. The safety profile of Iressa® is more acceptable than that of any other chemotherapy which may be considered in this situation" (45 p2). (In 2009, the drug was deemed to have met its conditions after a new study showed non-inferiority, that is, survival after taking it was no worse compared with another chemotherapy drug (47).)

Some drugs have been on the market for more than 10 years without fulfilling their conditions, leaving both clinicians and patients in the dark about how effective the products actually are (48, 49). (See Table 3.2.) The longer companies take to complete these postmarket studies, the greater the number of patients who receive treatment from drugs with no clearly established benefits (50) and the more money is paid out for these possibly useless drugs. What the NOC/c policy demonstrates is a lack of rigour in ensuring that companies provide the data for full approval and a failure on the part of Health Canada to remove those that don't make the grade.

Contracting out reviews of new drug submissions

All the government reports that called for speedier drug approval stressed that safety should not be compromised (26, 30, 51), and the pharmaceutical industry echoed this message (9). However, at the same time, the government has a goal of minimizing "the cost to government of the drug product licensing program by optimum utilization of extra-governmental resources" (20 p5). In practice, this policy of minimizing the costs to Health Canada has meant contracting out some reviews of new drug submissions to external reviewers.

Senior figures in Health Canada expressed confidence that the use of outside reviewers would not compromise safety (52, 53), but that viewpoint was not shared by former Health Canada employees, nor

Table 3.2 Length of time drugs approved through a Notice of Compliance with conditions (NOC/c) are on the market before fulfilling their conditions, as of 12 December 2015*

	Conditions fulfilled (years)				Conditions not fulfilled (years)				NOC/c revoked, suspended, not fulfilled, removed, product removed from market
	0–2	2–4	4–6	>6	0–2	2–4	4–6	>6	
Number of drugs	7	15	9	6	9	4	3	8 (2 for more than 10 years)	8

Sources: Law M. The characteristics and fulfilment of conditional prescription drug approvals in Canada. Health Policy. 2014;116:154–61; Lexchin J. Notice of compliance with conditions: a policy in limbo. Healthcare Policy. 2007;2:114–22.

* 69 NOC/c issued for new products or new indications for old products (53 separate products)

by people who have done some of the reviews. A former senior drugs manager was of the opinion that "this [outside-review] system will never work because too many interests are thrown into the pot and some people don't have the proper training to do an objective and thorough job" (53 pB2). Dr Anne Holbrook, a pharmaco-epidemiologist at McMaster University, who has done two independent external reviews, was also sceptical that proper standards could be maintained (52). Margaret Catley-Carlson, a deputy minister in the Department of Health and Welfare, dismissed the suggestion that a conflict of interest could arise under this system: "It does not give me discomfort to think that people we are working with might also be doing tests on behalf of pharmaceutical companies" (52 pA6). At the same time, several staff in Health Canada and outside reviewers felt that the potential for conflict of interest was significant (52), and several instances raise serious questions on this point. In one case, an Ottawa neurologist who participated in drug-company-funded studies later reviewed the same product for Health Canada, and after the product was approved, appeared at a press conference to promote the drug (53). Based on the 2011 auditor general's report, Health Canada is doing a reasonable job of monitoring conflicts of interest for its internal staff (54), but the publicly available policy about how conflicts of external reviewers are evaluated is vague and not very informative (55).

The lack of transparency in the drug approval process

Transparency is a term that is often invoked when it comes to drug regulation. When Health Canada uses the term, the meaning that it gives it is reassuring – "Canadians also want to better understand the decision-making process undertaken by the regulator. Health Canada must provide greater and more meaningful transparency by enabling easier access to information, as well as providing information in a format that is easy to understand and provides value to the end user" (56 p12). Understanding decision making means two things – providing the information that was used to make the decision and disclosing in detail the reasoning process behind the decision. In practice, this means that Health Canada should make public the efficacy and safety information that it receives from drug companies and the reports from its reviewers about the quality of that information. In the past, Health Canada failed to do either in an acceptable fashion, and it has not made any serious attempt to reform its practices. One early example of Health Canada's failure to take transparency seriously was the 1992 Gagnon Report. Out of 152 recommendations, none made any mention of openness or transparency (26).

The Canadian Association of Journalists deemed Health Canada the most secretive of all government departments and in 2004 awarded it its fourth annual "code of silence" award for showing "remarkable zeal in suppressing information" and "concealing vital data about dangerous drugs" (57). In early September 2011, Toronto doctor Nav Persaud applied to Health Canada for all of the information that it had on Diclectin (doxylamine and pyridoxine), a widely used drug for morning sickness. Six months later, Health Canada told him that it was "negotiating with the third party [Duchesnay, the maker of the drug] on which records they wish us to protect." Finally, after more than a year, he received 359 pages of which 212 were completely censored, and "other pages had blacked-out sections under titles such as 'Adverse Events,' because they were deemed confidential business information" (58). In addition, Health Canada required Dr Persaud to sign a confidentiality agreement that prevents him from revealing what is in the documents that he received. As part of that agreement he also has "to destroy the documents after he's reviewed them and to notify Health Canada in writing that he has done so" (58). Should he fail to meet these requirements Health Canada has threatened him with legal action (59).

My experience with Health Canada reinforces the delays that Dr Persaud experienced. I made an initial request for information in December

2014. A number of times I was told that my request was being prioritized or that Health Canada was trying to resolve it as quickly as possible. In spite of regular follow-ups, as of May 2016, I have not yet received the full complement of requested information. Health Canada has a long history of making specific promises to address problems with transparency, but these promises have, unfortunately, never been realized. Box 3.1 details some of these past promises.

The main rationale used by Health Canada to support secrecy is that it regards virtually all information that it receives from a drug company as commercially confidential, and it cannot be released without the expressed permission of the company. Not surprisingly, companies typically invoke their right to withhold information. An investigation into the reasons that information was not released by the Canadian government concluded that "across instances in which all or some information

BOX 3.1 FAILED OR SERIOUSLY DELAYED TRANSPARENCY INITIATIVES

December 1995

- Dann Michols (director general, Drugs Directorate) makes this statement: "A Canadian Summary Basis of Approval is also being considered as we streamline and standardize the review practices ... In addition, a project on the role of the Drugs Directorate in information dissemination to consumers and health practitioners is underway."

April 1998

- A Stakeholder Letter from Therapeutic Products Directorate requests input into a proposal to make public names of drugs in approval process.
- Nothing further is heard about this proposal.

June 1998

- Dann Michols once again referred to development of a Canadian Summary Basis of Approval: "additional time [to prepare such a document] is difficult to justify as the Programme strives to meet existing performance targets for all submission types."

is withheld on the basis of an exemption contemplated by the Access to Information Act, third-party information is by far the category of exemption most frequently invoked" (60 p195). The list of information that cannot be disclosed without permission of the company includes the name of a drug in the review process, any clinical trial data on the safety and efficacy of the drug, the names of drugs that were denied approval and the reports produced by Health Canada reviewers. (Starting in 2015 Health Canada began listing the names of drugs under review along with their therapeutic area – see http://www.healthycanadians.gc.ca/drugs-products-medicaments-produits/authorizing-manufacturing-autorisation-fabrication/review-approvals-evaluation-approbations/submissions-under-review-presentations-cours-examen-eng.php.) Companies are strongly in favour of this level of secrecy, arguing that if this information became public knowledge, it would harm their economic interest. This line of reasoning was reflected in a 2004 article authored by a vice-president of Merck, one of the largest pharmaceutical companies in the world. Writing in the *Canadian Medical Association Journal*, he stated that "Merck (like other companies) is obliged to protect proprietary information and intellectual property, including aspects of the design of clinical trials of investigational agents and the very existence of certain studies" (61 p482).

Secrecy is also a problem in other countries, but the regulatory agencies in the US and the European Union are considerably more open than is Health Canada. The FDA releases redacted reports from its reviewers (62) that, although lengthy, inconsistently organized, and weakly summarized, still provide a fascinating insight into how reviewers make their final decision about benefits versus harms (63). Over the years, prompter, more complete, and less redacted access has occurred, partly as a result of the Freedom of Information Act litigation against the FDA, brought by groups such as Public Citizen to force such disclosures (some examples of the information available can be found at http://www.citizen.org/Page.aspx?pid=3306&q=FOIA and FDA and litigation). The EMA releases the names of drugs that are not approved (64) and, as of 2014, was supposed to make publicly available all the clinical trial data it received (65), although in the end the EMA backed off somewhat from this commitment (66). Although Health Canada fairs poorly compared with these two agencies, it is no worse than those in Australia, France, and the United Kingdom in terms of information on its website (67).

Health Canada primarily uses two arguments to explain how it treats what it terms confidential business information. First, it cites the Access to

Information Act (68), Health Canada's interpretation of the Act means that it "will seek the sponsor or manufacturer's consent if it intends to publish" virtually any information it received directly from the company about a regulated product (69 p10). Health Canada "considers it inappropriate to post information concerning clinical trials, special access or products with notices of compliance with conditions on the basis that this information is incomplete or open to misinterpretation" (35 p8).

Subsection 20(6) of the Act would actually allow Health Canada to release much of the data it currently keeps secret on the grounds that "disclosure would be in the public interest as it relates to public health ... and, if the public interest in disclosure clearly outweighs in importance any financial loss or gain to, prejudice to the competitive position of or interference with contractual or other negotiations of a third party" (68) but for reasons that are not clear Health Canada has never chosen to try to use this section of the Act.

The second argument against transparency is based on Health Canada's reading of the requirements in the free trade agreements that Canada has signed, specifically the North American Free Trade Agreement and the Agreement on Trade-Related Aspects of Intellectual Property Rights. According to a Health Canada proposal for legislative renewal, these agreements "provide that the government must protect the confidentiality of undisclosed test or other data provided by the applicant to determine whether the use of such products is safe and effective, where the origination of such data involves considerable effort." In light of this interpretation, during one set of consultations on health protection legislation renewal in 2003, Health Canada was only willing to propose that a summary of the safety and effectiveness data submitted by the manufacturer would be made generally public. If consumers or health professionals want to see the full set of data, the proposal called for a "reading room where people could review all the data submitted by the manufacturer but not transcribe or copy it, or otherwise make that data available to interested members of the public" (70 p76).

The arguments brought forward by Health Canada to justify its position on secrecy were soundly rejected in a report by its own Science Advisory Board. The 2000 report stated, "in our view and that of many stakeholders, the current drug review process is unnecessarily opaque. Health Canada persists in maintaining a level of confidentiality that is inconsistent with public expectation and contributes to a public cynicism about the integrity of the process" (71 p9). To remedy this situation, the report recommended "that HPB [Health Protection Branch, now

Health Products and Food Branch] should set new standards of access to information at all stages of the drug review process, enhancing transparency and public confidence. We perceived no justification for current levels of delicacy regarding 'commercial confidentiality.' We would note: (a) Canada can at least emulate the standards of openness of our nearest and largest trading partner [the United States]" (71 p9–10).

The use of trade agreements as a reason to keep information confidential again appeared in the spring of 2008, when Bill C-51 was introduced. (See Chapter 5 for an analysis of how Bill C-51 would have affected drug safety.) This legislation, which died before reaching a Parliamentary vote, would have allowed the minister of health to "disclose to the public information about the risks or benefits that are associated with a therapeutic product," a positive move in terms of transparency. At the same time, it contained a provision that would have allowed the minister to impose regulations to enforce trade agreements, such as the North American Free Trade Agreement that Canada had entered into, reinforcing a rationale already used by Health Canada for keeping information secret (72).

Herder comments on how these rationales from Health Canada play out in the real world based on his participation in a series of technical meetings between October 2010 and January 2011 held to discuss regulatory modernization at Health Canada: "Each proposal put on the table by Health Canada to increase transparency – from making final decisions regarding applications for market authorization publicly available, to creating an online register of therapeutic products – was met with proprietary claims from MEDEC [Canada's Medical Technology Companies], BIOTECanada [the national biotechnology industry association] or Rx&D, the respective associations of medical device, biotechnology and pharmaceutical companies in Canada. Each time, Health Canada acknowledged that the law controlled what they could and could not disclose" (60 p194), and "the moderator noted the issue on a flip chart dubbed the "parking lot' and urged participants to stick to the agenda" (60 p198).

The NOC/c approval process is another example of Health Canada's reluctance to release basic information. A senior policy analyst articulated Health Canada's position regarding the conditions that need to be fulfilled: "specific conditions associated with approval under the NOC/c policy are negotiated on a case-by-case basis and due to their proprietary nature, cannot be released by the department without prior consent by the drug sponsor" (Tara Bower, personal communication with Alan

Table 3.3 Release of documentation about drugs with new active substances

Document	Description	Posting timeline	Number reviewed	Number posted within timeline
Product monograph	Describes the health claims, indications, and conditions for the safe and effective use of a drug. It also includes other important information, such as safety warnings, precautions, adverse reactions, and interactions with other drugs.	At the time of market notification	28	28 met the timeline
Notice of decision	Outlines in a one-page summary the authorization received and general information related to the approved drug.	Within 6 weeks of drug approval	31	20 met the timeline 11 took an average of 3 weeks longer
Summary basis of decision	Outlines the scientific and benefit or risk considerations that factor into Health Canada's decision to approve a drug.	Within 20 weeks of drug approval	31	15 met the timeline15 took an average of 12 weeks longer 1 was not yet posted

Source: Auditor General of Canada. Report of the auditor general. Ottawa: Office of the Auditor General of Canada; 2011. Chapter 4, Regulating pharmaceutical drugs – Health Canada.

Cassels, 20 November 2002). Further, the complete details about the trials necessary to fulfil the conditions are not made publicly available, and no information is published about whether trials have been undertaken or their progress.

The release of information about drugs containing new active substances (NAS) is particularly important for public safety and appropriate drug use, as a NAS is a molecule that has never been marketed before in any form in Canada. No Canadian experience with the drug can be drawn on to guide clinicians and patients. Table 3.3, taken from the auditor general's report, shows that Health Canada is often delinquent in its timely release of documentation for this group of drugs.

One case is the exception to Health Canada's policy of keeping information secret. In this instance, in 2012, Health Canada released information about Singulair (montelukast), a Merck product for asthma, over the company's objection. Merck took Health Canada to court but lost at the level of the Supreme Court. Even then, not all the information was released. Out of 850 pages, 90 were deemed confidential, 55 were redacted, and the rest released (73).

Summary Basis of Decision

In 2004, Health Canada announced the Summary Basis of Decision (SBD) project, something it had been talking about since 1995 with phase one of this initiative starting on 1 January 2005. The SBD is a document issued after a new drug or medical device is approved and explains the scientific and benefit-risk information that was considered before approving the product (74). Particularly valuable for health care professionals is the third section, which contains a description of the premarket clinical trials examined by Health Canada, and a summary of the final benefit-risk assessment for the product. Health Canada's position is that because of this initiative, "Canadian healthcare professionals and patients will have more information at their disposal to support informed treatment choices" (74 p8). At a 2004 workshop where the announcement was made, officials were confronted with an analysis of two pilot documents that showed the limitations of the SBD, primarily that the documents contained very little information about the conduct and results of the clinical trials. Health Canada officials defended the proposal by noting that this was phase one of a proposed three-phase model. Subsequent phases would examine the interpretation of the term "confidential information" and "*may* [emphasis added] see the inclusion of additional information" and "disclosure of negative outcomes or withdrawals [refusals to approve new drugs or new indications for older drugs, companies withdrawing submissions before a decision has been made] would be *explored* [emphasis added]" (74 p14). There were intimations of more to come, but their exact form was deliberately kept vague. Health Canada's explanation for the vagueness was that this was a new venture and each step needed to be carefully evaluated.

An analysis of all 161 SBDs (containing the results of 456 clinical trials) released from the beginning of the project until the end of April 2012 showed that clinical trial information was presented haphazardly, with no apparent method. In the majority of SBDs (126 of 161), at least one-third of the potential information about patient trial characteristics (e.g., age, sex, whether they were inpatients or outpatients) and the benefits and risks of tested treatments is missing. Although basic details of clinical trials were more frequently described, any omissions or ambiguities were especially troubling given the straightforward nature of the information, for example, the number of patients per trial arm, whether the trial took place at a single or at multiple sites, and whether a unique trial identifier was included (75). The need for objective information about new drugs, particularly drugs that use an entirely new mechanism of action, is especially acute in the period after they have been approved; the only published scientific information about them tends to come from the premarket clinical trials that are typically short and may involve only small numbers of patients (76). A second reason that objective information is needed is that when clinical trials are published in medical journals, they often contradict the information that the companies give to regulatory authorities about the same trial, and Health Canada does not disclose this discrepancy. In the United States, out of 24 negative studies submitted to the FDA about a variety of antidepressants, not only were 16 not published, but 5 of the 8 that were published claimed that the product was effective (77).

September 2012 saw the start of phase two of the SBD project, with a promise that the new documents "will contain a significantly increased focus on Health Canada's risk/benefit analysis for both drugs and medical devices" (78 p2). Whether that will produce more meaningful and complete information awaits a detailed analysis of these second-phase documents. One positive feature will be a post-authorization activity table that will provide ongoing information about approved products, including one-paragraph summaries of activities that affect the safe and effective use of the product (78). Also included are post-authorization submissions filed to fulfil conditions for drugs authorized under the NOC/c policy (78). For the first time, doctors, researchers, and other interested parties can freely access via the Health Canada website new information about the products that they are researching, prescribing, or taking.

Bill C-17

Bill C-17, which was signed into law in November 2014, offered a further opportunity to improve transparency, but instead took baby steps towards that goal. (See Chapter 5 for an analysis of how Bill C-17 might affect drug safety.) The Bill gives Health Canada the power to recall drugs from the market for safety reasons and gives the minister of health the authority to "order a person to provide ... information ... to determine whether the product presents" a serious risk of injury to human health (79 pE288).

What the legislation does not do is require Health Canada to publish the rationale for decisions concerning all drugs approved for sale, drugs refused for reasons of safety or efficacy, and the names of drugs that are suspended or recalled (79). However, a press release issued by the government on the passage of C-17 said that the regulatory decisions about drugs refused market authorization would be published (80). On the other hand, C-17 does echo the defunct Bill C-51 in that it gives the minister the authority to impose any regulations that are deemed necessary under the auspices of the free trade deals Canada has signed (81). These regulations could include the power to limit access to information based on the government's reading of the requirements of agreements such as NAFTA and the Agreement on Trade-Related Aspects of Intellectual Property Rights. These limitations were pointed out to a House of Commons committee studying the bill, and amendments were included and passed that allow the minister to disclose confidential business information if it presents a risk of serious injury or to protect or promote human health. However, disclosure of confidential information applies only to releasing the information to other governments, persons from whom the minister is seeking advice, and other persons carrying out functions related to the protection of human health. It is not clear if this provision will also apply to doctors, independent researchers, and the public (Matthew Herder, personal communication, 18 June 2014).

Clearly, manufacturing information should be protected by Health Canada for some good reasons. This is proprietary knowledge, and if it became public, it could adversely affect the financial status of a company by providing competitors with an unfair advantage. Personal data can include the identity of individual patients or health professionals, as well as information on the illness from which the patient is suffering; information that might lead to the identification of individual patients or health professionals should also not be disclosed to any party (82). However, these restrictions do not apply to data about the safety and effectiveness of medications. As Herder convincingly argues, Canadian law "does not, in principle, preclude Health Canada from disclosing data on safety and efficacy associated with pharmaceuticals, biologics and medical devices, including data on the designs and results of clinical trials" (60 p194).

Finally, no good evidence shows that the interests of companies would be harmed by the disclosure of this type of information; specifically, confidentiality is not necessary to foster research and innovation (83). Research builds on the work of others; hindering the transfer of knowledge may lead companies to repeat mistakes, causing research to take longer and cost more. On the other hand, nondisclosure has serious disadvantages for Health Canada, health professionals, and the public. If information submitted to regulatory agencies is never disclosed, then these data never enter the normal peer review channels and are, therefore, not scrutinized by independent scientists. Without this type of feedback, Health Canada reviewers may be more prone to misjudge the accuracy or usefulness of the data submitted; the scientific atmosphere in the agency may be stifled and the professional growth of its staff severely inhibited. Deprived of any independent access to information, health professionals have to accept Health Canada's judgment about the safety and effectiveness of products. For well-established drugs, this is probably not much of a concern, but it may be different with new drugs, where experience is limited (82, 83).

Health Canada held a consultation on the new powers conferred under Bill C-17 from 25 March to 8 June 2015, during which 25 stakeholders responded, including those from industry, health care professional associations, and academia. According to Health Canada, "all comments were considered and the final Guide incorporates changes to improve the clarity and precision of language to better reflect the legislative provisions" (84). But exactly how many of the comments will be used is unclear. Health Canada's remarks about comments on how to define confidential business information and what information Health Canada will make public all ended with phrases such as "Health Canada is considering comments received as the Department moves forward on further policy and process developments and will provide more information to stakeholders in the coming months" (84).

Harmonization of drug regulation

All regulatory agencies in countries in the Global North agree that before drugs are marketed, they should be safe, relative to the condition for which they are going to be used, and efficacious (i.e., they should work under ideal circumstances). Therefore, in theory at least, it makes sense to develop a common set of standards that can be applied across the Global North. Similarly, it seems reasonable for countries to draw on each other's strengths in regulation so that tasks are not unnecessarily duplicated. In Canada's case, resources and capacity are limited compared with those of other leading regulatory authorities, such as the FDA and the EMA, although all three agencies perform essentially the same functions when it comes to drug regulation and for a similar number of products. For 2009, the FDA's budget for its human drugs and biologics programs was just under US$1.1 billion, and it employed 4816 full-time equivalents (FTE) (85, 86) compared with C$98 million and 1040 FTEs for Health Canada (87). The EMA coordinates the scientific evaluation of applications and related work with the national regulatory authorities of the 28 member states in the European Union (EU) and has over 4500 experts listed in its database (88, 89).

The main driving force behind international harmonization is the International Conference on Harmonization of Technical Requirements for Registration of Pharmaceuticals for Human Use (ICH), an organization with only six voting members – the brand-name industry trade associations and the regulatory agencies from the European Union, Japan, and the United States. In addition, Canada, the European Free Trade Association, and the World Health Organization sit as observers. The secretariat for the ICH is housed in the Geneva headquarters of the International Federation of Pharmaceutical Manufacturers and Associations (IFPMA). There are notable absences from the groups that are allowed to participate in the ICH process: "ICH does not include representatives from professional associations, patient or consumer advocacy groups, the governments or health authorities of developing countries, companies specialising in generic drugs, or from groups producing pharmacopoeias" (90 p184). ICH was created because companies were concerned about the inconsistencies between national regulatory standards that produce "wasteful duplication in drug testing," which drives "up drug development costs and create[s] 'barriers to trade'" (91 p116). The rationale that regulatory agencies use to justify their participation is that it will improve safety and lead to greater protection of public health (91).

Harmonization of drug approvals has been a Canadian aspiration for many years. It was discussed in the 1992 Gagnon Report (26), and a 1999 document from Health Canada made it clear that the organization saw pursuing international agreements as a priority: "Regulatory cooperation now means going beyond the exchange of information and personnel and is heading towards the sharing of issues, the development and implementation of cooperative and global solutions, and the establishment of cooperative mechanisms" (92 p2). At the same time, the document emphasized the need to maintain high safety standards: Health Canada "must actively participate in and influence harmonization initiatives such as the development of international standards and guidelines to ensure that the high level of safety and quality standards currently applied in Canada are maintained or enhanced" (92 p2). While Health Canada was emphasizing safety, at least on paper, in 1999 it was also consulting with the pharmaceutical industry about international regulatory cooperation. In those consultations, it was evident where industry's priorities lay (93). The drug companies saw the benefits of harmonization first in economic terms – faster market authorizations and reduced regulatory costs – and only secondarily as giving Canadians faster access to therapeutic products and high standards of safety and quality. An early example of Canadian harmonization, and an example of how industry's economic priorities seemed to take precedence over concerns with safety, was the push to shorten the time taken to approve Phase I clinical trials, as documented in Chapter 2. According to a spokesperson for Rx&D, "unless Health Canada can show that an independent review process is essential to the health and safety of Canadians ... why not piggyback [with the United States]?" (94).

Harmonization is also consistent with smart regulation (see Chapter 1). The Expert Advisory Committee (EAC) on Smart Regulation "decided to focus its recommendations on how international regulatory cooperation can improve Canadians' access to new drugs by speeding up the drug approval process" (95 p80). The message was that Canadians are losing out because Health Canada is relatively slow in undertaking drug reviews. In the words of the EAC, making the Canadian economy more efficient "requires the removal of regulatory impediments to an integrated North American market and the elimination of the tyranny of small differences ... In cases where regulatory differences are insignificant or present low risk, it may be in the public interest for Canada to be pragmatic and simply align its approach with that of the United States. The Committee believes that the smart approach, in these cases, is to avoid unnecessary duplication and focus regulatory resources on situations that warrant a unique Canadian solution" (95 p21).

At a Health Canada meeting to discuss changes in the regulatory system regarding, among other things, licensing requirements, industry representatives asked "whether there have been discussions with the ICH to align our rules with theirs, as there may not be much value in setting entirely new and Canadian rules if there are already appropriate ones in place at ICH" (96). When the discussion moved to postmarketing study commitments, industry encouraged Health Canada to use flexible and harmonized rules and advised against developing "Canadian only" rules. Of course, no one is directly talking about lowering safety standards and, in fact, the EAC says safety is paramount. On the other hand, there is no explicit talk about harmonizing upwards to the highest standards, just harmonizing.

Health Canada often has a contradictory attitude towards harmonization, viewing it through a very selective lens. As Chapter 2 showed, Health Canada has failed to harmonize its requirements for clinical trial registration with the much more stringent ones in the United States. When patients receive prescriptions in Canada, they may be presented with an information leaflet about the product. However, including these leaflets with each prescription is not mandatory and the content of these leaflets is not approved by Health Canada. The leaflets are individually produced by commercial companies, and as such the quality of the information varies across leaflets (97, 98). In contrast, the EMA has required all prescriptions to have patient leaflets since 1999 (99).

Finally, the ideology behind harmonization is that it is about establishing the same technical requirements for regulatory agencies. However, drug regulation is more than just technical specifications. As Daemmrich points out, regulatory frameworks are a reflection of the therapeutic culture that has developed in an individual country. These "therapeutic cultures arise from networks of actors that produce regulatory policy, determine testing standards, and ultimately decide on market access for new drugs. The principle actors in medical policy (regulatory agencies, physicians, pharmaceutical companies, disease-based organizations) form a rather fluid and flexible network that sustains intense debates and very serious differences of opinion" (100 p11). It would be a serious mistake to think that national networks are the same across different countries. It misses the point that drug regulation is the intersection between values, science, medical culture, patient needs and expectations, and politics.

Conclusion

Drug regulation is not an exact science. Many areas of uncertainty call for judgments to be made about effectiveness and safety when deciding whether to approve a new drug or remove an old one from the market. As in any policy area, available resources are limited, be they monetary allocations or personnel, while the array of tasks in drug regulation is almost endless. How these limited resources are distributed often reflects the priorities of the regulatory agency. Regulatory agencies are privileged with a wide range of data about the products that they supervise – releasing that information might have negative economic consequences for regulated industries but a positive one for public health. Having laws and regulations in place is necessary in a regulatory environment, but they are not sufficient if the authority chooses not to enforce them.

At the extreme, there are two competing visions of what the prime function of a drug regulatory authority should be. The one put forward by the pharmaceutical industry holds that the main function is to facilitate industry's efforts to develop new products and to approve them as quickly as possible. In this view, medications are commodities and the regulatory authority exists to provide a service to the industry. The second view, espoused by consumer groups, health care professionals, and public health activists, sees the primary purpose as appropriately evaluating products to ensure a high standard of effectiveness and safety. Here, medications are seen as an essential element of the health care system and the regulatory authority exists to provide a service to the public. This chapter has shown that when private profit and public values clash, the decisions that Health Canada has made have typically favoured the former.

4 Regulating promotion or licensing deception?

Sections of the Food and Drugs Act and Regulations are in place to guard against pharmaceutical companies underplaying the negative effects of their products and overemphasizing the positive. But in practice Health Canada has turned over the day-to-day regulation of promotion to a combination of industry, an independent external group with strong industry representation, and private sector agencies. (See Table 4.1 for a summary of regulatory codes.) This chapter looks at whether this type of regulation is sufficient to ensure that doctors and patients get accurate and objective information about the products being marketed.

Drug promotion by companies involves a wide range of activities to convince doctors to prescribe their products and patients to ask for and use those products. This chapter will cover medical journal ads, visits to doctors by sales representatives, gifts and meals for doctors, physician meetings and events, promotion of over-the-counter (OTC) drugs, and direct-to-consumer advertising (DTCA) of prescription drugs. (Other forms of promotion are free samples provided to doctors and, increasingly, e-promotion through social media and websites.)

Between 1960 and 2004, spending on promotion was consistently many times the amount companies spent on research and development in Canada (see Table 4.2).

The differences in the amounts give an idea of the relative priority that industry assigns to developing new drugs versus promoting their use to doctors. Table 4.3 gives some details about the money and effort that companies are willing to put into promoting individual drugs to Canadian doctors. The pharmaceutical companies would not be spending the sums that they are if they were not getting a good return on their money.

Table 4.1 Codes regulating drug promotion

Organization	Title of code	Areas covered	Compliance	Penalty for violation	Last updated
Rx&D (Canada's Research-Based Pharmaceutical Companies)	Code of Ethical Practices	Business meetings and discussions, clinical evaluation packages ("samples"), conferences and congresses, consultant meetings, displays, learning programs for health care professionals, loan of medical equipment, market research, members' employees, patient programs, post registration clinical studies, provision of funding, retaining the services of a stakeholder, scientific exchanges, service-oriented items	Mandatory for all members of Rx&D	Violations in a 12 month calendar year: First violation: publication of the infraction on the Rx&D website and a fine of $25,000; Second violation: publication of the infraction on the Rx&D website and a fine of $50,000; Third violation: publication of the infraction on the Rx&D website, a fine of $75,000, and, the chief executive officer must appear before the Rx&D board of directors, at which time he/she must provide a detailed explanation of the violations and a comprehensive written action plan to ensure remediation; Each additional violation after a third one: publication of the infraction on the Rx&D website and a fine of $100,000; and all postings will remain on the website for 24 months from the date of the final decision.	2012
Pharmaceutical Advertising Advisory Board	Code of Advertising Acceptance	All advertising/promotion systems for health care products and corporate messages directed to licensed members of the professions of medicine, dentistry, naturopathy, homeopathy, nursing, pharmacy, and related health disciplines and institutions and to	Voluntary but mandatory for all members of Rx&D	Stage 1: Company has 10 days to provide a written response to a complaint Stage 2: If complainant is not satisfied with response and if an agreement between complainant and advertiser is thought to be feasible, the commissioner may recommend further dialogue, a face-to-face meeting, or other conciliation attempts. If none is possible, the commissioner will issue a ruling, rejecting or accepting all or part of the complaint and as part of this ruling may withdraw clearance for the advertising/promotion system	2013

		patient information that will be distributed by or recommended by a health care professional		Stage 3: Either the complainant or the company may appeal a Stage 2 ruling. The appeal will be heard by a review panel comprising three qualified individuals selected by the commissioner. If the ruling goes against the company, the commissioner may set out penalties against the company for Code violations. The appropriate penalty will be selected in accordance with the degree of the Code violation. Examples of penalties include immediate withdrawal of offending advertising, notices in annual reports or newsletters, and public letters of apology.	
Pharmaceutical Advertising Advisory Board or Advertising Standards Canada	No code	Gives advice to companies on direct-to-consumer advertising of prescription drugs	Voluntary	Complaints referred to Health Canada; the nature of penalties imposed by Health Canada unclear	Not applicable
Agencies wanting to review advertising can self-attest compliance	No code, minimal standards set by Health Canada	Advertising of over-the-counter products	Unclear	No penalty specified	Not applicable

Sources: Code of ethical practices. Ottawa: Canada's Research-Based Pharmaceutical Companies; 2013; Pharmaceutical Advertising Advisory Board. Code of advertising acceptance. Pickering (ON): PAAB; 2013; Health Products and Food Branch. Guidance document: consumer advertising guidelines for marketed health products (for nonprescription drugs including natural health products). Ottawa: Health Canada; 2006.

Table 4.2 Industry spending on promotion and research and development, selected years, 1960–2004

Year	Amount spent on promotion (C$000,000)	Amount spent on research and development (C$000,000)
1960	31.5	9.6
1964	33.0	5.5
1981	153.3	57.0 (1982)
2004	2380–4750*	1170

Sources: Royal Commission on Health Services. Provision, distribution, and cost of drugs in Canada. Ottawa, Health Canada; 1964; Parliament of Canada. Minutes of proceedings and evidence no. 4: Hearing before the House of Commons Special Committee on Drug Costs and Prices (June 16, 1966). Ottawa: Queen's Printer and Controller of Stationery; 1966); Parliament of Canada. Minutes of proceedings and evidence no. 5: Hearing before the House of Commons Special Committee on Drug Costs and Prices (June 23, 1966). Ottawa: Queen's Printer and Controller of Stationery; 1966); Commission of Inquiry on the Pharmaceutical Industry. Report. Ottawa: Health Canada; 1985; Patented Medicine Prices Review Board. Annual report 2004. Ottawa: PMPRB; 2005; Gagnon M-A, Lexchin J. The cost of pushing pills: a new estimate of pharmaceutical promotion expenditures in the United States. PLoS Medicine. 2008;5(1):e1.

* For comparison, in the United States companies spent US$57.5 billion on promotion in 2004 (1). About US$4 billion out of the US$57.5 billion was for direct-to-consumer advertising, which is not allowed in Canada. The calculations below are made on the assumption that if US$1 was spent in the United States, then C$1 was spent in Canada. The value of samples in the United States is US$15 billion, but drug prices are about 40% lower in Canada. A reasonable estimate of promotion in Canada without including the value of samples would be ($57.5 billion – $4 billion – $15 billion)/10 = $3.85 billion. The value of samples is (60% × 15 billion)/10 = $0.9 billion. Therefore, total annual promotion spending in Canada is about $3.85 billion + $0.9 billion = $4.75 billion. This is an upper limit. Figures from CAM (M-A Gagnon, personal communication, 16 August 2006) put the amount spent on promotion in Canada for 2005 at $1.066 billion. However, in the United States, the CAM numbers underestimate the amount spent on samples. The CAM figure for samples in Canada is $152 million. Subtract this amount from $1.066 billion and then add the $0.9 billion figure (see above) and you have $1.814 billion. CAM also estimates that in the United States, there is an additional 30% of promotion spending that it doesn't audit. Therefore add 30% to $1.814 billion and you get $1.814 billion + $0.544 billion = $2.358 billion. This might be a lower limit.

According to one American study, for drugs with annual sales greater than $500 million, for each dollar spent on sales representatives, journal advertising, and physician meetings/events, companies increased sales by $11.6, $12.2, and $11.7, respectively (2).

Table 4.3 Spending on the top-five most-promoted drugs in Canada, 2000

Product	Promotional expenditures ($000)	Number of advertisement pages in medical journals	Number of visits by sales representatives to doctors (000)	Number of samples left with doctors (000)	Number of minutes spent by sales representatives with doctors (000)
Vioxx	6286	1090	48	1060	216
Celebrex	6064	613	77	988	303
Effexor	5262	974	48	410	236
Lipitor	4385	559	65	513	246
Baycol	3952	361	54	281	231

Source: CBC News: Disclosure. Targeting doctors – Graph: top 50 drugs by promotion dollars (5 Mar). 2002. Reproduced by permission of IOS Press.

Use of promotion and its effects

Evidence has consistently shown that even though doctors do not necessarily think that promotional information is reliable, they use that information to make prescribing decisions. Angus Reid polled 787 Canadian doctors in 1990–91 about how they viewed the credibility of various sources of information and, importantly, how frequently they used those same sources. Although sales representatives and journal ads ranked low in credibility, they were the second and fourth most frequently used sources, respectively (3). By 2008, 92% of doctors still accepted visits from company salespeople, and 88% saw them because they believed that they received relevant information (4). Doctors in Montreal and Vancouver who were surveyed after they had just seen a sales representative reported that 63% of the time, they were somewhat or very likely to start or increase prescribing a drug after the visit (5). As reported in the *Canadian Medical Association Journal* (*CMAJ*) in 1995, fewer than one-third of medical students, interns, and residents doing psychiatry rotations in Toronto thought that pharmaceutical representatives were a source of accurate information about drugs, but 71% didn't want them banned from making presentations, and 56% believed they could receive gifts from companies without the gifts affecting their prescribing (6). In a study published in 2004, 81% of students studying medicine at Western University were not opposed to interacting with drug companies while they were in medical school, and most were willing to take gifts of small value and even gifts of larger value if those gifts had a medical education value (7). No more recent surveys of medical students are available to see if attitudes have changed in the last decade. In contrast to their frequent use of promotional material, doctors rarely consult the official product monograph, the Health Canada approved summary of information about a drug, according to a 2007 publication (8).

The acceptance and use of promotional material would not be a concern if it led to better prescribing, but that is not the case. A systematic review of 58 studies looked at the effect on prescribing after doctors received information directly from pharmaceutical companies. Ten of the 58 studies examined the quality of prescribing, and half found an association between exposure to pharmaceutical company information and lower-quality prescribing; 51 looked at the frequency of prescribing, and 38 found an association with higher frequency of prescribing (higher indicating poorer prescribing); and 5 of the 10 studies found evidence for an association with higher prescribing costs (less price sensitivity, fewer prescriptions for low-cost generics) (9).

Government regulation of promotion

The reliance on promotion and its negative effects on prescribing strongly support the need to regulate the form and content of promotion to protect public health. The Food and Drugs Act (F&DAct) and Regulations give the government the authority over the promotion of both prescription and OTC drugs and ban DTCA. In addition, as noted in Chapter 3, Canadian law prohibits advertising of treatments and cures for a set of listed conditions (Schedule A diseases) (10, 11). The F&DAct is part of Canada's Criminal Code, and consequently, the Health Products and Food Branch Inspectorate has a range of measures available for a serious breach. In carrying out enforcement actions, the Inspectorate considers a number of factors, including risk to health and safety, the manufacturer's compliance history, premeditation, likelihood of recurrence, expected effectiveness, effects on public confidence in Health Canada, and the Inspectorate's priorities and available resources (12). But despite having the nominal control over promotion, over the past century Health Canada and its predecessors have never shown much interest in exercising that power. Health Canada's position is that "it's not our policy to treat advertising as the definitive source of information with respect to drugs" (13 p19) and therefore, it only does informal spot checks on drug advertising. No penalties were imposed on any pharmaceutical company for illegal advertising between 1978 and 1984 (14), and there is no public record of any since then. The Regulatory Advertising Section within the Marketed Health Products Directorate, the part of Health Canada charged with regulating drugs (and other health products) already on the market, oversees regulated advertising activities, but the exact nature of its activities is opaque. Despite an extensive search on Health Canada's website there is no information about the number of personnel in the Section or its level of resources. According to the minutes of a meeting between Health Canada and various external agencies involved in controlling promotion (15), there is an Annual Statistical Report of Regulatory Advertising Activities (complaints and requests for information) issued by the Section, but with Health Canada's well-documented penchant for secrecy (see Chapters 2, 3, and 5) this report is not publicly available.

The case for nongovernmental regulation of promotion

Ichiro Kawachi at Harvard University and I looked at the rationale for non-governmental regulation of promotion. Government regulation has two major theoretical drawbacks: one financial, the other practical (16). Increasingly, fiscal pressures in almost all countries have prevented government agencies from effectively policing pharmaceutical promotion. Government regulatory agencies rarely have the resources to make it economically rational for individual firms *not* to cheat. The other major drawback to government regulation is that the government is content with relying on industry expertise and has made a political decision not to hire people with the knowledge and experience to do the job. Voluntary self-regulation, therefore, seems an attractive option because, lacking government-industry adversariness, it could be a more flexible and cost-effective option. Government regulators also reason that in a highly competitive industry, the desire of individual companies to prevent competitors from gaining an edge can be harnessed to serve the public interest through a regime of voluntary self-regulation run by a trade association in which member companies police each other. However, although misleading advertising may, to some degree, inhibit competition by either making false claims about the advertiser's product or unfairly disparaging a competitor's product, it is far more often good for business.

The mission of trade associations is primarily to increase sales and profit. From the business perspective, self-regulation is mostly concerned with the control of anti-competitive practices. Therefore, when industrial associations draw up their codes of practice, they deliberately make them vague or do not cover certain features of promotion to give companies wide latitude. Self-regulation works well when anti-competitive promotional practices happen to coincide perfectly with government regulators' notions of misleading advertising. Most often, however, the fit is far from perfect because far from being anti-competitive, many misleading advertising tactics are good for business. Therefore, from the public health perspective, the results of voluntary self-regulation are suboptimal. This theoretical analysis of self-regulation is reinforced by an examination of the functioning of the self-regulatory systems in the United Kingdom and Sweden, two countries often cited as examples of self-regulation. The study concluded that "the prevalence and severity of breaches testifies to a discrepancy between the ethical standard codified in industry Codes of Conduct and the actual conduct of the industry ... We interpret the arguably high rate of code violations as evidence that self-regulation has failed to sufficiently deter industry from engaging in frequent and sometimes serious unethical practices, as judged by the industry's own standards" (17).

The attitude that industry is better able to regulate its own promotional activities than is government is consistent with the clientele pluralist relationship between Health Canada and the pharmaceutical industry. In line with this philosophy, Health Canada turned over enforcement of promotion to the industry, and the Canadian Pharmaceutical Manufacturers Association produced the first version of its *Principles of Ethical Drug Promotion* in 1959 (18). By the start of 1966, this code had morphed into the much larger and comprehensive *Code of Marketing Practice.* The preamble to the code is a statement of ethics with phrases such as "The calling of a pharmaceutical manufacturer is one dedicated to a most important public service, and such public service shall be the first and ruling consideration in all dealings" (19 p332). The industry says these ethical principles guide its conduct, but others have a more cynical view as to why the 1966 code was adopted: "The Kefauver Act in the United States provided for the regulation of advertising in that country. And since Canada was an extension of the US market and the US drug corporations, the Kefauver legislation introduced some element of responsibility into the advertising techniques of Canadian subsidiaries through the international nature of the drug industry. In effect what has happened is that, in this respect, Canada has become governed by legislation passed by the Congress of the United States. It has also given the pharmaceutical manufacturers the right to say 'we [the Canadian pharmaceutical industry] have a code now as of January 1966 ... are we not nice, we have got a code of honour'" (20 p113).

The code once again changed its name in 1998 to the *Code of Ethical Practices*, and another edition was published in 2012 (21). (A revised version of the code was published in 2016, too late to be analyzed here.) The opening statement from the Rx&D president, Russell Williams, in the 2012 version is similar to the opening of the 1966 code and sets out the tenor of the document: "Members have embedded corporate ethics and responsibility into the very fabric of their organizational cultures. The changes to the Code mark a renewed pledge that the Members of Rx&D are committed to ensuring their behaviour benefits patients and enhances the practice of medicine" (21). Membership in Rx&D is conditional on compliance with the code.

Early history of the PMAC code

The consistent tone in the industry's code may be one of corporate ethics, but the early history of the PMAC/Rx&D code showed that this was mostly a rhetorical stance. The 1966 version of the code said, "Claims for the usefulness of a product must be based on acceptable scientific evidence and must reflect this evidence accurately and clearly ... Advertising copy should reflect an attitude of caution particularly with respect to the use of drugs which have not been studied for prolonged periods" (19). In practice, ads frequently highlighted only the positive points about a drug, expanded the scope of use, used emotionally resonant material, and abandoned the "attitude of caution." For example, one ad for Valium (diazepam), that appeared about the same time as the 1966 version of the code was inaugurated, offered the following assessment of when Valium should be used: "In clinical practice, symptoms of psychic tension, such as insomnia, fatigue, restlessness, hyper-irritability, hostility and agitation, often appear as part of a symptom complex which may include anxiety, depression, muscular spasm, organic or functional disorders. Valium® Roche, an important psychotropic agent, spans a wide therapeutic spectrum of psychic tension ... Valium Roche relaxes mind and body" (22 p53). When it came to illustrations in ads, the code said they "should be in good taste and should present the facts in an unequivocal manner." A 1973 ad for Atarax (hydroxyzine) promised that the drug will "restore normal behaviour rapidly, effectively and safely" for a child who is a "troublemaker, bed-wetter, picky eater" or who has a "nervous stomach." A 1975 ad for the antidepressant/neuroleptic combination

Etrafon (perphenazine/amitriptyline) just shows a housewife with her back against a wall surrounded by a giant diaper pin and vacuum cleaner (22). One particularly offensive ad in February 1974 showed a glowering bus driver over the caption: "He is suffering from estrogen deficiency." Turn the page, and you see a distraught middle-age woman presumably suffering from symptoms of menopause, and "She is the reason why."

The Pharmaceutical Advertising Advisory Board and its Code of Advertising Acceptance

In the face of this type of medical journal advertising, a 1973 meeting of federal and provincial health ministers recommended that the federal government "review controls on the advertising of drugs with the aim of strengthening them where necessary" (23 p27). In response, Marc Lalonde, then the federal minister of health and welfare, issued an ultimatum to the industry to reform its practices or face the prospect of government action. PMAC, as might be expected, was very much in favour of self-regulation over direct control by government and initiated a sequence of events that resulted in the creation of the Pharmaceutical Advertising Advisory Board (PAAB) in 1975. The first chair of the PAAB board was also an employee of the Upjohn company, and the PMAC promotion code formed the basis for the one adopted by PAAB (23). PAAB was given the responsibility for advertising and promotion systems, that is, the media presentation of promotion in all forms – print, audio, visual, audiovisual, and later electronic and computer means of communication. Before they can be used, advertisements in any of these forms have to be submitted to PAAB for preclearance to ensure compliance with the provisions of its code (24). The PMAC code retained responsibility for all other forms of promotion, including sales representatives, gift giving. and the sponsorship of meetings. The PMAC code also mandates compliance with that of PAAB (21).

Despite the nominal independence of PAAB from industry, its board includes a representative of the Association of Medical Advertising Agencies, the Canadian Association of Medical Publishers, Canadian Generic Pharmaceutical Association, Consumer Health Products Canada, Rx&D, and BIOTECanada, meaning that 6 of the 14 members come from organizations that, in one way or another, benefit from advertising (25). Since changing the code takes a two-thirds majority of the board, it is unlikely that anything that is unacceptable to industry will ever be passed. PAAB is self-financing from fees that companies pay to have their advertisements reviewed. Importantly, PAAB's code is not legally binding; its decisions are not legally enforceable; and as a voluntary, independent body, PAAB is not accountable for its actions to government or any other organization. PAAB will occasionally refer complaints about ads to Health Canada for final resolution. This method of regulating advertising is apparently acceptable to Health Canada, as it is an ex-officio member of the board, demonstrating again the clientele pluralist relationship between Health Canada and industry.

Early versions of the PAAB code had significant weaknesses. A 1991 survey of 111 different advertisements in 11 medical journals, two pharmaceutical journals, and one nursing journal found that while benefits were discussed in 91% of the ads, risks were mentioned only 53% of the time, and in the ads that mentioned risk, 94% referred to the product as free of certain risks or side effects. Moreover, risks and benefits were included on the front page of advertisements in just 39% of cases. Prescribing information accompanied the ad 18% of the time; in the remainder, it was at the end of the journal, far from the ad (26). Until January 1993, the sole provision in the code that directly applied to the pictorial, or non-textual, content of an advertisement was a statement that it must not imitate the ads of other firms. PAAB did not see the final version of the pictorial part of an ad, so in practice no effective control over illustrations existed. In January 1993, a revised edition of the PAAB code came into effect. Companies were then obliged to send in proposed illustrations, as well as text copy, for preclearance (27), although the code did not offer any substantive guidelines as to how the illustrations would be assessed. As of February 2015, it is still not clear whether the material PAAB sees will be "copy ready" or a draft because its code does not deal with this question.

Until the mid-1990s, the only information about complaints that PAAB released was found in an annual report that was sent to Health Canada and to the PAAB board of directors. Other distribution of the report was on an ad hoc basis. The report listed the total number of complaints handled during the year and the number of retraction letters that companies were required to send. Otherwise, little information about the complaints was given: the companies involved were not identified, the complainant was not identified except to give the number of complaints made by pharmaceutical companies and others, the nature of the violations was not described, the product involved was not named, when the violation took place was not disclosed, and reasons for the commissioner's decision were not given (28). Today, complaints with this previously missing information are now published in PAAB's quarterly newsletter, available online (29).

The early 1990s version of the PAAB code required all reference materials, both published and unpublished (data on file), to be the most recent available and consistent with current medical opinion. All references, except those classified as confidential by the advertiser or the author, had to be made available to health practitioners when they requested them. Along with a colleague, I examined 22 ads in issues of the *Canadian Medical Association Journal* published in 1992 for their use of references, and we requested 114 references from the 22 companies. Two companies, both PMAC members and responsible for 27 references, did not respond to the requests at all, and of the remaining 87 references, 78 (68%) were provided. The mean methodologic quality score, a measure of the methodological soundness of the reference, was 58%, and the mean relevance score, which evaluated whether the reference was appropriately cited, was 76%. The poor rating for the methodologic quality score was primarily a result of the use of low-quality review articles and "other" references, such as data on file at the company (30).

The only provision in the 1997 version of the PAAB code about the use of statistics was that they "must be presented so as to accurately reflect their validity, reliability and level of significance" (31). Changes in outcomes that result from drug and other types of therapy can be presented in a number of ways: relative risk reduction (RRR), absolute risk reduction (ARR), and number needed to treat (NNT). A RRR is the percentage reduction in the risk of targeted complications between two groups: a drop in mortality from 50% to 25% would be a RRR of 50%. An ARR is the absolute percentage difference in the risk of targeted complications between two groups: a drop in mortality from 50% to 25% would be an ARR of 25%. The NNT is the number of patients that have to be treated to prevent one complication of their disease: a drop in mortality from 50% to 25% would be a NNT of 4 (100/ARR) (32). Evidence shows that physicians' enthusiasm for a treatment modality varies depending on how the results are presented; specifically, the inclination to use a particular drug therapy is greatest when results are given as a RRR and lowest when they are given as a NNT (33–35).

This lack of specificity in the PAAB code about how statistics should be presented in ads allowed companies to use RRRs rather than ARRs or NNT. A study of 22 ads found that was what companies typically did. None of the ads gave an ARR or a NNT. In 11 of the ads, results were reported solely as a RRR. In two other cases, RRRs were used, but it was possible to calculate an ARR or NNT. In nine cases, no measure was reported but it was possible to calculate a RRR, ARR, or NNT (36). After the publication of this study, the PAAB code was changed to require that if results were reported as a RRR, "they must also include an indication of the absolute treatment effect. This can be presented as absolute risk reduction (ARR), number needed to treat (NNT) and/or the actual comparative clinical results or rates" (24).

A major continuing weakness in the PAAB code is that it does not require any information in ads beyond what appears in the product monograph (PM) approved by Health Canada. The use of surrogate outcomes in ads shows the problem with this limitation. Many drugs are approved by Health Canada solely based on surrogate outcomes. A surrogate outcome could be a change in tumour size, in a physiologic measurement, such as blood pressure; or in a laboratory value. However, surrogate outcomes do not necessarily translate into what matters for patients, a change in morbidity or mortality, a hard clinical outcome. In some instances, drugs approved based on surrogate outcomes later had to be pulled from the market because they did more harm than good. For example, Enkaid (encainide) was initially approved because it suppressed irregular heart rhythms but was eventually found to increase overall mortality (37).

If the PM lacks a statement saying that the medication has not been shown to reduce morbidity or mortality, then advertisements are not required to contain a similar statement. The ads will just mention the changes in surrogate outcomes. However, because doctors rely so heavily on promotion, the absence of a statement about the lack of changes in morbidity or mortality can be a problem. Doctors may believe that claims about positive changes in surrogate outcomes translate into a reduction in morbidity or mortality. Evidence from the United States shows that doctors generally are not aware of the FDA-approved indications of routinely prescribed drugs (38), that is, what a drug has and has not been shown to achieve, and the situation in Canada is likely the same. This ignorance about official indications may be one reason behind off-label prescribing, that is, prescribing for an indication that has not been approved by Health Canada. About 11% of primary care prescribing for adults in Canada is for off-label use, and in 79% of cases, this type of prescribing lacks strong scientific support (39).

I raised concerns about the use of unmodified surrogate outcomes in journal ads with PAAB in 2011 when it was reviewing its code. PAAB "believe[d] the suggestion [to require a statement about the lack of hard clinical outcomes in ads] may have merit due to international movement to recognize outcomes as more important in clinical decisions than mere surrogate marker measurement" (40). However, the position of the organization was that since its rules about the content of advertisements follow what is in the PM, the issue should more properly be discussed with Health Canada through a request for a modification in the contents of the PM. As a result, I sent a letter to Health Canada in early April 2012 requesting that when products are approved by using surrogate endpoints, the PM include a statement that the medication has not been shown to have an effect on a hard clinical endpoint (Letter to Health Canada, 2 April 2012). The issue was discussed at a meeting between Health Canada and Canadian advertising preclearance agencies, including PAAB. Health Canada's position was that "non-indications ... will continue to be added, based on an individual assessment" but that "lists of non-indications clutter the text of the Product Monograph and may contribute to confusion and be incorrectly recalled later by a prescriber as an actual indication" (40). Health Canada's reference to "non-indications" meant that it refused to require a statement in the product monograph that a drug did not have a positive result on a clinical outcome; that is, it was not going to require a statement that the drug had not been shown to actually help patients.

In 2004, I raised concerns with the PAAB regarding the small size of type for safety information that the code allowed to be used in ads in medical journals. The response included the claim that since doctors prescribe medicines for their benefits, the main message should be about benefits. The PAAB also said that if the font size was increased the ads would consist of nothing but information about potential harms and that pharmaceutical companies were already complaining about how difficult it was to put all of the content on a one-page ad. The PAAB did not take up my suggestion that it convene a sample group of doctors to consult on the appropriate type size for safety information compared to information about the drug's benefit.

The latest revision of the PAAB code took place in July 2013 but both the organization and its code continue to have features that raise concerns. The composition of the board of directors of the organization and the limitations that creates on the stringency of the organization's code has already been mentioned. In its January 2014 newsletter (http://www.paab.ca/newsletters.htm), the PAAB stated that it "regularly monitor[s] journals, the Internet, and receive[s] direct-mail/detail aid materials collected by health professionals as part of its monitoring program. When Code violations are discovered, PAAB sends a letter to the advertiser seeking their cooperation to meet the requirements of the Code." However, there is no further information given about the monitoring program or the letters that the PAAB sends.

The current version of the code requires a "fair balance of risk to benefit" but there is still no specific requirement that equal space in the ads be devoted to harms and benefits, nor for the font size for benefits and harms to be equal in size. The PAAB code allows the detailed prescribing information to be separated from the actual ad, a practice that is not allowed in US journal advertising. While the font size for the print in an ad does have a lower limit, the generic name of the drug is not required to be the same size as the brand name; additionally, the generic name does not have to be used each time that the brand name is given, despite evidence that use of the generic name leads to better prescribing (9). Companies are allowed to make statements in journal ads about effects of drugs, even if the clinical significance of those effects is unknown, as long as the ad also includes that caveat. Finally, and maybe most significantly, the only sanctions explicitly listed for violating the code are "immediate withdrawal of offending advertising, to notices in annual reports or newsletters, to public letters of apology." In fairness to PAAB, Canadian medical journal advertising is no worse than in other developed countries (41).

The PMAC/Rx&D Code of Marketing Practice/Code of Ethical Practices

Over 50% of the amount that companies spend on promotion goes towards the expenses of their salespeople, the men and women who visit doctors in their offices and clinics and hospitals (1). Historically, the importance of these people has been recognized by the industry, as can be seen in the testimony of the president of the PMAC to the House of Commons Special Committee on Drug Costs and Prices: "by far the heaviest marketing expense that must be borne is the cost associated with sending highly-trained professional representatives into the field to make our medical people aware of the existence of new drugs, of their indications and contra-indications, of their side effects and therapeutic potential" (42 p95). The various versions of the marketing and ethical codes from the industry have all had sections dealing with the role of these representatives. The 1966 code, when almost all representatives were men, asserted, "He will be honest in all his dealings and should provide professional contacts with full and factual information on his products, with no attempt at misrepresentation or exaggeration ... His statements must be accurate and complete and must not mislead either directly or by implication. His product knowledge should be maintained at a level which will enable him to fluently converse with the professions and supply necessary information on his products. His assertions must be scientific and backed up with medical evidence. Such professional standards of honesty and accuracy are to be maintained at all times so that a high professional stature will be accredited to the individual sales representative, his company and the industry as a whole" (19 p336). Similar statements appear in the current code: "All employees should have sufficient knowledge of their subject matter, reflecting the requirement of their professional practice. Employees interacting with Health Care Professionals must have sufficient knowledge of general science and product-specific information to provide accurate and up-to-date information ... Members must provide full and factual information on products, without misrepresentation or exaggeration. Statements must be accurate and complete. They should not be misleading, either directly or by implication" (21).

In 1969, the industry founded the Council for the Accreditation of Pharmaceutical Manufacturers Representatives of Canada, now the Council for Continuing Pharmaceutical Education. Sales representatives are required to complete the Council's accreditation course within two years of commencing their employment (21). Accreditation involves 250–300 hours of study in two units – anatomy and physiology, and pathophysiology and pharmacology – and ends with a multiple choice exam with a minimum passing grade of 60%. Initially, the course was one year with final exams held at a Canadian university. The result, in the opinion of the director of the Council, was supposed to be a graduate who could "provide accurate information supported by adequate documentation on all topics of the physician's concern as they relate to drugs" (43 pA8). Dr Norman Eade from McGill University investigated the Council in the 1970s. He reported that the Council had no teachers and conducted no classes; all coursework was done by mail. The functional staff consisted of one administrator and a secretary. The "Canadian university" where the exams were written was a room rented at a university. The Council refused to make a copy of the text or core material available for

Dr Eade's inspection. A representative exam was largely of the true-false variety, including questions on the rates of profit of various industries and other matters unrelated to the safety or efficacy of drugs (44). Dr Eade concluded: "This program is a ploy to make the detail men more convincing in their presentations. Doctors are often very naïve and they don't have much time to review data on drugs" (43 pA8).

The actual behaviour of sales reps is far from the ideal implied by Rx&D's code and the Council for Continuing Pharmaceutical Education. Here is a brief summary of how one Victoria area sales rep functioned between 1989 and 2006. He distributed gifts like pens and notepads (no longer allowed under the Rx&D code), brought in meals, or took doctors and clinic staff out for meals. He organized luxurious weekend "medical education" events featuring drug company-paid speakers in beautiful BC locales like Whistler. Another Victoria area rep who worked between 2002 and 2009 once met with a physician who was heading an institute. They discussed the drug company possibly funding research chairs in return for its drugs being prescribed by all the institute's doctors (45, 46).

As noted above, the current Rx&D code requires company sales representatives to "provide accurate and up-to-date information" (46) presumably including information about how to safely use the product they are promoting. This provision in the code is reinforced in a statement about the value of detailing: "Conversations between health care providers and representatives of Canada's research-based pharmaceutical companies focus on the appropriate use of medicines" (47). Whether the representatives do this in practice was recently investigated by having general practitioners in Montreal and Vancouver fill in survey forms after they had seen a representative. The primary outcome measure was the presence of "minimally adequate safety information," defined a priori as mention of ≥1 approved indication, ≥1 serious adverse event, ≥1 common non-serious adverse event, ≥1 contraindication, *and* no unapproved indications or unqualified safety claims (e.g., "this drug is safe"). "Minimally adequate safety information" was provided in 5 of 412 (1.2%) promotions in Vancouver and 7 of 423 (1.7%) in Montreal. Representatives did not provide any information about harms (a serious adverse event, a common adverse event, or a contra-indication) in 66% of interactions (5).

According to the 1991 version of the PMAC code, companies were to mail essential professional product information on new products to drug information (DI) centres a minimum of two weeks before market launch

(48). A one-year study by one DI centre found that product information was mailed to it two weeks or more before marketing for only 3 of 28 new prescription drugs and for none of 27 new prescription drug dosage forms or strengths. No product information was received for 10 of 28 new prescription drugs and 21 of 27 new prescription drug dosage forms or strengths (49).

The code has always allowed pharmaceutical companies to fund continuing medical education (CME) but says "the organization, content and choice of speakers must be determined by the healthcare professional organizers" (48). This provision is supposed to apply to events "organized under the auspices of the company either directly or through a third party" (47). In December 1991, Burroughs Wellcome paid for a meeting in Toronto to discuss the use of AZT (zidovudine) in early HIV disease. A for-profit New Jersey company called CME Inc selected the speakers. CME Inc had no physicians on staff (50). Scientists who disagreed with the early use of AZT in HIV patients were not invited to speak.

It is a common practice for companies to organize evening symposia on a variety of medical topics. In dealing with this area, the code stated that "social functions ... shall neither compete with nor take precedence over the central events ... Judgement should be exercised to ensure that the scientific content is the primary focus of the meeting, not the venue nor social activities" (48). Bristol-Myers Squibb sponsored an event in March 1991 for Toronto physicians entitled "Depression as Seen by the Primary Care Physician." Part of the evening consisted of a meal at a downtown Toronto restaurant where the usual price per couple was $120. An educational grant from Hoechst paid for another evening symposium that consisted of a one-hour reception preceding a one-hour talk, which was then followed by a meal. The total time for the social functions, therefore exceeded the time for the talk (27). The 2012 version of the code allows for "the provision of reasonable meals and refreshments" but "reasonable" is not defined (21).

The Rx&D code has never made any provision for monitoring of promotional activities in any of the areas regulated, so violations are discovered through a complaints mechanism. Information about compliance with the code used to appear in the *PMAC Bulletin* and then its successor, *PMAC News*. It now can be found on the website (51). To assess compliance with the code in the first part of the 1990s, I searched the print publications from 1 November 1991 to 31 December 1995. Over the 45 months for which figures were available, 157 violations occurred. Thirty-six companies had at least one code violation, but the majority committed five or fewer. Two companies had 24 and 19 violations, respectively, and six other companies had more than five infractions. No information was published about the total number of complaints, who complained about the violation, when the complaint was made, when the violation took place, the product involved, the nature of the offence, or sanctions imposed, or about alleged violations that were not upheld. The lack of any details about either the nature of the infraction or the sanctions imposed made it impossible to determine how serious the violations were and whether the guilty companies were being appropriately disciplined (28).

The information about violations as of mid-September 2014 deals with those that occurred between 2008 and 2011 (51). Of the 14 complaints, half were upheld. The validity of complaints is decided by the Industry Practices Review Committee (IPRC). The permanent members of the IPRC are two company representatives and two external health care professionals appointed by the Rx&D board of directors, a representative appointed by the Rx&D president, and Rx&D's general counsel. In addition, the committee has one or two ad hoc members: one individual appointed by the Rx&D president, one representative from PAAB, as required, and one external representative from the scientific community, as required, as appointed by the IPRC (21). In effect, unless a PAAB member is on the IPRC, the committee has no people completely independent of the industry. If a violation is confirmed, the penalty ranges from $25,000 for the first one in a 12-month period to $100,000 for the fourth. After the third violation the chief executive officer of the company is required to appear before the Rx&D board of directors to provide a detailed explanation of the violations and a comprehensive written action plan to ensure remediation. The most that a company could be fined in a year is $250,000. Considering that in 2000, companies were spending upwards of $6 million promoting a single product, $250,000 might be regarded as a price of doing business.

OxyContin promotion: Exposing the weaknesses in the codes

The widespread abuse of OxyContin (oxycodone) was a serious health and crime problem in parts of Canada. As an example, the Government of Newfoundland and Labrador, recognizing the dire consequences associated with the use of the drug, commissioned an OxyContin Task Force that issued a comprehensive report in 2004 (52). It included reports about how the diversion of OxyContin for non-medical purposes was widespread in the province and how abuse among adolescents was growing. Opioids are in the top-three most-popular substances of abuse for youth. They seem accessible and are perceived as safer than street drugs because they are prescription drugs (53). OxyContin was a drug of choice and the addict profile was a young male, in school or working, from a suburban family (54). The addition of OxyContin to the Ontario drug formulary was associated with a fivefold increase in oxycodone-related mortality and a 41% increase in overall opioid-related mortality (55).

Part of the blame for the problems that OxyContin caused may well be laid at the feet of the weaknesses of both the PAAB and the Rx&D codes. PAAB prescreened and allowed a 2000 ad for OxyContin from Purdue Pharma that used the pain scale from the World Health Organization without noting that the scale was developed for pain from cancer and not for chronic non-cancer conditions. The same ad also contained the claim, allowed by PAAB, that "drug abuse is not a problem in patients with pain for whom the opioid is appropriately indicated" (56). Because the OxyContin product monograph originally had the statement that the long-acting formulation had a lower risk of abuse compared with other opioid analgesics (55), under the PAAB code this statement was also allowed to appear in ads.

It is not clear if the Rx&D code covers the industry's role in medical education of health professional students, although the code does say, "All interactions with Stakeholders are to be conducted in a professional and ethical manner. We must be cognizant of potential conflicts of interest and manage them appropriately" (21). This management of conflict of interest did not seem to be implemented by some companies that marketed opioid analgesics. As part of their regular curriculum, in the mid-2000s, medical students at one Canadian university were required by their medical school to attend a series of pain pharmacotherapy lectures "supported by pharmaceutical companies that market[ed] opioid analgesics in Canada, and the guest lecturer was a member of speakers bureaus of the same companies. These conflicts of interests were not fully disclosed. A reference book that reinforced some of the information in the lectures and that [contained potentially misleading information] was paid for by a sponsoring company and was made available to students" (57).

Promotion of over-the-counter products

Canada has always permitted companies to promote over-the-counter (OTC) products directly to consumers on the assumption that the products are relatively safe for the intended condition of use and that members of the public can readily identify the condition (e.g., a fever or a cough). Until the end of February 1997, Health Canada was directly responsible for regulating this type of promotion. Print advertisements were assessed only based on complaints, whereas scripts for broadcast ads needed to be submitted to Health Canada before they were aired unless they did not make any claims for the product. A 1993 review showed that two-thirds of sampled magazine ads failed to comply with the regulations. "Minor" violations included exaggerations of benefits and inadequate risk information, in other words, misleading and inaccurate information about the products' characteristics and health effects; major violations were not defined. The review of broadcast advertisements included only scripts submitted for review, not full commercials that were heard and seen by the public; approximately one-third of these scripts failed to comply with regulatory requirements (58).

It is interesting, and rather disturbing, to note that Health Canada is not willing to regard breast milk substitutes as OTC products and regulate their promotion despite clear instances of violations of the World Health Organization's *International Code of Marketing of Breast-milk Substitutes* (59). Health Canada's position is that "Consumer Advertising Guidelines for Marketed Health Products would not apply to human milk substitutes (infant formulas) as those products are regulated as food products (and not as drugs or natural health products)" (Ann Sztuke-Fournier, personal communication, 6 July 2006). In addition, and for the same reason, PAAB will not accept complaints about advertisements for infant formula in medical journals, although it has prescreened such ads and allowed the advertiser to affix the PAAB logo to the ad (Mark McElwain, personal communication, 5 August 1996).

At the start of March 1997, the responsibility for preclearing consumer-directed broadcast and mass media print advertising for OTC drugs was transferred to Advertising Standards Canada (ASC), a national association committed to ensuring the integrity and viability of advertising. Importantly, the document issued by Health Canada that announced this transfer emphasized that the role of ASC was to **review** not to **regulate** (the emphasis on these two words was in original). Health Canada retained the role of setting "the minimum standards to be met in drug advertising by establishing the terms of product authorization, by developing appropriate regulations, guidelines and policies and by bringing these standards to the attention of ASC" (60 p4) but would no longer adjudicate complaints. Finally, although Health Canada "strongly encourages all market authorization holders to have the advertising material for their authorized health products 'precleared' prior to dissemination" it emphasizes that preclearance is voluntary; that is, companies are not required to have their advertising material reviewed before they use it (61).

After this transfer of responsibility, no public record is available of any evaluation of the adequacy of the new system in terms of complying with Health Canada's regulations. Despite this absence, in August 2006, Health Canada announced its intention to further delegate control over this type of advertising. Under the new proposed system, Health Canada would no longer endorse specific agencies performing these preclearance activities. Rather, it would establish criteria representing the minimum standard recommended to successfully preclear advertising and then let agencies self-attest that they could meet these criteria (62). ASC itself pointed out the weaknesses in what Health Canada was proposing: "In this new regime ... rather than Health Canada evaluating agencies to ensure they meet the established criteria, agencies are being asked to self assess and self-qualify. This self-qualification process could ... result in the mistaken belief [that agencies] possess the requisite knowledge, expertise and systems to perform this function. This lack of understanding and expertise could lead to review errors that compromise consumer health and safety. A competitive preclearance marketplace opens the door for 'clearance shopping', i.e., advertisers 'shopping' different agencies until an approval number is garnered from one ... Unless an agency has a significant portion of the preclearance volume, its ability to meet all of Health Canada's criteria, particularly those that do not produce revenue, will be seriously compromised" (63 p2). As of the end of 2015, two agencies have self-attested that they meet Health Canada's criteria: ASC and Extreme Reach Toronto (64).

As part of the move to change the oversight of OTC promotion, Health Canada also held a June 2006 invitational roundtable on the inclusion of risk information in advertising. At the roundtable a wide variety of opinions were expressed as to how much safety information should be included in advertisements: some wanted more detailed information provided, others advocated for "black box" warnings for certain drugs, and still others felt that labels and inserts should be more user friendly. Health Canada's position was that it "need[s] to find mechanisms to present fair and balanced representations in advertising, **when appropriate** [emphasis in original], in order to enable consumers to make informed decisions *without imposing undue impediments to industry*" (emphasis added) (65).

Ultimately, Health Canada went ahead with its self-attestation proposal (66). A year after it implemented this change, in correspondence with

Dr Barbara Mintzes from the University of British Columbia, Health Canada's position was that it "remains confident that the move to the attestation system was a sound decision and that the preclearance agencies are working diligently towards providing a high standard in advertising preclearance" (Marketed Health Products Directorate, personal communication to Dr Barbara Mintzes, 12 December 2007). As of 2014, the only safety information typically found in OTC ads on television is a statement in small print at the bottom of the screen, which is visible for different times for different products and says something to the effect that "to be sure this product is right for you, always read and follow the label."

Direct-to-consumer advertising of prescription drugs

Over the past two decades, Health Canada has become increasingly tolerant of direct-to-consumer advertising (DTCA), despite the prohibition of this type of advertising in the Food and Drug Regulations (11). In addition, Section 9(1) of the F&DAct prohibits deceptive or misleading advertising: "No person shall label, package, treat, process, sell or advertise any drug in a manner that is false, misleading or deceptive or is likely to create an erroneous impression regarding its composition, merit or safety" (10). The F&DAct defines advertising as "any representation by any means whatsoever for the purpose of promoting directly or indirectly the sale or disposal of any food, drug, cosmetic or device" (10). This definition is broad and focuses on the intent to stimulate sales. It does not limit advertising to paid communication or specific media (67).

The first, and relatively innocuous, change in Health Canada's position occurred in 1978 when price advertising was allowed through an amendment to the Regulations with the following wording: "Where a person advertises to the general public a Schedule F Drug, the person shall not make any representation other than with respect to the brand name, proper name, common name, price and quantity of the drug" (11). The reason for the amendment was to allow people to do price comparisons among different pharmacies. In 1996 and 1999, Health Canada held workshops on DTCA, followed in the winter of 2003–04 by a series of public consultations on advertising of health products under the Health Legislation Renewal proposal. (See Chapter 1 for an in-depth discussion of this initiative.) During these workshops and hearings, Health Canada communicated a fundamental change in the way that the 1978 regulation was interpreted. A 1996 Health Canada policy statement defined the boundary between "information dissemination" and "advertising" (68). In practice, this interpretation meant that unbranded "help-seeking" advertising was no longer illegal, as long as neither the brand nor the manufacturer's name was stated. These help-seeking advertisements mention a condition and suggest viewers "ask your doctor" about a treatment (67).

In November 2000, Health Canada published a second administrative policy paper that allowed branded "reminder advertisements" for prescription-only medicines targeting the public (69). A reminder ad is a form of DTCA that states the name of the product but does not mention its indication or make health claims. Following the November 2000 interpretation, Health Canada began to allow branded reminder ads on television, on billboards, in print advertising, and on Canadian Internet sites. It is still illegal in Canada to mention both the name of the drug and its indication in the same advertisement.

Although Canada is generally somewhat more restrictive than the United States when it comes to DTCA, there is one significant anomaly. Despite the US generally allowing DTCA, where both the drug and the disease it treats are mentioned in the same promotion, it does not allow DTCA for drugs with a "black box" warning, the strongest regulatory warning of serious harmful effects that the Food and Drug Administration imposes. In Canada, as a consequence of the way that Health Canada regulates DTCA and what information it requires in an ad, many of the drugs that are advertised to consumers in Canada, such as Celebrex (celecoxib) and Alesse (levonorgestrel/ethinyl estradiol), are ones with black boxes and could not be advertised to consumers in the United States (70).

In parallel with Health Canada's loosening of the restrictions around DTCA, industry's position has also undergone significant changes since the statement in 1961 from the Canadian Pharmaceutical Manufacturers Association that "the release to the lay public of information on the clinical use of a new medicinal agent or the new use of an established drug prior to adequate clinical assessment and presentation to the medical profession is not in the best interests of the medical profession or the layman" (18 p2009–10). By 1996, Merck was asserting that it had a constitutional right to engage in DTCA (71), a position that Rx&D supported with the statement "Canada's Research-Based Pharmaceutical Companies believes it can provide valuable information to consumers and encourage Canadians to learn more about prescription medicines that are approved for use in Canada" (72). In concert with its changing position on DTCA, industry spending increased dramatically. (See Figure 4.1.)

Figure 4.1 Industry spending on DTCA in Canada, 1995–2006

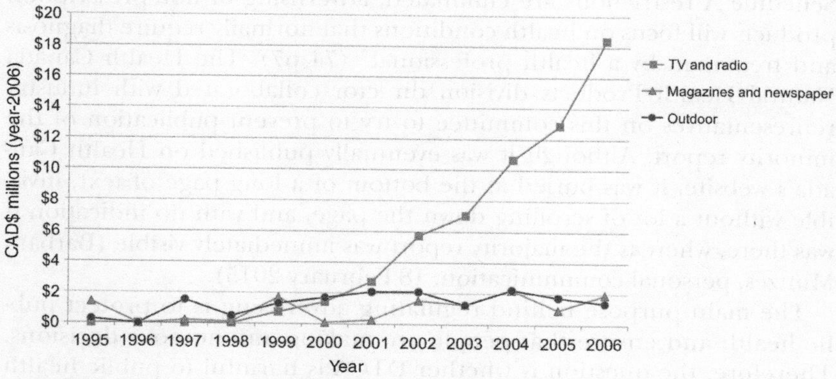

CAD$ millions (year-2006)
$0 $2 $4 $6 $8 $10 $12 $14 $16 $18 $20
1995 1996 1997 1998 1999 2000 2001 2002 2003 2004 2005 2006
Year
TV and radio
Magazines and newspaper
Outdoor

Source: Mintzes B, Morgan S, Wright J. Twelve years' experience with direct-to-consumer advertising of prescription drugs in Canada: a cautionary tale. PLoS One. 2009;4(5):e5699.

Another example of Health Canada's change in its position on DTCA is illustrated in what happened to Section 3 and Schedule A of the F&DAct. These parts of the F&DAct set out a list of diseases for which preventatives, treatments, or cures may not be advertised to the public: "The prohibition in Schedule A covers all product health claims, not just prescription drugs. The rationale is a recognition that people who are seriously ill may be vulnerable to unscrupulous marketing of medicines in a way that differs from people who are buying a new pair of jeans or a television set" (67 p6–7). Section 3 and Schedule A were amended in 2008. Many of the diseases listed in Schedule A, such as alopecia (hair loss), dysentery, gout, hypotension (low blood pressure), and impetigo (a relatively minor skin infection), were removed and others were modified; for example, heart disease was replaced by congestive heart failure. The Section 3 amendment permitted companies to make risk-reduction and symptomatic treatment claims for their products for diseases listed in Schedule A (73). Although this amendment did not apply to prescription drugs, the representatives from Women and Health Protection and Union des consommateurs on the committee that recommended the changes produced a minority report opposing the change. Their concerns were that most non-governmental committee members recommending the change to Section 3 had financial ties to the industries that stood to gain from expanded health product advertising and that "if Schedule A restrictions are eliminated, advertising of non-prescription products will focus on health conditions that normally require diagnosis and treatment by a health professional" (74 p7). The Health Canada Natural Health Products division director collaborated with industry representatives on this committee to try to prevent publication of the minority report. Although it was eventually published on Health Canada's website, it was buried at the bottom of a long page of text, invisible without a lot of scrolling down the page, and with no indication it was there, whereas the majority report was immediately visible (Barbara Mintzes, personal communication, 18 February 2015).

The main purpose behind regulating advertising is to protect public health and ensure that people are making autonomous decisions. Therefore, the question is whether DTCA is harmful to public health and whether individuals are making misinformed decisions; that is, does DTCA lead to people receiving medications unnecessarily or the wrong medications and, ultimately, is people's health made better or worse? These questions were last addressed in a 2012 systematic review of the literature on DTCA. The conclusion was that DTCA leads to increased prescribing volume and patient demand, prescribing becomes less appropriate, there is a shift to less cost-effective treatment, unsubstantiated claims about improved treatment adherence are provided, and there is no evidence of improved treatment quality or early provision of needed care (75).

Manufacturers who would like advice on whether their messages directed to consumers on prescription-only drugs are consistent with the law can check with either PAAB or ASC (64). If PAAB has prescreened an advertisement and considers it acceptable, the advertiser may include the PAAB logo on the ad. However, if a complaint is made about a pre-approved advertisement, neither PAAB nor ASC will consider the complaint, although both agencies have complaint resolution procedures for other forms of advertising. Health Canada instead reviews all complaints about DTCA. Beyond this complex system of delegated enforcement to various agencies, ultimately Health Canada is responsible for enforcing the law and can step in if a threat exists to public health. In practice, the agency rarely does.

Barbara Mintzes and I have examined how well Health Canada is regulating DTCA (76). We used a case study approach and looked at 10 examples of DTCA involving 8 different drugs that appeared to contravene Health Canada's policy on DTCA. (See Table 4.4.)

Table 4.4 Health Canada and regulation of DTCA

Regulatory issue	Drug	Company	Problem identified	Outcome
Failure to act on promotion of off-label indication	Xenical (orlistat)	Roche	Ads promoting the drug as appropriate for women who want to lose weight for cosmetic reasons	Health Canada did not consider the ads to violate Canadian law
	AndroGel (testosterone)	Abbott	Ads promoting use of AndroGel for symptoms of normal male aging	Message judged not to fall within the definition of advertising
Financial inducement to use a drug	Zostavax (zoster vaccine live, attenuated)	Safeway Pharmacy	Ad offered 100 bonus Air Miles to customers who got a Zostavax	Health Canada regarded the inducement as related to pharmacy practice and outside of its jurisdiction
Fear mongering	Lipitor (atorvastatin)	Pfizer	Ad played on people's fear of death from heart disease	Health Canada regarded ad as a help-seeking message and not promotion
Products with serious safety concerns	Diane-35 (cyproterone acetate and ethinyl estradiol)	Berlex	Concerns about effects on liver and increased risk of venous thromboembolism	No action on successive ads over a five-year period
	Celebrex (celecoxib)	Pfizer	Concerns about gastrointestinal bleeding and cardiovascular risks	Company allowed to run reminder ads without any mention of the need for caution in use of product

(*Continued*)

Table 4.4 (Continued)

Regulatory issue	Drug	Company	Problem identified	Outcome
Effectiveness of enforcement actions	Zyban (bupropion)	GlaxoSmithKline	Ads combined name of product with indication in violation of Food and Drugs Act	Health Canada issued repeated warnings but company ignored them
	Alesse (levonorgestrel and ethinyl estradiol)	Wyeth-Ayerst	Company used techniques to combine name of product with its use in separate, related ads	Health Canada recognized ads violated Food and Drugs Act and issued warnings but company ignored them
	Diane-35 (cyproterone acetate and ethinyl estradiol)	Berlex	Ads implied use of drug for off-label indication	Multiple efforts to achieve compliance over five years but no move to prosecute the company
Transparency in decision making	Diane-35 (cyproterone acetate and ethinyl estradiol)	Berlex	Posters advertising talk about sexual activity featured Diane-35 logo although drug not indicated for contraception	Health Canada judged the activity to be in violation of the law but the decision was not made public

Source: Lexchin J, Mintzes B. A compromise too far: a review of Canadian cases of direct-to-consumer advertising regulation. International Journal of Risk and Safety in Medicine. 2014;26:213–25.

Our conclusion was that Health Canada had adopted a narrow approach to enforcement and ignored broader concerns, such as off-label promotion, targeting of vulnerable groups, and poor safety profiles of products. Only one enforcement tool was used: negotiation with the company; fines, sanctions, requirements for remedial action, or prosecutions have not been used.

In answer to a question from the federal New Democratic Party, Rona Ambrose, the minister of health, said that between 2003–04 and 2013–14 there had been 359 complaints about promotion targeting consumers but that none of those complaints had resulted in penalties or fines. Reflecting the pattern that we have seen in other areas of regulation, Ambrose said Health Canada was able to work "collaboratively" with the companies to achieve compliance (77). In October 2014, Health Canada started listing all of the complaints that it received about health product advertising on a publicly accessible website. As of 10 November 2015 there were 53 active complaints and 99 closed complaints about natural health products, medical devices, and non-prescription and prescription drugs. As with most Health Canada efforts at transparency, this is a half-hearted venture; no details are given about the nature of the alleged violation and the typical "Action" listed is that a compliance letter has been sent. None of the 152 actions involved any fines (78).

The federal government has also not taken any action to stem the flow of televised DTC ads from the United States that come into Canada via satellite and cable, although it has the jurisdictional authority to require that the ads be removed. As a result, English-speaking Canadians are frequently exposed to DTCA originating in the United States. Michael Law from the University of British Columbia and his colleagues (79) found a link between exposure to US DTCA for Zelnorm (tegaserod) in English-speaking provinces and territories and an increase in prescribing that did not occur in Quebec, where residents watch much less US television. This drug was later withdrawn from the market because of cardiac risks.

Although the federal government, through Health Canada, has largely neglected its regulatory duty when it comes to DTCA, it was willing to defend the principle that it has a right to regulate this practice. In December 2005, Canwest Mediaworks Inc sued the federal government under the Charter of Rights and Freedoms, arguing that the ban prohibiting ads that name both the drug and the indication for the drug contravened a Charter provision that guarantees "freedom of thought, belief, opinion and expression, including freedom of the press and other media of communication." In addition, Canwest's position was that the ban limits information that patients "have a right to receive" and is paternalistic, anachronistic, and too broad (80). The case ultimately collapsed after Canwest went into receivership.

Conclusion

Health Canada's approach to the regulation of promotion of any type is a clear reflection of the clientele pluralist relationship that it has with the pharmaceutical industry. It theoretically is able to regulate all types of promotion, but it has historically chosen not to and has assigned that role to various industry associations or organizations with strong ties to industry. One way of looking at this abdication of responsibility is by comparing legal action taken against the drug companies in the United States and Canada because of illegal promotion. In the United States, since 1991, 239 settlements for $30.2 billion have been reached between federal and state governments and pharmaceutical companies to resolve allegations of numerous violations, primarily illegal off-label marketing, that is, marketing drugs for indications that have not been approved by the Food and Drug Administration (81). Several companies prosecuted for illegally marketing unapproved uses in the United States sell the same products in Canada, but a Health Canada spokesperson told the *Toronto Star* that it "has not been made aware of any specific similar issue in Canada and has not received complaints concerning these companies promoting off-label uses of their products in Canada" (81). Despite repeated requests by the *Star*, "Health Canada provided no evidence it has ever investigated, prosecuted or fined a single drug company for off-label promotions" (82).

As Barbara Mintzes and I note (76), the way that Health Canada regulates DTCA demonstrates an astonishing degree of discordance with public health priorities. Health Canada never offered a public health rationale for the introduction of "reminder" and "help-seeking" ads. Because no shift in law occurred, their introduction bypassed democratic processes, including a parliamentary debate and vote, and any possibility of open public discussion about the pros and cons of more widespread DTCA. More generally, since the federal government has absolved itself of any role in providing objective information about the appropriate prescribing and use of medications, by virtue of not regulating promotion, it has allowed industry to dominate the provision of information to both health professionals and to the public. Industry driven by commercial motivation has constructed weak regulatory codes with little enforcement and negligible penalties. Ads are persuasive and are carefully crafted to sway the opinion of health care professionals and the public; they represent a danger to considered decision making in the case of medicine use, and little to nothing is done to prevent this. The result has been an adverse impact on the way that doctors prescribe and consequently an adverse impact on the health of the people who receive the prescriptions or buy OTC products.

5 Health Canada and drug safety: How safe are we?

Drug safety raises many questions: What kinds of resources are devoted to postmarket safety? How does Health Canada monitor drugs for safety problems? How are problems communicated after they are recognized? How effective are Health Canada's methods of communication? How much information does Health Canada release about what it finds? This chapter examines all these issues to see how well Health Canada is doing in keeping people who use prescription drugs safe.

In the United States, adverse drug reactions (ADRs) were estimated to be the fourth to sixth leading cause of death in the 1990s, contributing to an estimated 76,000 to 137,000 deaths and 1.5 million hospitalizations yearly (1). The Institute for Safe Medication Practices places the number of annual deaths in the United States that are due to ADRs at 128,000 based on analysis of reports to the Food and Drug Administration (2). A comparable estimate comes from the Commission of the European Communities (3). Since the Lazarou and colleagues' estimate (1) was made in the late 1990s, reported serious ADRs increased from 34,966 in 1998 to 89,842 in 2005 and fatal ADRs increased from 5519 to 15,107 during the same period, while the total number of outpatient prescriptions went up by only 40% (4).

Lazarou et al. calculated that fatal ADRs occurred in about 0.32% of all hospital admissions. In the early 1990s, I conducted a systematic review of the Canadian literature about ADRs in hospitals and estimated that approximately 15% of hospitalized patients suffered an ADR and that about 1.5% of those patients died (5). Thus, my estimate of fatalities in 0.23% of admissions is quite close to that of Lazarou and colleagues'. A more recent study of all adverse events (AEs), not just those related to drugs, in Canadian hospitals reported that they occurred in

7.5% of admissions with about 1.5% of those suffering an AE dying (6). Using other figures in the study, I calculated that about one-quarter of the drug-related AEs (0.03%) in hospitalized patients resulted in death. The Canadian Institute for Health Information reports 2,446,700 hospital admissions in 2012–13 (7) and, therefore, depending on whether the 0.03% or 0.23% figure is used, somewhere between 735 and 5625 patients could have died from an ADR. Of course, many of these deaths are not preventable, but that number exceeds the 2075 Canadians who died in traffic-related incidents in 2012 (8) and is a number that cannot be ignored.

Between 1990 and 2009, about 4% to 5% of all new drugs approved by Health Canada in four different five-year periods (1990–94, 1995–99, 2000–4, 2005–9) subsequently needed to be withdrawn from the market for safety reasons (see Figure 5.1) (9). Although the percentage of withdrawals has remained relatively stable, aggressive marketing of new drugs by companies means that an increasing number of people may be exposed to these products before they are removed from the market. Despite significant safety concerns, evidence shows that Health Canada is not monitoring safety adequately. Two of the five most heavily promoted drugs in Canada in 2000 – Vioxx (rofecoxib), used for pain and inflammation, and Baycol (cerivastatin), used for high cholesterol – were subsequently withdrawn because of safety issues (9).

The length of time that drugs have been on the market does not correlate to their safety. Sometimes safety issues are not recognized for many decades (10). Nor are all drug withdrawals preceded by safety warnings. Half of the 22 drugs withdrawn in Canada between 1994 and 2013 did not have a preceding safety warning, raising questions about how much Health Canada knew about their safety. On the other hand, the extremely short intervals between the approval of a drug and a serious safety warning and between a safety warning and removal of a drug from the market raise questions about how the situation could change so rapidly. Bextra (valdecoxib), a drug used for pain and inflammation, went from approval to a safety warning in 20 days. Cerivastatin went from a safety warning to being withdrawn from the market in 23 days (9).

Surprisingly, Health Canada does not keep a specific summary record of drugs that have been withdrawn for safety reasons. As a result, acquiring such information requires searching multiple Health Canada databases. The absence of such a list means that Health Canada cannot easily look for or track trends in drug withdrawals; it cannot examine how long it takes to identify serious safety problems and whether this situation is

Figure 5.1 Percentage of drugs eventually withdrawn for safety reasons relative to all new active substances approved in various five-year periods, 1 January 1990 to 31 December 2009

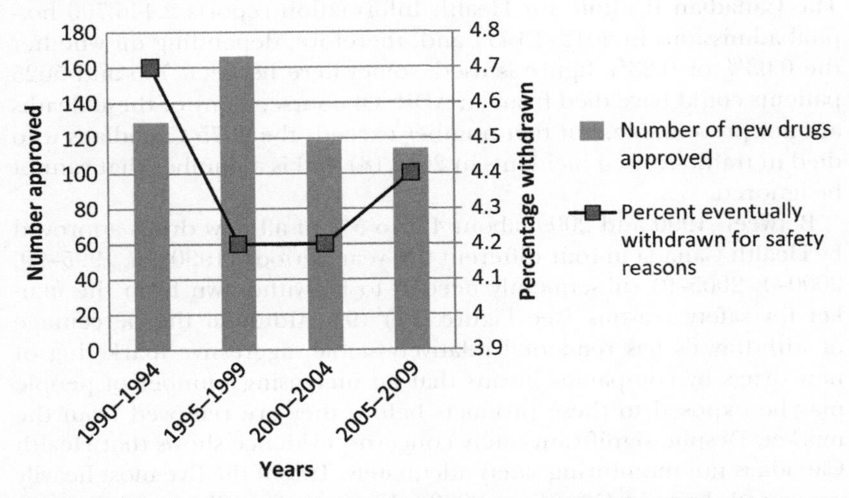

Source: Modified from Lexchin J. How safe are new drugs? Market withdrawal of drugs approved in Canada between 1990 and 2009. Open Medicine. 2013;8:e14-e19. Reproduced under the Open Government License – Canada (http://open.canada.ca/en/open-government-licence-canada).

worsening or improving; and it cannot see if some manufacturers have drugs with more safety problems than others.

Attitudes of industry and Health Canada towards drug safety

Industry maintains that its first priority is the health and well-being of Canadians (11), and likewise "Health Canada's vision is to continually promote high standards of product vigilance for the protection of the health and safety of Canadians" (12 p1). However, despite such pronouncements, in the past both parties have often not acted promptly when safety issues became apparent. Chapter 3 discussed Lilly's behaviour related to its arthritis drug Oraflex. Entero-Vioform (iodoquinol) is another example of the neglect of safety. In the mid-1950s, increasing numbers of people in Japan were becoming ill with a neurological disorder that produced degenerative and often irreversible changes, leaving people paralysed and blind. This new disease acquired the name subacute myelo-optic neuropathy or SMON. Eventually, an estimated 20,000 Japanese were affected (13). By 1975, both Norway and Sweden banned the drug Entero-Vioform (iodoquinol), made by Ciba-Geigy (now part of Novartis), which was implicated in causing SMON. The Canadian reaction was to do essentially nothing, and Entero-Vioform remained available on prescription. Why was the Canadian reaction so muted? One of Ciba-Geigy's defences was that SMON was a "Japanese disease." Canadian officials seem to have accepted this claim. A senior official in Health Canada was quoted as saying that Entero-Vioform and related drugs "really were not found to be causing any serious problems [in Canada]. This is what's so queer about it, it's all directly related to Japan" (14 pA6). The basis of that statement was apparently the fact that Health Canada knew of only 10 minor and 2 serious reactions in Canada to Entero-Vioform. Were there more reactions? How many? How many were serious? Those questions were never investigated.

A third historical example of Health Canada's apparent cavalier attitude to adverse drug reactions was its response to the harms to female fetuses that were exposed in utero to DES (diethylstilbestrol) between 1941 and 1971. DES is a synthetic estrogen, sold by multiple companies in Canada, that was prescribed because it allegedly prevented miscarriages, although this was never actually proven in any clinical trials. In 1971, it was banned for use in pregnancy in Canada because it caused a rare form of cancer and reproductive tract abnormalities in the daughters of women who used it while they were pregnant. (DES is now marketed in Canada only for veterinary uses.) The notice that Health Canada sent out at the time downplayed the risk, saying the drug "was not widely adopted in Canada" and the "Canadian Tumour Reference Centre has no record of any such cases [of clear cell carcinoma]" (15 p158). In reality, an estimated 200,000 to 400,000 women had been prescribed the drug (16). Health Canada required companies making DES to include a warning about use in pregnancy but never made the companies notify doctors of the problems. From 1971 to 1983, Health Canada issued a single press release to the public about the dangers from DES.

How Health Canada acquires "evidence" and interprets signals

Health Canada documents about what triggers a safety action are quite vague and provide little transparency or specifics regarding how decisions are made. For example, Health Canada states, "The determination of the seriousness of risk (probability of health hazard and probability of occurrence) and urgency of risk communication is based on sound scientific judgement" (17). Further, the agency states that "regulatory actions ... are taken according to the regulatory framework in place. This implies an evaluation of the signal and the appropriate benefit-risk review of the information available" (18 p6).

Chris Turner, the head of the Marketed Health Products Directorate (MHPD), the part of Health Canada charged with monitoring the safety of drugs already marketed, wrote a letter to the *Toronto Star* defending Health Canada's drug safety program, saying, "Health Canada has highly trained specialists who use Canadian adverse reaction data as well as other sources of information to systematically monitor, analyze and act on safety issues" (19). But another, unnamed, Health Canada official is quoted as telling the *Toronto Star* that "it is primarily the [drug company's] responsibility to monitor the safe use of their products" (20).

In May 2005, Christiane Vellemure, the director of the Office of Business Transformation, Planning and Administration at Health Canada, showed a PowerPoint presentation looking at the progress that had been made in setting up a new Health Product Safety Board that was designed to "encourage public input in regulatory decision making, strengthen public accountability in regulation and risk management of health products [and] provide independent advice on health product safety issues as a permanent part of the Health Canada decision making process" (21). By the time this body had its first meeting in November 2007, it had morphed into the Expert Advisory Committee on the Vigilance of Health Products with a mandate to provide objective external expert advice on broad strategic policy and program issues involving marketed therapeutic health products for human use (22). The committee met two to three times per year until 2011 (23), but since then it has held no further meetings, despite an announcement on the website of a meeting in October 2012 (24). According to one anonymous member of the committee, it advised the minister of health just once. This same member recounts that the committee asked Health Canada to define how safety signals were determined and what criteria or weighting was used in deciding about communicating safety problems. The committee never heard back from Health Canada (committee member, personal communications, 24 October 2010 and 11 January 2015).

An imbalance in resources for drug safety and its consequences

Health Canada seems to place safety at a lower priority than its mandate to get new drugs onto the market. Table 5.1 shows that in 2004, the arms of Health Canada that approved drugs (Therapeutic Products Directorate, TPD, and Biologics and Genetic Therapies Directorate, BGTD) were getting about seven times as much funding and had about seven times as many personnel as the MHPD. The 2004 imbalance did not seem to be important to the government. Out of $40 million allocated to Health Canada in 2003–4 for its drugs programs, just $2.5 million went to monitoring postmarket drug safety (25). A 2006 investigation by the auditor general documented that drug program managers felt that they were unable to meet the regulatory requirements for monitoring the safety of marketed drugs because of a lack of funds (26). Between 2004 and 2010 the situation improved somewhat, but by the latter date, more than three times the number of personnel and amount of funding were still going to the directorates reviewing drug applications (TPD and BGTD) compared with the one charged with monitoring safety (MHPD).

This mismatch in personnel and resources may be one reason that some provincial officials in charge of drug plans raised concerns about how thoroughly Health Canada examines the safety data that it receives. One official noted that the path between the information that Health Canada collects and what happens because of that information is opaque when it comes to labelling changes about safety. Another provincial official remarked that, in some instances, Health Canada seemed to take longer than it should in disseminating the safety information that it does collect, and it was not transparent enough in its rationale for issuing warnings and regulatory decisions. Some of these same officials were as critical of the pharmaceutical companies as they were of Health Canada, believing that pharmaceutical companies failed to disclose crucial safety information. Some felt that the activities of the companies contributed to the unsafe use of medications. Other provincial plan administrators suggested that companies delayed the disclosure of safety information because of the potential loss of revenue (27).

This imbalance in personnel and resources at Health Canada is also reflected in a power imbalance. Although the MHPD monitors safety, it does not have the authority to send out safety warnings or to withdraw products from the market. Those decisions remain with the TPD and the BGTD, the parts of the agency that authorized the marketing of the

Table 5.1 Comparison of personnel and resources of Health Canada directorates

	Annual operating cost base ($000,000)		Number of full-time equivalent employees	
	Year ending 31 March 2004	Year ending 31 March 2010	Year ending 31 March 2004	Year ending 31 March 2010
Therapeutic Products Directorate*	38	44.9	423	514.5
Biologics and Genetic Therapies Directorate†	22	29.7	228	312.2
Marketed Health Products Directorate‡	8	23.6	90	213.9
Total	68	98.2	741	1040.6

Source: Wiktorowicz M, Lexchin J, Moscou K, Silversides A, Eggertson L. Keeping an eye on prescription drugs ... Keeping Canadians safe: active monitoring systems for drug safety and effectiveness in Canada and internationally. Toronto: Health Council of Canada, 2010.

* Reviews applications for approval for prescription and non-prescription drugs derived from chemical manufacturing and medical devices.

† Reviews applications for approval for biological and radiopharmaceutical drugs including blood and blood products, viral and bacterial vaccines, genetic therapeutic products, tissues, organs, and xenografts.

‡ Monitors the safety of all health products on the market, including prescription and OTC drugs, medical devices, and consumer items, such as sunscreen and toothpaste.

drugs; therefore, to take action these directorates have to be willing to admit that they may have made a mistake. (Of course, not all drug safety problems can be anticipated at the time that drugs are being considered for marketing.) Whether this division of authority leads to tensions within Health Canada has not been explored.

Lack of transparency about releasing safety information

While the resources devoted to getting new drugs onto the market and monitoring their safety once they are being sold may be mismatched, Health Canada is consistent in its reluctance to release safety information. In the early 1990s, the Medicines Control Agency (now the Medicines and Healthcare Products Regulatory Agency) in the United Kingdom revoked the licence of Halcion (triazolam), a Valium-like drug used as a sedative. This decision was based on its reassessment of earlier trials and reports of adverse drug reactions in the United Kingdom (28). This action triggered a review of Halcion in many other countries, including Canada. The Canadian review was conducted with the advice of "six prominent Canadian clinical experts" and resulted in some changes to the product labelling and the introduction of a patient package insert for each package of Halcion (29). No one outside Health Canada, aside from the six experts, appears to have been consulted, and the evidence that the agency used in making its recommendations was never made public. (Halcion is still sold in Canada but is not widely prescribed.)

A second example concerns the short-acting version of Adalat (nifedipine), a calcium channel blocker that was widely prescribed for hypertension and angina in the 1980s and 1990s. It was originally marketed in Canada in 1982, but since the late 1980s, evidence pointed to serious adverse effects (30). After delaying taking any action for a number of years while the evidence mounted, Health Canada finally convened an expert committee of cardiologists in 1995 to examine the issue, and eventually a "Dear Doctor" letter was sent to all Canadian physicians. While perhaps lacking a sense of urgency about the problem, the letter did advise caution about prescribing short-acting nifedipine (31). However, the information used in producing this letter was not made public. Subsequently, Ken Rubin, an Ottawa researcher, attempted to use a subsection of the Access to Information Act to see this safety review but was unsuccessful. The courts ruled against him on the grounds that since the release of information was discretionary, the minister was not obligated to do so (32).

Health Canada and the Food and Drugs Act and drug safety

The Food and Drugs Act and its Regulations theoretically give Health Canada considerable authority in dealing with safety issues, but the legislation also has significant limitations. One of the most important of these is that the Food and Drug Regulations assign the primary responsibility for ensuring the safety and effectiveness of drugs to industry, including recalling a drug; Health Canada has no authority to order the recall of a drug that it judges poses an unacceptable risk (33). All it can do is request that the company involved recall the product. Health Canada's only direct power is to suspend the Notice of Compliance (NOC, marketing authorization) and cancel the drug identification number (DIN, which uniquely identifies each drug product sold in a dosage form in Canada) for any unsafe product. Without a NOC or DIN, a drug cannot be sold, and if the DIN is cancelled, then Health Canada inspectors can seize the drug from pharmacies. However, the only recent situation where this power was actually exercised concerned Adderall XR (amphetamine, dextroamphetamine mixed salts) a product used in treating attention deficit hyperactivity disorder in children. Health Canada suspended the marketing because of international reports of sudden deaths in children, even when the drug was being used at recommended doses (34). Health Canada subsequently appointed an expert review committee to examine the safety of Adderall XR, and the committee concluded that there was not enough evidence that Adderall XR was any more likely to cause an increased risk of sudden cardiac death compared to other treatments for attention deficit hyperactivity disorder. Following this report, Health Canada allowed the sale of Adderall XR to resume (35). In all other situations where Health Canada felt that a drug was too unsafe to remain on the market, it has preferred to negotiate with drug companies and have them remove the drug voluntarily.

The pharmaceutical industry, as represented by Rx&D, does not support legislation expanding Health Canada's powers to give it unilateral authority to remove unsafe drugs from the market. The opinion of Russell Williams, its president, is that while "'patient safety is the first priority of Canada's research-based pharmaceutical industry' ... recalls are only one of several 'escalating responses' drug companies take when a drug problem has been identified ... 'To this end any proposed legislation should direct Health Canada to continue to pursue the possibility of mutually acceptable voluntary undertakings before resorting to the power to recall. In exceptional circumstances where there is disagreement, a rapid means of dispute resolution should be available'" (36).

Health Canada can issue a public warning about a drug without the agreement of the company involved, but it cannot directly compel the company to revise the label of its product to reflect new safety information. However, Health Canada can notify the manufacturer that without adequate changes, the NOC or the DIN will be suspended. Whether Health Canada has ever used this threat to get a company to change labelling is not known. Health Canada's inability to directly order a recall was dramatically brought to light in the spring of 2013, when a delay occurred in recalling birth control pills because of faulty packaging that could have led to unwanted pregnancies. Health Canada not only delayed warning women about the problem but also had to rely on the manufacturer to physically remove the drug from pharmacies (33).

Although these are serious deficiencies in Health Canada's powers, its most significant limitation is that after a drug is on the market, Health Canada cannot require the manufacturer to undertake any new studies into the product's safety, and Health Canada fully recognizes this lack of authority (37). (Manufacturers are required by law to report all ADRs that they become aware of to Health Canada. The period for reporting varies depending on whether the reaction is known or unknown and whether it is serious.) The one exception is in the case of drugs approved under a Notice of Compliance with conditions (NOC/c). In this instance, Table 3.1 in Chapter 3 shows how long it can take before those studies are done.

Faster drug approvals and drug safety

In an effort to ensure that promising therapies for serious illnesses can reach Canadians in a timely manner, Health Canada has developed two pathways for approving new drugs more rapidly – priority reviews and the Notice of Compliance with conditions (NOC/c) policy. (See Chapter 3 for a discussion of these.) A priority review reduces the review period from the standard 300 days to 180 days. If companies apply for NOC/c status when they file the new drug submission, and Health Canada agrees, then drugs are reviewed in 200 days. If companies do not initially apply for NOC/c status, then drugs are reviewed in either 180 or 300 days, and Health Canada may grant NOC/c status at the end of the review.

An important question is whether the shorter priority review period and the approval of drugs under the NOC/c policy leads to products having more serious safety issues after they are marketed. The answer seems to be yes. A drug that has a standard review has a 20% chance that either Health Canada will issue a serious safety warning about it or the drug will be withdrawn from the market because it was unsafe. For drugs approved with a priority review, that figure rises to 34% (38). For drugs approved through the NOC/c policy, just under 41% either had a serious safety warning or were withdrawn (39). For both NOC/c and priority review drugs, the increased safety problems weren't balanced by an increase in benefits.

A closely related issue is tying review times to the amount that the regulatory agency receives in user fees, as is done in Canada and the United States. As the deadline approaches, reviewers may inadvertently speed up their examination of the evidence and overlook safety issues to avoid a loss in revenue. Carpenter and colleagues examined this question in the United States (40, 41), where the FDA has a statutory requirement to complete its review of 90% of new drug applications within set times. If the FDA fails to meet that obligation, then renewal of legislation that allows it to collect user fees from industry may be endangered. The conclusion reached was that when drugs are approved within two months of the deadline, a substantially higher rate of withdrawals or safety labelling changes occurred compared with drugs approved when the deadline was not an issue.

Similarly, cost recovery fees paid to Health Canada will also suffer if reviews of new drug applications are not completed within the targeted time. If Health Canada takes too long to review applications for new drugs in one year, then the next year it will be forced to reduce user fees. For example, if review times are 20% over time in 2012, then fees will drop by 20% in 2013 (42). Faced with the prospect of penalties, Health Canada might follow the pattern set by the FDA and perhaps rush to approve new drugs that are approaching the deadline to avoid incurring a financial loss in the next year. The equivalent would be putting a time limit on how long the Transportation Safety Board had to investigate an airplane crash, and if it exceeded that limit, its funding would be cut. As of February 2015, the change tying review times to user fees in Canada is too new to be able to determine if it has had any effect on Health Canada's revenue from cost recovery.

Communication standards

The 2011 auditor general's (AG) report investigated how well Health Canada ensures the safety of the drugs that it approves (43). The AG found that a lack of standards in areas such as the amount of time a potential safety issue might wait before an assessment begins and the amount of time an assessment might be placed on hold. Thus, it took Health Canada at least one year to complete 34 assessments and more than two years for five medium-priority assessments. A medium-priority assessment is one for which a labelling change will likely be necessary. Officials who recommend labelling changes are not the same as those who are responsible for working with the drug manufacturers to implement the changes. This latter group of officials often do not document whether they agree or disagree with recommended labelling updates or how they intend to implement the recommendations, including what the proposed timelines are for implementation. In 12 out of 38 cases, it

Table 5.2 Frequency of use of various sources of information about new safety issues by health care professionals, 2007

	The Canadian Adverse Reaction Newsletter (%)	DHPLs* from drug manufacturers (%)	DHPLs from Health Canada (%)	Drug safety advisories (%)	Med-Effect e-Notice (%)	Regional adverse reaction centres (%)
Frequently	16	17	15	14	20	17
Occasionally	51	52	45	45	46	43
Rarely	31	30	39	38	27	37
Have not used	1	<1	–	3	7	3
Didn't know/ no answer	1	1	2	1	–	–

Source: Environics Research Group. Adverse reaction reporting – survey with health professionals. Ottawa: Environics Research Group; 2007. Reproduced with permission.

*Dear Health Professional Letter

took Health Canada between 3 and 20 months to notify manufacturers about the needed changes.

In 11 out of 24 cases where it was necessary to issue risk communications to the public, it took Health Canada more than two years to assess the potential safety issue, update the drug's label (where necessary), and issue the risk communication. Even more worrisome, Health Canada had no standards for monitoring the effectiveness of its communication strategies with either the public or health care professionals, although it told the AG that it is taking steps to do so (43). Surveys of the public show that citizens are generally unaware of, and did not consider, Health Canada public advisories and warnings and its website as important sources of new drug safety information. Only 1% made use of the former and 3% of the latter, and just 8% of consumers reported having used the Health Canada website for this purpose over a six-month period (44). With such low use, their effectiveness is clearly in question, although the public may receive information in other ways. Use by health care professionals is somewhat better, but they too seldom use these sources. (See Table 5.2.)

Whether doctors use these safety warnings may be largely irrelevant, as single letters or website announcements about safety problems have shown little to no impact on prescribing rates (45, 46). Atypical antipsychotic use among seniors increased, albeit more slowly than predicted, despite three advisories from Health Canada warning prescribers of an increased mortality rate associated with the use of these products in nursing-home patients (47). On-the-other hand, DDAVP (desmopressin) use in children for bedwetting decreased markedly following two safety advisories (48).

Health Canada is aware of its lack of knowledge regarding the effectiveness of its communication strategies, and in 2014 it commissioned the Council of Canadian Academies to provide an evidence-based and authoritative assessment of the state of knowledge on measurement and evaluation of health risk communication about therapeutic products. The Council released its report in June 2015 (49), but it is too early to know if and how it will influence the way that Health Canada communicates with health care professionals, patients, and the public.

Inspections for good manufacturing practices

As discussed in Chapter 1, Health Canada has long had a system for the inspection of drug manufacturing facilities (good manufacturing practices, GMP), co-developed with the cooperation of the pharmaceutical industry. Like other aspects of drug operations, plant inspections have in the past been compromised by a lack of resources. The Field Operations Directorate within Health Canada that was charged with drug plant inspections and the drug sampling program had to make cutbacks in response to government-wide fiscal restraint in the mid-1980s. A study team looking into the Canadian Drug Safety, Quality and Efficacy Program documented a 15% drop in the number of regular plant inspections between 1983–84 and 1985–86, with a corresponding increase in the number of partial inspections (50). According to the study team, "it is not clear whether Partial inspections cover the right area on an annual basis ... the split between Partial and Regular inspections has resulted in a biased data base on company compliance history. This in turn creates difficulties in planning for future inspections" (50 p17). In late 2012, amid considerable fanfare, then health minister Leona Aglukkaq announced that these inspection standards were being strengthened by extending the requirements for GMP to include active ingredients, that is, the active material in the drug (51).

The only report about the results of Health Canada's inspection program covers 2006 to 2011 (52). (As of 2006, program managers at

Health Canada did not believe that the agency was allocating sufficient resources for the inspection of manufacturing facilities (26).) The document breaks down the findings into gross categories, such as the number of inspections performed, the percentage of inspections where various problems were found, and the most common problems. It contains no information about any specific inspection, no comment about what actions, if any, were taken to correct the problems, and nothing about the individual products involved. To find information about problems in specific Canadian manufacturing facilities requires filing a Freedom of Information Act request with the FDA in the United States. The FDA inspects not only domestic plants but also foreign plants that ship drugs into the United States. (Health Canada does not have the resources to do many foreign inspections and so has developed mutual recognition agreements with 26 international partners to ensure that drugs manufactured in these jurisdictions and imported into Canada comply with GMP (43)). According to the *Toronto Star*, FDA inspections have found serious manufacturing violations in 40 Canadian plants since 2008 (53). This information is available because the FDA makes inspection dates and results available to the public on its website, whereas Health Canada does not give any details of the problems, if any, that it finds during individual inspections and won't make public "the names of the 20-plus companies that have been cited since 2012 for severe manufacturing violations" (53). Health Canada told the *Toronto Star* that it would need to consult with the companies in question before releasing that type of information. Following an inspection of a plant in Bangalore, India, owned by the Canadian generic manufacturer Apotex, the FDA banned the importation of drugs made at that plant into the United States. In contrast, Health Canada, after being made aware of the inspection findings, eventually allowed the same drugs into Canada. It initially asked Apotex to stop importing the drugs, but the company refused the request twice; after Apotex agreed to do additional quality control tests, Health Canada dropped its request (54).

A couple of months after the *Toronto Star* stories appeared, Health Canada released inspection reports that showed that "nearly one-third of all Canadian drug plants inspected since 2013 have terms and conditions on their licences" (55). However, there are still ongoing gaps in what Health Canada is willing to make public: "While the disclosures show the date and location of the inspection, and whether the inspection led to regulatory action, Health Canada has not yet released details of the problems it found in all but one case. [The story in the *Toronto Star* did not say what that case was.] And while the new data shows that 13 facilities received a non-compliant rating and no longer have a licence, Health Canada refused to say whether in these cases it revoked the licence or the company voluntarily shut down post-inspection" (55). Even now that Health Canada is posting individual inspection reports on its website (http://www.hc-sc.gc.ca/dhp-mps/compli-conform/gmp-bpf/summary-sommaire-eng.php) anyone interested has to send an email requesting details about any terms and conditions that may have been imposed. The website promises someone will to try to respond within 10 working days, but when I asked for information, it took 24 days and that was only after another department in Health Canada interceded for me, and I had made two phone calls to inquire about what was happening. The information that I eventually received was minimal: "The terms and conditions imposed ... relates to a foreign site listed on the licence and restricts the scope of the activity 'test.' One of the foreign sites listed ... is authorised to conduct chemical and physical testing only." However, Health Canada's website does have two detailed inspection reports, and some vague language indicates that more of this type of report will become available.

In addition, Health Canada has started posting a small amount of information about potential health and safety issues that it is tracking with companies that fabricate, package/label, test, wholesale, distribute, or import drugs for sale in Canada (http://www.hc-sc.gc.ca/dhp-mps/pubs/compli-conform/tracker-suivi-eng.php).

Adverse drug reaction reporting

The backbone of Health Canada's system for monitoring the safety of drugs already on the market is the reporting of adverse drug reactions (ADRs) through MedEffect Canada (http://www.hc-sc.gc.ca/dhp-mps/medeff/index-eng.php). The number of reports that Health Canada receives has been increasing dramatically in recent years, as Figure 5.2 shows, with over 53,000 reports in 2012. Health Canada maintains a searchable online database that lists all the adverse drug reports that it has ever received (56), but the 545,000 foreign ADR reports it received in 2012 (43) were not entered into this database because of a lack of resources, thereby potentially missing important information that could identify unsuspected problems or confirm suspected problems. (This same problem was noted by the auditor general as far back as 2000 (57).) Although Canada was the first country to post its ADR database online (58), Health Canada strongly resisted doing so. As part of a series on

Figure 5.2 Number of domestic reports of adverse drug reactions received by Health Canada, 2002–2012

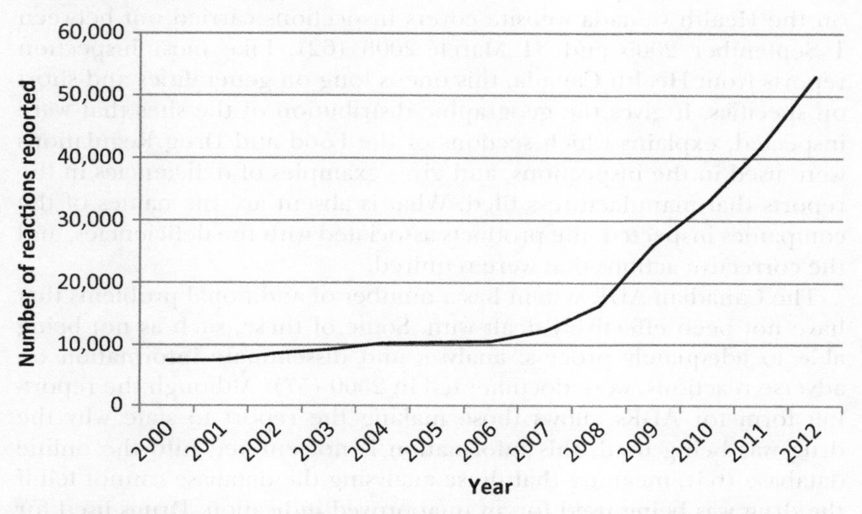

Source: Adverse reaction and incident reporting, 2012. Canadian Adverse Reaction Newsletter. 2013;23(3):2–5.

drug safety that the Canadian Broadcasting Corporation (CBC) ran in early 2004, the broadcaster used the Access to Information Act to obtain ADR reports and then posted this information online from 1965, when the ADR program started, to the end of September 2003 (59). Health Canada's immediate reaction was to issue a statement that read in part, "Health Canada is concerned that the Canadian public may misinterpret this adverse reaction information posted on the CBC website ... The subset of adverse reaction information posted on the CBC website represents the reporter's [i.e., the person filing the report] observations and opinions, and does not reflect any Health Canada assessment of association between the health product and the reaction(s) ... The adverse reaction data posted on the CBC website cannot be used on its own for the evaluation of a health product's safety" (60 p1). The database from the CBC remained in place until the end of May 2005, when Health Canada itself made the information publicly available online (61).

In addition to receiving voluntary reports of ADRs from various sources, including doctors, pharmacists, and the public, Health Canada also has an inspection system to ensure that drug companies are appropriately reporting the ADRs that they become aware of. The results of these inspections are available in a report, but the last one on the Health Canada website covers inspections carried out between 1 September 2005 and 31 March 2008 (62). Like most inspection reports from Health Canada, this one is long on generalities and short on specifics. It gives the geographic distribution of the sites that were inspected, explains which sections of the Food and Drug Regulations were used in the inspections, and gives examples of deficiencies in the reports that manufacturers filed. What is absent are the names of the companies inspected, the products associated with the deficiencies, and the corrective actions that were required.

The Canadian ADR system has a number of additional problems that have not been effectively dealt with. Some of these, such as not being able to adequately process, analyse, and disseminate information on adverse reactions, were documented in 2000 (57). Although the reporting form for ADRs allows those making the report to state why the drug was being used, this information is not entered into the online database (63), meaning that those analysing the database cannot tell if the drug was being used for an unapproved indication. Drugs used for unapproved indications may produce side effects that are unanticipated, because the scientific data for many of these unapproved indications is very weak (64). Contrary to New Zealand, where after each report has been assessed, letters providing relevant information about the ADR are sent to the reporter (65), Health Canada provides no feedback to reporters (66). Finally, drug companies are required to report ADRs that they become aware of, within specified periods, depending on the seriousness of the reaction and whether it was previously known. However, this requirement applies only when the company has linked the problem with a drug. Here is what Health Canada says in its guidance to industry on reporting: "Every MAH [Market Authorization Holder] is required to report ARs [adverse reactions] known to them involving their marketed health products in accordance with the requirements of the Food and Drugs Act and the Regulations" (67 p2). The Health Canada requirement seems to be based on its adoption of the standards set by the International Conference on Harmonization. (See Chapter 3 for an explanation of the ICH and its role.) In contrast, the FDA has rejected the ICH approach and, instead, all adverse events/experiences must be reported, regardless of any potential causal relationship with the treatment (68). This requirement would further increase Health Canada's workload, but on the other hand, it might also mean that adverse events that are unexpected would be flagged earlier.

New initiatives in drug safety

The National Pharmaceuticals Strategy (NPS) was part of the 2004 First Ministers' 10-Year Plan to Strengthen Health Care, in which provinces and territories agreed to make a variety of improvements to their health care systems, accompanied by additional annual payments from the federal government (69). One element in the NPS was a 2004 federal-provincial/territorial initiative intended to address drug safety by improving the way that medicines are monitored after they have been marketed (70). Few details were provided in the initial announcement, but according to a 2006 progress report, four interdependent strategies were being worked on: (1) supporting collaboration and priority setting by using a national oversight body composed of key stakeholders and representatives from all jurisdictions; (2) strengthening existing capabilities by establishing a network of pharmaceutical research centres of excellence; (3) building front-line participation and new opportunities through the active engagement of primary care and hospital-based teams; and (4) establishing clear standards and transparency of evidence by strengthening linkages among regulatory and health system decision-making experts, frameworks, and processes (71). The next steps in the process were to involve completing a business plan for a pharmaceutical research network, engaging stakeholders on the four interdependent strategies, and using a discussion paper to outline the full scope of safety and effectiveness issues. The only concrete outcome was the July 2008 launch by the federal government of the Drug Safety and Effectiveness Network (DSEN), an arm's-length network operating under the umbrella of the Canadian Institutes of Health Research (CIHR). DSEN was designed to connect researchers throughout Canada in a virtual network to conduct postmarket drug research independent of pharmaceutical companies (72) and to stimulate research in studying the impact of drug use in the real-world setting (73). DSEN is a positive initiative from the government, and its steering committee draws from a broad range of independent academics and others, including a patient representative. Although Health Canada is now commissioning studies from DSEN, it is still too early to tell how much influence the organization will have on Health Canada's priorities and activities when it comes to drug safety.

Earlier in this chapter, I discussed the problems that the AG identified with Health Canada's annual safety reports, but until mid-2014, these safety reports were not publicly available. The change was precipitated by what happened with Diane-35 (cyproterone acetate and ethinyl estradiol), an acne medication that was widely prescribed off-label as an oral contraceptive. In the wake of a number of deaths in France linked to the drug, its sale in that country was suspended (74). Subsequently, Health Canada undertook its own investigation of the benefits and harms from the product and, in the end, concluded that the drug should remain on the market but refused to make its findings public (75), citing "confidential business information" as the reason (76). The negative publicity about Health Canada's decision precipitated a change in the organization's position about releasing safety reports. In October 2013, the minister of health announced that she asked Health Canada to "take the steps necessary to begin publishing drug reviews transparently to ensure Canadians and medical professionals have the information they need and want" (76) as part of the government's Regulatory Transparency and Openness Framework for Health Canada (77). The first of these safety summaries to be released was the one for Diane-35, but its content was criticized by Dr Barbara Mintzes, an epidemiologist from the University of British Columbia. Mintzes said, "Generally the report fails to address the question of whether this drug is providing any substantial advantages to health that outweighs the additional potential for harm, as compared to low-risk oral contraceptives or other alternatives for acne ... It is mainly providing a rationale for the decision not to withdraw it from the market based on two things: the risks having been a concern for a long time rather than being a new problem; and the existence of other birth control pills that also have a poor safety profile in terms of risks of blood clots." (78).

These safety reports have other problems besides their content. The release of safety reports will not be made retroactive. Only the safety reports that were triggered by alarms raised by foreign regulators, medical or scientific literature, or Health Canada's routine monitoring activities are eligible for release. The others, 128 out of 152 done in 2013, will be kept confidential because they contain material supplied by drug manufacturers, including risk management plans for prescription drugs, reports of side effects, and usage data (79). Finally, Periodic Safety Update Reports, reports containing a comprehensive assessment of the worldwide safety data on a marketed health product and prepared by the manufacturer, will also remain confidential (67, 79).

Progressive licensing, Bill C-51, Bill C-17, and drug safety

At present, after a new drug is approved for marketing, Health Canada is significantly limited in terms of its ability to demand that companies generate new safety information. To change this situation, since 2006, Health Canada has been talking about progressive licensing (80). The aim of progressive licensing is to move from an all-or-none situation – either license the drug or don't – to a position where the safety and efficacy of drugs is followed throughout their entire life cycle. Here is what Health Canada says about progressive licensing on its website: "Progressive Licensing means that Health Canada would assess the benefits and risks of a product before and after it reaches the market, establishing a stable regulatory standard that reflects a lifecycle approach to drug regulation" (81). The promise of this new system is that ongoing re-evaluation of the risks and benefits of medications will pick up serious safety issues earlier and help to better target drug therapy. In April 2008, the Canadian government unveiled new legislation (Bill C-51), incorporating the principles of progressive licensing (82). Although this legislation died when a federal election was called in the fall of that year, some of its principles reappeared in 2014 with Bill C-17, which I will discuss shortly.

Under Bill C-51, Health Canada was to be given the new authority to issue the market authorization for a drug, subject to additional terms and conditions, and suspend the authorization if the company did not follow through on its obligations (83). In practice, these new powers likely meant that Health Canada would be able to require companies to carry out postmarket studies to look at potential safety problems. Although in theory this additional information would be valuable in assessing where new products fit into the therapeutic armamentarium, in reality there are worries about relying on industry-funded studies. A systematic review published by the Cochrane Collaboration, an independent, non-profit, non-governmental organization consisting of a group of more than 31,000 volunteers in more than 120 countries, has shown that commercially sponsored research is much more likely to result in positive outcomes than research funded from any other source. If a study was sponsored by a company, the results were 2.15 times as likely to be positive, and the conclusions were 2.67 times as likely to be positive compared with studies with other sources of funding (84). In addition, as Chapter 3 pointed out, the provisions about releasing information that were contained in Bill C-51 were ambiguous, and so it is not clear that, had it passed, that information about the progress and results of any postmarket trials would have been made public.

The latest piece of legislation to try to deal with the question of postmarket safety is Bill C-17, also known as Vanessa's Law, which was signed into law in November 2014. The following is based on an analysis of the proposed legislation that was published by Herder and colleagues, including me, in the *Canadian Medical Association Journal* (*CMAJ*) (85). Once the regulations for Bill C-17 are written and the legislation comes into force, it will correct the flaw in the current Food and Drugs Act whereby only the manufacturer can remove a drug from the shelves. Bill C-17 gives the minister the explicit authority to issue a recall, without prior consultation with the manufacturer, if the minister "believes that a therapeutic product presents a serious or imminent risk of injury to health" (86). Like Bill C-51, Bill C-17 also gives the minister the power to require postmarket studies when a NOC is issued. In a potentially very positive step, Bill C-17 contains provisions to enhance the transparency of clinical trial information by giving the minister the power to release such information where risk of injury is suspected or for the protection and promotion of health. In addition, the minister has the power to make regulations that require companies to make "prescribed information" transparent, and the regulations, once written, could extend the definition of prescribed information to postmarket studies.

Rx&D's position on how much power Bill C-17 should give Health Canada to unilaterally recall drugs was not initially clear. In his opening remarks to a House of Commons committee studying the bill, Walter Robinson, the vice-president for government affairs at Rx&D, said, "We also note that, prior to any specific powers now proposed in C-17, Rx&D members have and will continue to work closely with Health Canada to recall products, update or change labels and implement any other important safety-related actions either of our own accord or those deemed warranted by Health Canada" (87). A few months later, testifying before the Standing Senate Committee on Social Affairs, Science and Technology, Robinson was clearer; any disclosure of information must be done in a way to protect "confidential business information," which Rx&D defines as "any information that has economic value to a business or its competitors and that is not usually publicly available" (88). The only exception acceptable to Rx&D would be when there is an imminent and serious threat to human health. Rx&D proposed amendments at the Senate hearings that would have considerably narrowed the reasons for disclosure, instead of allowing disclosure "if the Minister believes that the product may present a serious risk of injury to human health" (89). Rx&D also proposed changing "if the purpose of the disclosure is related to the promotion or protection of human health" to read "if the purpose of the disclosure is necessary for the protection of human health" (88). Neither those proposals from Rx&D nor a number of amendments proposed by those who wanted to strengthen the bill by, for example, replacing the discretionary word "may" with the more prescriptive term "shall" (90) were approved by the Senate.

Conclusion

Absolute drug safety can never be achieved. The variability in human biology and the fact that all biologically active agents likely have multiple effects – some desired and some not – means that all drugs will have safety problems in some people. The task for regulatory authorities, such as Health Canada, is to identify as many of these problems as possible before drugs are released onto the market and then to continue to monitor drugs after approval to ensure that any new safety issues are documented. Finally, Health Canada has the responsibility to be sure that this information is disseminated effectively so that practitioners prescribe and patients use medicines in the safest and most beneficial way possible.

The Food and Drugs Act gives Health Canada significant powers, but the agency has typically chosen not to use these regulatory powers. Instead, it has opted for negotiations with the pharmaceutical industry, despite the fact that the profit-seeking goals of the industry are in conflict with Health Canada's mandate to protect the public. In the words of an editorial in the *CMAJ*, "drugs are allowed to continue on the market virtually without oversight ... incredibly [Health Canada] requires an exceptionally high degree of certainty before it chooses to force a drug company to comply" with a request to suspend sales of a drug or to withdraw an unsafe drug from the market (91 p1125). Attempts to correct limitations in the Food and Drugs Act in the form of Bill C-51 and Bill C-17 are, at best, partial solutions and still leave significant gaps in the agency's ability to ensure the safety of drugs that are allowed onto the market. Thus, as Maor has noted, Health Canada's approach to drug safety is that of a "shadow regulator" as, usually, it does not take independent action on drug safety but generally shadows or mirrors that of other agencies (92). Witness Canada's stance on the oral hypoglycemic agent Avandia (rosiglitazone) (93), when it waited until the FDA made a decision on whether to remove the drug from the market before issuing its own advice, and when it initiated its own investigation of the oral contraceptive Diane-35 only in the wake of an inquiry by France (94).

The way that Health Canada has exercised its legislative authority is mirrored in the priorities that it has adopted and vice versa. The agency has not fully abandoned its obligation to protect the Canadian public, but neither has it fully embraced it, which can be seen by looking at how it allocates its resources and how it treats the information that it receives. The organization has accepted the language and, more important, the ideology of the private sector and has tailored its activities to ensure that, in the language of its own Business Transformation Strategy, it "reduce[s] the administrative burden on business" (95).

6 Is intellectual property a right?

This chapter examines the paramount importance that the industry places on intellectual property rights (IPRs), the patents and other rights that give drug companies a temporary monopoly on the drugs that they produce and make some drugs immensely profitable.

IPRs are the key factor in driving revenue and profits for pharmaceutical companies. IPRs encompass several different kinds of property, including patents, copyright, trademarks, and trade secrets. In the contemporary pharmaceutical context, the primary (but by no means only) IPRs are the patents over the processes by which drugs are made, the patents over the products themselves, and the data that the companies generate when they conduct premarket clinical trials to evaluate the safety and efficacy of their products. Generally, the stronger a country's IPRs, the longer the companies have a monopoly on their products and the more money they can make from them. When the top 10 drugs in Canada each generate more than $220 million annually in sales (1), then even a few extra days of patent life can mean millions more in revenue. Chapter 3 pointed out that each day that Lipitor (atorvastatin) was on the market earned Pfizer $870,000 just in Ontario. Even though in the 1960s, individual drugs were bringing in only a fraction of the amount that they do today, it's not surprising that in its 1966 brief to the House of Commons Special Committee on Drug Costs and Prices that the Pharmaceutical Manufacturers Association of Canada (PMAC) was diametrically opposed to the proposal to weaken patent rights and called it "a misguided step" (2). Drug companies have always defended IPRs as being essential for research and continued investment. Embedded into the 1972 PMAC Principles and Code of Marketing Practice was the statement, "The respect of industrial property rights as represented by patents ... is the essential foundation for progress in research and therapeutics in the pharmaceutical industry" (3).

Drug companies also make it explicit that investment in Canada is contingent on respecting IPRs. In 1994, the Ontario government was considering listing a generic equivalent of one of Merck's drugs on its formulary to reduce the $36 million that the provincial government was paying for the drug. In a letter to the provincial premier the president of Merck Frosst Canada said, "You will appreciate that our investment activities are affected by our revenues. Actions such as that being considered by the Health Ministry could not only impact on our ability to invest, but could also be seen nationally as well as internationally as an indication of a change in your government's protection of intellectual property" (4 p160).

This attention to the IPRs and how long they protect companies from competition is often at the centre of industry reports when it pushes for longer and stronger patent protection (see the table in the Introduction). In 2001, Rx&D was claiming that the first 10 years of patent life were taken up with doing the laboratory and clinical testing for a new drug and then getting it through the regulatory system, leaving 10 years of patent life remaining (5). Ten years later, according to Rx&D, market exclusivity, that is, the time without competition, had dropped to seven to nine years (6). The numbers from Rx&D contradict data from other sources, calling into question the industry's figures. A 2003 Industry Canada document that examined the market exclusivity period for 73 drugs calculated the mean and median times at 12.9 and 11.4 years, respectively, although a few products had effective patent lives as short as 3 to 5 years and others had lives of 24 to 36 years (7). In addition, between 2001 and 2011, the time products spent in the review system dropped from a median of 561 days to 349 (see Table 3.1). Finally, the Patented Medicine Prices Review Board reported that out of the 115 new patented medications that it reviewed in 2013, 10 (8.7%) had been marketed before they were patented (8). It's not possible to determine exactly how much market exclusivity these 10 products will have, but it could potentially be the entire length of their patent life, that is, 20 years from the time that the patent application is filed.

Evergreening

The ability to extend the monopoly on a product and avoid losing sales to generic products is the reason companies commonly engage in a tactic known as "evergreening" (9). In some cases, they develop new formulations of products, such as extended release versions that can be taken once a day instead of two to three times per day as is required with the original product. Other times companies may combine the existing product with a second active ingredient. Typically these "new" drugs are marketed just before the patent on the original medicine is due to expire in a bid to switch prescribing from the original version to the new version before generic equivalents to the original medicine appear (10). A slight variation of evergreening involves using a racemic mixture (i.e., one that has two mirror-image molecules, only one of which is the active ingredient) and marketing the active molecule as a new drug. Examples of this practice are Losec (omeprazole) and Nexium (esomeprazole), and Celexa (citalopram) and Lexapro (escitalopram) (10, 11). Companies can take out a patent on a second indication for a medication as Pfizer did for its antidepressant Zoloft (sertraline). Although the patent for the treatment of depression had expired, Pfizer still had valid patents for Zoloft's use in obsessive-compulsive disorder and panic disorder. Therefore, to avoid the possibility of being sued for patent infringement, the Ontario government listed the generic versions of the drug in its formulary only as an antidepressant. Pharmacists were forced to find out why the drug had been prescribed, and if it was prescribed for either of the last two conditions, then they had to dispense the brand-name version (12). Finally, brand-name companies introduce pseudo-generics a few months before their patent on the brand-name product expires. Pseudo-generics are generic-style drugs produced by the brand manufacturer on the same production lines and to the identical formulation and standards as the brand product, but labelled under a generic name and priced to compete against other generics. Although the pseudo-generics are sold by nominally independent companies, the brand-name firm "controls all aspects of the manufacture, distribution, promotion, and sale" of these drugs (13 p23). Hollis showed that because pseudo-generics enter the market earlier than "real" generics, they control about 40% of generic sales in the first few years of generic entry. For each 10% increase in the pseudo-generic share of overall generic sales, brand prices are about 1% higher and therefore, pseudo-generics can drive up brand prices by about 4% (14).

Suppression of independent reports

The obsession with maintaining market exclusivity and keeping competitors from capturing market share may partly explain the aggressive behaviour that some companies have exhibited when they feel that their sales are threatened by reports that question the superiority of their products.

The Canadian Coordinating Office for Health Technology Assessment (CCOHTA, now the Canadian Agency for Drugs and Technologies in Health) released a report in October 1997 comparing the safety and effectiveness of the statin group of drugs in lowering cholesterol. The report concluded that all the statins available at that time were equivalent in their benefits. Bristol-Myers-Squibb (BMS), makers of Pravachol (pravastatin), took CCOHTA to court to stop the release of the report. In its lawsuit, BMS contended that the CCOHTA report was "negligently misleading" for stating that there was a class effect for the statins. Although the case was thrown out when it finally was heard by a judge, it delayed the release of the report by a full year and cost CCOHTA 13% of its annual budget on lawyers' fees (15).

Dr Anne Holbrook of McMaster University was hired by the Government of Ontario in 1999 to produce a report on gastrointestinal medications. Her report concluded that AstraZeneca's drug, Losec (omeprazole), a drug used for disorders such as ulcers and reflux ("heartburn"), was no better than two less expensive products in the same drug class. As a consequence of her conclusion, she received a letter from a law firm representing AstraZeneca, claiming that if her report was released, she would be contravening the Food and Drugs Act and that "in the event that you proceed notwithstanding this warning you should assume that our client will take appropriate steps including the commencement of appropriate legal proceedings in order to protect its interests and to obtain compliance with the law" (16 pA1). AstraZeneca quickly apologized to Dr Holbrook and claimed that the letter had been misdirected to her and should have instead been sent to the Ontario government (17).

It's hard to escape the conclusion that, in both cases, the main aim of the companies involved was to suppress the release of any reports in the future that might threaten the sales of their products, however valid the information in those reports might be.

Compulsory licensing

During the 1960s, three reports all pointed out that drug prices in Canada were among the highest in the world, and all three reports identified patent protection as one of the major reasons (18–20). The dominance of branches and subsidiaries of multinational companies, chiefly US companies, and the widespread use of drugs developed in the United States meant that the drug trade in Canada operated under the US patent system. As a result, drugs were marketed at a price at least as high as that charged in the United States. The Canadian public, therefore, was paying prices set by the laws of the United States.

In 1969, the Liberal government added Section 41(4) to the Patent Act, thereby extending its ability to issue compulsory licenses for drugs. In essence, a compulsory licence is a permit which effectively negates the patent. Theoretically, the company owning the patent on a drug would be a monopoly seller until the patent expired. However, if other companies apply for, and are granted, a compulsory licence against a drug, they can then market their own version of that drug before the patent has expired. The compulsory aspect means that the company owning the patent cannot block the licence from being granted. Drugs sold through compulsory licences are generally referred to as "generics" even if they have their own brand name, and the companies that market them form "the generic drug industry." (The nine major generic players in Canada with sales of $5.2 billion annually are represented by the Canadian Generic Pharmaceutical Association, CGPA (21). Ironically, given the hostility that often exists between generic and brand-name companies, some of the members of the CGPA are owned by brand-name companies.)

Compulsory licensing for drugs in Canada dates back to 1923, when Section 41(3) of the Patent Act was amended to allow individuals or corporations to apply to the commissioner of patents for a compulsory licence to use a patented process to manufacture a drug in Canada. The intention behind this legislation was to encourage multiple companies to manufacture the same drug. In a marketplace with many sellers, it was hoped that the companies would engage in competitive pricing to gain market share. However, the amendment was largely unsuccessful in its goal. From 1923 to 1969, only 49 applications for compulsory licences were submitted, and only 22 of these were granted (22). Gorecki (23) details the reasons that compulsory licensing initially failed, but the main factor was the requirement that the drug be manufactured in Canada. The Canadian market was simply too small to support manufacturing. What Section 41(4) did was allow companies to receive a licence to import a drug into Canada, rather than having to manufacture it here.

The PMAC mounted an intense campaign from 1967 to 1969 against legislation allowing compulsory licensing to import (initially Bill C-190 and then after that bill failed to pass because of an election, Bill C-102), which cost $200,000 to $250,000 annually (24). Ultimately, the PMAC effort failed and the bill passed in March 1969. It was immediately challenged in the courts by American Home Products, and although that action failed, it delayed implementation of the legislation by a year. By 1971, of the 69 licences issued, there had been 43 appeals before the courts. Court challenges to the law continued sporadically up to 1985. In addition, the multinational companies employed other tactics in an attempt to blunt the effects of compulsory licensing. They questioned the quality of generic products through letters to physicians and instituted price cuts and production increases just before the generic products' entry into the market (22).

Generic companies took greater advantage of compulsory licensing to import than of compulsory licensing to manufacture, primarily because importing a drug was considerably less expensive than manufacturing it. Consequently, between 1970 and 1978, 142 compulsory licences were issued on 47 prescription drugs (23), and ultimately, between 1969 and 1992, 1030 applications to import or manufacture medicines under such licenses were made, of which 613 were granted (25).

Despite the strong and deeply rooted opposition to compulsory licensing from the multinational companies, the evidence that their economic position was adversely affected by it was not convincing. Partly as a result of the continual opposition from the industry to compulsory licensing, the Liberal government set up the Commission of Inquiry on the Pharmaceutical Industry (the Eastman Commission) in 1984 (26). When Eastman reported a year later, he produced evidence that by 1983 the multinationals had lost only 3.1% of the Canadian market to generic competition. Eastman found that, with the exception of the United States, profit levels in Canada were generally higher than in most other countries in the Global North. Comparing overall growth and development in the pharmaceutical industry in Canada to that in the United States yielded, according to Eastman, "the straightforward conclusion that growth has been more buoyant in Canada than it has been in the United States since 1967" (26 p68).

FTA, NAFTA, TRIPS, and Bills C-22 and C-91: The end of compulsory licensing

By the time Eastman's report was released, the federal election had been won by the Progressive Conservatives led by Brian Mulroney. During the election campaign, Mulroney made statements very favourable to the multinationals' position against compulsory licensing (27). However, the most important change in favour of the multinationals was the Conservatives' commitment in 1985 to a free trade deal with the United States. This decision opened up the federal government to intense pressure from the US government, the US-based multinational pharmaceutical companies and their lobbying organization, the Pharmaceutical Manufacturers Association (PMA), and the Conservative Members of Parliament from the Montreal area, where most of the multinational companies were located.

In 1981, US president Ronald Reagan appointed Ed Pratt to head the US government's top private sector trade advisory panel. Pratt was also president of Pfizer Inc, a US multinational drug company, and he quickly moved the issue of IPRs and patent protection for pharmaceuticals to the head of the US trade agenda (28). When Reagan met with Mulroney at the "Shamrock Summit" in Quebec City in March 1985, one of the key items discussed was drug patents. In October of that year, the annual report of the US trade representative on trade irritants with its trade partners listed Canada's drug legislation. The chief US trade representative, Clayton Yeutter, rebuked the Conservatives for failing to make the long awaited changes in Canada's drug patent laws. George H. Bush, US vice-president at the time, publicly complained about the delay in the changes when he visited Ottawa in June 1986 (27).

The Conservatives vigorously denied that there was any connection between the free trade agreement and changes in compulsory licensing (29–31), but the facts make their denials hard to believe. Bill Merkin, the US deputy chief negotiator in the free trade talks, said: "Ottawa didn't want it [intellectual property] to be in the free trade negotiations. They didn't want to *appear* to be negotiating that away as part of the free trade agreement. Whatever changes they were going to make, they wanted them to be *viewed* as, quote, 'in Canada's interest.' ... It was a high priority issue for us. We were not above flagging the importance of resolving the issue [to the Canadian negotiators] for the success of the overall negotiations" (emphasis in original) (28 p136). The Americans gave the final proof of the linkage between the two issues the day after the successful conclusion of the free trade talks. A US summary of the agreement said the accord contained a clause "to make progress toward establishing adequate and effective protection of pharmaceuticals in Canada by liberalizing compulsory licensing provisions" (32 pG2). Only after Conservative politicians demanded the removal of that section was it dropped from the final text of the agreement.

In return for free trade with the United States (the Free Trade Agreement, FTA), the Conservatives produced Bill C-22 and eventually passed it in December 1987. The essence of the bill was that it gave companies introducing new drugs a minimum of seven years of protection from compulsory licensing. After seven years, the company receiving the compulsory license would have to manufacture the necessary fine chemical, that is, the active ingredient, within Canada. If the fine chemical was imported, then new drugs had 10 years of protection. One senior official in the US administration said, "We want better than that [bill] in a free-trade agreement," while to another senior official it was "barely acceptable." The PMA was willing to support the bill, but said that the US industry "would like to see a similar level of protection as in Western Europe and the U.S. ... Canada's out of synch" (33 pA1).

The final demise for routine compulsory licensing came with the passage of Bill C-91 in 1993. In this case, Canadian eagerness to sign the North American Free Trade Agreement (NAFTA) and the Agreement on Trade-Related Aspects of Intellectual Property Rights (TRIPS) coincided with the interests of the drug industry. (Compulsory licensing is allowed under TRIPS in certain circumstances.) In introducing Bill C-91, the minister of industry and science argued, "The pharmaceutical industry is in the process of restructuring globally ... The degree of patent protection provided for innovations is the most critical factor. With our current system of compulsory licensing we could not hope to attract these investments" (34 p13).

A final feature of Bill C-91 was that it allowed companies to file product patents for their drugs rather than just process patents. Since the same product can often be produced in multiple ways, process patents are regarded as a weaker form of protection than product patents. Canada was far from an exception among Global North countries as to when it adopted product patents. For example, Austria and Norway only accepted them in 1992 (35).

Bill C-91 had a four-year review built into it and, while they were in Opposition, the Liberals campaigned strongly against Bill C-91. But by 1997, once they were in power again and the review was imminent, their attitude had changed and the position was "we are now part and parcel of the international community in terms of our commitments to NAFTA. And I [David Dingwall, minister of health] don't want to raise a false expectation that with the review of Bill C-91, which is coming up in 1997, that we are going to flush the intellectual property rights which Canada has supported from day one and will continue to support" (36). The House of Commons Industry Committee's deliberations on the review were cut short by a federal election and, in a hastily written report, it recommended the continuation of the 20-year patent period (34, 37).

After Canada signed the TRIPS Agreement, two separate challenges were launched against Canadian pharmaceutical patent legislation. The European Union (EU) complained about a provision in the Canadian patent law that allowed generic drug companies to begin testing, manufacturing, and stockpiling drugs for sale before patents expired. When Canada changed from a 17- to a 20-year patent term for drugs approved after 1 October 1989, the change was not made retroactive. In a second complaint, the United States charged that a group of about 30 drugs patented before October 1989 should receive an additional three years of patent life. (The complaint by the United States did not just cover drugs but also patents on all products that were granted before October 1989 and were still valid.) Canada lost the case filed by the United States (38), and the World Trade Organization (WTO) ruled that generic companies could not stockpile drugs for sale before the patent expired (39). Because of these decisions, in mid-2001, Canadian patent laws were further amended with the passage of Bill S-17. The extension of the patent term on the 30 drugs added an estimated $40 million to Canada's prescription drug costs, according to the Canadian Drug Manufacturers Association, the predecessor of the CGPA (40). Prohibiting generic companies from stockpiling drugs until the patent expires delayed the marketing of generic products for weeks. A report prepared for the CGPA that looked at a group of 34 generic products estimated that each day of delay in reaching the market was associated with a cost of almost $5500 per product (41). Rx&D countered with a quote from the minister of industry to the effect that the implications of the changes were negligible: "The maximum amount of lost savings would be less than one tenth of one per cent of drug sales over the eight-year period during which affected Old Act patents expire." (5 p7).

Notice of compliance linkage regulations

Besides extending the time for patent protection and abolishing compulsory licensing, Bill C-91 also established the Notice of Compliance (NOC) "linkage" regulations. Under this provision, regulators at Health Canada cannot issue a NOC for generic products until all the relevant patents on a brand-name product have been proven to have expired (42). When the generic company submits its application to get a product approved, it also sends a Notice of Allegation (NOA) to the patent holder, claiming that no patents are being infringed. The patent holder then has 45 days in which to seek an order from the Federal Court of Canada to prohibit Health Canada from issuing a NOC to the generic manufacturer for 24 (originally 30) months. The matter may proceed to a court hearing. The stay expires either after 24 months when the patent expires, or when the court case is decided, whichever comes first (43).

The government's explanation for the linkage regulations was that they were part of its pharmaceutical patent policy that sought "to balance effective patent enforcement over new and innovative drugs with the timely market entry of their lower priced generic competitors" (44 p1510). This explanation for the necessity of introducing these regulations was echoed by the brand-name industry (45). One part of the "balance" was allowing generic companies to begin testing their products before the patent had expired on the original product, allowing the generic product to enter the market as soon as possible after patent expiry. Having allowed testing of generics before the patent expired, the linkage regulations were introduced "to ensure that this new exception to patent infringement [was] not abused by generic drug applicants seeking to sell their products during the term of the competitor's patent" (44 p1510).

The CGPA claims that "not only is this abuse [i.e., the linkage regulations] of Canada's patent regime extremely harmful to Canada's generic pharmaceutical industry, the Canadian public loses out on millions of dollars in savings by having to pay for the higher-priced brand-name version for an extended period of time. The delays caused by these needless court battles have cost Canadians, their governments and private insurers hundreds of millions of dollars" (46 p1). Canada's Research-Based Pharmaceutical Companies (Rx&D) counters that these regulations are necessary because without them, brand-name companies would have to try to get injunctions to prevent the marketing of generics; statistics show that injunctions are available in pharmaceutical cases approximately half as often as in other industry patent cases. Therefore, according to Rx&D, "to prevent the complete destruction of their intellectual property rights and market share, the linkage regulations are the only means for Canada to meet its international obligations to provide an effective enforcement mechanism for patents" (5 p10).

The final report from the Commission on the Future of Health Care in Canada (Romanow Commission) recommended a review of the NOC regulations. In June 2002 the House of Commons Industry Committee voted 10–1 for such a review (47), but the next year when the committee was due to hold the hearings, the Liberal government brought in two members of Parliament as alternate committee members, and the committee voted to push back the hearings in the hope that they would end up being cancelled (48). When the four days of hearings were finally held in June 2003, the generic and brand-name companies both gave their usual messages. The generics argued that Canada was losing foreign investment because of unnecessarily restrictive rules on patented medicines that favoured brand-name drug companies and that this form of evergreening let patent-holders quash competition and keep drug prices high (49). The brand-name companies countered that relaxing patent regulations in favour of the generic companies could put Canada in violation of international trade agreements on intellectual property (50). The most interesting, and controversial, testimony came from Andrei Sulzenko, assistant deputy minister of industry, who claimed that the rules about when generic drugs can come to market are carefully balanced so as not to favour either the brand-name or generic companies and that changing the rules would lead to investment dollars from the brand-name companies disappearing. However, he also admitted that no studies had been done on the economic impact of eliminating the NOC regulations (51). The hearings ended when the House of Commons adjourned for the summer, and the committee never issued a report.

Initially, the NOC regulations allowed companies to file sequential patents that forced repeated delays in the appearance of generics. As one example, in August 1997, the generic drug firm Apotex served a Notice of Allegation on the four patents listed on the Patent Register for Paxil (paroxetine), an antidepressant, made by GlaxoSmithKline. Predictably, GlaxoSmithKline opposed these notices, but while the issue was before the Federal Court the company listed four additional patents; after 28 months, when the court ruled in favour of Apotex on the initial notices, Apotex had to file an additional notice triggering another automatic stay. This "strategy of triggering an automatic stay, listing new patents and appealing an earlier unfavourable ruling was repeated several times, ultimately delaying Apotex's market launch until October 2003 ... GlaxoSmithKline's strategy thus prolonged Paxil's market exclusivity by four years, earning it an estimated $300 million in extra sales revenues, despite the federal court siding with Apotex in its review of each of the Notice of Allegations" (52 p546).

In October 2006, the Canadian federal government recognized that some brand-name companies had been abusing the NOC regulations. The government passed new regulations that prevented new patents filed after a generic company had submitted an application from being considered in the NOC regulations process. Moreover, the new regulations made it clear that patents covering areas without direct therapeutic application could not be used to delay generic approval (44). Less than two months later, the Supreme Court of Canada also recognized that the brand-name companies had been abusing the NOC regulations by adding irrelevant patents (53).

Although the change described above was favourable to the interests of the generic companies, they viewed other changes less favourably. To discourage abuse of the linkage regulations by brand-name companies, Section 8 of the regulations had previously allowed generic companies to collect "damages or profits" from the brand-name company when the generic drug was wrongfully kept off the market by the automatic 24-month stay. One of the 2006 amendments removed the words "or profits" from Section 8, meaning that brand-name companies no longer had to repay profits acquired when they abused the automatic stay provision. The CGPA's position on this change was that "the Government of Canada has essentially made it less economic for anyone to make the investment necessary to challenge the brand-name company's monopoly, and introduce a low-cost generic product to market" (54 p1). The regulations were further amended in 2008 when an unanticipated Federal Court of Canada ruling changed the intent of the 2006 amendments. These new changes exempted patents submitted for listing that conformed to the pre-2006 rules from coming under the 2006 changes (55).

The Pharmaceutical Research and Manufacturers of America (PhRMA), the organization representing the brand-name companies in the United States (previously PMA), also entered into the dispute about the NOC linkage regulations. PhRMA's position was that the regulations had serious and systematic deficiencies on three points: brand-name companies had no effective right of appeal; the listing of valid patents had limitations; and patent infringement proceedings needed strengthening because the judicial review was aimed only at determining if the allegation was justified, which placed limits on introducing evidence and cross-examination (56). In light of these (and other) problems with respect to the way that Canada dealt with IPRs, PhRMA requested "that Canada be placed on the **Priority Watch List** for the 2014 Special 301 Report, and that the U.S. Government continue to seek assurances that the problems described herein are quickly and effectively resolved" (emphasis in original) (56). The Special 301 Report is an annual publication issued by the United States trade representative that examines in detail the adequacy and effectiveness of IPRs in countries around the world. Based on this report, countries are categorized by how seriously their IPRs are damaging US companies and their products. At the highest category, a country may be subject to US trade sanctions to pressure it to "strengthen" its IPRs. Although Canada was put on the Watch List in 2014 (one of the middle categories) for a number of reasons, the way it administered its NOC linkage regulations was not one of them (57).

Data protection

To gain marketing approval, generic companies typically demonstrate that their product is bioequivalent to a patented product (i.e., the generic is chemically similar and works the same in the human body) and then rely on the patented product's efficacy and safety data to earn approval. Back in 2003, Rx&D noted that Canada protected registration (efficacy and safety) data for 5 years compared with 6 to 10 years in Europe, depending on the particular regulatory agency (45). (The European Community now gives companies eight years of data protection, another two years of market exclusivity, and one additional year for new indications on original products. Generic companies can start testing during this period but cannot market their products.) In the United States, companies get five years of data protection, three more years for new indications for existing medicines, and 12 years of data exclusivity for biologics (58, 59). Rx&D viewed Canadian data protection as inadequate and believed Canada had a "practice of accepting drug submission from generic manufacturers that rely upon the innovator's data within the allotted five year period." Rx&D contended that policy "effectively undermines the intent of the current data protection provision" (43 p1).

Rx&D's criticisms were echoed by its sister organization in the United States. Based on PhRMA's reading of Article 39.3 of the TRIPS Agreement, Canada was not offering enough protection of the registration data, arguing that "Canadian authorities allow parties other than the right holder to effectively gain marketing approval in direct reliance of protected confidential data. This violates TRIPS Article 39.3 as it eliminates the TRIPS requirement to prevent 'unfair commercial use' of protected data" (60 p92). Although Article 39(3) of TRIPS does require WTO member countries to adopt measures to protect undisclosed test data submitted by pharmaceutical companies against "unfair commercial use," the length of that protection is not specified. Although generic companies cannot use this data, neither TRIPs nor NAFTA prohibit regulatory authorities from relying on the data in their possession for the approval of competing products, a practice that falls outside the definition of unfair commercial use (61). Further, what Rx&D and PhRMA do not point out is that prolonged data protection means that generic companies would have to redo certain clinical tests to generate information that is already known. Not only does this delay the appearance of the generic product, but it would also waste resources because generic companies would be repeating testing and, much more important, subjecting patients or volunteers to unnecessary risks in duplicating the safety data.

Because of the lobbying efforts by the pharmaceutical industry, Canada amended its regulations on data protection to allow for eight years of data exclusivity, with an extra six months possible if the company marketing the drug is able to get an indication for its use in children. In the government's words, "eligible innovative drugs ... will thus receive an internationally competitive, guaranteed minimum period of market exclusivity" (44 p1522). These changes were made despite "innovative drugs" being defined in the Food and Drug Regulations as drugs never marketed in Canada and it making no mention of new indications, whether for children or any other group (62).

Eli Lilly, NAFTA, and the Canadian courts

One of the most controversial sections of NAFTA is Chapter 11, the part that covers what is known as investor-state dispute resolution (63). Under this chapter, investors or companies are allowed to sue foreign governments for the loss of expected future profits and to demand taxpayer compensation. These cases are not processed through the court system but are heard by a tribunal of three private-sector lawyers (64). In the past, US corporations have cited provisions in Chapter 11 in claims against the Canadian government in several health-related cases. In one case, the Ethyl Corporation, a chemical company, forced the Canadian government to back down on its ban on the importation of MMT, a gasoline additive suspected of being a neurotoxin. In a second case, SD Myers, a waste disposal company, challenged Canada's temporary ban on the export of toxic PCB wastes and was awarded $5 million plus interest in compensation (65). Eli Lilly is currently using Chapter 11 to sue the Canadian government for $500 million over how Canadian courts have interpreted patent law with respect to two of its products (66).

Canadian patent law has what is known as a "promise doctrine," whereby patents will be awarded if the promise regarding an invention's utility is demonstrated or soundly predicted at the time of filing. In the case of Strattera (atomoxetine), a drug used to treat hyperactivity attention deficit disorder in children, a Federal Court judge ruled that "the clinical trial used to demonstrate the drug's utility – a seven-week, double-blind placebo-controlled study of 22 patients – was 'too small and too short in duration to provide anything more than interesting but inconclusive data.'" In the case of Zyprexa (olanzapine), a judge found that the drug did not meet Lilly's implied promise that it was a superior treatment for schizophrenia. When the Supreme Court refused to hear an appeal from Lilly, the company took the route of a NAFTA tribunal, contending that its "exclusive rights" had been expropriated by the court decisions (67). The chair and CEO of Lilly claimed that Lilly had lost $1 billion in revenue, was forced to shed 280 Canadian jobs, and could even leave Canada entirely (68). Effectively, through its suit Lilly is trying to define what Canada's standard of patentability policy should be. According to the US consumer group Public Citizen, "this is a critical point: Eli Lilly is asking the NAFTA investor-state tribunal to award compensation for a violation of its investor rights because Canada enforced its patentability standards, even though the underlying NAFTA provisions covering patents provide signatory countries flexibility to determine their own substantive standards for patentability" (69 p4). In response to the suit, the Canadian government filed a 178-page defence accusing Lilly of applying for patents based on guesses and of "blast[ing] away with patent applications in every direction, and claim whatever gets hit" (70).

Comprehensive Economic and Trade Agreement between Canada and the European Union

The pharmaceutical industry has accumulated a number of powerful allies in its push for stronger IPRs, including, among others, the Canadian Chamber of Commerce (6), the Conference Board of Canada (71), the Macdonald-Laurier Institute (72), former Liberal deputy prime minister John Manley (73), and former Conservative prime minister Brian Mulroney (74). Because of friends like these and the Conservative government's push for a free trade agreement with the European Union (EU) – the Comprehensive Economic and Trade Agreement (CETA) – the industry has achieved some, but not all, of what it wants. The CETA was finalized in September 2014, although ratification by Canada and the EU will take a few more years. As with all trade deals, multiple elements affecting a wide variety of industries were up for negotiation and, in the government's view, the concessions that Canada made about IPRs were offset by the gains in other areas. According to the government "the agreement will [bring] ... a $12-billion annual increase to Canada's economy ... this is the economic equivalent of adding $1,000 to the average Canadian family's income or almost 80,000 new jobs to the Canadian economy" (75).

The following analysis of the IPR provisions in the CETA draws heavily on the work of the Canadian Centre for Policy Alternatives (76). Canadian negotiators made unilateral concessions in the CETA that affect only Canada and will not require changes to the intellectual property rights regime for pharmaceuticals in the European Union. The EU and particularly Rx&D were pushing Canada to extend patents for up to five years. Rx&D's position was that longer patent life would be good for investment by and employment in the pharmaceutical industry (77). Canada rejected this demand but agreed to an extension of two years. This extension is designed to compensate brand-name drug manufacturers for the time between the filing for patent protection and the granting of market authorization by Health Canada, based on the assumption that the entire responsibility for the delay rests with Health Canada. (As of 2013, Health Canada was approving new drug submissions more quickly than the European Medicines Agency, 340 days versus 478 days (78). Most of the difference in when drugs are marketed in Canada versus Europe occurs because companies apply for marketing later in Canada than in Europe (79), probably because of the difference in the size of the market.) However, patents can still be extended even if the patent holder is responsible for the delay; for example, by filing an incomplete new drug submission. Moreover, brand-name companies will be able to choose the most favourable patent for extension, that is, the one that they feel will give them the longest period of monopoly marketing.

Canada rejected the EU's push for a 10-year period of data protection but agreed to lock in its current 8- to 8.5-year term, making it virtually impossible for any future government to shorten this time period since amending CETA requires the agreement of all parties. Before the CETA, if a brand-name company lost the summary proceedings in court under the NOC Linkage Regulations, it had no right of appeal, whereas the generic company did have this right of appeal. The CETA stipulates that brand-name manufacturers must be provided an equal right of appeal, and this could mean a delay of 6–18 months before generics appear, while the appeal makes its way through the court system. Finally, Canadian negotiators failed in their efforts to exclude court decisions regarding patents from the CETA's contentious investor-state dispute resolution mechanism. Consequently, we may see more companies challenging Canadian court decisions by using tribunals, similar to what Lilly is currently doing. The eventual effect of the IPR provisions in the CETA on overall drug expenditures in Canada could be $795 million annually or 6.2% of spending on patented drugs (76, 80).

Costs and benefits of intellectual property rights

Almost every publication that comes out from Rx&D talks about the economic benefits that arise from a strong patent system, including the overall investment that companies make, the number of direct and indirect jobs that are created, and the high quality of those jobs. For an example of these claims, see the report *Improving the Health of Canadians* (81). Similarly, Industry Canada is upbeat about the value of a healthy pharmaceutical industry to the Canadian economy (82). One of the reasons that Canada was willing to accept the increases in expenditures that will probably accompany the CETA was because the government believed that the higher spending would be offset by more drug development and job creation (83), a topic that I will deal with shortly.

Interpreting the validity of claims about improved economic activity is problematic because of the way that much of the relevant data is gathered. As one example, Statistics Canada data about certain aspects of the pharmaceutical industry uses the North American Industry Classification System (NAICS) that categorizes each company according to its core activity. In the case of pharmaceuticals, NAICS does not list pharmaceutical companies as a category but, instead, lists pharmaceutical and medicine manufacturing, meaning that only companies with pharmaceutical manufacturing as their core activity are included. Companies like contract research organizations (see Chapter 2) or human health biotech companies are often listed in different categories that include other types of companies, making it very difficult to extract accurate information specific to pharmaceuticals (84). Read the following analysis about profits and employment with this caveat in mind.

Relative to all non-financial companies, profits in the pharmaceutical industry have been falling recently (see Table 6.1), but it is difficult to know what these numbers mean because firms may employ what is known as transfer pricing to shift profits to jurisdictions with lower tax margins. Under transfer pricing, if a local subsidiary of a multinational imports products into Canada, then the subsidiary pays its parent for those goods.

Table 6.1 Profits as a percentage of capital employed,* 2008–2012

	2008	2009	2010	2011	2012
Pharmaceutical industry	6.2	5.2	7.6	6.6	6.1
Total non-financial industries	7	6	7.2	7.8	7.3

Source: Statistics Canada. Table 180-0003 – financial and taxation statistics for enterprises, by North American Industry Classification System (NAICS), annual (dollars unless otherwise noted) [Internet]. Ottawa: Statistics Canada; c2014 [cited 2014 Oct 2]. Available from: http://www5.statcan.gc.ca/cansim/a26?lang=eng&id=1800003.

* Capital employed is the capital investment necessary for a business to function.

If the multinational wants to move profits out of Canada, it can increase the transfer price that it charges its own subsidiary (85). Moreover, the profit figures from Statistics Canada do not distinguish between brand-name and generic companies, so it is impossible to know exactly how profitable the brand-name subsidiaries operating in Canada actually are.

Documents from Rx&D point out the value added from employment in the pharmaceutical industry and that average overall remuneration in the pharmaceutical industry is second only to that in the oil and gas industry (81). But remember that about half of all employment in the brand-name pharmaceutical industry has nothing to do with either manufacturing or R&D. In fact, using 2003 Rx&D data, more people are employed in marketing and selling (9111 jobs) than in either R&D (3863) or manufacturing (5427) (86). In addition to direct employment by drug companies, there is also indirect employment in non-manufacturing firms primarily engaged in activities related to pharmaceutical research and development (R&D, 10,000 jobs) and the wholesale and distribution of pharmaceuticals and pharmacy supplies (26,000 jobs) (86). The value added from these jobs is not known.

Statistics Canada data shows that direct employment in the brand-name and generic industries combined fell slightly from 2009 to 2013 from 28,138 to 26,983 (87). (About 35% of total direct employment is in the generic industry (86).) Looking just at the brand-name industry alone, Gagnon and Gold estimated total direct and indirect employment in 2009 at 19,400 and 29,100, respectively, with 8148 direct jobs in manufacturing and research and almost the same number in marketing, 7954 (84). Their data shows that those directly employed are paid $89,806 annually, while those with indirect employment earn significantly less, $50,717 annually (84).

Table 6.2 Trade balance in pharmaceuticals ($ million), 2004–2013

	2004	2005	2006	2007	2008	2009	2010	2011	2012	2013
Total exports	4,011	4,337	5,442	6,802	6,768	7,569	6,158	5,207	5,549	6,067
Total imports	9,563	10,030	11,369	12,336	12,687	14,539	13,331	13,597	13,497	13,716
Trade balance	−5,551	−5,693	−5,926	−5,534	−5,919	−6,971	−7,173	−8,390	−7,948	−7,650

Source: Industry Canada. Trade data online [Internet]. Ottawa: Industry Canada; c2014 [cited 2014 Oct 2]. Available from: https://www.ic.gc.ca/app/scr/tdst/tdo/crtr.html?naArea=9999&searchType=KS_CS&hSelectedCodes=|3254&customYears=2004|2005|2006|2007|2008|2009|2010|2011|2012|2013&productType=NAICS&reportType=TB&timePeriod=|Custom+Years¤cy=CDN&toFromCountry=CDN&countryList=ALL&grouped=GROUPED&runReport=true.

Not only is employment declining slightly, but Canada's trade balance in pharmaceuticals, the difference between imports and exports, is also going deeper into the red, as Table 6.2 shows.

Lost in trying to interpret all these numbers is the basic question of whether stronger IPRs lead to a better Canadian economy, as the industry claims. Gagnon and Gold would say no. In their view, as far as employment goes, the direct and indirect public support that the industry gets is far greater than the employment related investment from the industry (84).

When 34 senior executives from 14 research-based pharmaceutical and biotech companies were asked what factors were influential in making their investment decisions, they spoke of four general factors: history – where companies already have substantial stock of assets; disinvestment – rationalizing and consolidating investments; stability – low tax, low bureaucracy, a can-do attitude, and a flexible labour market; and political stability over the long term. Pharmaceutical market conditions may have a subtle influence, but no credible economic mechanisms suggested that market characteristics were of overriding importance in making investment decisions. When it came to decisions specifically about where to locate manufacturing facilities, the executives cited the need for quality (a culture of good clinical practice and the ability to produce credible data) as a must have, and after quality was assured, then cost became important – low taxes, labour flexibility, and other components of cost. The only mention of IPRs was in the context of locations where key steps of IPRs are taxed and the rules for taxing IPRs in the relevant jurisdiction (88). No evidence suggested a relationship between whether a country had data exclusivity and the amount of investment in the country by the pharmaceutical industry (89).

While there is little evidence that stronger IPRs have generated investment in Canada by drug companies, significant costs are associated with IPRs. Baker and Chatani itemize five ways that patent protection leads to wasteful rent-seeking behaviour by pharmaceutical companies (90). The first is the amount spent on researching and developing copycat drugs that offer no new therapeutic benefits but are marketed to cash in on lucrative markets. The second is the billions of dollars spent on promotion to try to persuade doctors to prescribe drugs to increase sales while the drugs are still under patent protection. The third is trying to gain a competitive edge on rival firms by restricting the dissemination of research findings or falsifying research results until all the patents that could prove profitable have been obtained, thereby slowing scientific progress. In the United States, 27% of faculty in university life science academic departments who received industry support delayed publication of their results for more than more months, compared to 17% without such support. Eighty-one per cent of life science companies with relationships with academic institutions reported keeping results secret for longer than was necessary to obtain a patent (91). Communication is the lifeblood of science, and if it is impeded, so is scientific research. Without knowing what others are doing, scientists may be needlessly repeating work, wasting money and resources. Fourth are the direct legal costs associated with filing and protecting patents and the indirect costs that result from successful efforts such as evergreening that stall the marketing of generic drugs. The estimate is that over 100 Federal Court cases are heard each year because of the NOC Linkage Regulations, costing generic and brand-name companies over $100 million, costs that are ultimately passed on to consumers and drug plans as higher prices for drugs (52). Finally, industry in Canada also spends money lobbying at the federal level to ensure that its views are heard. A search of the federal Registry of Lobbyists between 9 September and 12 September 2008 found 163 individual lobbyists representing both Rx&D and individual drug companies (92).

Neoliberalism and stronger IPRs

The increasing willingness of Canadian governments to accommodate stronger IPRs needs to be seen within the context of the neo-liberal environment that has evolved in the past 30 years. Stronger IPRs have become integral to so-called free trade agreements, despite the fact that strong IPRs are the antithesis of free trade, because they allow companies to maintain monopolies and inhibit competition. IPRs, however, are consistent with neo-liberalism in emphasizing private interests over public concerns, as they tend to grant exclusive rights to private individuals – and, more recently, to corporations, under the legal fiction that grants them the status of individuals. Countries in the Global North that are home to major corporations that are the prime knowledge producers, consumers, and exporters seek to expand IPR protection domestically and internationally to benefit these corporations (93).

The link in Canada between neo-liberalism and the need to have stronger IPRs is articulated in the report of the Expert Advisory Committee on Smart Regulation. One element that the committee envisions in a regulatory system is the support for innovation by enhancing "market performance ... competitiveness, entrepreneurship and investment in the Canadian economy" (94 p14). Concretely, when it comes to IP protection and biotechnology, this vision means that "IP protection is important to the development and commercialization of biotechnology products. Inadequate patent protection causes market uncertainty, likely resulting in an outflow of funds and expertise" (94 p92). The consultations before the development of the 1998 Canadian Biotechnology Strategy "revealed, among other things, the need for better coordination within government to address issues affecting many departments ... One of these ... concerned modernizing Canada's intellectual property laws" (94 p91).

Conclusion

From an economic point of view, what the pharmaceutical industry does to protect and strengthen IPRs makes perfect sense. After all, the companies are in business to make money for their shareholders. Therefore, we should not be surprised by actions such as evergreening, suppressing information and making complaints to various trade bodies. But to misquote Erwin Wilson, the former head of General Motors when he was being confirmed before the US Senate as President Eisenhower's secretary of defence, what is good for the industry is not necessarily good for the country (95). Aside from the experiment from 1969 to 1987 with loosening the rules about IPRs, both Liberal and Conservative Canadian governments have not made this distinction between what is good for the pharmaceutical industry and what is good for Canada and have consistently pushed to enact stronger IPRs. That support has come in the form of longer patent periods, more protection for brand-name drugs against generics through the NOC Linkage Regulations, or stronger data protection. At times, these measures were part of a larger trade picture, but the government has never seemed reluctant to meet the requests of the brand-name industry for more vigorous IPR protection. The main beneficiaries from the IPR system that Canada has put in place for pharmaceuticals have been the companies. These changes allowed them longer periods during which to charge monopoly rents. The benefit to the Canadian economy has been minimal at best, and it is possible that stronger IPRs have harmed the Canadian economy as a whole.

The fundamental question is what should be the role of the patent system in the area of pharmaceuticals. Patents are said to be necessary to stimulate economic activity, to lead to the development of products that then compete on prices with established drugs, and to generate the profits that are necessary for the R&D of new innovative therapeutic products. Chapters 7, 8, and 9 will discuss whether the IPR system has been successful in these objectives by examining the effects of IPRs on Canadian drug prices and spending, R&D activity in Canada, and Canadian foreign policy when it comes to promoting access to drugs in countries in the Global South.

7 How revenue is generated: Prices, volume, mix, and overall spending

Galexos (simeprevir) and Sovaldi (sofosbuvir) are new treatments for hepatitis C; the price for a course of therapy for the former is $36,000 and for the latter, $55,000 (1). Kalydeco (ivacaftor) treats one form of cystic fibrosis at $300,000 per year (2) (the price paid by provinces and territories has now been reduced by an undisclosed amount) and the current most expensive drug in the world, Soliris (eculizumab), is a highly effective therapy for atypical hemolytic uremic syndrome, a genetic disorder that affects about 60–90 Canadians, but it costs $700,000 per year for each person (3). Why these prices exist, what contributes to the overall expenditure on drugs, and how Canada has tried to control prices and expenditures are the themes explored in this chapter.

Complicating the problem with high prices and increasing spending on prescription drugs is the fact that Canada is the only country in the Global North with a national health care system that does not also cover drug costs. This book is not the place for a detailed analysis of why the 1966 legislation that added physician coverage to existing hospital coverage and created what we now call medicare did not also cover drugs, but a brief synopsis is necessary for understanding the present realities of drug prices and expenditures in Canada today.

As Morgan and Daw describe it (4), Canada opted to establish health coverage in stages with the Royal Commission on Health Services (Hall Commission) (5), which was the catalyst for physician coverage, recommending that pharmacare should follow after doctors' services were insured. Although pharmaceutical expenditures in the mid-1960s were small by today's numbers, the use and costs of medications were growing following the post–World War II therapeutic revolution. The Hall Commission's report noted the challenges "of establishing a drug benefit program in the face of excessive patient demand, excessive prescribing, too many repeat prescriptions, [and] the lack of historic plateau or benchmark of use or average prescription price" (4 p16) and recommended that pharmacare be delayed until drug spending levelled off. Opting for a piecemeal approach to health care coverage matters "in policy development because of the mechanisms put in place by the pace of change. A lack of consensus on big policy ideas contributes to a slow process of policy development, and this process in turn reinforces limited policy ideas" (6 p446). Once the idea that pharmacare was an "extra" became entrenched in the minds of politicians, policy leaders, and, eventually, the public, it became more and more difficult to envision implementing such a policy nationally (6). Therefore, each province and territory developed its own system for public payment, with the resultant provincial variation in what drugs are covered, what groups of the population are eligible for public insurance, and what level of copayment, deductibles, and user fees are levied.

To make the Canadian situation even more complex, while the provinces and territories control prices for generic drugs, prices for patented drugs, that is, brand-name drugs, are set at the federal level.

Prices and expenditures: what's the connection?

When we talk about money, prices, expenditures, and drugs two points count above all else when it comes to public policy. The first is the relationship between how much companies spend on research and development (R&D) and the price of a drug. The second is the distinction between drug prices and overall spending. Although average figures from industry show how much companies spend on R&D for each new drug that they market (see Chapter 8), the amount spent on an individual drug is almost impossible to determine because much of the basic research can be used in the development of multiple medications. Manufacturing costs are also unknown because the companies will not divulge that information even to committees of the House of Commons because of what they term "competitive reasons." Witness this exchange between Rob Merrifield a MP from the Canadian Alliance (now the Conservative Party of Canada) and Terry McCool, the vice-president of corporate affairs for Eli Lilly (Box 7.1).

Even if Mr McCool had provided the information to the committee, it wouldn't have helped the committee to determine whether the price of

BOX 7.1 EXCHANGE ABOUT MANUFACTURING COST OF DIFFERENT FORMS OF INSULIN

MR ROB MERRIFIELD: I have just one quick question for Mr McCool, going back to the same line of questioning that Ms. Brown started with. I have a business background as well. I could care less about the retail price of either the synthetic or the animal; I'm interested in the actual cost of production. Can you tell me the cost of production of the human insulin compared with the beef insulin, or the pork insulin?

MR TERRY MCCOOL: I can't tell you the cost of production. That's information we don't share for competitive reasons ...

MR ROB MERRIFIELD: Can you give me a comparison between the two?

MR TERRY MCCOOL: No, I can't, because I don't have it ...

MR ROB MERRIFIELD: Okay. Can you find that out and give us that information?

MR TERRY MCCOOL: What I'm saying is, I cannot share that manufacturing information for competitive reasons.

MR ROB MERRIFIELD: Okay. So it's not that you can't, it's that you won't.

MR TERRY MCCOOL: Right.

MR ROB MERRIFIELD: And it's not that you don't know, it's that you won't reveal it.

MR TERRY MCCOOL: It's both. I personally don't know, and if I did know, I couldn't share it.

Source: House of Commons Standing Committee on Health. Evidence. Ottawa: Parliament of Canada; c2003 [updated 2003 Apr 29; cited 2014 October 5]. Available from: http://www.parl.gc.ca/HousePublications/Publication.aspx?Language=E&Mode=1&Parl=37&Ses=2&DocId=850659&File=0.

insulin was reasonable. The simple reason is that no relationship exists between what it costs to research and produce a drug and what companies charge for the product. The determining factor is what the companies think that the market will pay. When asked to explain the prices for asthma medications, Michele Meixell, the United States spokesperson for AstraZeneca, had this to say in an email: "Our pricing is competitive with other asthma treatments currently on the market" (7). Hank McKinnell, the former CEO of Pfizer, was quite direct about saying that

Table 7.1 Comparison of R&D costs and annual prices

Therapeutic indication	Average R&D cost for a drug for this indication ($)*	Drug therapy for indication (generic name in brackets)	Approximate annual Canadian cost of drug per person ($)†	Year approved
Rheumatoid arthritis	1,203,000,000	Remicade (infliximab)	17,330	2001
Alzheimer's disease	1,161,000,000	Ebixa (memantine)	1,710	2004
Asthma	951,000,000	Singulair (montelukast)	560	1998
Breast cancer	784,000,000	Herceptin (trastuzumab)	49,920	1999
HIV/AIDS	616,000,000	Prezista (darunavir)	7,930	2006

* Prices for average R&D costs from a mix of provincial formularies and websites.

† Annual cost per person from Mestre-Ferrandiz J, Sussex J, Towse A. The R&D cost of a new medicine. London (England): Office of Health Economics; 2012.

R&D costs had nothing to do with drug prices: "[I]t's a fallacy to suggest that our industry, or any industry, prices a product to recapture the R&D budget" (8).

A great deal of dispute occurs about the exact amount spent on R&D per product (see Chapter 8), but there is general agreement that costs might vary by about a factor of two, depending on the primary therapeutic indications for a drug (9). Table 7.1 compares the R&D costs of developing a new drug in five different therapeutic classes with the annual cost per person of representative drugs in those classes, which were all approved at roughly the same time. There is a twofold difference in R&D costs but an 89-fold difference in annual costs: the cost to develop a new drug for asthma is just slightly more than the cost to develop a new drug for breast cancer, but the annual cost per person for Herceptin is 89 times that of Singulair.

Finally, when setting prices, corporations must use what is known as the "best interests of the corporation" principle. This principle is a legal duty, now a fixture in the corporate laws of most countries, that says that corporation managers and directors have to put shareholders' interests

Table 7.2 Total spending on prescribed drugs ($ million), 2000–2012

	2000	2001	2002	2003	2004	2005	2006
Current dollars	11,725	13,167	14,751	16,414	17,858	19,111	20,831
Constant dollars*	11,725	12,806	13,991	15,266	16,307	17,013	18,156

	2007	2008	2009	2010	2011	2012
Current dollars	22,000	23,407	24,814	25,898	26,887	27,734
Constant dollars*	18,849	19,378	20,704	21,238	21,382	21,791

Source: Canadian Institute for Health Information. Drug expenditure in Canada, 1885 to 2012. Ottawa: CIHI; 2013.

* Base year = 2000 (Bank of Canada. Inflation calculator. Ottawa: Bank of Canada; c2014 [cited 2014 Oct 5]. Available from: http://www.bankofcanada.ca/rates/related/inflation-calculator/).

above all others and that they have no legal authority to serve any other interests (10), including those of patients who may not be able to afford expensive drugs. Translated into practical terms, this means that prices are set to achieve the highest level of profit possible.

Publications from Rx&D, the organization representing the brand-name companies in Canada, invariably point out that the yearly increase in the price of individual drugs is almost always less than the rate of inflation, and Rx&D cites this finding as an indication that drugs are not too expensive (11). This statement is not only true but also a truism. Prices for patented drugs in Canada are set in such a way that they can never go up faster than the rate of inflation (12). Furthermore, prices, while important, are only one component in determining how much is spent on medications. That's why, despite the stability of prices of individual drugs, overall spending on prescription drugs in Canada rose from $11.7 billion in 2000 to $27.7 billion in 2012 (Table 7.2), an increase of 137% in 12 years. Even accounting for inflation, overall spending has still risen by 86% in the 12 years, although in the past few years it has dropped to under 4% annually as blockbuster drugs have gone off patent and lower priced generics are now available (13).

At over $700 per person per year (US$ purchasing power parity), Canada spends more per capita on pharmaceuticals than any other country in the world, except the United States (14). Similarly when measured against comparator countries in the Organisation for Economic Co-operation and Development (OECD), Canada's growth in drug spending per capita (in real terms) between 2000 and 2009 was 4.3% per year compared with the OECD average of 3.5%. Although this rate fell to −0.3% per year from 2009 to 2011, the OECD average fell even further to −0.9% (14). The high per capita expenditure, despite the control over introductory prices for patented drugs and the limitation on the rate of rise of their price, emphasizes the fact that the price of individual drugs is only one factor influencing expenditures. The other factors are population growth, population aging, general inflation, price effects, volume effects, and mix effects. Of these, volume effects was the largest, accounting for an average annual increase of 6.2%, followed by general inflation and mix effects at 2.6% and 2.0%, respectively. Price effects, the change in the price of individual drugs and the entry of generic drugs, were responsible for a decrease in annual spending of 2.7% (15). Volume effects reflect the number and size of prescriptions purchased to treat conditions and rise and fall based on the prevalence and treatment of disease, as well as changes in treatment guidelines. Mix effects are factors that change the average cost of treating a given condition because of changes in the drugs prescribed. A person starting on or switching to a higher-cost drug in a therapeutic class would increase the mix effect. Price, volume, and mix effects are influenced by the activities of the pharmaceutical industry and can be addressed by government. I will shortly examine each of them.

Industry (non)explanations for high prices

As the previous chapter pointed out, drug prices in Canada were among the highest in the world in the early 1960s, primarily because of patent protection. Even representatives of the brand-name drug industry, such as William Robson, president and CEO of Smith Kline and French Canada, conceded that "drug prices probably were higher than they should have been in the 1960s" (16 p15). At times, industry defended the prices by comparing the number of hours of work required to pay for drugs in different countries, as was the case with the Pharmaceutical Manufacturers Association of Canada (PMAC) brief to the House of Commons Special Committee on Drug Costs and Prices: "The plain fact is that if we consider the *real* cost of any product or service – the hours of labour necessary to earn the money for the purchase – we find that Canadians come off well in terms of the pharmaceuticals necessary to our national health and well being. A Canadian citizen is obliged to work fewer hours than the peoples of most other countries for the ethical drugs needed for the maintenance of his and his family's health" (emphasis in original) (17 p94). This argument, however, raises the question of whether the prices were reasonable with respect to research and manufacturing costs and profit levels. Equally fallacious were claims about the comparative cost of drugs in relation to the benefits derived. The modern day version of this argument is in a 2013 pamphlet from Rx&D: "Medicines keep people out of hospital and in their homes. They cure ailments and stave off infections. Vaccines offer significant public health and economic benefits by preventing illness from happening in the first place" (18). Again, this tells us nothing about the reasonableness of the price. The third common argument from the industry is typically the cost of the R&D that goes into bringing a new drug to market, but as we have already seen, the price has no relationship to how much is spent in this area.

Compulsory licensing

As detailed in the preceding chapter, the first serious attempt to control drug prices was the 1969 change to the Patent Act that allowed for compulsory licensing to import active ingredients. This legislation led to the growth of the generic drug industry in Canada and the introduction of generic equivalents to brand-name products at substantially reduced prices within five to seven years after the brand first appeared. Generics generally entered the market 20% below the price of the brand-name drug, and when more than one generic was available, the price difference was even more dramatic, up to a 60% discount (19).

When generic companies started to use the new provision in the Patent Act to bring products onto the market, the brand-name pharmaceutical companies tried to impugn the effectiveness or safety of the generics and to question their quality. To this end, a booklet published by the PMAC marshalled quotations from 13 different authorities, all designed to convince the reader that generic drugs cannot be trusted to be therapeutically equivalent to brand-name ones. The booklet ends with the sermon: "*Conscientious physicians and pharmacists consider it part of their obligation to the patient to select manufacturers who will supply the drug required in a proven, therapeutically effective form*" (emphasis in original) (20 p23–5). Upjohn published a book entitled *Basics of Bioavailability* that also was

Figure 7.1 Relation between number of companies marketing a drug and the cost of the least expensive version as a proportion of the cost of the most expensive version

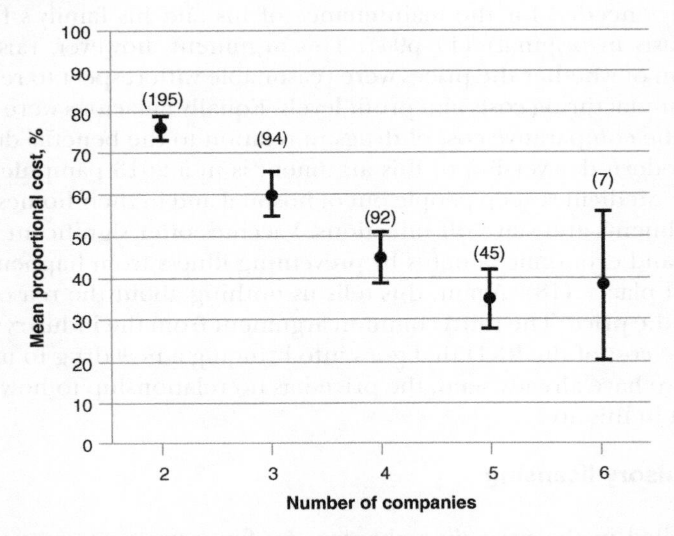

Source: Lexchin J. The effect of generic competition on the price of prescription drugs in the province of Ontario. Canadian Medical Association Journal. 1993;148:35–8. Reproduced with the permission of the Canadian Medical Association.

Lines represent 95% confidence intervals; number of products are in parentheses.

intended to raise doubts about whether generics and brand-name drugs were interchangeable. Dr Allan Dyer, Director of Drugs and Therapeutics of the Ontario Ministry of Health, commented on the book: "We are aware of much of the literature quoted in Upjohn's paper and, as you probably know, most of it is not relevant to the subject of interchangeability of comparable dosage forms. It is unfortunate that data like this is presented as representing comparative bioavailability of like formulations since most of the references relate to 'unlike' formulations" (21 p41–42). A 1982 ad from Ciba-Geigy claimed that Anturan was "the only sulfinpyrazone available to Canadian physicians that has been subjected to extensive world-wide clinical investigation" and below a prescription for the drug were the words "no substitution" (22 p214). Companies have now developed new tactics to try to avoid competition from generics. They are offering payment assistance cards to patients – handing them out to doctors and pharmacists to give away and advertising them directly to patients on television. More than 100 brand-name drugs are now covered by these cards, including many bestselling products, such as birth control pills. Patients present the card to the pharmacist when they have a prescription filled. The card cues the pharmacist to fill the prescription using the brand-name drug, even though it can cost much more than the generic version. Drug companies are supposed to pay the difference, but increasingly patients are paying some of that extra cost because drug companies have started to cut back on the amount of rebate they will pay. As a bonus for the companies, because the card information is entered into the pharmacy computer along with the patient's personal information, companies now have access to demographic information about patients who are using their drugs (23).

The report from the Commission of Inquiry on the Pharmaceutical Industry highlighted just how dramatic the effect of compulsory licensing was on spending. It pointed out that the generic companies had introduced a vigorous level of competition with the average generic price at 51% of the brand-name price. The consequence of compulsory licensing was that Canadian consumers and taxpayers paid $211 million less in 1983 (out of a total drug bill of $1.6 billion) than they would have done for the same drugs in its absence (24).

Price effect and the Patented Medicine Prices Review Board

The government, having used patent status as the basis for controlling drug prices through compulsory licensing, continued to deal with prices at the federal level through the patent system when Bills C-22 and C-91 did away with compulsory licensing. Bill C-22 established the Patented Medicine Prices Review Board (PMPRB), and C-91 gave it additional powers. After a drug receives a patent and is marketed in Canada, it comes under the jurisdiction of the PMPRB. The PMPRB's independent Human Drug Advisory Panel looks at the clinical value of the product and then, based on how much therapeutic innovation the drug offers, the PMPRB applies a variety of tests. It compares the intended price with the prices in seven other countries and compares the price of the new drug with the prices of existing drugs in the same therapeutic class. The PMPRB uses this information to set a maximum introductory price for the drug and then limits the rate of increase in the price to the rate of inflation (25). Companies can still charge whatever they want, but if the PMPRB believes that the price is too high, based on its guidelines, then it can hold a public hearing, and if the conclusion is that the price is excessive, then the PMPRB recover any excess revenue that the company may have accrued (26).

One early attempt by brand-name companies to circumvent the authority of the PMPRB was to dedicate patents, in effect to voluntarily surrender the patent for public use. The logic behind this tactic was that once the patents were surrendered, the PMPRB no longer had any authority over the price of the product. From 1 January 1988 until the practice was stopped in January 1995, 449 patents on 136 drug products were dedicated. A report from the PMPRB revealed that following the dedication of patents, at least 43 of the 136 were priced above the level allowed by the PMPRB, with an estimated cost to Canadian consumers of almost $40 million (27).

Companies still occasionally try to evade the jurisdiction of the PMPRB. The most recent example involved Celgene's attempt to claim that the PMPRB had no jurisdictional authority over the price of Thalomid (thalidomide) used in the treatment of multiple myeloma, a type of cancer. Between 1996 and 2005, the price of the drug had increased ninefold and was costing $4500 per person per month. Brian Gill, Celgene's director of corporate communications, said Thalomid was priced relatively low when compared with other drugs used to treat multiple myeloma, adding that "it truly reflects its therapeutic value in the marketplace" (28 pA1). (This statement about pricing Thalomid relative to other drugs on the market for the same disease confirms that the production cost of drugs does not determine their price.) The PMPRB did not challenge the price of Thalomid until 2006, when Celgene obtained a Canadian patent. After thalidomide was withdrawn from the Canadian market back in 1962, no company ever reapplied for approval, and therefore Thalomid has never been approved for use in Canada. It is supplied through the Special Access Program, a program developed by the federal government to ensure that Canadians have access to drugs that are not approved for marketing in Canada. Celgene claimed that the place of sale for the drug was its headquarters in New Jersey and not Canada; since the drug was not "sold" in Canada, the PMPRB had no authority over its price (29). The dispute between Celgene and the PMPRB went all the way to the Supreme Court, where the Court unanimously ruled that the PMPRB did have jurisdiction (30).

The regulations governing the PMPRB require it to use seven specific countries for price comparison purposes: France, Germany, Italy, Sweden, Switzerland, the United Kingdom, and the United States. These

Table 7.3 Average foreign-to-Canadian price ratio at market exchange rates for patented drugs, 2005

	Country	Ratio
PMPRB comparator countries	France	0.85
	Germany	0.96
	Italy	0.75
	Switzerland	1.09
	United Kingdom	0.90
	United States	1.69
Non-comparator countries	Australia	0.78
	Finland	0.88
	Netherlands	0.85
	New Zealand	0.79
	Spain	0.73

Source: Gagnon M-A, Gold R. Public financial support to the Canadian brand-name pharmaceutical sector: a cost-benefit analysis. Ottawa: Health Canada; 2011. Reproduced with the permission of Marc-Andre Gagnon.

countries were chosen because the federal government hoped Canada would match them in terms of R&D spending as a percentage of revenue. They also happen to include some countries with the highest prices worldwide, and since the Canadian price is set at the median of the international price, the legislation effectively positions Canadian patented drug prices at the fourth highest in the world (31). Between 2005 and 2013, Canadian prices rose against six of the seven countries, with the United States being the only exception, and since 2001, Canadian prices have exceeded the median international price (26). Using other comparator countries could significantly affect the Canadian price. In 2006, the PMPRB conducted bilateral comparisons of the price of patented drugs in Canada and 11 other OECD countries, including 6 of the 7 comparator countries that it uses. (Sweden was excluded.) The mean of the average prices for the six comparator countries compared with the Canadian price was 1.04, whereas had all 11 countries been used the mean would have been 0.91 (Table 7.3) (32).

When calculating the maximum Canadian price, if the PMPRB had used all the countries above, rather than only the seven designated comparators, the average price of patented drugs would have been about 11% lower than it was. Since $12.9 billion worth of patented drugs at ex-manufacturer prices were sold in 2009 (26), this would have saved Canada $1.42 billion in patented drug costs in that year alone (32).

Some inherent deficiencies in the PMPRB process contribute to the high per capita expenditure level in Canada. When generic equivalents are marketed in Canada, the brand-name companies do not reduce their prices or try to compete on price (33). Since the PMPRB allows companies to set prices for new patented medicines up to the highest amount charged for other medicines in the same therapeutic market (12), by not lowering brand-name prices, companies thereby enable new entrants into the same therapeutic market to charge higher prices. This feature of the regulations governing the PMPRB concretely affects introductory prices. The mean introductory price of 33 new medications marketed in Canada between 1994 and 2003 was 95.9% of the price of existing brand-name products and 91.5% of the price of the most expensive brand-name product in their classes (34). As biologics like Kalydeco and Soliris costing hundreds of thousands of dollars keep coming on the market, this PMPRB regulation about how introductory prices are calculated means that the biologics that follow them will cost at least as much.

The PMPRB is also ineffective in dealing with situations such as the one, described in an article by Roberts and colleagues (35), that people with Wilson's disease recently faced. Wilson's disease was an invariably fatal neurologic disorder associated with liver cirrhosis, but it is now treatable. The second-line drug for this illness is Syprine (trientine). Syprine has no drug identification number (DIN) since it never received regulatory approval in Canada, and doctors have to apply for access to trientine through Health Canada's Special Access Program. Since the drug lacks a DIN, it is not eligible for subsidy in most provinces, and, therefore, the cost is usually borne by the patient. Until the end of 2013, the price of Syprine in Canada was about $963 per month. But a few years earlier, Valeant acquired the licence to manufacture Syprine in the United States and began to increase the price in that country and in Canada to $13,244 per month. The reason Valeant offered for this price increase was purely financial. In a letter to physicians and pharmacists, Valeant noted that making Syprine "available free of charge [through a compassionate use program] ... was no longer sustainable ... From that date [1 January 2014], Syprine™ was only available at the commercial US price, as the product is not commercially available in Canada." After hearing opposition from hematologists, doctors in the specialty that treats people with Wilson's disease, Valeant lowered the Canadian price of Syprine back to its previous level (35).

Price effect, provincial plans, and industry reaction

In 1972, the New Democratic Party (NDP) government of Manitoba came out with a study highly critical of many aspects of the drug industry (36). Highlighted in the report was a recommendation to set up a committee to prepare a Manitoba formulary of equivalent brand-name drugs and list the prices of these medications. A Crown corporation was proposed for province-wide central purchasing, and distribution to pharmacies, of the most widely used drugs on this list. Pharmacists would have been required to use these centrally purchased drugs instead of the more costly equivalents. In the end, the government did not go ahead with bulk purchasing but did pass a law making it mandatory for pharmacists to substitute cheaper generic drugs for those named on prescriptions, unless prohibited by the physician writing the prescription. Furthermore, the substitute could not be sold at a price higher than that of the lowest priced equivalent drug. After this legislation passed, the president of the PMAC made a thinly veiled threat to the Manitoba government: "It will remain to be seen how much value would be put on the Manitoba market by research-oriented companies. It is each company's decision whether the size of their Manitoba market will merit the cost of properly servicing that market. If they can't meet the prices they could be forced out of business" (37).

In 1995, in the face of annual cost increases of 16% for the provincial Pharmacare plan, the BC government brought in its Reference Drug Program (38). Under this system, also used in many European countries and New Zealand, a reimbursement price is set for a therapeutic category of drugs, and patients are required to either accept the reference product or pay any difference between the cost of the product prescribed and the reference price, unless they have a valid medical reason for needing the more costly drug. Therapeutic categories are selected where expert advice indicates that all the available medications are equally effective and have similar safety profiles. In these cases, the most cost-effective form of prescribing is to use the reference product. Just as drug companies use promotion to shift prescribing patterns to newer, more expensive drugs, in British Columbia the aim was to shift prescribing to less expensive but equally safe and effective products.

Four months before the policy came into effect, PMAC placed a series of ads in major BC newspapers in an attempt to discredit the policy, proclaiming, "The Provincial Government wants to change your medication" and "RBP [reference-based pricing] has begun. Where will it end?" (38). PMAC charged that the reference product was usually an older therapy that had largely been superseded by newer products that offered better efficacy or side effect profiles for many patients, with the likely effect that overall health costs would rise, offsetting any drug savings (39). However, aside from some anecdotal evidence, PMAC never produced any concrete data to back up its claims. The Supreme Court of British Columbia and the BC Court of Appeal both rejected a 18 December 1995 suit filed by PMAC and seven of its member companies "to stop the Minister of Health and Pharmacare from implementing all reference drug policies." (38 p15). In February 1998, the Supreme Court of Canada denied PMAC leave to appeal the case further (40).

Compare the reaction from the brand-name industry to Manitoba's and British Columbia's attempts to control prices with what it had to say about Quebec's 15-year rule. As part of its industrial strategy to attract new pharmaceutical investment into the province and retain existing R&D and manufacturing capacity, in 1994 Quebec brought in its 15-year rule. Under this rule, the régime général d'assurance-médicaments (Quebec's public drug program) reimbursed patented drugs at their full cost for 15 years after their placement on the provincial formulary, even if the patent had expired and generics were available. The net effect of the rule meant that Quebec was forgoing more than $100 million in annual savings that it could have realized from the earlier use of generic products (32). That money instead went to the brand-name companies. An Rx&D publication was enthusiastic about this rule for obvious reasons: "For many years, successive governments have ensured that patients have access to innovative drugs for 15 years post market launch. This policy, known as BAP 15, is unique in Canada" (41 p6). As we will see in Chapter 8, the 15-year rule did not protect R&D jobs in Quebec.

Volume and mix effect and public/private coverage

Without the ability to significantly raise the prices for drugs already on the market, companies must use other means to increase revenues, including getting products onto provincial drug formularies quickly so that they will be reimbursed, reaching doctors to convince them to increase prescribing, expanding the range of conditions that can be potentially treated with drug therapy, and enlarging the parameters of illnesses that justify treatment.

In the past, drug companies dangled jobs and investments as a way to keep drugs on provincial formularies or get new ones listed. In Thomas Walkom's book about the left-of-centre NDP being in power in Ontario in the first half of the 1990s, he documents the negotiations between the government and Eli Lilly, which in 1991 ranked as the most profitable company in Canada, with a 107% rate of return on shareholders' equity (42). The NDP was trying to rationalize which antibiotics it was willing to publicly cover. One antibiotic being considered for delisting was Ceclor (cefaclor), a drug that had no particular advantage over other less expensive drugs on the formulary, but one that was generating $8 million annually in revenue for Lilly. Lilly was naturally eager to keep the drug on the formulary and made statements that its continued investment in Ontario was contingent on several factors, including keeping Ceclor on the formulary, successfully passing Bill C-91, and guaranteeing that the Ontario provincial government would be quick to add new Eli Lilly products to the formulary. The president of Lilly's Canadian subsidiary, Nelson Sims, warned the premier, Bob Rae, that the government's failure to comply with these demands would "most certainly negate [Eli Lilly's planned] investment in Ontario" (42 p152). A letter jointly drafted by Eli Lilly and government officials and signed by Rae guaranteed that Ceclor would remain on the formulary for at least two years and that "the Drug Reform process [a provincial examination of all of its drug programs] is specifically considering ... the role which investment and economic development considerations should play in the Formulary approval process" (42 p154). In other words, drug listings would no longer just depend on the therapeutic value of the drug. On 7 December 1992, Rae, Sims, and the federal minister of finance announced Eli Lilly's decision to invest $170 million over five years to expand its Toronto operation, including a $50 million expansion of its plant and a North American mandate for certain kinds of drug production that would generate 150 new jobs. Fifteen months later, Lilly decided against expanding its manufacturing facility and claimed the 150 jobs anticipated would be created if Lilly's business improved. The $170 million investment was still supposed to go ahead, but it was not clear what form it would take.

To highlight what it sees as an unjust delay in getting new drugs on provincial formularies, Rx&D and organizations that generally support its positions, such as the Canadian Health Policy Institute, periodically produce reports comparing provinces in terms of the percentage of new drugs that they list on their formularies and how long the listing process takes (43, 44). Similarly, Rx&D has a yearly publication that compares public coverage for drugs in Canada and other countries. The message in all these publications is essentially the same; provinces don't list enough new drugs and are slow to list the ones that they do. The cumulative effect, according to the industry, is that Canadians are not getting the best care possible. Box 7.2 provides the tenor of these reports.

BOX 7.2 INDUSTRY VIEWS OF PUBLIC DRUG COVERAGE IN CANADA

Rx&D, 2002

Cost-containment pressures are forcing provincial governments to curtail drug expenditures through policies that control or influence drug utilization, pricing, and the pace of adoption of new medicines. As a consequence, patient access to new medicines is increasingly restricted ... To maintain a health care system that is the envy of nations throughout the world, Canadians must have unrestricted access to the best available treatments.

Rx&D, 2012

This access deficit is perhaps most acute for new "first-in-class" drugs, highlighting a substantial missed opportunity: Canadians do not appear to benefit from access to the full range of new pharmaceutical innovations ... Canada continues to be near the bottom of the rankings for all categories; from a high of 21st place (out of 32 countries) for the Non-CDR [Common Drug Review] and iJODR [interim Joint Oncology Drug Review] drugs to a low of 27th place for the CDR reviewed drugs.

Canadian Health Policy Institute, 2014

However, it is important to put the performance of all public drug plans in the context of benchmarks set by private sector insurance plans. Other CHPI research confirms that all public drug plans in Canada provide much lower quality of coverage for new drugs when compared to private sector drug insurance plans.

Sources: Rx&D. Access to medicines: a critical health care issue. Ottawa: Canada's Research-Based Pharmaceutical Companies; nd; CHPI. Comparing access to new drugs in Canada's federal and provincial public drug plans. Annual series: how good is your drug insurance. Canadian Health Policy. 2014 (June); Rx&D. 2011–2012: the Rx&D international report on access to medicines. Ottawa: Rx&D; 2012.

These quotations may give the impression that the Canadian market is unattractive for companies from an economic point of view, but another side of the picture shows that the Canadian market is internationally competitive for brand-name companies. In 2005, new products that had been launched in the previous five years had captured about 22% of the Canadian market, which was close to the equivalent percentages for the French, German, and Australian markets; above that for the Italian, Swiss, British, and Japanese markets; but below the US market share (45). Eight years later, in 2013, patented drugs that were marketed within the previous 5 years still had 22% of the $13.6 billion in sales (26).

A number of assumptions are made in the statements from Rx&D and its allies that deserve a critical examination. First is the notion that after Health Canada has approved a new drug, it should automatically be paid for through taxpayer-supported provincial drug plans. Arguments often erupt about whether the public should cover the expensive new drugs that come onto the market, for example, the annual $300,000 per person price tag for the cystic fibrosis treatment Kalydeco (2), but generally most people accept that drugs that offer significant new therapeutic benefits should be covered by provincial and federal plans, and only a few such drugs are added every year. The comparison between what drugs are covered in Canada and in other countries implicitly assumes that the more new drugs that are covered, the better off is the health of the country's people, but no good information exists to back up this assertion. Claims that more new drugs or more spending on drugs equates to better health (46) are open to question (47).

The brand-name companies also promote the idea that since private plans cover a wider range of drugs than the public ones do, the latter are inferior to the former and that public plans should meet the standards of the private ones. But if anything, the reverse is true – public plans are better managed and more cost-effective. Historically, private drug plans have never seriously attempted to control costs. In the mid-1990s, only 16% of 401 companies had introduced generic substitution, and even fewer were using other methods, such as formularies and caps on dispensing fees (48). Two decades later, little had changed. From 2003 to 2012, private expenditures rose faster than public expenditures in 8 of the 10 years (13). One key reason that private insurers pay little attention to costs is because "the majority of private drug benefit plans are administered for companies by outside firms – mainly insurance companies – that are often paid a percentage of plan costs" leaving them no incentive to rein in prices (49). Private plans often pay prices that are in excess of the manufacturer's list price. Although some provinces try to ensure that generic prices are equivalent in the public and private sector, a Competition Bureau report found that prices in private plans are 10% higher than those in public plans for non-patented brand-name drugs and 7% higher for generic drugs (50). This difference in prices extends to patented brand-name products. In a "claims review of a large employer, drug prices submitted by pharmacies for certain brand drugs ranged from 9.2 percent to 37.2 percent more than the ... list price; and certain generic drugs were priced between 45 percent and 102.9 percent more than the ... list price. In other words, some pharmacies charged 102.9 percent more for the same drug, in the same quantity, to the same drug plan" (51 p7) and the plan paid that price. Since private drug plans pay 30% of the cost of prescription drugs in Canada (13), the overpayment by private plans is probably costing billions of dollars per year.

Although all public drug plans require mandatory generic substitution, only 67% of employees belonged to private plans that had this requirement, and only 19% of employees were part of a private plan that used a multitiered formulary, that is, a formulary that places drugs into different pricing tiers, with the first tier requiring the lowest copayment and typically including mostly generic drugs (52). According to Law and colleagues, "the very limited use of managed formularies – a list of the drugs covered by the Plan – in the past by private drug plans ... has made it difficult, if not impossible, for insurers to negotiate ... preferred discounts or rebates in exchange for preferential listing status. Industry estimates also suggest that the limited use of formularies resulted in private plans paying $3.9 billion more for drugs in 2012 where equally effective therapeutic alternatives were available" (53 pE473).

Volume and mix effect and the Common Drug Review

Coupled with the industry's negative view of provincial plan coverage is an equally critical opinion about the Common Drug Review (CDR). The CDR is an organization housed within the Canadian Agency for Drugs and Technology in Health and funded by federal, provincial (except Quebec), and territorial governments. Since 2003, it has provided advice regarding comparisons of the clinical efficacy and cost-effectiveness of a drug against other drug therapies, to all the provincial drug plans (except the one operated by Quebec), the three territorial, and six federal drug plans so that public funds are optimally used (54). CDR bases its recommendations on a systematic review of all relevant published and unpublished randomized controlled trials and, in addition, examines and critiques the manufacturer's pharmacoeconomic evaluation. The participating drug plans that receive these recommendations still make the final decision about coverage (55). The pan-Canadian Oncology Drug Review uses a process similar to the one used by CDR for providing advice about oncology drugs.

Rx&D's views about the value of the CDR were summed up by its CEO Russell Williams when he testified before the House of Commons Standing Committee on Health: "Today I will make it clear to the members of this committee that the CDR process is, at best, a duplication and, at worst, a barrier for patients' access to medicines ... Every time CDR says no to innovative medicine, it removes a treatment option for seniors, low-income families, and others who rely on these public drug plans ... What we find incredibly troublesome is how CDR makes a negative listing recommendation after Health Canada has recognized the value of an innovative medicine" (56). The essence of the problem from the viewpoint of Rx&D was that the CDR process delayed listing on formularies, that its recommendations were flawed, and that it didn't approve full funding for every drug before it. The last point was examined in a comparison between the CDR and similar agencies in Australia and Scotland that I led. Our conclusion was that no difference existed among the three agencies in terms of the number of drugs recommended for full or restricted listing or where listing was opposed. Where differences occurred at the individual drug level, these appeared to be due to pharmacoeconomic evaluations and were likely reflective of discrepancies among countries in national markets and health systems (57).

The reason behind Rx&D's concerns about listing and how quickly it takes place is simply the forgone revenue when provinces decline to list new drugs or delay doing so. The drugs most likely not to be listed are the ones that are regarded as having little or no additional therapeutic value or the ones that do not have a more favourable cost-effectiveness ratio compared with existing drugs. These drugs are by far the bulk of those approved yearly, but they are very attractive for companies since the average price for a prescription for brand-name drugs increases much faster than does the price for a prescription for generic drugs. Between 2003 and 2013, the price for a prescription for drugs in the former group went from $58.25 to $80.88, compared with a small decrease in the prescription price for generic drugs – from $22.44 to $22.11 (58). The net result of the confluence of these factors – the number of new patented drugs listed on formularies, their little if any new therapeutic benefit, and the cost of a prescription for a patented drug – is that in British Columbia,

80% of the increase in drug expenditure between 1996 and 2003 was due to the use of new, patented drug products that did not offer substantial improvements compared with less expensive alternatives available before 1990 (59).

Volume and mix effect and the control of information

One way that drug companies increase sales is by targeting specific doctors who are already prescribing their products and sending sales representatives to their offices to try to convince them to increase the number of prescriptions written. In this practice, they are aided by the services of IMS Canada, the Canadian branch of a multinational company. IMS collects prescriptions from thousands of pharmacies across Canada. Although it removes patients' names from the prescriptions, the names of the doctors who wrote the prescriptions are recorded along with a variety of other information about the drug and the doctor. This data is then aggregated into groups of 10 or more doctors, but individual physicians are identified within these groups along with their level of prescribing (60, 61). This information is then sold to pharmaceutical companies that arm their sales representatives with detailed knowledge about the prescribing practices of individual doctors. The CBC TV news show *Disclosure* interviewed a former sales representative about how this information was used: "What that tells a rep is how many prescriptions Dr. X is writing of my specific drug. It's very, very detailed ... I think a lot of companies, what they try to do is to target their efforts ... So I am selling an antibiotic and I know doctors in the 'A' class tend to prescribe a lot of antibiotics – that's where I want to focus all of my efforts" (61).

In a variation on direct-to-consumer advertising, companies also create or recruit patient and health professional groups to lend legitimacy to their promotional campaigns directed at consumers. When Glaxo Canada launched its new treatment for migraine, Imitrex (sumatriptan) in 1995, the company began giving substantial grants to the Canadian Migraine Foundation, a patient group that had been dormant for some time. When that group became uncomfortable with Glaxo's involvement in the educational campaign, Glaxo simply found another organization to fund, the Canadian Association of Neuroscience Nurses. Glaxo's goal was to "create a demand for a product before it was actually released" (62). Denis Morrice, the president of the Arthritis Society of Canada, was present at the launch of Celebrex (celecoxib), and is quoted in the *Toronto Star* as saying, "This is truly a breakthrough. Something is happening and it is quite frankly long overdue" (63 p1). The logo of the Canadian Lipid Nurse Network appeared on a series of ads about the dangers of high cholesterol. These ads were, in fact, paid for by Pfizer, the maker of Lipitor (atorvastatin). Until Lipitor went off patent it was generating in excess of $1 billion annually for Pfizer in Canada. The URL (www.lipidnurse.ca) for the Lipid Nurse Network listed on Pfizer's website (64) links web pages that have nothing to do with that organization. The best known of the cholesterol ads is the one termed the "toe tag" ad that features a woman's corpse lying on a stretcher in a morgue; on her toe is a tag listing the cause of death as "heart attack" (65, 66). A similar campaign ran in France from February to April 2003. In response to those ads, Jonathan Quick and others from the Department of Essential Drugs and Medicines Policy at the World Health Organization wrote to the *Lancet*. Among other problems with the ad, including its sole focus on high cholesterol as a cause of cardiovascular disease and the fact that it was "neither accurate, informative, or balanced," the authors pointed out that the ad "could have worried patients"; in other words, it could be perceived to be using the fear of disease to promote its message (67). As part of the theme of using others to get the message across, Pfizer recruited former hockey star Guy Lafleur to act as a spokesperson for Viagra (sildenafil) to tell Canadian men that even virile athletes may one day need to use the drug (68).

Another way to change prescribing for a condition, and to potentially increase sales, is to influence when and how that condition should be treated. The most seemingly objective way of achieving this end is through clinical practice guidelines. These are recommendations on how to treat a problem that are supposed to be based on objective summaries of the medical literature. Drug companies recognize the potential advantages for them from these guidelines and either fund guideline creation directly or establish a relationship with people who sit on guideline committees. For example, the Canadian Thoracic Society's 2012 update on its guidelines on asthma management received "unrestricted grants [from] ... AstraZeneca Canada, Boehringer Ingelheim Canada, GlaxoSmithKline Inc., Pfizer and Talecris." According to a statement in the guidelines, funders did not play "a role in the collection, review, analysis or interpretation of the scientific literature or in any decisions regarding the recommendations or key messages presented in this document" (69 p163). On the other hand, speaking of the 2010 version of these guidelines, Dr Niteesh Choudhry, who has previously investigated the conflicts of interest of guideline authors, said,

"Collectively, the physicians on the CTS Asthma Committee have on at least one occasion acted as consultants for, received research funds from, and received speaker's fees from these pharmaceutical companies" (70 pE139). The Canadian Diabetes Association's (CDA) website states that the "Association maintains editorial independence and operational separation from our corporate sponsors" (71), but it's not readily apparent who the sponsors are of its 2013 Clinical Practice Guidelines for the Prevention and Management of Diabetes in Canada. Ninety-three people were involved in producing the 2008 version of the CDA guidelines, 78% of whom had conflicts of interest. All 23 panel members of the Canadian Cardiovascular Society who were involved in its 2009 guidelines had conflicts (72). The message is not that funding and conflicts automatically produce bias, but as Choudhry notes, "We wonder whether academicians and physicians underestimate the impact of relationships on their actions because the nature of their professions is the pursuit of objective unbiased information ... Unfortunately, bias may occur both consciously and subconsciously, and therefore, its influence may go unrecognized" (73 p615).

In the US context, some evidence suggests that a relationship may exist between conflicts and a bias in the recommendations in the guidelines for the treatment of major depression in the outpatient setting. All six members of the guideline development committee declared conflicts with pharmaceutical companies, with an average of 20.5 relationships per member. Less than "half (44.4%) of the studies supporting the recommendations met criteria for high quality. Over one-third (34.2%) of the cited research did not study outpatients with major depressive disorder, and 17.2% did not measure clinically relevant results. One-fifth (19.7%) of the references were not congruent with the recommendations" (74 p674).

Finally, drug companies use ghostwriters to control the information that doctors receive. Ghostwriters are people hired either directly or indirectly through medical information companies to write scientific articles (commentaries, reviews, or research papers) and then the drug company or the medical information company finds prominent doctors or researchers who are willing to put their names to the articles, a practice referred to as "guest authorship" (75). In one instance, SmithKline Beecham (now GlaxoSmithKline) hired the public relations agency Ruder-Finn to prepare publications to counter negative claims from Eli Lilly about SmithKline Beecham's antidepressant Paxil (paroxetine). Ruder-Finn ghosted a letter that appeared in the *Journal of Clinical Psychiatry* under the signature of Dr Bruce Pollock, a psychiatrist from the University of Toronto. The letter did not acknowledge that SmithKline Beecham or Ruder-Finn had any role in writing it, nor that Dr Pollock had any financial relationship to SmithKline Beecham (76). In a second instance, Dr Barbara Sherwin, a psychologist at McGill, was formally reprimanded, but not sanctioned, by the university for failing to acknowledge the role of a ghostwriter hired by the drug company Wyeth Pharmaceuticals (now part of Pfizer) in an article about hormone replacement therapy (77). Back in 2003, the CBC television show *Marketplace* investigated ghostwriting and found one ghostwriter who was willing to talk on camera under the pseudonym Blair Snitch. According to Snitch, he is "given an outline about what to talk about, what studies to cite. They [the drug companies] want us to be talking about the stuff that makes the drug look good ... There's no discussion of certain adverse events. That's just not brought up." In answer to the question about how much pressure there was from the drug company to write something favourable, he said, "You're being told what to do. And if you don't do it, you've lost the job" (78). An analysis of ghostwriting policies at all 17 Canadian medical schools found that while 8 had restrictive policies, 9 had either no policy or a permissive policy (79).

Attempts to address the price, volume, and mix effect: National Pharmaceuticals Strategy

The forces driving spending on prescription drugs – price, volume, and mix – do not stop at provincial or territorial borders and as such cannot be fully addressed by the actions of a single province or territory or even several acting in unison. At a minimum, they require federal leadership, along with federal-provincial-territorial cooperation for a number of reasons. Some matters, such as prices for patented medicines, are under federal jurisdiction; other times provinces and territories work at cross-purposes, for example, competing incentives from Ontario and Quebec to attract pharmaceutical investment (see Chapter 8); and finally federal contributions are needed to make a national pharmacare plan, that would provide drug coverage to everyone in the country, a reality.

The National Pharmaceuticals Strategy (NPS) was one such attempt at federal leadership and federal-provincial-territorial cooperation. The NPS was established as part of the 2004 Health Accord, the First

Minister's 10-Year Plan to Strengthen Health Care, in part to address issues around affordable access to pharmaceuticals for all Canadians (80). The main areas in the strategy relevant to prices, affordability, and expenditures were developing options for catastrophic drug coverage, finding ways to reduce the costs of prescription medications to governments and individual Canadians; and ensuring that all Canadians had access to the same prescription drugs through their government drug plans, based on a common national drug formulary (81). Health ministers were directed to establish a ministerial task force to develop and implement the NPS and report on progress by 30 June 2006. But the progress report showed little evidence of any significant movement on these objectives. The principles behind catastrophic insurance were enunciated, but beyond studying options for attaining these principles, nothing further had been achieved. Similarly, work was to continue on designing a national formulary, but no formulary was created, and "a non-regulated, business-management approach to drug pricing issues," with priority on non-patented, that is, generic, drugs, was going to be pursued (82 p12). The progress report contained nothing about prices or expenditures on patented brand-name drugs that, in 2006, made up almost 68% of all drug sales (26). Possibly the sole major achievement by the NPS was that it led to the expansion of the use of the CDR to all provinces and territories, except Quebec. By the time the Health Council of Canada issued its evaluation of the NPS in 2009, the overall tone was pessimistic about any measureable changes happening (83). The fade-out for the NPS was sounded by both the health minister, Leona Aglukkaq, and the deputy minister at Health Canada, Glenda Yeates, when they appeared before the Standing Senate Committee on Social Affairs, Science and Technology in November 2011 (84) (See Box 7.3.).

BOX 7.3 LEONA AGLUKKAQ'S AND GLENDA YEATES'S TESTIMONY TO THE SENATE

Leona Aglukkaq

The challenge we had at the time [the process started] was that in order to have a national plan there had to be a national agreement. There was not always consensus around what that would look like ... Since there was no agreement on the national plan, from the west side, three or four jurisdictions put plans together to do bulk purchasing to reduce the cost of managing pharmaceuticals ... We have to be mindful that the accord is not over yet. We are in 2011, so work is still progressing in areas that had been identified by jurisdictions. In a nutshell, that is where that program is at.

Glenda Yeates

There was no agreement at that working-group level to move forward, so in a sense the work is suspended. We have said as a federal government we are willing to continue to talk on the national pharmaceutical strategy, but in the sense that was not the consensus that made moving forward something that anyone pursued. It is essentially just suspended at this point.

Source: Standing Senate Committee on Social Affairs Science and Technology. Proceedings. Ottawa: Parliament of Canada; c2011 [cited 2014 Oct 14]. Available from: http://www.parl.gc.ca/content/sen/committee/411/SOCI/08EVB-49206-E.HTM.

Pan-Canadian Pharmaceutical Alliance

With the failure of the NPS, the most recent attempt to deal with the inadequacies in the control of drug prices and expenditures is the provincial initiative, the Pan-Canadian Pharmaceutical Alliance (PCPA), recently renamed from the Pan-Canadian Pricing Alliance. Initially, 9 out of 10 provinces and Yukon were participating in the PCPA (85), and in the fall of 2014 Quebec announced that it would join. The idea is to combine the bargaining power of the provincial and territorial drug plans to negotiate a lower price for both brand-name and generic drugs. By the summer of 2014, negotiations by the PCPA had reduced prices on 43 brand-name drugs and 10 generic drugs, with a savings of over $260 million (86), but that amount represents less than 1% of total spending on prescription drugs. The PCPA will consider negotiating prices on all drugs coming forward for funding from either the CDR or the Pan-Canadian Oncology Drug Review. One prominent success from the PCPA was the reduction in the price of Kalydeco from the initial price of $300,000 per annum that Vertex Pharmaceuticals was charging. The exact price reduction that was achieved is not publicly accessible, but it was enough that Ontario reversed its decision and started paying for the drug (2).

The PCPA initiative is promising, but it has to deal with the realities of Canada's fragmented drug payment and coverage system – provinces and territories structure their drug plans differently to reflect their priorities and goals, some provinces or territories enter into confidential pricing agreements with companies, and final decision-making on whether to cover a particular product is still made at the provincial or territorial level (87). One additional glaring deficiency is the absence of any of the private drug plans that pay over 35% of prescription drug expenditures (13). The absence of these plans significantly reduces the bargaining power of the PCPA especially, since, as previously noted, most private plans are not interested in controlling expenditures.

Rx&D's view of the PCPA is not completely clear. In a 2010 *Toronto Star* story, Russell Williams, Rx&D's CEO, "said each province uses drugs in different ways and centralizing everything in a way that focuses on driving down the bottom line could hinder quality and access" (88 pA1), a possible sign that the industry was worried about losing revenue from lower prices for its products. Three years later, Rx&D asked "that all stakeholders – patient groups, life science organizations and industry – be provided with the opportunity, through meaningful consultations, to contribute to the development and evolution of the Council of the Federation's Pan-Canadian Drug Pricing Alliance" (89).

Conclusion

Because of the federal government's historical reluctance to set up a national program, the task has been left to the provinces and territories, with the result that there is a hodgepodge of programs with variable coverage for groups within the population. Provincial and territorial plans pay 37% ($10.68 billion) of total prescription drug costs in Canada, federal and social security funds pay an additional 6.0% ($1.65 billion), leaving private insurance to cover 30% ($9.83 billion) and out-of-pocket payment at 17% ($5.58 billion) (13). While provincial and territorial drug plans are the largest payers, they cover only about 25% of the population (90). Simulations based on provincial drug plans as of December 2006 showed that for the same package of drugs for diabetes, hypertension, and insomnia, a 65-year-old woman could pay between $8 and $504 annually depending on what province she lived in. Not surprisingly, cost-related non-adherence is significantly related to income and having insurance coverage: for those with a high income (annual household income > $80,000) and insurance it was 3.6%, while for those with a low income (annual household income < $20,000) and no insurance it was 35.6% or 10 times as great (91).

This situation is not caused only by drug prices and overall levels of expenditure. One reason that politicians have failed to act on a national pharmacare plan with first dollar coverage, that is, no copayments or user fees, is the size of the national drug bill. The amount that we pay in this country is intimately linked to the direct and indirect effects of the intellectual property rights system, including the limitations in the policies of the PMPRB, and to the failure to develop mechanisms to control the effects that the pharmaceutical industry has on the volume and mix of drugs that are prescribed.

8 Who gets the value from research and development?

This chapter returns to the topic of drug research, but this time from an economic perspective, and asks who gets the most benefit from the research and development (R&D) undertaken in Canada.

Based on what industry spokespeople and reports have to say, research into the discovery and testing of new drugs is the industry's primary purpose. According to Dr William Wigle, the president of the Pharmaceutical Manufacturers Association of Canada (PMAC), in his opening testimony before the House of Commons Special Committee on Drug Costs and Prices in 1966: "This is a research-based industry that spends internationally something in the order of half a billion dollars a year to provide us with the new life-saving drugs that have in the past two decades all but revolutionized the practice of medicine" (1 p95). Almost 40 years later, the same theme was found in a report from Canada's Research-Based Pharmaceutical Companies (Rx&D) advocating for a new innovative pharmaceutical strategy for Canada: "Through the development of innovative medicines, the research-based pharmaceutical industry has: enabled the treatment of disease conditions not previously manageable, shortened hospital stays, reduced the need for surgical interventions, and enhanced patients' quality-of-life" (2 p2). In September 2014, the website for Rx&D prominently said "most importantly, new medicines represent some of the most scientifically advanced, safest and most effective treatments available to help Canadians live longer, better and more productive lives" (3).

Besides the value of new drugs for the health of Canadian patients, drug company publications also promote the value of clinical trials for Canadian scientists, for people to gain access to new medications, and for the Canadian economy. Aventis highlighted the 64 ongoing or planned trials it was sponsoring and how these trials were helping Canada to attract and retain its best scientists (4). Another industry publication touted the domino effects from clinical trials: healthier Canadians, job creation, and a strengthened economy and health care system (5). These messages were repeated at the 2011 Canadian Clinical Trial Summit partly sponsored by Rx&D and Canadian Institutes of Health Research (6). A 2013 publication from Rx&D talks in glowing terms about how clinical trials from companies such as GlaxoSmithKline, Lundbeck, and Novartis "give Canadians access to new, potentially life-saving medications" (3 p2).

The value of research and development should not be underestimated. Modern pharmaceuticals underlie many of the important advances in health care (7). Although some of the industry's claims are exaggerated (8), drugs have made HIV a chronic illness rather than a death sentence (where these drugs are affordable), and many children's cancers are now curable because of drugs.

Industry tends to play the research card when it feels threatened by the prospect of government action to lower prices or when it wants to pressure government for more favourable conditions around issues, such as intellectual property protection (see Chapter 6) or a higher number of products listed on formularies (see Chapter 7). Following the 1969 passage of legislation allowing compulsory licensing to import (see Chapter 6), the industry began an intensive lobbying campaign to get the law repealed. Companies claimed that before its passage, research and development (R&D) was flourishing in Canada in the 1960s and that the changes to the Patent Act were responsible for the low level afterwards (9, 10). The position taken by vice-president of marketing for Ayerst was that "anyone thinking of opening a pharmaceutical research and development centre [in Canada] has rocks in their head" (11 p97). While talking about the benefits from the research, industry was also careful to remind readers that "research in the pharmaceutical industry is 'virtually an investment in faith' since there is little tax incentive nor effective patent protection to do so" (12 p18).

In the past, pharmaceutical companies threatened to withdraw their investment of R&D in Canada when governments proposed policies that the companies regarded as not in their interest. Before the Patent Act was amended to allow for compulsory licensing, Dr Wigle wrote to the *Canadian Medical Association Journal* threatening that if this recommendation were acted on, the large companies operating in Canada would close down their plants (13). After Dr Gordon Guyatt reorganized the general internal medicine training program at McMaster University in the early 1990s to restrict contact between pharmaceutical industry sales representatives and medical residents, he was visited by an industry official who suggested that research funding at McMaster might be compromised. When Dr David Sackett, also from McMaster, requested funding from the industry to help with research done by medical residents, the response from a senior official with a Canadian subsidiary of a multinational company was that "recently, access to many of these key people [health care professionals at McMaster] has become limited, including the medical residents. Without this contact, it is very difficult for a partnership to develop. Consequently, it is not easy for [our company] to justify philanthropic donations to research when there is limited or no access to researchers, and no hand in the type of research project selected for support. Unfortunately, at this time we will have to decline your request" (14 p952).

The cost of R&D

One of the main ways that industry defends industrial policies to support R&D is to stress the expense of research into new drugs. Using figures from a 1993 study, brand-name companies claimed that it costs over US$800 million to bring a single new drug to market (15), and now with inflation that number is US$1.2 billion. Further, they note that only 1 in 10,000 original compounds ever makes it through the 12-year research, development, and approval cycle (16). (In late 2014, the same group at the Tufts Center for the Study of Drug Development that produced the 1993 figure, upped the amount spent on R&D cost for a new drug to US$2.6 billion (17). The Tufts Center receives about 40% of its funding in unrestricted grants from the pharmaceutical industry (18).) Impressive as the dollar amount is, and although it is widely quoted, its calculation rests on data and sampling that have been seriously challenged, most notably by Light and Warburton. These authors claim that the conclusions from DiMasi and colleagues should not be accepted at face value because of six factors: (1) cost data used was proprietary and confidential and, therefore, readers cannot know how each company collected its data or what was counted as research costs; (2) the companies surveyed had an incentive to deliberately and systematically overstate costs in their survey responses because they knew the purpose of the study; (3) the small, non-random firm sample (n = 10) and drug sample (n = 68) introduce a potentially large source of variation and error into cost estimates; (4) the findings applied only to new drugs that were solely discovered, researched, and developed in-house by US companies; (5) estimates of company spending on drug development were presented without deducting (or at least identifying) government subsidies for this work; and (6) the cost estimates are not adjusted for tax deductions and credits (19). (For more on the debate between DiMasi/Hansen/Grabowski, the Tufts Center researchers, and Light/Warburton see (20–22)).

Another factor that is often overlooked in the debate about how much it costs to bring a drug to market is how much of that cost a company needs to recover from an individual national market. This question can be approached in several ways. One is that a country's share should be computed based on its overall level of wealth, for example, its gross domestic product per capita or on the purchasing power of its currency versus the currencies of other nations. A second approach is that countries should contribute based on their share of the world market in drug sales. On this measure, since Canada is 2.6% of the world market (23), if R&D actually does cost $1.2 billion, companies need to recoup only $31 million of that cost from this country.

Commission of inquiry into the pharmaceutical industry

The Commission of Inquiry on the Pharmaceutical Industry (Eastman Commission) (24) reported in 1985 that the expenditures on intramural R&D in the pharmaceutical industry were on a par with that in other industries and surpassed spending in the chemical industry, contradicting the industry's claims about the effect of compulsory licensing on R&D. (See Chapter 6 for more details about the Eastman Commission and Chapter 7 for compulsory licensing.) The conclusion was detecting any significant effect on R&D from compulsory licensing was difficult. Here, Eastman was in agreement with an earlier report from the Economic Council of Canada. According to that report, "there has *not* been a massive reduction in R&D activity in Canada ... Indeed, the weaker inference that R&D has declined is not supported" (emphasis in original) (25 p161). If account is taken of inflation, then the growth in research spending stopped in 1973, dropped slightly, and subsequently levelled off, before declining somewhat in the late 1970s. However, the amount spent in 1980, in real terms, was above what was spent in 1969. This pattern of spending, in fact, just mirrored what happened in R&D expenditures in

Canadian industry generally (26). The Eastman Commission was relatively optimistic about Canada's potential for clinical research. But when it talked about the future potential for basic R&D in Canada, the type of R&D that identifies new biological pathways or new molecular receptors and forms the basis for developing new drugs, it concluded, "Canada does not now possess either the scientific manpower or the physical infrastructure that would make it a major world centre for basic pharmaceutical research. Nor, in the opinion of the Commission, would it be wise for governments to seek to create such an environment in competition with heavily supported long-established centres in other countries" (24 p423).

Foreign control and research spending

Indeed, to the extent that research spending in Canada was suppressed in the latter half of the twentieth century, it appeared to be largely due to the foreign-owned nature of the Canadian industry. Commenting directly on the Canadian situation, the authors of a report for the Organisation for Economic Co-operation and Development (OECD) said that "an additional factor which must be considered in assessing the relatively low proportion of funds directed to pharmaceutical R&D in Canada is that technology and the results of innovation from parent corporations have been so readily available and so economically attractive in the short term, that the growth of national innovative technological capacity has been severely inhibited" (27 p173). A 1980 study for the federal Department of Industry, Trade and Commerce reported that the degree of foreign ownership of a country's drug industry exercised a strong negative effect on the R&D intensity in that country (28). Even executives in the industry agreed that companies tended to concentrate their R&D where their home offices were. Donald Davies, chair of Ayerst McKenna and Harrison said, "Virtually all companies do most of their research in their home country ... That's just the way it is." Nor was compulsory licensing the reason why Ayerst shut down most of its Canadian research. The shutdown was part of a process of corporate consolidation (29 pB1). More recent data backs up the contention that having a home-based multinational is necessary to generating a significant amount of R&D. Between 1991 and 2004, Canadian owned-companies consistently were responsible for fewer than 3% of the new drugs introduced on an annual basis (30).

The abolition of compulsory licensing and its impact on research spending

In response to the 1987 move by the government to limit compulsory licensing, industry pledged to increase spending on R&D to 10% of sales by 1996 (31). The federal government's goal was for R&D expenditures in Canada to reach the same level as in a group of seven leading industrialized countries that all had established industries: France, Germany, Italy, Sweden, Switzerland, the United Kingdom, and the United States. According to two Conservative ministers of consumer and corporate affairs, Canada would become a "leader in pharmaceutical development" (32) and Canada would have the potential to undertake pharmaceutical research and development on a world scale once compulsory licensing was abolished (33).

Initially, the industry substantially increased the percentage of total sales spent on R&D (Figure 8.1) so that by 1993 it was already above the promised 10% mark. The rise in spending as a percentage of sales was also matched by an increase in the overall amount being spent, going from $165.7 million in 1988 to over $1 billion in 2001 (34). The rise was due to two factors: the amount of money spent per company was going up, and more companies were investing in R&D (35). The question that remains unanswered is whether the increase was due to the change in the patent regime or was a reflection of PMAC's political promise to the government (36). We also need to remember that even with this increase in R&D investment, companies were spending at least double the amount on promotion – see Table 3.1.

Despite the increase in spending, some questions were raised about how valuable all that new research money was. Forty key medical figures engaged in pharmaceutical research in Canada were surveyed in 1990 and asked about how they viewed the additional research money that was available. They were generally pleased about the increase in funds, but they also expressed a number of misgivings about drug industry funding: 90% foresaw a likely conflict of interest; 80% deemed pharmaceutical clinical research as "me too" research; while 75% saw it as "might as well" research; and 40% were worried about a potential delay in the publication of unfavourable results (37). Anecdotally, other researchers believed that Bills C-22 (the one that weakened compulsory licensing) and C-91 (the one that abolished compulsory

Figure 8.1 Research and development spending as a percentage of total sales, 1988–2013

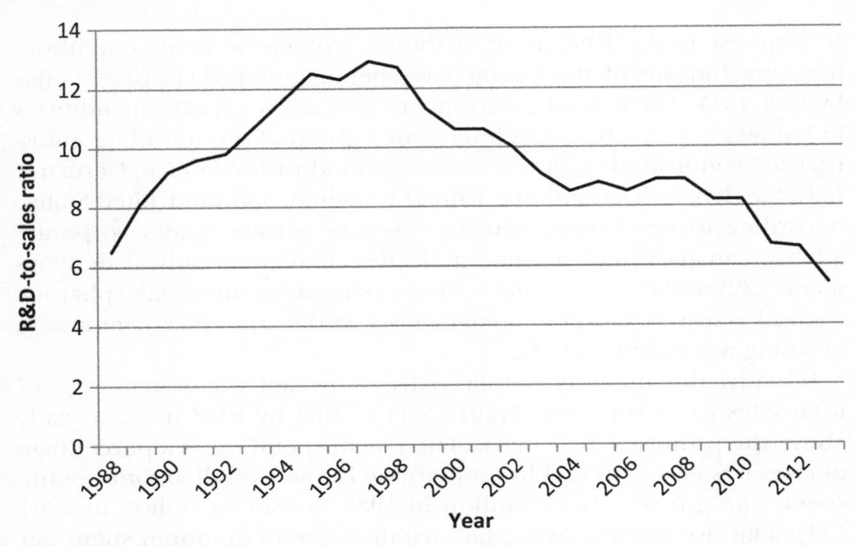

Source: Patented Medicine Prices Review Board. Annual report 2013. Ottawa: PMPRB; 2014. Reproduced with the permission of the Patented Medicine Prices Review Board, 2014.

licensing) were essential for a positive change in the Canadian R&D environment (36).

The rise in the amount of money going into research was matched by an increase in the number of research personnel employed (Table 8.1). What's more, the greatest increase in employment between 1997 and 2006 was in the number of professionals, that is, scientists (38). Based on an analysis of data from the Patented Medicine Prices Review Board (PMPRB) and Statistics Canada, Grootendorst and Di Matteo believed that between 1998 and 2002, drug R&D spending increased by $4.4 billion compared with, at most, an increase in spending on medications of $3.9 billion, meaning that, in cost-benefit terms, the change in the Patent Act had a net benefit for Canada (39). This conclusion was challenged on a number of grounds, including the decision to compare R&D in the pharmaceutical industry with that in the automobile industry and the failure to recognize that global factors play a significant role in the siting of R&D facilities (40–42).

Table 8.1 Number of research personnel in the pharmaceutical industry, 1997–2012

Year	Professionals	Technologists & technicians	Other support staff	Total
1997	1516	715	508	2739
1998	1596	719	422	2737
1999	1907	762	502	3171
2000	2115	799	666	3580
2001	2349	1142	855	4346
2002	2617	1404	971	4992
2003	2890	1543	1114	5547
2004	3123	1509	1070	5702
2005	3067	1990	749	5806
2006	3440	1395	1055	5890
2007	3138	1622	995	5755
2008	2252	1100	1325	4677
2009	2072	1032	1251	4355
2010	2069	866	915	3850
2011	1645	770	692	3108
2012	1822	719	790	3332

Source: Statistics Canada. Industrial research and development: intentions, 1999–2014 (Cat. No. 88-202-X). Ottawa: Statistics Canada; 2015.

This table should be interpreted with some caution because the figures include employment not just in companies that are members of Rx&D but also in generic companies.

Other changes in industrial policy to attract R&D spending

In addition to changing Canadian rules about intellectual property rights, Canadian federal and provincial governments also developed a variety of other industrial policies to encourage R&D. Industry Canada has cited a number of reasons that companies should undertake research in Canada including a 7.4% cost advantage over the US for clinical trials (43). The Life Sciences Branch of Industry Canada has produced promotional documents encouraging companies to use Canada for their clinical trials, and governments have structured the federal-provincial corporate income tax system into one of the most favourable in the world in its treatment of R&D (44).

Although these inducements apply to all R&D done in Canada, from the mid-1990s to the mid-2000s, "successive governments and regional agencies have worked hard to convince global companies that Canada has the right infrastructure and conditions to promote innovation and encourage new drug development" (45). By international standards, in 1999 Canada provided the most attractive environment for R&D among 11 countries (Australia, France, Germany, Italy, Japan, Korea, Mexico, Sweden, the United Kingdom, and the United States). Its federal R&D tax incentives included an immediate write-off for current costs, R&D machinery, and equipment costs, as well as a 20% level-based and taxable tax credit. Federal R&D tax provisions were generously strengthened by provincial R&D tax incentives (46). Four years later, while acknowledging that companies had difficulty accessing the tax incentives at times when the need for financial support for R&D programs was most acute, and that other countries were also aggressively using tax incentives to support R&D, the conclusion was still that Canada was providing one of the most generous R&D tax treatments (47). Taking into account the various provincial encouragements, Gagnon and Hébert showed that the net cost for pharmaceutical companies per dollar spent on R&D could be as low as $0.33 in Quebec. Overall, the $1274 million spent by the industry in 2007 translated into $521.2 million after tax subsidies (Table 8.2).

The 2014 report from the accounting firm KPMG that looked at the tax competitiveness of various countries when it came to R&D reported that Canada, France, and the Netherlands had R&D tax incentive programs that effectively produced negative income taxes because refundable tax incentives are greater than corporate income taxes (48). Furthermore, overall, out of 10 countries, Canada had the second-lowest business costs, 7.2% lower than the United States (49). An internal survey of Rx&D members, conducted by the accounting firm PriceWaterhouseCoopers, determined that in 2003, companies recovered 48% of their research expenditures through provincial and federal tax credits for R&D (50). (For a much more detailed discussion about tax credits for R&D, see the report by Marc-Andre Gagnon and Richard Gold (51).)

Besides R&D tax credits, provincial governments have provided other incentives to attract pharmaceutical company investments in R&D. Quebec's 15-year rule for reimbursing brand-name products (see Chapter 7) extended market exclusivity by approximately 3.6 years for drugs paid for by the public plan (51). When the rule was abolished in 2013, it was replaced by an increase in the refundable tax credit for R&D salaries

Table 8.2 Tax subsidies in Canadian R&D spending by patented pharmaceutical companies, 2007

	Region				
	Western provinces	Ontario	Quebec	Atlantic provinces	Canada
Effective tax rate for R&D (%)	−108.1	−112.7	−202	−117.9	
Net R&D cost per dollar spent by industry	0.48	0.47	0.33	0.54	
Government subsidy portion of each dollar spent by the industry	0.52	0.53	0.67	0.54	
Gross R&D expenditures by the patented pharmaceutical industry ($ millions)	124	567.8	561.7	20.5	1274
Net R&D expenditures by the patented pharmaceutical industry ($ millions)	59.5	266.9	185.4	9.4	521.2
Government subsidy portion of total R&D ($ millions)	64.5	300.9	376.3	11.1	751.8

Source: Gagnon M-A, Hébert G. The economic case for universal pharmacare: costs and benefits of publicly funded drug coverage for all Canadians. Ottawa: Canadian Centre for Policy Alternatives; 2010. Reproduced by permission of the Canadian Centre for Policy Alternatives.

from 17.5% to 27.5%, as well as matching funding of $125 million over five years for research partnership projects with pharmaceutical companies (52). This infusion of money was on top of the 2009 Stratégie biopharmaceutique québécoise that was designed to spend between $122.77 and $176.77 million over three years, including between $81 million and $135 million as subsidies to the private pharmaceutical sector. The 2009 investment by Quebec was in response to Ontario's 2008 biopharmaceutical investment strategy that made $150 million available over five years to attract pharmaceutical investments including R&D (51).

The BC provincial government pandered to the pharmaceutical industry's obsession with the Therapeutics Initiative (TI) in an attempt to attract industry investment. The TI is an independent group, separate from government, the pharmaceutical industry, and other vested interest groups, at the University of British Columbia with a mission to provide physicians and pharmacists with up-to-date, evidence-based, practical information on prescription drug therapy. The TI provides independent assessments of evidence on drug therapy to balance the drug-industry-sponsored information sources (53). Because it has often offered critical views about medications – for example, about Celebrex (celecoxib) (54) – the pharmaceutical industry was extremely hostile to it. To appease the industry, the provincial government appointed a task force to examine the recommendations about the therapeutic value of medications made by the TI. On the task force were the president of Rx&D and the vice-president of Angiotech Pharmaceuticals Inc, a BC-based pharmaceutical company (55).

Decline in R&D spending since the mid-1990s

Despite these various programs, Figure 8.1 and Table 8.1 both show a significant fall in spending on R&D and R&D employment, the former since 1997 and the latter since 2006. Since 2010, the Montreal area alone has lost over 800 R&D jobs from the closure of research facilities by AstraZeneca, Johnson & Johnson, Merck, Pfizer, and Sanofi (56–59). (A 2012 Secor-KPMG report sponsored by Rx&D predicted that rebound in R&D jobs would occur within a few years as more biologic medicines were marketed (16).) A report prepared for Industry Canada attributes these closures to facilities that were engaged in therapeutic areas that were no longer subjects of global corporate focus or to outsourcing and in-licensing to minimize costs and risks associated with in-house product development (60). The report also commented that research was being consolidated into clusters located closer to company headquarters or located in attractive geographic markets with a favourable infrastructure and government incentives, such as taxation (60).

In 2002, Canadian pharmaceutical R&D as a percentage of gross domestic product ranked 10th out of 19 OECD countries (61), and in 2006 its ranking had fallen to 16th out of 24 (62). By 2011, Canada's R&D-to-sales ratio was poorer than that for any of the seven countries that the PMPRB uses for comparison (34).

Kalant and Shrier compared the major Canadian subsidiaries with their multinational parent firms regarding the number of publications and number of patent applications before and after the Patent Act was changed in 1993. Except in the case of Merck, the subsidiaries had many fewer publications and patent applications per dollar of R&D, and no increase occurred in the total number of important new drugs introduced per year after 1993 in Canada. In contrast, the number of new drugs in the United States increased by 63% for the same period (1998–2004) (63). However, the interpretation of these figures is not completely clear because the proportion of pharmaceutical patents filed in Canada that were granted to Canadians went up from 1.61% between 1967 and 1987 to 3.36% between 1988 and 1993 (36). Whether this increase was due to more R&D investment secondary to the patent change is an open question. By 2010–12, slightly more than 5% of patents in the pharmaceutical and medical device industries were being filed by Canadians, a figure that was interpreted as showing a "relatively weak Canadian presence." The comparable figure for all industries was more than twice as large (64). Therefore, although a report from the Canadian Council of Academies looked at the global number of pharmaceutical patents being filed from Canada as indicating strength in industrial R&D (65), most of these patents were coming from multinational subsidiaries, not from Canadians per se. As the CD Howe Institute notes, Canada might be in a better position to absorb foreign technologies where there is higher domestic innovation capacity (64).

Overall, the trend in R&D spending and research productivity bears out a caution issued by the OECD that whenever governments have deliberately tried to encourage pharmaceutical innovation in countries where it exists only on a low level, "the results have been disappointing" (27 p232).

The Canadian industry's response to the figures showing declining R&D investment is to claim that the PMPRB figures fail to take into account all types of R&D spending. The legislation setting up the PMPRB specified that it should report on expenditures that would qualify for scientific research and experimental development (SR&ED) tax credits as they were defined in 1987. To qualify, these expenditures must be made in Canada and the work carried out in Canada. In general, the type of spending that qualifies falls into three categories: basic research, applied research, and development. Spending in such categories as market research or sales promotion; quality control or routine testing of materials, devices, or products; or the commercial use of a new or improved process is excluded (66). Rx&D commissioned the accounting firm KPMG to calculate what it believes is the true figure for R&D spending (67) and claims that the KPMG data show that 46% of industry spending is being overlooked by the PMPRB because it is using an outdated measure of what constitutes R&D. This under-reporting matters, according to Rx&D, because attracting investment hinges on Canada's ability "to create and sustain an environment with the right policies that allow [the country] to compete globally and drive our knowledge-based economy. Accurately tracking and reporting this investment is an important part of that environment" (68). Among the items that Rx&D thinks should be counted in R&D spending are the management of clinical trials that take place outside Canada, research in bioethics or other social sciences and humanities, regulatory and administrative costs for applications for clinical trials, the cost of drugs that are donated, and contributions that support the arts and other cultural activities in Canada (67).

While advocating for a change in the way that R&D spending is measured, the industry also acknowledges that R&D spending in Canada is facing serious challenges as it tries to compete on the world stage (69). The reason is that "Canada is not globally competitive when it comes to its intellectual property regime" and the obvious solution from the perspective of Rx&D is to reverse that situation by strengthening it (69). This is a message that Rx&D has been repeating since at least 2004 (2). According to Gagnon and Gold, this type of move would be folly. They calculate that the current patent regime and the drug prices that it generates (see Chapter 7), plus the various other direct and indirect subsidies, mean that Canada is spending an additional $2.257 billion to generate $662 million net of tax credits of direct R&D spending by the drug companies (51). Nor would raising prices be of any help in attracting more R&D money. Several countries have prices that are lower than those in Canada and have better R&D-to-sales ratios (a standard index to measure R&D) intensity (70). In its latest annual report, the PMPRB is quite blunt in its assessment of the impact of this change: "There are a multitude of factors that drive the location of pharmaceutical R&D. These include where companies can find the best science base at reasonable cost and ready access to a quality clinical trials infrastructure. Although price levels are often cited as an important policy lever for attracting R&D, the data has not supported this link domestically or internationally" (34 p38). An examination of the effect of stringent drug price regulation in 27 European countries between 2002 and 2009 found only a weakly significant association with a decline in R&D investment (42).

The same set of senior pharmaceutical executives who were asked about factors influencing their decisions about where to locate manufacturing (see Chapter 6) were asked the same question about choosing sites for R&D in general and clinical trials in particular (71). Among the factors they were asked about were the quality of the science in the country, the intellectual property regime, the spread of facilities (different sites for different research activities to take advantage of local scientific expertise), public funding for basic research, cost factors (including R&D tax credits and capital grants), and regulatory factors. For the sites for R&D in general, by far the most important driver was a location in which they could do good science by accessing world-leading scientists. They said that sensitive research would not be undertaken in countries that were perceived to have inadequate systems for the protection of intellectual property and gave as examples India and China. Cost factors were relatively unimportant. When it came specifically to the location for clinical trials, it was important to locate clinical trials in major commercial markets to familiarize key opinion leaders with the new products being tested. In addition, they sought places that were cost-efficient to run and patient recruitment was timely. These opinions bolster the quote from the PMPRB that a patent regime like Canada's is very unlikely to be a significant factor in influencing research decisions positively or negatively (71).

The value of commercial R&D

Although the amount spent by the pharmaceutical industry on R&D has declined, the absolute value of what companies spend is still considerable. Among the top 100 corporate R&D spenders in Canada are 22 pharmaceutical companies (see Table 8.3).

How valuable are the drugs that come out of the R&D, and what is the impact of industrial focused R&D on the way that public bodies, such as the Canadian Institutes of Health Research (CIHR), hospitals, and universities, function? To answer these questions, it is necessary to address two issues: the meaning of innovation and the consequences of the corporatization of research and its impact on public values. Both government and industry use the term *innovation* frequently. The report from the Expert Advisory Committee on Smart Regulation spoke about how "a key area for multilateral cooperation is the approval of new and innovative products and technologies" (72 p23) and "that [Canada needed to be sure that] innovation is not stifled" (72 p40). In its blueprint for legislative renewal, Health Canada emphasized "new and innovative drug products" (73 p23). Rx&D repeats the word *innovation* in its communications; for example, in the eight-page pamphlet *Saving Lives – Transforming Care*, the word appears 18 times (3). The drug companies recognize that not every product that they market is a major breakthrough, but they still regard every new drug as "innovative" in the sense that it adds to the choices that doctors have, and they claim that significant therapeutic improvements result from multiple small innovations.

The definition of innovation, as a new molecule, is not one that is shared by everyone. The International Society of Drug Bulletins (ISDB)

Table 8.3 Pharmaceutical companies' spending on research and development, 2011–2012

Rank (out of all companies doing R&D)			R&D spending			Revenue	Research intensity
2012	2011	Company	FY 2012 ($000)	FY 2011 ($000)	Percentage change 2011–2012	FY 2012 ($000)	R&D as a percentage of revenue
13	13	Apotex Inc	207,745	174,003	19.4	1,265,624	16.4
24	15	Sanofi	122,408	151,695	–19.3	596,116	20.5
26	18	GlaxoSmithKline Canada	112,266	118,433	–5.2	947,818	11.8
28	28	Novartis Pharmaceuticals Canada Inc	98,808	90,008	9.8	No data	–
31	20	Pfizer Canada Inc	89,920	113,544	–20.8	1,517,214	5.9
33	37	Valeant Pharmaceuticals International Inc	79,020	64,971	21.6	3,545,207	2.2
34	36	Amgen Canada Inc	74,215	65,186	13.9	No data	–
38	32	Boehringer Ingelheim (Canada) Ltd/Ltée	66,658	75,258	–11.4	449,053	14.8
40	41	Janssen Inc	64,053	55,204	16.0	1,267,934	5.1
54	53	Cangene Corporation	41,873	36,706	14.1	110,985	37.7
55	60	Pharmascience Inc	35,994	30,917	16.4	673,378	5.3
61	71	Oncolytics Biotech Inc	31,403	23,387	34.3	0	
64	45	QLT Inc	24,568	43,058	–42.9	25,465	96.5
65		Medicago Inc	24,232	11,965	102.5	5,540	437.4

67		Bayer Inc	23,743	10,193	132.9	858,877	2.8
71	69	AEterna Zentaris Inc	21,463	24,629	−12.9	33,652	63.8
73	79	Bioniche Life Sciences Inc	20,549	19,782	3.9	31.797	64.6
74	40	AstraZeneca Canada Inc	19,773	55,258	−64.2	1,074,324	1.8
76	93	Resverlogix Corp	19,730	13,979	41.1	0	
81	78	Tekmira Pharmaceuticals Corporation	18,032	19,920	−9.5	14,107	127.8
82		Trimel Pharmaceuticals Corporation	17,060	13,086	30.4	0	
86		MethylGene Inc	16,759	9,715	72.5	2	

Source: Re$earch Infosource Inc. Canada's top 100 corporate R&D spenders list 2014 [Internet]. Toronto: Re$earch Infosource; c2014 [cited 2014 Sept 22]. Available from: http://www.researchinfosource.com/top100_corp.php.

FY = fiscal year

issued a declaration where it distinguished between three forms of innovation: "the commercial concept: any newly marketed me-too product, new substances, new indications, new formulations, and new treatment methods; the technology concept: any industrial innovation, such as use of biotechnology, or the introduction of a new substance delivery system (patch, spray, etc.), selection of an isomer or a metabolite; [and] the concept of therapeutic advance: a new treatment that benefits the patient when compared to previously existing options" (74 p1). The ISDB came down squarely in favour of the third concept and defined therapeutic advance or innovation as a combination of efficacy, safety, and convenience. A systematic review of how the term *innovativeness* is defined also supports using therapeutic value measures as the best way to assess the effectiveness of investments in drug development (75). Viewed in this light, the number of drugs that are truly innovative or significant therapeutic advances is quite small. Industry likes to cultivate the impression that the research it does is innovating for unmet need. Witness the triumphal tone in one of its publications: "Canadian researchers at the University of Western Ontario have a clinical trial underway that, if successful, will lead to the world's first vaccine for HIV/AIDS; Scientists at the University of British Columbia are making steady progress toward vaccines that will minimize the impacts of traumatic brain injury and Alzheimer's disease; and, Vaccines at various stages of development offer promise to treat several types of aggressive cancers, including brain, cervical, colorectal and pancreatic cancers" (3 p3). The reality is that the companies respond to economic imperatives and invest in areas that will carve out a share of a lucrative market, not products that will necessarily result in significantly better health outcomes. The result is primarily drugs that are essentially minor variations on existing medications, for example, additions to the angiotensin-converting enzyme inhibitor group of drugs for treating high blood pressure and heart disease. Although there are occasional instances where drugs that were initially thought to have no or minor therapeutic gains turned out to be much more valuable than originally believed (76), overall only between 1 in 10 and 1 in 15 new drugs have any major new therapeutic value (77, 78).

The relationship between the pharmaceutical industry and the Canadian Institutes of Health Research

The increasing corporatization of research is evident in the relationship that the pharmaceutical industry has had, with the major health funding body in the country – the CIHR and its predecessor the Medical Research Council (MRC). The MRC supported the abolition of compulsory licensing in a brief that it "prepared to inform the research community about the patent law and its importance for the research community" (79 p1). The first collaboration in research funding between the industry and the MRC came in 1993, in the wake of the final abolition of compulsory licensing, with the development of the Pharmaceutical Manufacturers Association of Canada (PMAC)/MRC Health Program under which industry promised to invest $200 million over five years, complimented by $50 million from the MRC. However, this program was not run at arm's length from the PMAC. Contrary to the usual MRC practice, the program was administered separately from other MRC funds through a management committee of two representatives from the MRC and two from the PMAC (80).

Two years after the program was launched, the industry had delivered only $28 million out of a promised $80 million (81, 82). (The MRC also had spent only $8.55 million instead of $20 million.) At that point, MRC president Henry Friesen noted that the biomedical community was becoming extremely restless over the disparity between reality and PMAC's promise to open its enriched vaults for university research and training (83). The next half year saw some improvement so that by May 1996, program commitments from the industry had reached $60 million, and by the end of that year, it was expected that the industry would have spent $100 million (81, 82).

A number of reasons were proposed for the initial shortfall, including one that is particularly relevant to the corporatization of research: the two parties may have had different perceptions of the fund's purpose, with the MRC expecting that a larger share would go to basic research while the PMAC thinking that it should go to research with a commercial outcome (81). Although the PMAC and the MRC have been divided on the direction of research, Friesen saw research directed towards commercialization as one solution for a decrease in federal funding in the mid-1990s that cut the MRC's income by 10% over three years (84). Reflecting the outcome of the 1992 MRC strategic plan, *Investing in Canada's Health: A Strategic Plan for the Medical Research Council of Canada* (85), Friesen wrote that the MRC was becoming "a builder of productive alliances" by introducing a "major effort toward attracting more funding for research from industry" and improving the ability to "transfer new knowledge ... to the community and marketplace" (86 p2127, 2128). The strategy further saw the MRC committing "to partnerships with industry, focusing on industrial needs and resources, problems of technology transfer, intellectual property and ethical and other issues" (85). Others saw this as an "ideology of privatization" (87 p2138).

The contract between Rx&D, the new name for PMAC, and the CIHR was renewed in 1999–2000 for another five years (88). This renewal was shortly followed by the establishment by the CIHR's Governing Council of a National Working Group on Partnerships with "representatives of other agencies and, importantly, of industry" (89 p288). One of the four objectives of the program was to "contribute to economic development and job creation and to improved health and health care in Canada" (88 p4). The legislation that established CIHR listed eight goals for the organization in the preamble (90). Seven related to the promotion of health and research excellence and a single one referenced enhancing economic development and promoting growth and job creation. It was questionable how much priority that single goal should be given at the expense of the other seven.

The CIHR/Rx&D program provided matching funding for research training and industry-funded salary support and research grants. Writing a few years later about another matching grant program through Genome Canada, a group of researchers pointed out that co-funding can steer "resource allocation, as dictated by the partner entity, which may be to the detriment of some of the best science. In particular, co-funding is often biased against fundamental research that is far from commercialization and so at odds with the short-term goals of industrial partners" (91 p1867). In particular, the application for Genome Canada funding required up to 10 times as many pages of budgetary justification as the number for the scientific proposal. The draft CIHR strategic plan for 2009–10 to 2013–14 (92) was criticized for narrowly focusing on using science and scientists as a source of competitive advantage. Once again, the worry was that the requirement to get funding from commercial sources would bias the priority setting process against those who had little money to contribute (93). The plan also emphasized aligning CIHR priorities with the federal science and technology strategy (92). Under the heading "Mobilizing Science and Technology to Canada's Advantage," the strategy recognizes "that the most important role of the Government of Canada is to ensure a competitive marketplace and create an investment climate that encourages the private sector to compete against the world on the basis of their innovative products, services, and technologies (94 p10)." Nowhere is there any mention of mobilizing science and technology in the service of dealing with issues such as environmental causes of ill health.

The two most recent examples of the politicization of the CIHR research agenda are the appointment of a senior executive of Pfizer Canada to the governing board of the CIHR and the CIHR's withdrawal of its policy on clinical trial registration. In late 2009, the federal minister of health announced the appointment of Dr Bernard Prigent, vice-president of medical affairs for Pfizer Canada, to the governing council of the CIHR. Prigent is one of "the senior officers of Pfizer who are registered as lobbyists with the Office of the Commissioner of Lobbying of Canada, and CIHR is listed as one of the targets of Pfizer's lobbying activities" (95). The move was defended by Dr Alain Beaudet, president of CIHR and also a federal government appointee, on the grounds that Prigent was appointed as an individual and not as a representative of Pfizer (Dr Alain Beaudet, personal communication, 17 Nov 2009) and because, according to Beaudet, the agency wants "to ensure closer ties with industry, that they sit at the same table at the precompetitive level. We want to help industry to succeed and encourage them to invest" (96 pE256). The CIHR did not consider that there might be a conflict of interest in appointing someone with direct high-level corporate ties to its board.

In December 2010, CIHR posted its policy for clinical trial registration on its website. Any researcher who wanted to obtain CIHR funding had to comply with this policy, which contained some stringent provisions, including a requirement for publication of results within 12 months after the end of a clinical trial and the inclusion in these publications of reports of serious adverse effects. In addition, when the trial was registered, it had to contain a reference to the systematic review that justified the trial. A short three months after the policy went up, it was removed because, according to a form letter from CIHR, it would have created confusion with the recently released Tri-Council policy statement, *Ethical Conduct for Research Involving Humans.* However, the Tri-Council policy is significantly weaker than the one that the CIHR developed in several ways, including requirements about publication and the inclusion of safety information (97). Trudo Lemmens, who teaches law at the University of Toronto and is a member of the World Health Organization Expert Advisory Panel on the Clinical Practice Guidelines and Research Methods and Ethics, speculated that the CIHR policy was withdrawn because the CIHR was in negotiations with Rx&D about renewing the joint funding program, and industry was not favourable to clinical trial registries (97). As to the argument that the CIHR policy was not congruent with the one from the Tri-Council, Francoise Baylis and Jocelyn Downie from Dalhousie University pointed out that there are at least three other instances where CIHR's policies overlap with ones issued by the Tri-Council and where the two sets are not consistent (98), yet these CIHR policies have not been retracted.

Relying on industry funding and the consequences for the research community

It would be naive to think that industry funding can be dispensed with any time soon, and it would be foolish to deny that some of that money is well spent. But we need to be cognizant of the consequences of relying on industry for funding research. The case of Dr Nancy Olivieri is all too well known. Olivieri was doing research on L1, a product to be used in the treatment of iron-overload in patients with thalassemia, a blood disorder that requires frequent transfusions, but she had also signed a confidentiality clause with Apotex, the Canadian company with rights to the drug. The clause gave Apotex the right to control communication of trial data for one year after termination of the trial. When Olivieri became concerned about the safety of L1, she contacted Apotex and explained to the company that she needed to inform the patients in the trial of these new safety concerns. Apotex disputed the interpretation of her safety data, refused her request, and threatened to take legal action against her if she made her concerns public. At the same time, the University of Toronto, where she was a faculty member, was negotiating with Apotex for a large grant to help pay for the cost of a new building, and refused to defend her (99).

Over the past few decades, universities across Canada have established technology transfer/industry liaison offices in the hope of gaining much needed income through commercializing intellectual property and the physical products that come out of research on their campuses. One source of money that they are eyeing is the pharmaceutical industry, although it is responsible for just 5% of the amount of money that universities and teaching hospitals spend on R&D (see Table 8.4). The benefits from commercialization are easily recognized in the money that flows into the universities, although, on average, Canadian universities are netting less than $500,000 annually from commercialization of intellectual property (100). On the other hand, there is much less recognition of the harms that might come in terms of what is researched, how the research is carried out, and how it is interpreted and reported (101).

Little evidence suggests that Canadian universities, medical schools, and allied teaching hospitals have come to grips with dealing with the

Table 8.4 Industry contribution to health spending in the higher education sector

Year	Total health spending ($000,000)	Contribution from industry	
		Amount ($000,000)	Percentage of total
1997–8	1516.1	147.2	9.7
1998–9	1627.8	168.0	10.3
1999–2000	1822.5	172.4	9.5
2000–1	2103.9	144.6	6.9
2001–2	2382.6	159.6	6.7
2002–3	2955.6	139.8	4.7
2003–4	3086.8	127.5	4.1
2004–5	3584.6	148.2	4.1
2005–6	3767.1	164.1	4.4
2006–7	3780.9	188.0	5.0
2007–8	4013.6	177.1	4.4
2008–9	4379.4	162.1	3.7

Sources: Statistics Canada. Science statistics: estimates of research and development expenditures in the higher education sector, 2008/2009. Ottawa: Statistics Canada; 2010; Patented Medicine Prices Review Board. Annual report. Ottawa: PMPRB; 1999–2009.

The figures in this table should be read with caution for several reasons. First, Statistics Canada reports by the fiscal year whereas the Patented Medicine Prices Review Board reports by the calendar year. Second, the PMPRB tabulates R&D spending only by companies that have sold patented drugs in the previous year, and therefore an unknown amount of money goes unreported. Finally, industry also contributes in ways that are not counted as formal research dollars, for example, the establishment of a chair in medication adherence at the University of Saskatchewan (102) and the University of British Columbia professorship in sustainable health care funded by 10 pharmaceutical companies (103).

financial conflicts of interest (COI) that go hand in hand with industry research dollars. Williams-Jones and MacDonald defined five basic essential elements that should be in a university COI policy: the date the policy was approved and revised, the definition of COI, examples of COI, procedures to follow in the event of COI, and additional sources of further information on COI. They looked for these elements in the policies of the 13 leading Canadian research universities and found all five elements in policies from only two universities as of 2007 (104). A more detailed analysis looked for the presence of 61 different items in the financial COI policies of Canadian academic health centres between August 2005 and February 2006 (105). At that time, no single policy in any Canadian centre informed researchers about the broad range of investigator financial COI issues, and some areas, such as strategies for managing financial COI and publication rights, were not addressed at all. More than half of Canadian universities, half of medical schools, and more than a third of teaching hospitals had no institutional financial COI policy at the time of the survey (106). Out of 844 investigators who were surveyed at these centres, 269 personally experienced (n = 85) or witnessed (n = 236) a financial COI, and over 70% of these situations related to industry trials (107). COI policies at Canadian medical schools are unlikely to deter faculty who want to opt for close affiliations with industry, as the majority of schools have weak or permissive policies (108). In a series of surveys spanning over 20 years (1985 to 2007) in the United States, Blumenthal and co-workers showed that investigators who have industry funding are much more likely to take commercial considerations into account when choosing research topics than are those without commercial sponsorship (109–111).

Conclusion

Just as the decision to strengthen intellectual property rights had significant consequences for how much Canada spends on drugs, so too has it had a major impact on the direction of biomedical research. In pursuit of industry funding, the government and its agencies, such as the CIHR, have tailored industrial policies to align research spending with the objectives of industry. As the amount that industry spends decreases, calls will be made for further realignment of policy objectives to attract the remaining industry dollars.

Biomedical research should serve the public interest, not subvert it (112): "Research conducted in public institutions should not be decided by private interests simply because these interests predominate in the funding of research. Commercial funding can play a legitimate role in research in Canada, but active steps must be taken and mechanisms put in place to ensure that the participation of commercial firms does not skew research priorities and activities in universities and publicly funded agencies" (80). On a fundamental level, the value of pharmaceutical R&D to Canadian society should not be answered by counting the number of new drugs marketed or the amount of money spent. The question that needs to be asked and answered is, in what direction does Canadian society want to try to direct R&D? In the area of medical research, research funded by the pharmaceutical industry may leave many questions untouched. Do we want most of the money available for health research to be narrowly directed into the development of new patentable medications, the main priority of the pharmaceutical industry, or do we want to prioritize other areas, such as research that has the potential to improve population health but that cannot be easily, or at all, patented?

9 Canada, the pharmaceutical industry, and access to medicines in the Global South

Mean per capita expenditure on pharmaceuticals in low-income countries is just over US$20 per annum (1), and in some of these countries, purchasing basic medications, such as salbutamol for asthma or the antibiotic amoxicillin, would mean that up to 86% of the population would see its daily income fall below US$1.25 (2). Low-cost generic medicines were available from just 29.4% to 54.4% of public sector sites that were surveyed in 36 low- and middle-income countries (3).

Articles 12 and 2 of the International Covenant on Economic, Social and Cultural Rights, which Canada has both signed and ratified, commit countries to recognizing "the right of everyone to the enjoyment of the highest attainable standard of physical and mental health" (Article 12) and "to take steps ... through international assistance and co-operation ... with a view to achieving progressively the full realization of the rights recognized in the present Covenant" (Article 2) (4).

In light of these facts, it would seem that it is a moral imperative for Canada to support improved access to medicines in the Global South. This mandate was recognized in a report by a research consortium on the subject of Canada and health care in a globalized world for the Commission on the Future of Health Care in Canada (Romanow Commission), a federally appointed commission looking at the future of health care in Canada. The researchers contended that health as a human right must be Canada's overarching global commitment and the primacy of human rights should take priority over other elements of international law, including international trade and investment law as it applies to access to pharmaceuticals (5). In his final report, Romanow was quite emphatic that "it is time for Canada to use both its positive relationship with developing countries and its considerable expertise in health care to help improve health and health care around the world" (6 p243). As we saw in Chapter 6, in the past Canada used patent legislation to protect its own population from high drug costs. Given its own history, Canada might be expected to be sympathetic to the need for countries in the Global South to provide their people with affordable medications.

Susser (7) posits that health as a human right entails four components: equal access to appropriate services for all members of all groups, equity in health states for all social groups as an explicit aspiration, evaluative mechanisms to monitor the distribution of both states of health and specific needs for health, and equitable sociopolitical arrangements that give a voice to all groups in sustaining equity in health. The availability of low-cost essential drugs is key to the first two and to helping ensure that access means active support for the fourth component by helping those voices be heard.

Case studies: access versus IPRs

This chapter uses seven case studies to explore whether the normative goal of helping countries in the Global South to improve health and health care has actually been reflected in Canadian policy and examines the political ideology driving the decisions that Canada has made. In those cases where information is available, this chapter also looks at the position of the pharmaceutical industry in either supporting or opposing the actions of the Canadian government. Specifically, this chapter examines instances where improved access to safe and low-cost drugs in countries in the Global South came into conflict with support for intellectual property rights (IPRs). IPRs are clearly not the only limitation on access to medicines in the Global South. Other important factors include the infrastructure in the country to store and deliver medicines, the number of health care professionals and their training, and the diversion of medicines into illegal channels. The reason for focusing on IPRs is because they highlight the conflict between neo-liberal and social justice values, and the choices that the Canadian government made clearly defined which values it prioritized.

South Africa versus the drug companies

With the culmination of the Uruguay Round of trade negotiations in 1994, the World Trade Organization (WTO) came into existence on 1 January 1995 and with it the Agreement on Trade-Related Aspects of

Intellectual Property Rights (TRIPS), one of the three core agreements overseen by the organization. The other two are the General Agreement on Trade in Services and the General Agreement on Trade and Tariffs. All WTO member states must abide by the terms of these three agreements. The TRIPS Agreement harmonized patent terms worldwide for a minimum of 20 years from the time that the patent application was made and mandated the granting of patents in all fields of technology, including pharmaceuticals. Before TRIPS, many countries in the Global South either did not grant patents for pharmaceuticals or granted patents only on the process used to make the medication (8). As one medication can usually be made in many ways, lower cost generic versions were quickly available in countries with an active generic industry like India. Indian generics were then available for export to countries that did not grant patents on pharmaceuticals (9). Following TRIPS, this pathway to making generics available was going to be severely curtailed because these countries had to accede to TRIPS by 2005. By 2000, just as the AIDS crisis was exploding, many of these countries confronted prices for triple therapy for HIV of greater than US$10,000 per person per year, and access to low-cost generics was disappearing (10).

In the late 1990s, faced with increasing rates of HIV infection and the high prices for HIV treatment, the South African government passed the Medicines and Related Substances Control Amendment Act that allowed for generic substitution of off-patent medicines, transparent pricing for all medicines, and the parallel importation of patented medicines. (Once generics became available, the price of triple therapy for HIV tumbled. In June 2000, before generics appeared, treatment for one year with brand-name products was US$10,439. By March of the next year, after the first generics were marketed, the price was US$295, and brand-name products could be bought for US$727. As more generics were brought to market, the price continued to fall so that by June 2011, the price was US$65, a fall of more than 99% (11).) In response, 39 multinational pharmaceutical companies, with the support of the US government and the European Commission, took the South African government to court in 1998, alleging that the legislation violated both the TRIPS Agreement and the country's constitution. Eventually, in the face of widespread public opposition, the US government withdrew its support for the court case, and without the US support the companies dropped their lawsuit (12). Canada's position was that intellectual property should be "a balance between the need to provide incentives to spur innovation and the benefits derived by society to have maximum access to new creations" (13). Canada did not support the United States, but it also did not affirm the right of the South African government to take the steps that it did (5). Although Canada did not influence the outcome, its failure to come down firmly on the side of South Africa illustrates the contradiction between its positions on drug access internationally and nationally. At the same time that Canada was staying neutral in the South African case, it was also defending Canadian legislation before the WTO, arguing that provisions in the TRIPS Agreement "call for a liberal interpretation ... so that governments would have the necessary flexibility to adjust patent rights to maintain the desired balance with other important national policies" (14 p153–4). This disconnect between domestic and international positions is further highlighted in the next part of this chapter.

Canada and the Doha Declaration

In the lead up to the Fourth WTO Ministerial Conference in Doha in November 2001, countries from the Global South were pushing for more flexibility in how to interpret the IPR provisions of the TRIPS Agreement. The documentation from the Department of Foreign Affairs and International Trade (DFAIT) is decidedly ambiguous about exactly how Canada viewed this demand. A document tabled before the House of Commons Standing Committee on Foreign Affairs and International Trade recognized that these countries were "seeking a recognition that nothing in the Agreement ... shall prevent members from taking measures to protect public health, in particular in the context of access to essential medicines for handling pandemics such as HIV/AIDS, malaria and tuberculosis" (15). On the other hand, DFAIT did not seem committed to supporting this goal. Its official position was that it was necessary "to ensur[e] that the balance between creators and users is maintained in any future negotiation ... The provision of drugs and therapies is a complex question involving patent rights, the establishment of systems to deliver and monitor drug usage, cost and alternative mechanisms to finance drug purchases by developing countries" (16).

At the Doha meeting, Canada initially sided with Australia, Japan, Switzerland, and the United States in opposing a proposed resolution that would affirm that nothing in the TRIPS Agreement prevents WTO members from adopting measures to protect public health (5). As the meeting progressed, Canada reversed its position and ended up supporting the Doha Declaration that prioritized public health over trade.

Some observers contend that the Canadian attitude changed to avoid international embarrassment. A month earlier, Canada had threatened to violate Bayer's IPRs if the company was unable to provide enough ciprofloxacin to protect the Canadian population in the event of a widespread anthrax attack (17). Being willing to invoke compulsory licensing at home and denying the same right to other countries was too much of a contradiction.

One key provision of the Doha Declaration was the reaffirmation of the article in TRIPS stating that countries could issue compulsory licenses for medications. In addition, the Doha Declaration made it clear that in emergencies or other circumstances of extreme urgency, countries could choose to waive the normal requirement to first attempt to negotiate a voluntary licence on reasonable terms and conditions for a reasonable period. However, according to the TRIPS Agreement, generic production had to be predominantly for domestic consumption, leaving the problem of how to provide low-cost generic medicines to countries that lacked the facilities for domestic generic manufacturing. In negotiations to resolve this problem, groups of countries in the Global North offered two significantly different proposals. The European Union (EU) proposed a solution that would provide limited exceptions to patent rules that hindered the export of drugs under a compulsory license, while the United States backed a time-limited, conditional moratorium on WTO challenges to such exports. In general, countries in the Global South saw the EU initiative as a positive step, although they were concerned about certain elements, whereas the reaction to the US proposal was generally negative because it didn't offer a permanent solution to the problem. Canada backed the much more restrictive US position over the one put forward by the EU (18) and maintained its backing for months as negotiations progressed. It took two years of difficult negotiations before the WTO members, meeting in the WTO General Council, reached an agreement. The so-called "August 30, 2003" decision authorized the TRIPS Council to issue a waiver that allowed pharmaceutical producing nations to grant a compulsory license for the export of pharmaceutical products to nations with insufficient pharmaceutical production capabilities (8).

Canada's Access to Medicines Regime

Once the compromise around compulsory licensing was reached, Canada passed Bill C-9 in May 2004, becoming the first country to have legislation allowing for the production and export of generic drugs to countries that lacked their own manufacturing capacity. The chain of events that triggered this legislation included a speech in September 2003 by Stephen Lewis, then the United Nations special envoy to Africa for HIV/AIDS, and the desire of Jean Chrétien, then prime minister of Canada, to leave a legacy (19). The legislation, now called Canada's Access to Medicines Regime (CAMR), was initially called the Jean Chrétien Pledge to Africa. The initial reaction to the introduction of this legislation from the international brand-name pharmaceutical industry was hostile. Harvey Bale, the director-general of the International Federation of Pharmaceutical Manufacturers and Associations, was quoted in the *Globe and Mail* as saying that the initiative "won't solve a thing" and it will be a "negative black eye for Canada" that will "very well affect the investment climate" (20 pA1). However, two weeks later a more conciliatory message from both Bale and Rx&D offered support for the legislation and their commitment to solving the problems of the developing world (21).

Rx&D's brief a few months later to the House of Commons Standing Committee on Industry, Science and Technology echoed this sentiment: "Canada's Research-Based Pharmaceutical Companies (Rx&D) fully supports the humanitarian efforts of Bill C-9 ... Rx&D believes that Bill C-9 sets out the right policy framework for working with developing countries to provide affordable medicines, while respecting and allowing a role for the innovative pharmaceutical industry" (22 p3). At the same time, Rx&D also proposed changes to the bill that would have significantly altered its intent. One amendment would have given the patent holder a strong incentive to undercut any price offered by the generic manufacturer to maintain its market monopoly, effectively precluding the competition that is needed to bring prices down and keep them down. The second change would have created a legal obligation for a generic producer to notify a patentee of any contract negotiations it was undertaking. This would have allowed brand-name companies to identify and directly contact the country that was in negotiations to receive the generics and try to pressure the country to abandon its efforts. This proposal went beyond anything required in the TRIPS Agreement, something that Rx&D acknowledged (23).

Policy debates about Bill C-9 "were dominated by two themes overall: intellectual property rights and TRIPS compliance ... With the Departments of Industry Canada and International Trade as the lead institutions, the goals of protecting intellectual property and ensuring good trade relations with the United States appear to have taken priority over encouraging generic competition to achieve drug affordability" (24). As such, it is not surprising that when the legislation finally passed, it contained compromises that made it largely unworkable. Among the flaws in the legislation were the limited list of pharmaceutical products that were eligible for export, the limited list of countries a drug could be exported to, the short duration for a compulsory licence authorizing the export of a generic drug, and significant administrative roadblocks. A compulsory licence could be issued only after advance disclosure to the patent holder of the proposed recipient country, something that Rx&D had argued for, there was a fixed "maximum quantity" of the product to be exported in generic form and "a generic manufacturer had to file a [separate] application for every drug, for every amount produced and for every country to which it wanted to export a drug" (25 pE705).

Built into the legislation was the requirement for a review after three years. By April 2007, when the review took place, the Conservatives had replaced the Liberals as the government of Canada. At this time, CAMR had never been employed. Subsequently, the legislation was used to send a shipment of antiretroviral drugs to Rwanda (26). In the initial parliamentary debates in 2004 about CAMR, there was almost no mention about promoting the right to health through access to essential medicines or the need to deal with neglected diseases, and the absence of these themes carried over to the parliamentary review (24). While the Liberal government was primarily focused on protecting IPRs, it was not aggressively pushing this stance in its foreign policy dealings with countries in the Global South. This position changed under the Conservatives, as their view was that IPRs were taking on an increased importance in the knowledge economy and, according to Esmail and Kohler, under them Canada's foreign policy became much more favourable to IPRs. As one example of the more aggressive policy "the Department of Foreign Affairs and International Trade ... announced in 2007 that it was assessing its interests in protecting intellectual property as it initiated trade agreements in Peru, Colombia and the Dominican Republic" (24).

Because of this stance by the Conservative government, the conclusion of the review was that no amendments would be made to CAMR to improve its functionality. This conclusion was reached despite the 2006 pronouncement by Tony Clement, Conservative minister of health, that CAMR was a flawed piece of legislation (27). Instead the government touted a series of measures it was taking, including providing tax incentives for pharmaceutical donations to countries in the Global South, giving $100,000 to the University of Toronto's program to improve access to pharmaceuticals in Ghana and other West African countries, and its $450 million decade-long African Health Systems Initiative to support country-led efforts to strengthen health systems, improve health outcomes, and make progress towards the Millennium Development Goals (28). The benefits from these government-led initiatives would have been a good complement to an amended CAMR, a piece of legislation that would have had a relatively quick and meaningful impact on access to low-cost essential medicines, but they should not be seen as a substitute for amending CAMR. The government concluded the report by promising to monitor the situation with respect to CAMR and make amendments if necessary.

The Conservatives had a chance to act on their promise of amending the act in 2011, when a private member's bill to amend and simplify CAMR was the subject of a vote in Parliament. CAMR had not been used since the shipment to Rwanda by Apotex, and Apotex, the only generic company that had used the legislation, had stated that it would not use it again in its current form (25). Despite passing the House of Commons, the bill was delayed by the Conservatives in the Senate until it died with the calling of an election. Tony Clement, who had switched from health minister to minister of industry, sent a highly misleading memo to Conservative members in the Senate, urging them to vote against the legislation because it "would allow drugs that have not been certified by Health Canada to be shipped 'to unsuspecting populations, to their detriment.' The drugs, he wrote, could be redirected to the black market with proceeds going to non-humanitarian causes such as weapons, and the shipments could run afoul of domestic laws and traditions" (29). He further claimed that the legislation would lead to patent holders leaving Canada, thereby threatening Canadian research and development (R&D) (29). The inaccuracies in what Clement wrote are well documented in a memo released by the Canadian HIV/AIDS Legal Network and the Grandmothers Advocacy Network (30). Companies such as GlaxoSmithKline and Boehringer Ingelheim testified in Parliament against reforming CAMR, wrongly claiming that the reforms were not in compliance with Canada's obligations as a WTO member (31).

A second opportunity to amend the legislation came in the fall of 2012, but with a few exceptions, even the Conservatives in the House of Commons who had supported amending the legislation in 2011 yielded to the pressure from the government, and the almost unanimous vote by the Conservatives led to the defeat of the bill. The parliamentary secretary to the defence minister maintained that there were better ways to help people suffering from diseases in Africa and elsewhere and, once again, there were charges that Conservative members of Parliament were spreading misinformation about the effects of the bill (32).

United Nations High-Level Meeting on Non-Communicable Diseases

Over the past decade, recognition has been growing of the magnitude of the morbidity and mortality associated with non-communicable diseases (NCDs), not just in the Global North countries but also in countries in the Global South. In fact, the volume of NCDs in the Global South has been increasing owing, in no small measure, to actions of the Global North. They have been fuelling the epidemic of tobacco-related diseases by pushing countries to allow the giant multinational tobacco companies freer access to their populations (33) and refusing to do anything meaningful about climate change, thereby contributing to the rise of type II diabetes (34), to name but two ways. Aside from some regions in Africa, the global burden of disease from NCDs is greater than it is from infectious diseases (35) and almost two-thirds of the 36.1 million deaths per year from NCDs come from the poorest countries (36).

Because of numbers such as these, in September 2011 the United Nations convened a high-level meeting to develop with a strategy for how to deal with NCDs. The main outcome of the meeting was a political declaration on their prevention and control (37). In the lead-up to the meeting, Canada was instrumental in trying to weaken the final declaration by, among other things, pressing for the exclusion of a pledge to support universal health care, advocating for the removal of a section about conflict of interest that would have limited the involvement of food and alcohol companies in developing public health policies, and not addressing trade-related barriers to global health. Although IPRs were not directly mentioned in the final statement from the meeting, they are intimately linked with trade through the provisions of the TRIPS Agreement. The absence of any mention of trade-related barriers could negatively affect the ability of countries in the Global South to access low-cost drugs for NCDs.

Anti-Counterfeiting Trade Agreement

Undoubtedly, counterfeit drugs are a significant problem in countries in the Global South. The World Health Organization estimates that

10% of the drugs in these countries may be counterfeit (38), but the estimate is complicated because of conflicting definitions of what counterfeit means. As Attaran and colleagues (39) point out, four groups of drugs are often lumped together as "counterfeits." True counterfeits are products that violate IPRs because of alleged infringement on patents, trademarks, or other forms of IPR. Substandard drugs are ones that unintentionally do not meet the necessary quality standards, perhaps because of impure ingredients or manufacturing problems. Unregistered medicines are those that are present in the country without the authorization of the regulatory authority, often because of theft or illegal diversion. Finally, deliberately falsified medicines are ones created with a criminal intent to violate quality standards, for example, by using fake ingredients. The pharmaceutical industry is primarily interested in taking action against drugs that violate their IPRs, that is, counterfeits, but for patients the main concern is with drugs that do not meet quality and safety standards, that is, ones that will harm their health (40).

In 2006, Japan and the United States started preliminary discussions about the Anti-Counterfeiting Trade Agreement (ACTA); in 2006 and 2007, Canada, the EU, and Switzerland joined these discussions, and when formal negotiations began in 2008, Australia, Korea, Mexico, Morocco, New Zealand, and Singapore were also parties. However, rather than focusing on how to stop the trade in medicines that might damage people's health, the main focus of ACTA was on trade in medicines that violate various forms of IPRs (41). If enacted, the terms in ACTA could also negatively affect access to generic drugs in countries in the Global South. The border-measures section excludes detaining products because of patent violations, but civil trademark infringements are included as a ground to detain generics passing in transit, that is, going through a third country on the way between the exporting and importing countries (42). This concern about generics being detained is not merely theoretical. The EU already has regulations about goods in transit that are similar to those in ACTA: "In 2008 and 2009 there were at least 19 detentions by customs authorities of medicines in transit through the EU from the source country [usually India] to destinations in Latin America and elsewhere ... These detentions took place under an EU regulation ... that permitted action against goods infringing intellectual property rights, including goods in transit ... even though the products were not patented in India or the destination country" (40 p4). Patents are included in the civil enforcement section of the treaty by default. Countries in the Global South could exclude them, but there is a well-grounded fear that these countries could be pressured into adopting the default position of including patents. Finally, "ACTA puts a broad group of third parties at risk of criminal and civil enforcement measures ... In the trade in generics, this group of third parties can potentially include suppliers of active ingredients for medicines or NGOs procuring and distributing legitimate generics for treatment" (42 p3).

Several of these concerns were raised in June 2009, when DFAIT held a roundtable with representatives of civil society about ACTA. At the meeting, officials from Canadian Border Services Agency stated that seizures at Canadian borders of generic drugs that were in transit were unlikely to happen because of Canada's differing legislation and practices compared with those in the EU. Regarding the point that ACTA was only intended to deal with IPR issues and not drugs that could compromise health, DFAIT's position was that "ACTA can make a contribution to the fight against counterfeit medicines by establishing international standards for trademark enforcement, but only as a part of Canada's broader approach" (43). However, Canada was not taking any initiatives to deal with substandard or deliberately falsified medicines nor had it publicly indicated its intent to do so. In addition, DFAIT was opposed to the idea of removing medicines from the scope of ACTA because its view was that ACTA is a non-sectoral agreement, that is, an agreement about counterfeiting in general, and removing pharmaceuticals would result in lower sectoral enforcement standards (43). Rx&D's only comment about the proposed treaty was to acknowledge the dangers from counterfeit medicines, but its letter to DFAIT did not define what it meant by counterfeit and contained nothing about the risk of generic drugs being stopped in transit (44).

Canada has signed ACTA although it has yet to ratify it (45), and at this point (September 2015), it seems as if the treaty is dormant if not dead, primarily because the European Parliament overwhelmingly rejected ACTA (46).

Negotiations for TRIPS extension for least developed countries

Least developed countries (LDCs), as defined by the United Nations, are those with a gross domestic product per capita of less than US$905, human resource weakness, and economic vulnerability. Currently, 49 countries have this designation (47). When the TRIPS agreement came into force on 1 January 1995 LDCs were granted a 10-year exemption from complying with its provisions, and this exemption was subsequently extended to 1 July 2013. (See Chapter 6 about data protection in Canada.) As the July 2013 deadline neared, the LDCs started lobbying for a further indefinite extension that would apply until a country no longer fell into the LDC category (48). This position echoed the recommendation from the Global Commission on HIV and the Law that "WTO Members must indefinitely extend the exemption for LDCs from the application of TRIPS provisions in the case of pharmaceutical products" (49 p87).

The US and the EU, backed by a group of the Global North including Canada, Australia, Japan, New Zealand, and Switzerland were opposed to an indefinite extension and, instead, argued for a time-limited extension of between 5 and 10 years. In addition, these countries were opposed to the elimination of the "no rollback" condition that was included in the 2005 extension (50). This clause prevented LDCs from repealing or revising any TRIPS-related IPR provisions that they had already implemented, thereby stopping them from being able to experiment with IPRs that were appropriate for their level of development (51, 52). The final compromise was for an eight-year extension. Although the no rollback clause was not eliminated, LDCs will be allowed to use the "flexibilities" in TRIPS to introduce measures such as compulsory licensing, but only if they "express their determination to preserve and continue their progress towards implementing the TRIPS agreement" (53). The EU is already interpreting this phrase in a much more restrictive manner than are the LDCs (54).

Extension of the transitional period for granting and enforcing medicines patents

Since the inception of the TRIPS Agreement, the world's LDCs have been granted a transition period from having to enforce intellectual property rules on drugs. This exemption, which was affirmed in the Doha Declaration, enables poor countries to export and produce generic drugs regardless of whether they are patented but was set to expire at the end of 2015. Although these countries had the general exemption from TRIPS provisions that was described in the previous section, the importance of this specific exemption for pharmaceutical products remained. Preliminary results of a study of the use of TRIPS showed "that during 2001–2009 at least 31 LDCs authorised the importation of generic antiretroviral medicines (ARVs) to treat HIV/AIDS with a reference to the ... extension." The continuing "ability of LDCs to not enforce patents through simple declarations is [still] of key importance. It provides much needed legal certainty for suppliers and procurement agencies ... [for HIV and other drugs] who seek to minimize the risk of patent infringement suits" (55).

Bangladesh, on behalf of the LCD members of the WTO, was pushing for an indefinite extension of the transition period until countries were no longer classified as a LDC. The LDCs, backed by nearly one hundred civil society and HIV/AIDS treatment groups operating in poor Asia-Pacific and sub-Saharan African countries, as well as the United Nations Development Programme and the Joint United Nations Programme on HIV/AIDS, argued that an indefinite extension was necessary because until a country graduated from the LDC designation, meeting the TRIPS pharmaceutical requirements would "limit its ability to address basic medical needs for its citizens and hinder efforts to lift them out of poverty. Tying the requirements to the LDC classification is in and of itself establishing a timeline by which a country must meet the pharmaceutical intellectual standards" (56). Even the European Commission, in a dramatic change of position, ended up supporting the need for an indefinite extension (57).

The main opposition came from the United States, which argued for a 10-year extension. Not surprising, given its position on the general TRIPS extension, Canada, along with Australia and Switzerland, backed the US position (58). In fact, Canada should not even have been taking a position on such a controversial issue since the extension was being debated during the 2015 Canadian election, a time when the government is supposed to be operating in caretaker mode and not making major policy decisions. The final resolution was a 17-year extension. According to one NGO activist, "The decision to extend the WTO waiver of drug patent rules for 17 years is a better outcome than the 10-year waiver proposed by the US Trade Representative Ambassador Michael Froman, but it is also a disappointment, and falls short of what was asked and needed" (59).

Canada and industry: the good and the bad

It would be a mistake to conclude that Canada has not done anything to help improve access to medications in countries in the Global South. Between 2001 and 2010, Canada contributed over US$874 million to the Global Fund to Fight AIDS, Tuberculosis and Malaria, ranking it seventh among individual country donors (60). Noticeably though, Canada is missing from the list of the top 12 donors for research into neglected diseases, whether measured by the absolute amount of money donated or in relation to gross domestic product; Brazil and India have both donated more than Canada (61).

Similarly, the pharmaceutical industry is not oblivious to the plight of countries in the Global South. One document, on the Rx&D website in February 2015, discusses a number of positive initiatives that the industry has undertaken in terms of providing assistance to these countries, including drug donations and the active support for the construction of hospitals, clinics, and even roads that facilitate the movement of imported medicines and vaccines to areas of need (62). IPRs are mentioned but not in the context of being a barrier to affordable medicines. Rather, the document talks about tiered pricing as a way to access an increased number of medicines and vaccines. Tiered pricing refers to selling drugs at reduced prices in countries in the Global South and, while it does make medicines more affordable, it is not as effective in lowering prices as generic competition (63). According to Rx&D, brand-name companies grant licences to generic manufacturers in countries in the Global South, and it cites the licences that Gilead has signed with Indian generic manufacturers for HIV drugs. Indeed, the access program for the HIV drug tenofovir has extended the use of this drug to 2.4 million people in low- and middle-income countries, but the program also has economic benefits for Gilead: "Even though pharmaceutical companies may market their access programmes as philanthropy on the basis of the associated price discounts and increased patient enrolment in developing countries, it is clear that in the case of TDF [tenofovir disoproxil fumarate] the programme also made good business sense. By stimulating the demand for formulated product, the programme dropped Gilead's input costs, off-setting any potential loss in revenue as a consequence of product discounts" (64 p6).

Gilead also has agreements with Indian companies for the production of drugs for hepatitis C, but these licences exclude 51 middle-income countries in which 50 million people are living with the disease (65). Furthermore, other companies that make drugs for hepatitis C, AbbVie, Bristol-Myers Squibb, and Johnson & Johnson, so far have not entered into any agreements to offer their drugs at lower prices. When generic drugs are produced through compulsory licences, brand-name companies are not as generous in their attitudes. Marijn Dekkers, CEO of Bayer, referred to compulsory licensing as "essentially theft," although it is legal under the TRIPS Agreement. In addition, in contrast to the noble statements by Rx&D about helping countries in the Global South to access medicines is the admission from Dekkers, when talking about his company's new and highly effective drug Sovaldi (sofosbuvir) for treating hepatitis C: "We did not develop this product for the Indian market, let's be honest. I mean, you know, we developed this product for Western patients who can afford this product, quite honestly" (66).

Strong IPRs are not for all countries

The Canadian prioritization of IPRs internationally is a reflection of what has been happening domestically in Canada for 30 years, as was seen in Chapter 6.

Internationally, the expectation by the Canadian government that the poorest countries in the world should adopt IPRs that are equivalent to those in the wealthy Global North countries ignores both historical and current economic realities. Many major western countries, including Canada, Denmark, Sweden, and Switzerland, did not adopt full IPRs for pharmaceuticals until the 1970s and 1980s when their gross domestic product per capita was in the range of US$16,000 to $36,000 (67). Expecting the same from countries with a per capita GDP of less than US$1000 is unreasonable and unjust (see Table 9.1). In the words of the Commission on Intellectual Property Rights, "It is our contention that intellectual property systems may, if we are not careful, introduce distortions that are detrimental to the interests of developing countries. Very 'high' standards of protection may be in the public interest in developed countries with highly sophisticated scientific and technological infrastructures ... but this does not mean the same standards are appropriate in all developing countries ... so far as possible developing countries should not be deprived of the flexibility to design their IP systems that developed countries enjoyed in earlier stages of their own development, and higher IP standards should not be pressed on them without a serious and objective assessment of their development impact" (68 p8).

Despite repeated claims that strong IPRs will benefit the LDCs, the opposite is true. Between 1975 and 2004, only 21 out of 1556 new marketed drugs were indicated for the neglected diseases, such as African trypanosomiasis, Chagas disease, and schistosomiasis, that occur largely or exclusively in the LDCs (69), affect roughly one billion people worldwide, and lead to 530,000 deaths annually (70). In the first half of the

Table 9.1 Year countries adopted product patents and gross domestic product

Developed countries			Developing countries		
Country	Year	Gross domestic product per capita (US$ 1995 exchange rate)	Country	Year	Gross domestic product per capita (US$ 1995 exchange rate)
Switzerland	1977	36,965	China	1992/1993	426
Italy	1978	13,429	Brazil	1996	4474
Netherlands	1978	20,722	Argentina	2000	8174
Sweden	1978	22,178	Guatemala	2000	1563
Denmark	1983	28,010	Uruguay	2001	6193
Austria	1992	24,844	Egypt	(2005)*	1250
Spain	1992	14,384	Pakistan	(2005)*	518
Portugal	1992	10,538	India	(2005)*	493
Greece	1992	11,114	Malawi	(2016)*	157
Norway	1992	30,598			

Source: Lanjouw J, Jack W. Trading up: how much should poor countries pay to support pharmaceutical innovation [Internet]. London (England): Center for Global Development; c2004 [cited 2014 Sept 30]. Available from: http://www.cgdev.org/publication/trading-how-much-should-poor-countries-pay-support-pharmaceutical-innovation

* Year scheduled to adopt full patent rights under TRIPS Agreement

2000s, 5 out of 12 of the top multinational companies were not conducting any research on neglected diseases, and these companies were unwilling to enter this area regardless of any incentives offered (71). Speaking to a reporter from the *Financial Times*, Daniel Vasella, then the CEO of Swiss multinational drug company Novartis, said, "We have no model which would (meet) the need for new drugs in a sustainable way ... You can't expect for-profit organization[s] to do this on a large scale. If you want to establish a system where companies systematically invest in this kind of area, you need a different system" (72). For countries in the Global South, there is no relationship between patent protection and investment in R&D (73). In addition, "the introduction of patents in developing countries has not been followed by greater R&D investment in the diseases that are most prevalent there" (74 p1157) and no relationship exists between whether a country adopts data exclusivity and the amount of investment by the pharmaceutical industry in the country (75).

The bottom line is that strong IPRs do not bring any economic benefits to countries in the Global South, and they do not foster research into diseases prevalent in these countries. Their main effect is to cut off the availability of generic drugs, leaving expensive brand-name drugs on the market. Brand-name drugs are typically more expensive than generics and less available (76). The net result is to make drug treatment much less affordable and, therefore, much more difficult to access.

Conclusion

What this chapter shows is that whenever a conflict has arisen between access to medications and supporting IPRs, the Canadian government, regardless of its political leanings, has at best been neutral, as in the South African court case, or consistently aligned itself with the interests of the pharmaceutical industry and backed stronger IPRs. The "goals of protecting intellectual property and ensuring good trade relations with the United States" have taken precedence over the need for safe, low-cost medications in poor countries (24). Similarly, and not surprisingly, the pharmaceutical industry has been equally strong in supporting IPRs. The triumph of IPRs over access as a human right is a demonstration that both Canadian governments and industry value neo-liberalism, as expressed through individual property rights, over the realization of collective security through access to essential medications. As a result, Canada, backed up by the pharmaceutical industry, has failed in its humanitarian duty to protect the human right to health in the form of safe and low-cost essential medicines for the people in the Global South. The government has not tried to ensure access to appropriate medications for all members of all groups, it has not supported other voices calling for access, and it has not pushed for equity in health states for all social groups.

10 Courage, my friends; 'tis not too late to build a better world (1)

This final chapter puts the conclusions about regulatory failure and the industry bias in economic and industrial policy into the context of the neo-liberal agenda as it pertains to deregulation and the prioritization of private intellectual property rights (IPRs) over public values. It then advocates for the systemic changes necessary to correct that situation.

This book shows that over nearly a hundred years, with a few exceptions, the Canadian state, as represented by the federal government, has sought cooperation with the pharmaceutical industry. Often, the government has gone beyond cooperation and actively promoted industry's interests through legislation and policies, even when the industry's interests conflicted with those of the public. In some areas, it has voluntarily turned over de facto regulatory power to industry.

The alliance of interests between the state and the industry has not been static and has markedly increased over the past two decades. As the neo-liberal agenda gained momentum in the mid-1980s, the deregulation trend in Canada accelerated, further deepening the relationship between Health Canada and the pharmaceutical industry. Neo-liberalism heralded a prioritization of IPRs over public values, affecting drug-pricing policies, the incentives offered for R&D, and Canadian foreign policy on access to drugs in the Global South. It is crucial to emphasize the point that neo-liberalism is not merely another incarnation of laissez-faire capitalism whereby the state stands back and gives the market free rein. Neo-liberalism involves the active participation in *facilitating* markets, that is, the state adopts a bias in favour of corporations.

The symbiotic relationship between the industry and Health Canada existed because, although the Food and Drugs Act and Regulations gave Health Canada significant power, that power was never matched with the necessary resources. The philosophy of cooperation was reinforced by the common culture that bound industry and Health Canada and the movement of government officials to industry. Added to this history was the power the pharmaceutical industry exercised through its lobbying activities and its influence in Quebec because of the significant investment by pharmaceutical companies in the Montreal area. But the primary factor in establishing and reinforcing the cooperative arrangement was the congruent interests of the multinational companies and governments in the United States and Europe that, in turn, used bilateral and multilateral trade deals to achieve their objectives. It would be a mistake to see the Canadian government as a passive victim of external pressure; rather, it actively cooperated by declining to adopt stricter regulatory measures and relinquishing national authority over IPRs.

Neo-liberalism is focused on the regulatory power of the market place and supports the diminishing of the role of the state in protecting its citizens by letting industry set its own regulatory standards and police them. Clientele pluralism had already established this practice of ceding its authority to industry when it came to the governance of promotion and the setting of standards around manufacturing practices. This acceleration in the deference to the industry is best understood in the context of corporate bias. The state did not completely surrender its regulatory role, but attempts to exert more authority, such as inspections of clinical trials, were undertaken in a half-hearted manner that avoided confrontation with industry and actually strengthened the position of industry.

The introduction of user fees from the pharmaceutical companies to help fund part of the drug regulatory process in the mid-1990s demonstrated how Health Canada prioritized the profit-based goals of the pharmaceutical industry over the goals of health protection and safety. User fees established the industry as the client of Health Canada with the obligation to meet the needs of the client, especially when it came to how quickly drugs went through the regulatory review process. Each day of delay in getting a drug onto the market could mean the loss of millions of dollars in sales. Not only were speedier drug reviews made a priority, but Health Canada also devised two mechanisms to get drugs through the system even faster: priority approvals and the Notice of Compliance with conditions (NOC/c). Both mechanisms were much more valuable for industry than for the health of the public. Drugs with marginal value were marketed more rapidly, and drugs that went through the priority review and the NOC/c processes were much more likely to receive serious safety warnings or be pulled off the market, further damaging the health of patients who took them. Focusing on the needs of the industry client also meant that Health Canada was not willing to devote the necessary resources to monitoring the safety of products once they were approved. Even if safety problems were identified, warnings about them could be subject to prolonged negotiations with companies. The value of communications that Health Canada issued to health care professionals and the public regarding safety was never evaluated. Innovation, as defined by Health Canada, was tailored to meet the needs of industry, emphasizing new drug molecules rather than better drug therapy.

Layered on top of poor regulation of clinical trials, faster drug approvals, and poor safety monitoring is the refusal of Health Canada to do anything effective about the way that medications are promoted to doctors and the public. When it comes to drug promotion to doctors, Health Canada never exercised the power that it had. Control over promotion to consumers of both over-the-counter and prescription-only drugs was progressively weakened and handed over to private interests, with little to no oversight by Health Canada. Complaints about regulatory violations in direct-to-consumer advertising of prescription drugs are ignored for months or longer and then dismissed. Despite serious flaws in the Pharmaceutical Advertising Advisory Board and Rx&D codes governing promotion of drugs, Health Canada stands on the sidelines, content to let industry or industry-influenced organizations continue to do a grossly inadequate job. Finally, Health Canada's position vis-à-vis the interests of industry versus those of the public is encapsulated by its obsessiveness in keeping information secret on the grounds that it is commercial business information. This willingness to guard information on behalf of industry, rather than to share it with health care professionals and consumers, is seen in numerous areas: how little information it releases about its inspections of plants and its inspections of the way that industry reports adverse drug reactions in clinical trials, in the minimal amount of safety and efficacy data it releases from industry-supported clinical trials, and in the lack of reporting about the progress of studies required under the NOC/c approval policy. Even the transparency initiatives of the past decade are significantly flawed. The clinical information in the Summary Basis of Decision documents is incomplete and haphazardly reported, the large majority of the drug safety reports produced by Health Canada will not be publicly released, and the long overdue clinical trial registry will not contain any results.

Davis and Abraham's conclusion about what needs to happen to regulation in the neo-liberal era in the United States and the European

Union is equally applicable to Canada: "Broadly speaking, the lesson from the neo-liberal era is that regulatory standards need to be raised and extended in the interests of public health, rather than lowered and loosened. In particular, the narrowly construed definition of regulatory efficiency as speed of regulatory review and marketing approval during the neo-liberal era has been misguided from the perspective of the interests of patients and public health, though it has served the commercial interests of industry" (2 p275).

When it comes to economic and industrial policy, the story is somewhat more nuanced than with regulation. In the 1950s and 1960s, the evidence is that Canada was not overly concerned about the economic health of the pharmaceutical industry. The 1960s were the heyday of economic nationalism, and since the last two Canadian-owned companies of any significant size had been sold to foreign interests, the Canadian government and Canadian society had little sympathy for the pharmaceutical industry. Moreover, the multinational subsidiaries were taking their cue from their parent companies and did not seem to understand that Canada was not simply an extension of the United States. As Lang puts it, "the PMAC was a civil service outcast. Even the sponsoring Department of Industry treated the PMAC as if it had become infected by some strange and infectious disease. Rather than enjoying a close, harmonious and mutually dependent status with a particular government department, the PMAC was shunned by all. The bureaucracy even went so far as to take measures which would shield its deliberations from the association" (3 p296).

By the 1980s, the situation had changed dramatically, as neo-liberalism and free market ascendancy ushered in the era of free trade agreements, with their emphasis on the importance of protecting and strengthening intellectual property rights. Neo-liberalism fitted well with the government's smart regulatory agenda and with the belief that providing the conditions for industry investment and research and development (R&D) would inevitably produce better drugs, better health, more economic activity, and more high-end jobs in the knowledge economy. The key, according to government thinking, was to make sure that companies could retain monopoly rights to the medications for long enough to generate the profits necessary to produce the next generation of "wonder" drugs. Though this arguably made economic sense, it made no sense at all in terms of protecting the public. And, of course, respect for IPRs as private property was a necessary component of this equation. Thus, federal governments from the right (Conservative) and centre (Liberal) were willing to cooperate with industry demands for longer and more stringent patent rights and better data protection and to put in place the NOC Linkage Regulations to delay the entry of generic products. The fact that these decisions might lead to higher drug expenditures did not seem to matter. Industry has used IPR as a bargaining chip in its relations with provincial governments, and at least some, eager for more investment, were supportive of industry. On the economic front, better IPR protection certainly benefits industry, but it is hard to demonstrate that it has helped the overall Canadian economy or the health of Canadians. However, it has generated costs in the form of legal expenses, longer monopoly periods with higher prices, vast sums spent researching and developing "me too" drugs, billions of dollars spent on drug promotion, and restriction on the dissemination of research results to maintain a commercial advantage.

The decision to abolish compulsory licensing as a way of controlling drug spending and to replace it with the Patented Medicine Prices Review Board (PMPRB) might seem reasonable on the surface, since the PMPRB has been successful in controlling the price of individual drugs. But that "control" has kept Canadian drug prices at the fourth highest in the world. New patented drugs are allowed to enter the market at prices equivalent to the highest-priced product in the therapeutic group, regardless of whether they are therapeutically better, the same, or inferior. Companies do not price products based on their R&D costs but rather on what they think that the market will bear. The more desperate the patients are for the drug, the higher the price. This is painfully evident in the price of Kalydeco for cystic fibrosis and Soliris for atypical hemolytic uremic syndrome at $300,000 and $700,000 per year per person, respectively. Moreover, the PMPRB is powerless to deal with the main controllable drivers when it comes to increasing drug expenditures – the techniques that industry has available to affect the mix and volume of drugs that are prescribed. These techniques involve using carrot-and-stick approaches with provincial governments; trying to suppress unfavourable reports; pushing for faster listing on provincial formularies because Health Canada has approved the drug, regardless of its actual therapeutic worth; disparaging the cost-effectiveness evaluations from the Common Drug Review; and funding seemingly independent groups that are willing to lobby on behalf of the products that companies make. The federal government initiated the National Pharmaceuticals Strategy (NPS) to try to deal with some of these issues, but once the Conservatives took over in Ottawa, the NPS died a slow death from neglect.

Policy decisions about R&D have been predicated on the assumption that more R&D is better and that stronger IPRs are necessary to achieve the desired R&D spending. Industry has encouraged that attitude with both threats of withdrawing investment and promises of increasing investment, all contingent on the amount of IPR protection that is offered. However, government has not been a neutral player and has consistently met industry demands, even in the face of shrinking R&D expenditures, in both relative and absolute terms, and declining R&D employment. Government has also failed to recognize the difference between the industry definition of *innovation* as a new molecule and the patient-oriented definition as a drug that substantially improves health. Finally, government has allowed the priorities of publicly funded research through the Canadian Institutes of Health Research (CIHR) to align with the commercial priorities of the drug companies. Funding priorities are unquestionably skewed in favour of the corporate sector rather than what will yield the greatest health benefits. Universities are eyeing the pot of gold at the end of the commercialization rainbow and are similarly in danger of having their public values undermined. Last, not only does the fetishization of IPRs affect domestic policy, but it has also influenced Canadian foreign policy when it comes to helping countries in the Global South access safe and affordable essential medicines. Over the past decade and a half, the Canadian position has been, at best, that of a neutral observer and, most of the time, it has actively worked to restrict access.

The problems we are seeing are, obviously, not the result of a group of malevolent people within the drug companies, Health Canada, or the government in general. In fact, many good people work in all sectors. The problems are structural and only system changes will help solve them. However, despite both parties – government and industry – being part of the problem, only one is part of the solution.

There's a fable about a scorpion and a frog. The scorpion comes to a river that she wants to cross, but being unable to swim, approaches a frog and asks if the frog will take her across the river on his back. The frog replies that the scorpion will sting him and kill him, but the scorpion points out that if she stings the frog while they are crossing the river, they will both die. The frog sees the logic in this and lets the scorpion climb on. As they are crossing the river, the scorpion stings the frog. As they are drowning, the frog asks why the scorpion did it, and she replies, "It's what I do, it's my nature." The drug industry is the scorpion and instead of stinging, it makes money for its shareholders. Indeed, investor-owned drug companies have a fiduciary responsibility to make as much money as possible. As Milton Friedman so famously said: "Few trends could so thoroughly undermine the foundation of our free society as the acceptance by corporation officials of a social responsibility other than to make as much money for their shareholders as possible (4 p133)." As long as companies do nothing illegal, then we should expect them to do everything they can to make money. But what is expected of Health Canada, and the Canadian government in general, is that its primary purpose is to protect the public interest, not to serve commercial interests. What we are seeing is institutional corruption. Here, I am using the term as defined by Lawrence Lessig: "Institutional corruption is manifest when there is a systemic and strategic influence which is legal, or even currently ethical, that undermines the institution's effectiveness by diverting it from its purpose or weakening its ability to achieve its purpose, including, to the extent relevant to its purpose, weakening either the public's trust in that institution or the institution's inherent trustworthiness" (5 p553). Health Canada has been corrupted by the combination of clientele pluralism, corporate bias, and now, the deregulatory culture that accompanies neo-liberalism.

To counter that corruption, any reforms need to deal with the underlying causes. The difficulty in proposing reforms is that they need to be realistic without sacrificing ideals, and they need to be sufficiently radical to significantly alter the current situation. I have tried to incorporate these principles into what I recommend. In line with the focus of this book on the federal government, the reforms will be directed at what that level of government should do and not deal with provincial governments. (See Box 10.1 for a summary of all of the recommendations for reforming pharmaceutical policy.)

BOX 10.1 SUMMARY OF RECOMMENDATIONS FOR REFORMING PHARMACEUTICAL POLICY IN CANADA

- Health Canada should be funded solely from parliamentary appropriations and user fees should be eliminated.
- Overall funding for Health Canada should be increased.
- Health Canada should require all clinical trials done in Canada to be registered and refuse to consider any new drug application where this has not been done.

- Registration data should at a minimum comply with standards set by the World Health Organization.
- Health Canada should conditionally approve new drugs until all results are reported in a publicly available manner.
- Health Canada should publicly release clinical study reports after a new drug is approved.
- Health Canada should publicly release all safety data regardless of whether a new drug is approved or denied.
- Health Canada should provide more information about the clinical trials that it requires for drugs approved under its Notice of Compliance with conditions policy.
- Health Canada should release redacted reports about new drug applications from Health Canada's reviewers.
- Health Canada should release records showing the process that it uses when it makes decisions about drug warnings or removing drugs from the market.
- Health Canada should stop negotiating with companies over the wording of safety advisories.
- Health Canada should involve the wider community in its decision-making about drug approvals and safety issues by holding public advisory committee hearings. Membership in these committees should be restricted to people without financial conflicts of interest with industry.
- Health Canada should create a public interest advisory committee comprising representatives of those consumer and patient organizations that are not industry funded.
- Health Canada should devote more resources to improving its accuracy in identifying new drugs that offer significant therapeutic advantages.
- Health Canada should intensively monitor postmarket safety for drugs approved in less than the standard 300 days.
- Health Canada should work with the United States Food and Drug Administration and the European Medicines Agency to require clinical trials to use active controls and placebo controls and to test me too drugs in people who have not responded to the usual therapy.
- Except in exceptional circumstances, Health Canada should require clinical trials with hard clinical outcomes.
- The Common Drug Review should make a recommendation for public funding conditional on the existence of clinical trials with both active controls and hard clinical outcomes.

- At a minimum, the funding for clinical trials should continue to come from pharmaceutical companies but that money should be managed by an independent organization, such as the Canadian Institutes of Health Research, that would select the researchers.
- The Canadian government should explore the feasibility of public funding for clinical trials.
- The Canadian government should institute a tax on the money that pharmaceutical companies spend on promotion and use that money to fund independent clinical trials.
- Health Canada should take action to stop the use of reminder ads and help-seeking ads.
- Cross-border advertising of prescription drugs should be stopped.
- Regulation of advertising of over-the-counter drugs should be taken out of the hands of private organizations, and all print and broadcast ads should be prescreened.
- All promotion should be governed by an independent agency that is established in legislation.
- The independent agency regulating drug promotion should use a pyramid of sanctions approach to penalize drug companies that engage in illegal promotion.
- The independent agency regulating drug promotion should explore different methods of funding for its activities.
- Newly approved drugs should be identified by a prominent marker on their packaging and all printed promotional materials to enhance reporting of adverse drug reactions.
- Health Canada should institute a prescription event monitoring system to increase its ability to detect new and unexpected adverse drug effects.
- Health Canada should work with provincial and territorial governments to ensure that all provinces and territories develop drug databases with fields to enter adverse drug reactions.
- Health Canada should undertake a thorough systematic review of how it communicates drug safety information to health care professionals and the public.
- The Canadian government should refrain from signing any new trade deals that impose stricter standards for intellectual property rights or investor-state dispute settlement mechanisms.
- The Canadian government should repeal the Notice of Compliance Linkage Regulations.

- The Canadian government should amend the Patent Act so that minor variations of an existing drug are not eligible for a new patent.
- The Patent Medicine Prices Review Board should amend its regulations so that new entries into an existing therapeutic class are priced to the level of generic drugs in that class.
- The Patent Medicine Prices Review Board should expand the number of countries that it uses to set Canadian prices.
- The Canadian government should develop a national universal pharmacare plan to help control drug prices through stronger bargaining power.
- The Canadian government should consider replacing the Patented Medicine Prices Review Board with a different mechanism to control drug prices and spending.
- The Canadian government should work with the provinces to develop mechanisms to improve the prescribing practices of health care professionals.
- The Canadian government should consider ways of providing objective prescribing drug information to health care professionals.
- The Canadian government should provide leadership in linking provincial and territorial databases to be able to evaluate how health care professionals prescribe.
- The Canadian government should implement a version of the US Sunshine Act requiring pharmaceutical companies to disclose payments to doctors.
- Decisions about whether to encourage pharmaceutical companies to invest in research and development in Canada should be part of a wide societal debate.
- The Canadian government should increase funding for biomedical research.
- The Canadian government should consider funding the equivalent of the Italian Mario Negri Institute for Pharmacological Research where independent research could be done.
- The Canadian government should stop appointing people with corporate interests to the board of the Canadian Institutes of Health Research.
- The Canadian government should revise the legislation creating the Canadian Institutes of Health Research to emphasize that its primary commitment is to improving public health and advancing health research.
- The Canadian government should support domestic and international policies that increase access to low-cost, effective medicines in the Global South.

Eliminate corporate funding to Health Canada

The history of a clientele pluralist relationship cannot be changed, and reforming the drug regulatory system will not get at the roots of neoliberalism, but the factors that have strengthened and deepened the relationship between the industry and Health Canada can be weakened. The first step is to address the dependence of Health Canada on industry funding for half the operating budget of the drug regulatory system. When the US Congress was debating renewing the legislation allowing user fees, Dr Jerry Avorn wrote that legislators believed that user fees were saving the public money (6). His conclusion, that in drug regulation nothing is free, applies equally well in Canada; either implicitly or explicitly the drug companies expect something for their money. Parliament needs to provide Health Canada with the resources needed to perform its assigned tasks without relying on corporate funding that leaves it vulnerable to biases. Besides fully funding Health Canada out of parliamentary appropriations, overall per capita funding should be increased to at least the level present in the United States. In 2013, the US Food and Drug Administration's (FDA) budget for the regulation of human drugs (excluding veterinary medicines) was US$1.04 billion or US$3.39 per capita (C$1.07 billion or C$4.29 per capita, based on the 2013 average exchange rate) (7). In contrast, in 2009–10 (the most recent available data), the regulatory branches of Health Canada had an operating cost base of C$98.2 million or C$2.91 per capita (8). If Health Canada had the same resources for drug product regulation as the FDA does, its budget would be $46.5 million larger.

Register all clinical trials done in Canada

The lack of transparency exhibited by Health Canada means no independent check is done on the quality of its work and Health Canada's reviewers have no way to get independent feedback. Information may be missed or misinterpreted, leaving clinicians and patients with incomplete and possibly misleading information on which to base their prescribing and drug-taking decisions. Health Canada needs to begin by requiring registration of any type of clinical trials done in Canada. All the information required by the World Health Organization (WHO) in a clinical trial registry (9) should be present, and Health Canada should refuse to consider any new drug application with incomplete data registration. It also needs to require reporting of trial results in registries, at a minimum to the standards in the draft WHO statement: "1. The main findings of clinical trials to be submitted for publication in a peer reviewed journal within 18 months of study completion and are to be published through an open access mechanism unless there is a specific reason why open access cannot be used, or otherwise made available publicly at most within 30 months of study completion. 2. In addition the key outcomes are to be made publicly available by posting to the results section of the primary clinical trial registry. Where a registry is used without a results database available, the results should be posted on a free-to-access, publicly available, searchable institutional website of the Regulatory Sponsor, Funder or Principal Investigator" (10). An up-to-date and comprehensive "registry of all clinical trials and their results would enable more comprehensive and less biased studies and meta-analyses of the clinical efficacy, off-label use, and safety of pharmaceuticals" (11 p2342). But passing laws is not enough; results are reported on time in the US National Institutes of Health's clinicaltrials.gov for fewer than one in eight trials and, although US law allows for imposing fines of $10,000 per day, there is no record of any fine ever being imposed (11). Complete registration would be more likely to happen if Health Canada gave drugs an initial conditional approval and converted that to a full approval only after all results were reported.

Automatically release clinical study reports when drugs are approved

Registration is only the first step in transparency. Clinical study reports are documents providing detailed information about trials and are often thousands of pages. Twice as much patient-relevant information is in these reports than is found in registries or any other publicly available source including journal articles (12). These documents, redacted to remove true manufacturing secrets and the identities of any individual patients, should be automatically released when a drug is approved.

Automatically release all safety data when drugs are approved or denied

Transparency applies equally as well to safety information. All the safety data that Health Canada receives and produces, including the company generated Periodic Safety Update Reports, need to be freely publicly available. New drugs or new indications for existing drugs may be initially refused approval but later granted approval. The new drug may be related to one already on the market and, therefore, if the new product has problems, those problems may also apply to the existing drug. Doctors may already be prescribing a drug off-label, and if the company marketing the drug applies to have this indication approved and approval is refused, either because the data shows that it is ineffective or unsafe, then patients' health is at risk, and this knowledge needs to be made public. The public and clinicians have a right to know why Health Canada changed its decision and that means that the agency needs to release the names of drugs that were denied approval and the reasons for those decisions. Finally, we need much more detailed information about the clinical trials that Health Canada requires for drugs approved under its NOC/c policy – what is the status of the trial, whether it has been delayed, and the reasons for the delay. Health Canada needs to not just publicly announce when the trials are completed but also to make sure that the results are either posted to a registry or published in a journal article, and information about how to access these results should be reported on the Health Canada website.

Transparency in how Health Canada makes decisions

Transparency also means being open about how decisions are made. Issues about drug safety and effectiveness are rarely black and white, but when Health Canada approves a new drug or a new indication for an existing product, that nuanced information is not conveyed to either clinicians or patients. Since there is no access to reviewers' reports, it is not possible to determine which drugs they were enthusiastic about and which ones they were sceptical about (13). The FDA releases redacted reports from its reviewers that contain detailed analyses of the data that companies have submitted, and Health Canada should do the same in a standardized format to make sure that the necessary information that is included is easily identified. Similarly, we need to see how Health Canada makes its decisions about safety issues. Health Canada should release records showing the process that it uses when it decides to issue a safety warning about a drug or withdraw a drug from the market, including its interactions with industry about these decisions. The agency needs to break with its current practice of negotiating safety letters and withdrawals with industry, because this negotiation process has the potential to water down or delay the message that needs to be transmitted, as an example from the United States shows. The FDA wanted to add a warning to the Vioxx (rofecoxib) label about cardiovascular risks in light of the findings from the VIGOR trial, but the pharmaceutical industry objected. The resulting negotiations took over a year, and rather than going into the "warning" section of the label, it ended up in the less prominent "precautions" section and was said to be of unknown clinical significance (14).

Institute a transparent system of public hearings and advisory committee meetings

Health Canada needs to involve the wider community in its decision making about drug approvals and safety issues. One of the few times that Health Canada held hearings before approving a new drug was when it was considering the controversial injectable hormonal contraceptive Depo-Provera (depot medroxyprogesterone). Strong protest came from women's groups across the country, as did a demand for public input into the decision. The concession from Health Canada was to appoint a panel to hold meetings in six cities to hear submissions about all methods of contraception. The hearings were not open to the public, and presentations of briefs to the panel were by invitation only. Even a list of invited participants' names had scrawled across the top of it, "Do not release to the media or the public. The meeting is *by invitation only*" (emphasis in original) (15 pA8). Health Canada's defence was that people would not come forward if the meetings were public.

Instead of replicating this flawed model for involving the public and outside experts, Health Canada should adopt the model used by the FDA for advisory committee hearings but improve on the negative elements. These hearings are held for about 25% of the new drugs the agency considers each year. Some of the circumstances that can trigger a hearing are when drugs are particularly controversial, when they might pose significant safety risks, or when they are exerting their effect through a new pathway. Near the middle of the meeting is a 60-minute open public hearing session, and any member of the public who has signed up in advance can make his or her opinion known about the drug. The public is also entitled to all the documentation previously made available to the experts who sit on the committee (16). But unlike committee members, who receive the information at least three weeks before the meeting, the public receives Internet access to this information usually just 48 hours before the meeting. Hearings should be held to discuss not only drug approvals but also drug withdrawals, unless the safety issue is so acute that the drug needs to be taken off the market immediately, but even in these cases Health Canada still needs to publicly explain its reasoning. Finally, as with the FDA, these committes should have voting consumer members to advocate from a consumer perspective.

In calling for Canada to emulate the FDA system of advisory committees, I am conscious of the failings of the US system, for example, ignoring committee recommendations for overtly political reasons, as was the case with the recommendation to allow Plan B, the so-called morning after pill, to be sold over-the-counter (17) or having people with financial conflicts of interest on the committees (18). Some potential committee members have been allegedly excluded because of an "intellectual bias" against the drug being considered (19). The opening public session, at times, has people that the company has brought in to testify in favour of the product under consideration (20).

Use "public interest" advisory committees with representatives of consumer and patient organizations

Along with expert advisory committees, there should be a "public interest" advisory committee comprising representatives of consumer and patient organizations that are not industry funded and have already proven themselves to have a special interest in medicines safety, plus some direct citizen participation based on statistical representation (21). Not only would such a committee expose Health Canada staff to opinions of non-experts, but it would also provide an opening for wider scrutiny of the documentation that companies submit when seeking approval for new drugs or additions to the indications for older ones. The National Institute for Health and Care Excellence (NICE), the body in the United Kingdom that evaluates health technology, has a Citizens Council of 30 members of the public that largely reflect the demographic characteristics of the United Kingdom. Members are recruited by an independent organization, serve for up to three years, and provide NICE with a public perspective on overarching moral and ethical issues that NICE has to take account of when producing guidance (22).

Intensify postmarket safety monitoring for drugs brought to market quickly

Health Canada should continue to make drugs with significant new therapeutic value available as quickly as possible, but at present its ability to identify these drugs is not well developed, and it needs to devote more resources to improving the accuracy of its decisions. Even if it is better able to identify the therapeutic value of the drugs, strong evidence shows that drugs approved in shorter times are much more likely to either need a serious safety warning or to be withdrawn because of safety problems. Therefore, all of these drugs brought to market more rapidly should be subjected to intensive safety monitoring so that if safety issues develop, they will be recognized early.

Refuse placebo-only trials and surrogate trials and require superiority testing

Many drugs are approved based on clinical trials against placebos, using surrogate endpoints and a non-inferiority or an equivalence design. Surrogate endpoints are measurements such as changes in the level of blood glucose or whether a tumour shrinks in size. The problem with trials using these designs is that they don't provide doctors and patients with any information about what the ultimate effect on health will be and on where the new drug fits into the therapies that are already available. Garattini and Bertelé argue that non-inferiority and equivalence trials are unethical and should not be allowed (23). A non-inferiority trial is one that compares the efficacy or safety of the new drug with the standard treatment (or placebo). The new drug is declared acceptable even if it is not as efficacious or safe, as long as the difference is within a predefined limit. Depending on the limit, this type of trial could be used to approve a product that is actually less efficacious or safe than the standard therapy. An equivalence trial aims to show that the new drug is not much worse than the comparator (as in non-inferiority trials) but also is not much better. These types of trials are typically used for what are commonly referred to as "me too" drugs, that is, drugs that are molecular variants of medicines already on the market. Drug companies argue that they don't need to show that the benefit to harm ratio of new products is better than those of existing products. They claim that the added value of the new drug is that some patients who will not respond to standard drug therapy might respond to the new one or that some patients will experience fewer side effects. This would be a reasonable argument, except that these trials are never done on non-responders but on the entire group of patients who need the particular type of treatment.

It is probably a good idea to have a choice of drugs in the same therapeutic class, but it is likely that in many cases the number of me too drugs is excessive. Norway had nine beta-blockers, a type of drug used to treat hypertension and heart disease, on the market in 1981, compared with 11 in The Netherlands, and only 1.6% of Norwegian cardiologists thought too few drugs of this type were available (24). In the case of non-steroidal anti-inflammatory drugs Norway had 7 versus 22 in The Netherlands in 1980, and three-quarters of Norwegian rheumatologists were comfortable with that number (25).

According to Garattini and Bertelé, non-inferiority studies betray the trust of patients who are enrolled in them, because they do not offer any possible advantage and expose patients to a treatment that may actually be worse than available therapies. Development of me too drugs serves a commercial interest much more than a health interest. In most cases, no adequate comparative evaluation exists in terms of efficacy or toxicity. Although new me too drugs may appear to be equivalent to existing ones, "the equivalence is only apparent because trials are small, the prototype drugs are sometimes not employed using the best dose and schedule of treatment, the evaluation is made with surrogate end-points (for example antihypertensive effect instead of cardiovascular severe events), the trials are of short duration in relation to the proposed length of utilization, and are too small and therefore not powerful enough to identify small differences" (26).

Chapter 2 discussed the problems with the use of placebo controls and the lack of comparative evidence when new drugs are approved. The requirement for comparative trials is a position increasingly supported by the European Medicines Agency (EMA), and it has recommended the use of trials involving standard treatments when a new drug might be associated with safety or inferiority concerns (27). Asking Health Canada to undertake such a change in requirements to get a new drug approved will require not only the agency but the entire government to make a 180-degree turn in its philosophy. In the past, Health Canada specifically rejected evaluating the advantages and disadvantages "to having as an additional approval criteria, the requirement of proof/evidence of improved effectiveness, less toxicity or less ADRs for all new drug submissions compared to products currently on the market for the same indication" (28 p167). The reason this question was not thought necessary to answer was that "any requirement for additional approval criteria would be the result of a political decision ... It seems unlikely that the present or any foreseeable Canadian government would be inclined to take such a decision" (28 p173).

Relying on surrogate trials as the sole basis for clinical decision making is, in most circumstances, fundamentally flawed. Only in very limited circumstances could surrogate endpoints reasonably be used, for example, in the case of very rare diseases, validation of hard endpoints may take an unreasonable time to complete. Surrogates may also be justified in guiding therapy in circumstances such as exposure to biological/chemical weapons, where it is ethically impossible to test candidate drugs (29). In all other circumstances, Health Canada should require the use of clinical trials with hard clinical outcomes.

On its own, Health Canada may not have the power to force a change in the design of clinical trials given the relatively small size of the Canadian market; but it is feasible for it to take the lead in working with the FDA and the EMA in pushing for changes whereby regulators would not accept trials against only placebos when effective treatments already exist and would demand that companies conduct superiority trials and use hard clinical outcomes instead of surrogate endpoints. For me too drugs, companies should be required to test them in people who have not responded to the usual therapy to show that these drugs actually have some additional value.

The Common Drug Review, the federal-provincial-territorial body that advises provincial and territorial public plans about whether to fund new drugs, has a role to play in pushing companies to do superiority tests with hard clinical outcomes. It should make a recommendation for public funding conditional on either the existence of these types of trials or else the commitment of the company marketing the drug to initiate and complete such a trial.

Sequester the money for clinical trials from their design, conduct, and analysis

These reforms still leave the design, conduct, and analysis of clinical trials in the hands of drug companies, with the possibility that commercial concerns will bias their outcome. British economist Alan Maynard notes, "Economic theory predicts that firms will invest in corruption of the evidence base wherever its benefits exceed its costs. If detection is costly for regulators, corruption of the evidence base can be expected to be extensive. Investment in biasing the evidence base, both clinical and economic, in pharmaceuticals is likely to be detailed and comprehensive, covering all aspects of the appraisal process. Such investment is likely to be extensive as the scientific and policy discourses are technical and esoteric, making detection difficult and expensive" (30). University of Manitoba bioethicist Arthur Schafer proposes a "sequestration thesis" or the complete separation of researchers from the process of commercialization, which would include isolating industry from clinical trial data as a way to avoid many of the biases associated with industry-financed and -run clinical trials (31). While companies would continue to develop and market their products and pay for the trials, they would be separated from the process of generating and interpreting the clinical data about them. This model would see the money for the studies go to an institution, such as the CIHR, that would then ask for proposals from independent researchers to design, organize, and manage clinical trials and the data that comes from them. Requiring companies to fund the trials would "discourage the wholesale testing of marginal drugs with little therapeutic value, or candidate medicines with little chance of clinical adoption" (32 p3).

A more radical version of the sequestration thesis would see a system whereby all clinical trials would be publicly financed and then non-exclusive licences sold to multiple companies, leading to the low prices that come with competition. The saving to public drug plans from much lower costs could then be used to fund the trials (33). Whether this latter version of sequestration would be feasible in Canada would need careful study.

Even without public funding for all trials, some will still need to be paid for using tax dollars, for example, studies for new uses of drugs that are off-patent and comparative trials, such as the ALLHAT study that looked at the effectiveness of different classes of antihypertensives in decreasing morbidity and mortality (34). One way of paying for these trials would be to adopt the Italian model of imposing a tax on drug-promotion spending and then using the revenue. Italy has a 5% tax that is used to finance independent research in three main areas: orphan drugs for rare diseases and drugs for non-responders to conventional treatment, comparative studies (including head-to-head comparison of drugs and therapeutic strategies), and studies on the appropriateness of drug use, pharmacovigilance, and outcome research. Between 2005 and 2007, 151 studies were approved for funding for about €78 million (35). With $2.38 to $4.75 billion spent on promotion annually in Canada (see Chapter 4), a 5% tax would generate between $119 million and $237.5 million annually.

Meaningful, independent regulation of drug promotion

Poor regulation of drug promotion is not just a Canadian problem; no country in the world does a good job at controlling it. Overall, the FDA receives 75,000 to 80,000 individual pieces of promotional material per year (36) and, as of 2008, had just 50 full-time staff and a budget of $9 million (37), an amount of money that is dwarfed by what the pharmaceutical industry spends on promotion. The FDA has acknowledged that it can't review all submissions because of the volume that it receives (38). Sales representatives in Australia routinely did not comply with provisions in the industry self-regulatory marketing code (39). Low quality in medical journal advertising is a global phenomenon (40).

Canada does not allow direct-to-consumer advertising (DTCA) that mentions both the name of the drug and its indication, unlike New Zealand and the United States, but its loose enforcement of existing regulations about DTCA means that ads that skirt the boundary of what is legal are common occurrences. The changes needed to current Canadian practices are clear-cut. Health Canada should repeal the interpretation of policies allowing reminder and help-seeking ads, ads that mention the name of a drug, and those that encourage people to see their doctor for a particular medical problem. The Canadian government has the jurisdictional authority to require media companies to remove cross-border DTCA advertising and it should exercise this authority. Regulation of advertising of OTC drugs should be taken out of the hands of private organizations, and all print and broadcast ads should be prescreened. All promotion should be governed by an independent agency that is established in legislation so that it has the legal authority to ensure compliance or, when compliance is lacking, to impose sanctions. Organizations independent of any groups that generate revenue from pharmaceutical promotion but are connected with drug therapy, for example, health professional organizations, patient and consumer groups, and guideline creation groups, could nominate representatives to this body with the final selection being made by government.

Ayres and Braithwaite argue in favour of an explicit enforcement pyramid (41). Defection from compliance is much more likely for a business facing a regulator with a single deterrence option, which is the case with many existing voluntary codes and for many government regulatory agencies, compared with a regulator with an explicit enforcement pyramid. This is true even where the one deterrence option available to the regulator is maximally potent, because it becomes politically impossible and morally unacceptable to use it with any but the most extraordinary offences. Using a pyramid approach, the range of sanctions could start with a simple warning letter for minor violations and range up to measures such as a requirement to send out remedial material, suspension of the ability to promote the product for a time, and fines and criminal prosecution, depending on the severity of the offence. Funding of this new regulatory agency needs to be based on two principles. First, revenue should be both stable and predictable so that the regulatory body can plan future activities, guarantee the maintenance of standards, and not be forced to cut back on its activities. Second, the level of financing must not be tied to performance criteria set up for the regulatory body to preserve the agency's independence; performance standards should reflect public health objectives, not financial requirements. Six possible non-mutually exclusive models are available to generate revenue for regulating promotion (42):

1 A fee paid by pharmaceutical companies for each unique piece of promotional material (pamphlet, direct mail, advertisement, written or visual content of company-controlled continuing education, etc.) that they create or an overall tax on promotion;
2 A fee paid by pharmaceutical companies to regulatory authorities when drugs are submitted for approval or annual fees paid for drugs already on the market;
3 A fee from payers (government, insurance plans, individuals) or pharmaceutical companies for each prescription dispensed;
4 A fine paid by pharmaceutical companies for violations of the regulatory code;
5 Public funding from general tax revenue;
6 Payment from social insurance and mutual insurance funds.

All these proposals have their strengths and weaknesses, and these need to be kept in mind in making any final decision. For example, levying a fee for each piece of promotional material would provide stable funding unless the volume of promotion fell off dramatically, but it might also create a conflict of interest similar to what exists between the industry and Health Canada in the drug-approval process (42).

Strengthen the ability to detect adverse drug reactions

Some reforms to enhance drug safety have already been discussed. Beyond these measures, much more needs to be done. Reporting adverse drug reactions needs to be encouraged by providing timely and useful feedback to people filing reports. Newly approved drugs should be identified by a prominent marker on their packaging and all printed promotional materials about them to let both patients and doctors know that limited safety information exists about these products. The United Kingdom has been using an inverted black triangle for this purpose for a number of years (43), and this measure could be easily adopted in Canada at minimal cost. Canada should adopt a prescription event monitoring (PEM) system to identify new and unexpected adverse effects. PEM is a system whereby all prescriptions issued for particular drugs over a specified time are collected, and the patients issued these prescriptions are tracked to look for any untoward events. The Intensive Medicines Monitoring Program based at the University of Otago in New Zealand uses a PEM system through prospective observational population studies of selected new drugs. The groups of patients are established from prescription data received from hospital and community pharmacies. Questionnaires are sent to the prescribers at regular intervals, requesting information on any adverse events that have occurred since the most recent prescription (44). PEM is also undertaken in the United Kingdom by the Drug Safety Research Unit (DSRU). An electronic copy of targeted prescriptions, written by general practitioners and submitted to the Prescription Pricing Authority for reimbursement, is transmitted to the DSRU. The DSRU requests prescribers of target medicines to voluntarily complete a "green card form" questionnaire for each patient detailing any adverse drug event(s), including death, following the prescription of newly marketed drugs (45, 46). Typically, 60% to 80% of questionnaires sent to doctors are returned (47–49).

Health Canada should work with provincial and territorial governments to ensure that all provinces develop drug databases with fields to enter adverse drug reactions so that this information is available to all health care professionals, with the permission of the patients. Finally, Health Canada needs to undertake a thorough systematic review of how it communicates drug safety information to health care professionals and the public and evaluate whether these methods lead to the desired changes in the way that drugs are prescribed and used.

Get IPR provisions out of trade agreements

IPRs have damaging effects on how much Canada spends on prescription drugs, have a negative economic impact when it comes to the methods that we use to encourage R&D, and have led Canada to lose sight of its humanitarian goals. Reforming IPRs in Canada will be even more difficult than dealing with deregulation. The scope and functions of a drug regulatory system are still a national decision, although the pressure to adopt guidelines agreed to by the International Conference on Harmonization can be very strong. IPRs are embedded into free trade agreements, the most prominent of which is the Agreement on Trade-Related Aspects of Intellectual Property Rights (TRIPS) administered by the World Trade Organization (WTO). Amending the TRIPS Agreement would require the unanimous consent of all 160 member countries. Therefore, the 20-year patent period for pharmaceutical products is not going to be altered soon. The importance of the point about embedding IPR provisions into trade agreements is particularly acute in Canada today because of the Comprehensive Economic Trade Agreement (CETA) between Canada and the European Union. As Chapter 6 describes, this agreement grants companies up to a two-year extension on their patents and embeds an eight-year data exclusivity period into Canadian IPR laws. Although the CETA has been signed, it has not been ratified and, therefore, theoretically it is still possible to remove the IPR provisions. Canada may want to extend patent rights and keep data exclusivity at eight years, but without being in the CETA they remain subject to change by a future Canadian government. Retaining them in the CETA means that, for all practical purposes, they can never be altered, and the same is true for the enhanced IPR provisions in the recently concluded Trans-Pacific Partnership (50). Canada should seriously consider trying to renegotiate these onerous clauses in both agreements and work to keep so-called TRIPS Plus provisions out of any future agreements it is party to.

The CETA also includes an investor-state dispute settlement (ISDS) mechanism that allows companies to sue governments for government actions that the companies see as threatening their profits. Eli Lilly is already using this provision in NAFTA to try to get around the way that Canadian courts have interpreted Canada's Patent Act. Including ISDS in other trade agreements would mean that companies based in a wider range of countries would also be able to challenge the way that Canada deals with IPRs.

Contrary to popular belief, the TRIPS Agreement does allow for compulsory licensing and does not list any specific conditions necessary for it to be used, and the Doha Declaration on TRIPS and Public Health (see Chapter 9) confirms that countries are free to determine the grounds for granting compulsory licences (51). Following the Doha Declaration, the Canadian government pledged not to use the decision to import drugs produced under a compulsory licence (52), but this pledge is not part of any legal obligation. Therefore, it would be theoretically possible for Canada to implement compulsory licensing once again, but this decision would be highly controversial and the likelihood of it happening is extremely small. Other reforms, while difficult, are more feasible. Aside from the United States, Canada is the only other country in the Global North to allow brand-name companies to delay the regulatory approval of generic drugs by claiming that their patents are being violated. Repealing the NOC Linkage Regulations would mean quicker access to lower cost generic products.

Section 3(d) of the India Patents Act says that "the mere discovery of a new form of a known substance which does not result in the enhancement of the known efficacy of that substance" is not a patentable invention, meaning that many forms of evergreening, such as producing minor variations of known drugs, could not be patented unless they are shown to be substantially more effective than the original drug. When Novartis challenged this clause in a case involving its drug Gleevec (imatinib) in the Indian court system, it ultimately lost at the Supreme Court (53). Amending the Canadian Patent Act with a similar clause would have a major effect in inhibiting evergreening and in allowing faster entry of generics.

Reform how Canada sets drug prices

The purpose behind the way that Canada sets prices for patented medicines is to encourage companies to invest in R&D and, in that respect, it has been a failure. Even if prices were successful in incentivizing R&D, because the PMPRB allows companies to price new drugs up to the level of existing products in the same therapeutic category, we would likely get more me too drugs rather than drugs for unmet medical needs (54). Regulations governing how the PMPRB sets maximum prices should be changed so that new entries into existing therapeutic classes are priced to the level of generic drugs in that class, unless the new product offers a proven therapeutic improvement. External reference pricing, that is, setting Canadian prices based on what other countries allow, is fraught with difficulties because it assumes that these countries have accurately assessed the value of new drugs. Moreover, drug companies typically introduce new drugs into the American and German markets first (55) because of the relative lack of price controls in those countries that allow them to charge high prices (56). Companies then use American and German prices as benchmarks for prices in other countries. Moving beyond the seven countries that the PMPRB currently uses and incorporating a wider range of countries would lower Canadian prices, as Chapter 7 showed. Reviving elements in the National Pharmaceuticals Strategy, such as catastrophic insurance (or better still a national first-dollar, universal pharmacare plan) and a national formulary would help with controlling prices because they would provide even stronger bargaining power than the pan-Canadian Pharmaceutical Alliance currently offers.

A more basic question is whether the PMPRB should continue to use external reference pricing as a means of establishing the price of patented medicines or whether the PMPRB should be abandoned and replaced by another means of controlling prices. Other methods are operating in different countries or have been proposed, but they would have to be carefully assessed to see if they are suitable for Canada. New Zealand probably has the most aggressive mix of tools to control drug prices, including internal-reference-based pricing, similar to the system used in British Columbia (see Chapter 7) but covering a much wider range of drug groups. It also uses multi-product agreements whereby companies agree to lower the price on a drug already covered to get a new one listed, tendering for drugs no longer under patent to generate price competition among companies, and expenditure caps that limit spending when there is uncertainty and potential risk around the likely uptake of the medicine (57). Without PHARMAC, the agency that manages the New Zealand drug budget, expenditures were projected to grow from NZ$517 million in 2000 to NZ$2.336 billion in 2012, but instead were only NZ$777 million (58). In talking about controlling drug prices in the United States, Finkelstein and Temin advocate for the creation of an independent, public, non-profit drug development corporation that would act as an intermediary to acquire new drugs that emerge from private sector R&D and then transfer nonexclusive rights to sell the drugs to a different set of firms, effectively generating price competition (59).

Deal with the volume and mix effects that drive drug expenditures

Besides dealing with the prices of drugs, a strategy needs to be developed for countering the volume and mix effects that drive expenditures. Many of the changes that are needed involve the provincial and territorial governments because they deal with the price of generic drugs or fall under the rubric of the practice of medicine and the practice of pharmacy that traditionally have been regulated by the provinces. Still, nothing is stopping the federal government from coordinating some of the reforms or providing money to the provinces and territories to help them do the coordination. For instance, academic detailing, where pharmacists (or other health care professionals) who are trained in educational techniques visit doctors to talk about ways to improve prescribing, has been shown to be successful in optimizing prescribing behaviour (60). However, at present only four provinces have province-wide programs, and the one in Alberta closed in 2010 because of lack of funding (61).

The federal government needs to help get comparative drug information to doctors and other prescribers across Canada, possibly through providing the *Compendium of Therapeutic Choices*, produced by the Canadian Pharmacists Association, free to all prescribers in Canada, just as the British government provides the *British National Formulary* free to health care professionals in that country. Although the Canadian government would subsidize the distribution costs, the actual material in the volume is under the control of the Canadian Pharmacists Association, removing suspicion that the main purpose of the book is to save the government money on drug costs.

Being able to analyse prescribing patterns could be a powerful tool in developing educational strategies for doctors, but that requires capturing all prescriptions that have been filled. Currently, most provinces and territories only collect data for people who are covered under their provincial drug plans. A minority of provinces have information about all prescriptions filled (62) and there is no way of linking the provincial databases. Federal leadership in linking databases would provide a powerful tool for evaluating how doctors prescribe.

Transparency in drug company payments to doctors

A critical element in ensuring appropriate prescribing is addressing the issue of conflict of interest between the medical profession and the industry, something that Health Canada has been loath to undertake. A hidden method of promotion is the payments that companies make to doctors for activities such as sitting on advisory boards and doing speaking engagements on behalf of drugs that the companies make. Many of these doctors also sit on committees that construct clinical practice guidelines that play a major role in guiding prescribing practices (63). Conflicts of interest lead to biases in the guidelines in favour of the companies with which doctors have relationships (64). While many guidelines have conflict-of-interest declarations from the people who developed them, declarations are not universal, and in Canada no publicly available way exists to find out which doctors have received payments from companies. The recently enacted Sunshine Act in the United States requires companies to disclose all payments to doctors of US$10 or more, or less than US$10 if they total US$100 or more per year (65). Some question how effective the Sunshine Act will be (66), but it provides a starting point for knowing about the interactions between doctors and drug companies that have largely remained hidden in Canada. The law would apply to any company doing business with the federal government, that is, any company whose drugs are covered by one of the various federal drug plans for the military, veterans, the Royal Canadian Mounted Police, prisoners in federal jails, and Aboriginal Canadians.

Rethink the value of pharmaceutical research and development

A couple of factors enter into the question of whether to encourage pharmaceutical industry investment in R&D in Canada. The most fundamental question revolves around whether to accept industry priorities in the direction of R&D. Canadian hospitals and universities have also invested heavily in training researchers who could be employed doing industry-financed research and unless there is an alternative source of funding for them, they may leave Canada to seek employment elsewhere. The resolution of these issues is not something that should be solely left to politicians or even the research community, but should be informed by a wider societal debate, perhaps led by an expansion of the citizens' panels similar to the NICE Citizens Council that was mentioned earlier.

Increase government funding for biomedical research

In Canada, the PMPRB has admitted that the patent system plays little role in influencing decisions about R&D (see Chapter 8) and according to the British Office of Fair Trading, neither do drug prices: "We find that there is very little evidence to link the price of pharmaceuticals in the UK with the overall attractiveness of the UK as a location for pharmaceutical R&D investment" (67 p48). The inducements from the federal and provincial governments through tax credits or other economic benefits do not seem to be effective, judging by the decline in R&D spending and employment over the past decade. Senior executives in the pharmaceutical industry are largely dismissive of incentives, such as R&D tax credits, as a significant factor in where to locate research activities. If we take them at their word, then the two significant factors are locations where they can do good science and public funding of a basic medical and science base (68). On the latter measure, overall health R&D funding from the federal government barely moved from 2003 to 2009, going from $1.031 billion to $1.339 billion. The CIHR budget has dropped in real terms from fiscal 2007–8 to 2010–11 (69). The US population is about nine times that of Canada, but funding for the National Institutes of Health in 2011 was US$30.6 billion (70) or 31 times the size of the CIHR's budget of $984 million (69). Canada has the capacity to do very good science but the federal government's funding of biomedical research is paltry compared with what happens south of us and in the United Kingdom and Australia (71). Increasing funding for biomedical research would have multiple positive effects. First, it would increase researchers' ability to independently investigate areas without worrying about the commercial value of their investigations and without having to attract matching commercial funding. Second, it would help universities avoid the conflict of interest that comes with the commercialization of research conducted in the academic setting, and finally, should a public debate decide that Canada needs to do more to foster R&D investment by the pharmaceutical industry, it would help to create the necessary conditions for that investment. If we decide against using government funding to encourage commercially oriented R&D, then that funding could help to create a Canadian equivalent of the Mario Negri Institute for Pharmacological Research in Italy. A book by Donald Light and AF Maturo details how the Institute works (72). It takes money from commercial and non-commercial sources for both basic and developmental research, but plans, conducts and analyzes the research entirely independently, files no patents, and concentrates on research that its scientists feel will have the greatest public health benefits, not the most lucrative commercial ones. As part of decoupling R&D from commercial considerations, the government needs to stop allowing corporate interests onto the board of the CIHR, and it needs to revise the legislation that created the CIHR to emphasize that its primary commitment is to improving public health and advancing health research; it should not be concerned with economic development and job creation.

Reaffirm the goal of humanitarianism

The Canadian government needs to remember the humanitarian goals it signed up for in documents such as the *Universal Declaration of Human*

Rights and the *International Covenant on Economic, Social and Cultural Rights* and support access to low-cost, effective medications over onerous IPRs. That was not possible under the previous Conservative government. It was a government that, among other things, was funding partnerships between non-governmental organizations (NGOs) and mining companies operating in the Global South (73), apparently on the assumption that the social justice goals of NGOs are no different from the economic goals of mining companies. It continued to support the export of chrysotile asbestos, a known cause of cancer, and twice blocked its inclusion on a list of hazardous substances under the United Nations' Rotterdam Convention (74). Canada, under the Conservatives, was the only country in the world to withdraw from the United Nations Convention to Combat Desertification (75); sided with China, Egypt, Iran, Pakistan, and Russia in aggressively opposing European endorsements of health policies aimed at reducing harms, such as HIV transmission, among drug users; and opposed the participation of NGOs in future United Nations policymaking sessions on illicit drugs (76). The Conservative government cut foreign aid to fragile states and crisis-affected communities from $788,201,000 in 2011–12 to $684,154,000 in 2015–16 (77). Whether the new Liberal government will do any better is an open question. The Liberals were responsible for the severely flawed Canada's Access to Medicines Regime (CAMR) when they were last in power.

A better world is possible

The quotation that is the title of this chapter comes from Tommy Douglas, the leader of the social democratic Cooperative Commonwealth Federation (now the New Democratic Party) who took power in 1944 in Saskatchewan, a province that was chronically poor and made even worse because of the Depression. Douglas had the vision and determination to establish, first, universal hospital insurance and later extend that to universal insurance for doctors' services. By himself, Douglas could never have achieved what he did. His election was the embodiment of the strength of the union movement, the history of farmers in the Prairie provinces who needed to cooperate to survive, and other groups committed to social change that were active in Canada at the time. If anything is to happen to radically change pharmaceutical policy, it will need to be the outcome of a public demonstration of the need for change. Douglas, with progressive forces at his side, showed that it is possible to change even entrenched systems, if we have the will and determination to challenge existing power structures.

Acknowledgments

After not only the work involved in writing my first book, *The Real Pushers: A Critical Analysis of the Canadian Pharmaceutical Industry* but also the challenge of getting it published, I decided that I would stick to writing journal articles, newspaper pieces, and chapters for other people's books. It was a lot less work and a lot less aggravating. Reinforcing my decision was the fact that sitting opposite my new partner while reading the page proofs of the book against the copy edited manuscript was hardly conducive to fostering a good relationship so soon after we started living together. So the idea of writing another book remained well and truly dormant for almost 30 years, until I was sitting in a very pretty quadrangle at the University of Queensland in Australia in May 2013 reading Dominique Tobbell's excellent book *Pills, Power, and Policy: The Struggle for Drug Reform in Cold War America and Its Consequences.* The idea occurred to me that I had something to say about pharmaceutical policy in Canada that could be said only through a book-length work. So was born the idea for *Private Profits versus Public Policy: The Pharmaceutical Industry and the Canadian State.*

This book is based on 35 years of researching, analysing, and writing about pharmaceutical policy but, of course, ideas don't just fall out of the sky. In my case, they came primarily from talking, arguing, and debating pharmaceutical policy online, in person, and by mail with a wide range of wonderful people. In alphabetical order, so as not to offend anyone, they are Elia Abi-Jaoude, John Abraham, Sharon Batt, Warren Bell, Lisa Bero, Alan Cassels, Janet Currie, Courtney Davis, Laura Esmail, Colleen Flood, Anne Rochon Ford, Colleen Fuller, Janice Graham, Paul Grootendorst, Ken Harvey, David Healy, David Henry, Hans Hogerzeil, Aidan Hollis, Richard Laing, Michael Law, Richard Lee, Trudo Lemmens,

Mitchell Levine, Don Light, Ruth Lopert, Peter Lurie, Dee Mangin, Mike McBane, David Menkes, Steve Morgan, Bob Nakagawa, Nancy Olivieri, Nav Persaud, Harriet Rosenberg, Paula Rochon, Libby Roughead, Larry Sasich, Adrienne Shnier, Sergio Sismondo, Robyn Tamblyn, Leonore Tiefer, Brett Thombs, Sari Tudiver, Mary Wiktorowicz, and Sid Wolfe. (My apologies to anyone I've forgotten.)

I've also had the opportunity to learn from reading some truly inspiring books written by John Abraham, John Abramson, Marcia Angell, Jerry Avorn, John Braithwaite, Howard Brody, Courtney Davis, Graham Dukes, Carl Elliott, Ben Goldacre, Peter Gøtzsche, Jerome Kassirer, Charles Medawar, and the late Milton Silverman. I can only hope that my book lives up to their standards.

For more than 25 years, Health Action International (HAI) has been part of my life, drawing me out of my cozy Canadian environment and into the world of international pharmaceutical politics and letting me meet people I otherwise never would have known. To my friends and colleagues, past and present, at HAI I owe an enormous debt of gratitude: Teresa Alves, Wilbert Bannenberg, Rose de Groot, Annelies den Boer, Patrick Durisch, Marg Ewen, Kathy Glavanis-Grantham, Anita Hardon, the late Lisa Hayes, Elina Hemminki, the late Andrew Herxheimer, Catherine Hodgkin, Beryl Leach, Charles Medawar, Tessel Mellema, Kirsten Myhr, Orla O'Donovan, Katrina Perehudoff, Tim Reed, Ancel.la Santos, Philippa Saunders, Jorg Schaaber, Staffan Svensson, Ellen 't Hoen, Bas van der Heide, and Christian Wagner.

Three people deserve special mention for their contributions to my thinking on all the issues that I discuss in this book and more: Marc-André Gagnon, Peter Mansfield, and Barbara Mintzes. Each in his or her own way has made me rethink some of my basic ideas, and even if I ended up disagreeing (I agreed with them much more than I disagreed), the exercise left me with a more nuanced understanding of what I wanted to say. Their intellectual abilities, energy, and enthusiasm are something that I truly admire.

After I completed the first draft of this book, I reached out to those who I thought could help me to improve what I had written. The response I got was overwhelming and I need to thank John Abramson, Michael Allan, Peri Ballantyne, Alan Cassels, Lisa Cosgrove, Peter Davis, Adriane Fugh-Berman, Marc-Andre Gagnon, Jerry Hoffman, Anne Holbrook, Don Husereau, Annemarie Jutel, Jillian Kohler, Donald Light, Abby Lippman, Peter Mansfield, Alastair Matheson, Catherine Oliver, Karen Palmer, Gordy Schiff, Sergio Sismondo, Geoff Spurling, Agnes Vitry, and

Terence Young for the time that they devoted to reading parts or all of the book and for their extremely helpful comments. For going above and beyond, my special thanks to those who read the entire manuscript and provided such detailed feedback: Janet Currie, Matthew Herder, Kelly Holloway, Kathy Moscou, and Adrienne Shnier. I incorporated most of what everyone said, and when I didn't, it was usually because either the information wasn't there to implement your ideas or it was beyond my intellectual abilities to integrate them into the manuscript. You have all made this book better than anything I could have done on my own. Any mistakes that remain are mine, unless I can blame them on our now deceased cat or on Mike Harris, former premier of Ontario.

The Brocher Foundation housed and fed me and gave me an office on the shores of Lake Geneva in the fall of 2014, where I wrote the first draft of this book. The staff there was wonderful and the atmosphere was perfect for writing. Whenever I tired of working on the book, I could just look out at the lake. Likewise, the other researchers who shared my time there were a great source of inspiration for me. The revisions to the book were accomplished while I was on sabbatical at the Charles Perkins Centre at the University of Sydney, avoiding the bitterly cold Toronto winter of 2014–15, and I am grateful to everyone there for making me feel at home, especially my colleague Lisa Bero.

There are two special friends that I want to mention. Neither is especially interested in pharmaceutical policy, although both are sympathetic to my point of view. What both of them did was be there for me whenever I needed support, friendship, or just someone to laugh with. Thank you, Bob James and Philip Berger.

When I initially approached University of Toronto Press with my idea for this book, I got an extremely warm reception from Eric Carlson, who helped arrange for the board to give me an advance contract without even seeing a sample chapter and who help guide the book to completion. After Eric left, I was ably assisted by his replacement, Stephen Shapiro. Dawn Hunter did an amazing copy-editing job that improved the readability of this book.

I cannot end without mentioning my two children, Esther Lexchin and David Oliver. Writing a book is not easy and neither is raising children, but you both, in your own ways, give me such pleasure. I could have done without writing this book but not without you two. Finally, there is my wife, Catherine Oliver, who stuck with me despite being forced to read the page proofs of my previous book back in 1983. I ambushed her at the late lamented Classics Bookstore on St Catherine Street in Montreal in the fall of 1982, and we have been together now for over 33 years. I can't imagine my life without her.

Some of the material in this book was previously published in journals and other publications; I thank the publishers and editors for their permission to reprint excerpts here.

Material from the following articles is reproduced by permission of SAGE Publishing:

Lexchin J. Canadian marketing codes: how well are they controlling pharmaceutical promotion? Int J Health Serv. 1994;24(1):91–104. http://dx.doi.org/10.2190/EKEP-D9JE-31A4-KTE5

Lexchin J. Clinical trials in Canada: whose interests are paramount? Int J Health Serv. 2008;38(3):525–42. http://dx.doi.org/10.2190/HS.38.3.h

Lexchin J. Harmony in drug regulation, but who's calling the tune? An examination of regulatory harmonization in Health Canada. Int J Health Serv. 2012;42(1):119–36. http://dx.doi.org/10.2190/HS.42.1k

Lexchin J. Hear no secrets, see no secrets, speak no secrets: secrecy in the Canadian drug approval system. Int J Health Serv. 1999;29(1):167–78. http://dx.doi.org/10.2190/RM7E-748K-K4XM-HHQP

Lexchin J. Pharmaceuticals, patents and politics: Canada and Bill C-22. Int J Health Serv. 1993;23(1):147–60. http://dx.doi.org/10.2190/UCWG-YBR3-X3L0-NWYT

Lexchin J. Who needs faster drug approval times in Canada: the public or the industry? Int J Health Serv. 1994;24(2):253–64. http://dx.doi.org/10.2190/NYKA-UH7E-WBQ4-RD1J

Material from the following articles is reproduced by permission of IOS Press:

Lexchin J. The relationship between pharmaceutical regulation and inappropriate prescribing: the case of psychotropic drugs in Canada during the 1960s and early 1970s. Int J Risk Saf Med. 1998;11(1):49–59

Lexchin J, Kohler JC. The danger of imperfect regulation: OxyContin use in the United States and Canada. Int J Risk Saf Med. 2011;23(4):233–40

Lexchin J, Mintzes B. A compromise too far: a review of Canadian cases of direct-to-consumer advertising regulation. Int J Risk Saf Med. 2014;26(4):213–25

Material from the following articles is reproduced under the Creative Commons Attribution licence:

Habibi R, Lexchin J. Quality and quantity of information in summary basis of decision documents issued by health Canada. PLoS One. 2014;9(3):e92038

Lexchin J. Canada and access to medicines in developing countries: intellectual property rights first. Globalization and Health 2013;9:42

Lexchin J. Canada's patented medicine notice of compliance regulations: balancing the scales or tipping them? BMC Health Serv Res. 2011;11(1):64

Mintzes B, Morgan S, Wright JM. Twelve years' experience with direct-to-consumer advertising of prescription drugs in Canada: a cautionary tale. PLoS One. 2009;4(5):e5699.

Material from Lexchin J. Use of surrogate outcomes in medical journal advertising in Canada. J Popul Ther Clin Pharmacol. 2013;20(2):e146–e148 is reproduced by permission of the journal.

Material from Lexchin J. Pharmaceutical policy: the dance between industry, government, and the medical profession. In: Raphael D, Bryant T, Rioux M eds. Staying alive: critical perspectives on health, illness, and health care 2nd ed. Toronto: Canadian Scholars' Press Inc, 2010:371–93 is reproduced by permission of Canadian Scholars' Press, Inc.

Material from Lexchin J. Health Canada and the pharmaceutical industry: a preliminary analysis of the historical relationship. Healthc Policy 2013;9(2):22–9 is reproduced by permission of Longwoods Publishing Corporation.

Material from Lexchin J. New directions in Canadian drug regulation: whose interests are being served? In: O'Donovan O, Glavanis-Grantham K eds. Power, politics and pharmaceuticals. Cork: Cork University Press, 2008:153–70 is reproduced by permission of Cork University Press.

Material from Light DW, Lexchin J, Darrow JJ. Institutional corruption of pharmaceuticals and the myth of safe and effective drugs. J Law Med Ethics. 2013;41(3):590–600 is reproduced by permission of John Wiley and Sons. Copyright 2013 American Society of Law, Medicine & Ethics, Inc.

Material is reprinted from *Social Science and Medicine*, 31(11), Lexchin J., "Drug makers and drug regulators: too close for comfort. A study of the Canadian situation," 1257–63, Copyright 1990, with permission from Elsevier Ltd.

Material is reprinted from *Health Policy*, 40, Lexchin J., "After compulsory licensing: coming issues in Canadian pharmaceutical policy and politics," 69–80, Copyright 1997, with permission from Elsevier B.V.

Material from the following appears with kind permission from Springer Science+Business Media: *Pharmaceutical prices in the 21st Century*, "Drug pricing in Canada," 2015, 25–41, Lexchin J., Copyright Springer International Publishing Switzerland.

References

Introduction: Why do we care about the pharmaceutical industry in Canada?

1 Industry Canada. Canada's pharmaceutical industry and prospects. Ottawa: Industry Canada; 2013.
2 Ford A, Saibil D, editors. The push to prescribe: women and Canadian drug policy. Toronto: Women's Press; 2009.
3 Young T. Death by prescription: a father takes on his daughter's killer. Toronto: Key Porter Books; 2009.
4 Lang R. The politics of drugs: a comparative pressure-group study of the Canadian Pharmaceutical Manufacturers Association and the Association of the British Pharmaceutical Industry, 1930–1970. Westmead (England): Saxon House; 1974.
5 Lexchin J. The real pushers: a critical analysis of the Canadian drug industry. Vancouver: New Star Books; 1984.
6 Regush N. Safety last: the failure of the consumer health protection system in Canada. Toronto: Key Porter Books; 1993.
7 Canadian Institute for Health Information. National health expenditure trends, 1975 to 2013. Ottawa: CIHI; 2013.
8 Lexchin J, Mintzes B. A compromise too far: a review of Canadian cases of direct-to-consumer advertising regulation. Int J Risk Saf Med. 2014;26(4):213–25. Medline:25420763.
9 Davis C, Abraham J. Unhealthy pharmaceutical regulation: innovation, politics and promissory science. New York: Palgrave Macmillan; 2013. http://dx.doi.org/10.1057/9781137349477.
10 Batt S. Who pays the piper? Industry funding of patients' groups. In: Ford A, Saibil D, editors. The push to prescribe: women and Canadian drug policy. Toronto: Women's Press; 2009. p. 67–89.

11 Health Products and Food Branch. Blueprint for renewal: transforming Canada's approach to regulating health products and food. Ottawa: Health Canada; 2006.
12 Health Products and Food Branch. Blueprint for renewal II: modernizing Canada's regulatory system for health products and food. Ottawa: Health Canada; 2007.
13 Therapeutic Products Directorate. Annual report 2007–2008. Ottawa: Health Canada; 2008.
14 Jasanoff S. Acceptable evidence in a pluralistic society. In: Mayo D, Hollander R, editors. Acceptable evidence: science and values in risk management. New York: Oxford University Press; 1991. p. 29–47.
15 Atkinson MM, Coleman WD. Corporatism and industrial policy. In: Cawson A, editor. Organized interests and the state. London: Sage; 1985. p. 22–44.

1. (De)regulation through cooperation

1 Daemmrich AA. Pharmacopolitics: drug regulation in the United States and Germany. Chapel Hill: University of North Carolina Press; 2004.
2 Sjöstrom H, Nilsson R. Thalidomide and the power of the drug companies. Middlesex: Penguin; 1972.
3 Atkinson MM, Coleman WD. The state, business, and industrial change in Canada. Toronto: University of Toronto Press; 1989.
4 Atkinson MM, Coleman WD. Corporatism and industrial policy. In: Cawson A, editor. Organized interests and the state. London: Sage; 1985. p. 22–44.
5 Potter R. Prescription drugs: the changing response of Canada's Food and Drug Act (Part 4). Can Pharm J. 1966;99(2):9–12, 39.
6 Davis C, Abraham J. Unhealthy pharmaceutical regulation: innovation, politics and promissory science. New York: Palgrave Macmillan; 2013. http://dx.doi.org/10.1057/9781137349477.
7 Johnson J. Speech at annual general meeting of CDMA [Canadian Drug Manufacturers Association]. 1991.
8 Clark C, McCarthy S. Drug-company donations to Manley spark controversy. Globe and Mail. 2003 May 14; Sect. A:8.
9 Expert Advisory Committee on Smart Regulation. Smart regulation: a regulatory strategy for Canada: report to the Government of Canada. Ottawa: Privy Council Office; 2004.
10 Hapman RA. The evolving role of the Canadian government in assessing drug safety. Can Med Assoc J. 1968;98(6):294–300. Medline:5636098

11 Parliament of Canada. Minutes of proceedings and evidence no. 4: Hearing before the House of Commons Special Committee on Drug Costs and Prices. 16 June 1966. Ottawa: Queen's Printer and Controller of Stationery; 1966.
12 Boothe K. Ideas and the limits on program expansion: the failure of nationwide pharmacare in Canada since 1944. Can J Polit Sci. 2013;46(02):419–53. http://dx.doi.org/10.1017/S000842391300022X.
13 Morrison A. The Canadian approach to food and drug regulations. Food Drug Cosmet Law J. 1975;30:632–43.
14 House of Commons. An Act to Impose Licence Duties on Compounders of Spirits and to Amend the "Act Respecting Inland Revenue" and to Prevent the Adulteration of Food, Drink and Drugs. Ottawa: House of Commons; 1874.
15 The 75th anniversary dinner. Food and Drug News. 1950;4(2):21–3.
16 Pugsley LI. The administration and development of federal statutes on foods and drugs in Canada. Med Serv J Can. 1967;23(3):387–449. Medline:4861831
17 Davidson A. The genesis and growth of food and drug administration in Canada. Ottawa: Department of National Health and Welfare; 1949.
18 Herder M. Denaturalizing transparency in drug regulation. McGill J Law and Health. 2015;8(2):S57–S143.
19 Parliament of Canada. Report of the committee: Hearing before the Standing Committee on Public Health and Welfare, 4 Dec 1952. Ottawa: Queen's Printer and Controller of Stationery; 1952.
20 Curran R. Canada's food and drug laws. Chicago: Commerce Clearing House, Inc; 1954.
21 Pharmaceutical Manufacturers Association of Canada. Submission to House of Commons Special Committee on Drug Costs and Prices. Ottawa: PMAC; 1966.
22 Parliament of Canada. Minutes of proceedings and evidence no. 2: Hearing before the House of Commons Special Committee on Drug Costs and Prices. Ottawa: Queen's Printer and Controller of Stationery; 1964.
23 House of Commons. Debates: official report (26 Oct 1962); 1962.
24 Potter R. Prescription drugs: the changing response of Canada's Food and Drug Act (Part 3). Can Pharm J. 1966;99(1):24–6, 37.
25 Hilts PJ. Protecting America's health: the FDA, business and one hundred years of regulation. New York: Alfred A. Knopf; 2003.
26 Regush N. Drug dangers elude our safety controls. Montr Gaz. 1982 Oct 23;Sect. A:1, 4.
27 Anderson J. Pressure groups and the Canadian bureaucracy. In: Kernaghan K, editor. Public administration in Canada: selected readings. 3rd ed. Toronto: Methuen; c1977. p. 292–304.

28 Goyer R. Regulatory aspects and their influence on pharmaceutical research and on the introduction of drugs in Canada: Background study for the Commission of Inquiry on the Pharmaceutical Industry. Ottawa: Supply and Services Canada; 1985.
29 Regush N. How a suspect arthritis drug evaded government checks. Montr Gaz. 1982 Oct 23;Sect. A:1, 6
30 Hollobon J, Lipovenko D. Begin plans no big changes in regulations for new drugs. Globe and Mail. 1982 Oct 28; Sect. A:5.
31 Eggertson L. Drug-approval process criticized: some Health Canada managers passed products despite reviewers' concerns, insiders say. Globe and Mail. 1997 May 28;Sect. A:10.
32 Abraham J. Sociology of pharmaceuticals development and regulation: a realist empirical research programme. Sociol Health Illn. 2008;30(6):869–85. http://dx.doi.org/10.1111/j.1467-9566.2008.01101.x. Medline:18761508
33 Regush N. Safety last: the failure of the consumer health protection system in Canada. Toronto: Key Porter Books; 1993.
34 Auditor General of Canada. Report to the House of Commons, fiscal year ended 31 March 1987. Ottawa: Office of the Auditor General of Canada; 1987.
35 Commission of Inquiry on the Pharmaceutical Industry. Report of the Commission of inquiry on the pharmaceutical industry. Ottawa: Supply and Services Canada; 1985.
36 Gagnon D. Working in partnerships: drug review for the future. Ottawa: Health and Welfare Canada; 1992.
37 Task Force on Program Review. Improved program delivery: health and sports. Ottawa: Supply and Services Canada; 1986.
38 Working Group on Drug Submission Review. Memorandum to the minister (the Stein Report). Ottawa: Department of National Health and Welfare; 1987.
39 Lexchin J. Drug makers and drug regulators: too close for comfort. A study of the Canadian situation. Soc Sci Med. 1990;31(11):1257–63. http://dx.doi.org/10.1016/0277-9536(90)90133-D. Medline:2291124
40 Health Canada. Shared responsibilities, shared vision: renewing the federal health protection legislation. Ottawa: Minister of Public Works and Government Services Canada; 1998.
41 Health Canada. Health Canada decision-making framework for identifying, assessing, and managing health risks: summary document. Ottawa: Health Canada; 1999.

42 Ford A, Saibil D, editors. The push to prescribe: women and Canadian drug policy. Toronto: Women's Press; 2009.
43 Legislative renewal - issue paper: confidential commercial information. Ottawa: Health Canada; 2003.
44 Health protection legislative renewal: detailed legislative proposal [Internet]. Ottawa: Health Canada; c2003 [cited 2014 Sept 11]. Available from: http://publications.gc.ca/collections/Collection/H21-218-2003E.pdf.
45 McBane M. Risk first, safety last! A citizen's guide to Health Canada's health and safety first! A proposal to renew federal health protection legislation. Ottawa: Canadian Health Coalition; 2003.
46 Women and Health Protection. Brief to the office of legislative renewal [Internet]. Toronto: Women and Health Protection; c2004 [cited 2014 Sept 11]. Available from: http://www.whp-apsf.ca/pdf/brief-mar31.pdf.
47 Health Products and Food Branch. Blueprint for renewal: transforming Canada's approach to regulating health products and food. Ottawa: Health Canada; 2006.
48 Health Products and Food Branch. Blueprint for renewal II: modernizing Canada's regulatory system for health products and food. Ottawa: Health Canada; 2007.
49 Women and Health Protection. Submission from WHP to Health Canada in response to blueprint for renewal: transforming Canada's approach to regulating health products and food [Internet]. Toronto: Women and Health Protection; c2007 [cited 2014 Sept 11]. Available from: http://www.whp-apsf.ca/en/documents/blueprint.html.
50 Evans P, Sewell W Jr. Neoliberalism: policy regimes, international regimes and social effects. In: Hall P, Lamont M, editors. Social resilience in the neoliberal era. Cambridge: Cambridge University Press; 2013. p. 35–68. http://dx.doi.org/10.1017/CBO9781139542425.005.
51 Pannell B. Anti-regulation bill will lull public's watchman to sleep. 1995 Oct 28. Gov Info in Canada. 1995;2(1) [cited 2014]. Available from: http://library2.usask.ca/gic/v2n1/pannell/pannell.html.
52 Auditor General of Canada. 2000 December report of the Auditor General of Canada. Ottawa: Office of the Auditor General of Canada; 2000. Chapter 26, Health Canada – regulatory regime of biologics; p. 26-1–26-21.
53 Dobbin M. Paul Martin: CEO for Canada? Toronto: James Lorimer & Co., Ltd; 2003.
54 Eggertson L. Federal labs to be shut down Ottawa closing facilities that did independent tests on pharmaceuticals, food safety. Globe and Mail. 1997 Jul 11;Sect. A:1.

55 Kondro W. Review of Canada's research cuts ordered. Lancet. 1997;350 (9074):347. http://dx.doi.org/10.1016/S0140-6736(05)63409-5.
56 Windsor H. Health branch 'transition' sparks questions. Globe and Mail. 1998 Sept 9; Sect. A:5.
57 Therapeutic Products Directorate. Business transformation progress report. Ottawa: Health Canada; (n.d.).
58 Governor General of Canada. The Canada we want: speech from the throne to open the Second Session of the Thirty-Seventh Parliament of Canada [Internet]. Ottawa: Library of Parliament; c2002 [cited 2004 Feb 15]. Available from: http://www.lop.parl.gc.ca/ParlInfo/Documents/ThroneSpeech/37-1-e.html.
59 External Advisory Committee on Smart Regulation. Risk management [cited 2004 Feb 2]. Available from: https://web.archive.org/web/20041223094703/http:/smartregulation.gc.ca/en/05/01/i4-01.asp.
60 Health Canada. Health protective legislative renewal: detailed legislative proposal. Ottawa: Health Canada; 2003.
61 Lee M, Campbell B. Putting Canadians at risk: how the federal government's deregulation agenda threatens health and environmental standards. Ottawa: Canadian Centre for Policy Alternatives; 2006.
62 Schafer A. A bitter pill: consultations on drug safety appear to be stacked in favour of industry, which could be bad news for the public, writes Arthur Schafer. Ottawa Citizen. 2011 Jan 19; Sect. A:11
63 House of Commons Standing Committee on Health. Drug supply in Canada: a multi-stakeholder responsibility [Internet]. Ottawa: House of Commons; c2012. [cited 2014 Sept 12]. Available from: http://www.parl.gc.ca/content/hoc/Committee/411/HESA/Reports/RP5640047/hesarp09/hesarp09-e.pdf.
64 Duffin J. Canadian drug shortage: recent history of a mystery. CMAJ. 2012;184(8):1000. http://dx.doi.org/10.1503/cmaj.120527. Medline:22529168
65 Rx&D. Remarks to House of Commons Standing Committee on Health. Ottawa: Rx&D; 2012 Mar 27.
66 Green J. Drug-shortage plan 'susceptible' to gaps; Health Canada staff feared voluntary reporting was risky, documents show. Toronto Star. 2012 Dec 28; Sect.A:1.
67 The Multi-Stakeholder Steering Committee on Drug Shortages in Canada. Protocol for the notification and communication of drug shortages [Internet]. Ottawa: Health Canada; c2013 [cited 2014 Oct 21]. Available from: http://www.drugshortages.ca/CMFiles/MSSC_Notification_Communication_Protocol_EN.pdf.

68 Health Canada. Information on drug shortages. Ottawa: Health Canada; 2014.

69 Lunn S. Drug shortages worsening as Health Canada starts study to address it: CBC News [Internet]. Toronto: CBC; c2014 [cited 2014 Oct 21]. Available from: http://www.cbc.ca/news/politics/drug-shortages-worsening-as-health-canada-starts-study-to-address-it-1.2652581.

70 Health Canada. Health Canada seeks input on notification of drug shortages [Internet]. Ottawa: Health Canada; c2014 [cited 2014 Oct 21]. Available from: http://news.gc.ca/web/article-en.do?nid=850509.

71 Government of Canada. Harper government announces requirement for reporting of drug shortages [Internet]. Ottawa: Health Canada; c2015 [modified 2015 Feb 10; cited 2015 Feb 12]. Available from: http://news.gc.ca/web/article-en.do?nid=930039.

2. Biased testing, hidden results, and the regulation of clinical trials

1 Pugsley LI. The administration and development of federal statutes on foods and drugs in Canada. Med Serv J Can. 1967;23:387–449.

2 Miller P. Institutional oversight of clinical trials and the drug approval process. Osgoode Hall Law J. 2006;44:679–725.

3 Health Canada. Background: Food and Drugs Act and Regulations [Internet]. Ottawa: Health Canada; c2006 [cited 2006 Nov 21]. Available from: http://www.hc-sc.gc.ca/dhp-mps/prodpharma/applic-demande/guide-ld/clini/cta_background-eng.php.

4 Wyatt J. Information for clinicians: use and sources of medical knowledge. Lancet. 1991;338(8779):1368–73. http://dx.doi.org/10.1016/0140-6736(91)92245-W.

5 Hersh AL, Stefanick ML, Stafford RS. National use of postmenopausal hormone therapy: annual trends and response to recent evidence. JAMA. 2004;291(1):47–53. http://dx.doi.org/10.1001/jama.291.1.47.

6 Austin P, Mamdani M, Tu K, et al. Prescriptions for estrogen replacement therapy in Ontario before and after publication of the Women's Health Initiative study. JAMA. 2003;289(24):3241–2. http://dx.doi.org/10.1001/jama.289.24.3241.

7 Standing Senate Committee on Social Affairs Science and Technology. Canada's clinical trial infrastructure. Ottawa: Senate of Canada; 2012.

8 Rx&D. Report to Canadians: a commitment to innovation, discovery, quality and safety – number of active clinical trials in Canada (p. 18) [Internet]. Ottawa: Rx&D; c2015 [cited 2016 Mar 11]. Available from: http://

innovativemedicines.ca/wp-content/uploads/2015/06/RxD-Magazine-FINAL-Online.pdf.
9 Leclerc J-M, Laberge N, Marion J. Metrics survey of industry-sponsored clinical trials in Canada and comparator jurisdictions between 2005–2010. Healthc Policy. 2012;8(2):88–106.
10 Regulations amending the Food and Drug Regulations (1024 – clinical trials). Canada Gazette. 2000;134(4):227–60.
11 Health Canada. Regulatory roadmap for health products and food [Internet]. Ottawa: Health Canada; c2012 [cited 2015 Feb 15]. Available from: http://www.hc-sc.gc.ca/ahc-asc/activit/strateg/mod/roadmap-feuillederoute/rm-fr-eng.php.
12 Karleff I. Canada may speed access to its human guinea pigs: ethicists queasy about plan to approve clinical trials in 48 hours. Globe and Mail. 1999 Oct 25;Sect. A:4.
13 Regulations amending the Food and Drug Regulations (1024 – clinical trials). Canada Gazette. 2001;135(13):1116–53.
14 Health Products and Food Branch. Review of the 2001 clinical trials regulatory framework: Part C, Division 5 of the Food and Drug Regulations (drugs for clinical trials involving human subjects). Ottawa: Health Canada; 2007.
15 National Council on Ethics in Human Research. The Canadian research ethics board (REB) list (as of 09-05-2014) [Internet]; c2014 [cited 2014 Sept 5]. Available from: http://www.ncehr-cnerh.org.
16 Food and Drug Regulations, C.R.C., c. 870, (2014).
17 Flood C, Dyke P. The data divide: managing the misalignment in Canada's evidentiary requirements for drug regulation and funding. Univ B C Law Rev. 2012;45:282–325.
18 Lemmens T, Miller PB. The human subjects trade: ethical and legal issues surrounding recruitment incentives. J Law Med Ethics. 2003;31(3):398–418. http://dx.doi.org/10.1111/j.1748-720X.2003.tb00103.x.
19 Beagan BL. 1: Ethics review for human subjects research: interviews with members of research ethics boards and national organizations. In: McDonald M, editor. The governance of health research involving human subjects (HRIHS). Ottawa: Law Commission of Canada; 2000.
20 Silversides A. The tribulations of community-based trials. CMAJ. 2004;170(1):33.
21 Munro M. Doctors buying ethics approval. Vanc Sun. 2004 Feb 27; Sect. A:5.
22 Lemmens T, Freedman B. Ethics review for sale? Conflict of interest and commercial research review boards. Milbank Q. 2000;78(4):547–84. http://dx.doi.org/10.1111/1468-0009.00185.

23 Canadian Institutes of Health Research, Natural Sciences and Engineering Research Council of Canada, Social Sciences and Humanities Research Council of Canada. Tri-Council policy statement: ethical conduct for research involving humans. Ottawa: Interagency Secretariat on Research Ethics; 2005.
24 Munro M. UBC broke federal ethics rules by failing to adequately warn patients. Vanc Sun. 2004 Feb 25; Sect. A:1
25 Walters J. Prozac research targets local girls. Hamilton Spectator. 2002 Nov 2; Sect. A:1.
26 New Canadian standard for research ethics oversight of biomedical clinical trials [Internet]. Ottawa: Public Works and Government Services Canada; c2013 [cited 2014 Sept 7]. Available from: http://www.tpsgc-pwgsc.gc.ca/ongc-cgsb/publications/nouvelles-news/nncvcb-ncsreo-eng.html.
27 Cornacchia C. Cozying up to drug firms disturbs some physicians. Montr Gaz. 2004 Feb 24; Sect. A:4.
28 Walker R. Why FP research works. The Medical Post. 1999 August 10.
29 Munro M. Drug firms pay $3,000 or more per patient for trials. Vanc Sun. 2004 Feb 24; Sect. A:4.
30 Marketplace. Drug trials: CBC; March 18, 2003 [cited 2008 Jan 20]. Available from: https://web.archive.org/web/20030403225617/http://www.cbc.ca/consumers/market/files/health/drug_trials/
31 Munro M. Doctors pressure human guinea pigs. Vanc Sun. 2004 Feb 23; Sect. A:1.
32 National Council on Ethics in Human Research. Welcome to the National Council on Ethics in Human Research [Internet]. Ottawa: National Council on Ethics in Human Research; c2014 [cited 2014 Sept 5]. Available from: http://www.ncehr-cnerh.org.
33 Travers J, Marsh S, Williams M, et al. External validity of randomised controlled trials in asthma: to who do the results of the trials apply? Thorax. 2007;62(3):219–23. http://dx.doi.org/10.1136/thx.2006.066837.
34 Wisniewski S, Rush A, Nierenberg A, et al. Can Phase III trial results of antidepressant medications be generalized to clinical practice? A STAR*D report. Am J Psychiatry. 2009;166(5):599–607. http://dx.doi.org/10.1176/appi.ajp.2008.08071027.
35 Lexchin J. New drugs with novel therapeutic characteristics: have they been subject to randomized controlled trials? Can Fam Physician. 2002;48:1487–92.
36 Rothwell P. External validity of randomised controlled trials: "to whom do the results of this trial apply?" Lancet. 2005;365(9453):82–93. http://dx.doi.org/10.1016/S0140-6736(04)17670-8.

37 Lippman A. The inclusion of women in clinical trials: are we asking the right questions? Toronto: Women and Health Protection; 2006.
38 Rochon PA, Berger PB, Gordon M. The evolution of clinical trials: inclusion and representation. CMAJ. 1998;159(11):1373–4.
39 Caron J. Report on governmental health research policies promoting gender or sex differences sensitivity. Ottawa: Institute of Gender and Health; 2003.
40 Health Canada. Guidance document: considerations for inclusion of women in clinical trials and analysis of sex differences [Internet]. Ottawa: Health Canada; c2013 [cited 2014 Sept 7]. Available from: http://www.hc-sc.gc.ca/dhp-mps/prodpharma/applic-demande/guide-ld/clini/womct_femec-eng.php.
41 Health Products and Food Branch. Guidance for industry: clinical investigation of medicinal products in the pediatric population: ICH topic E11 (Contract No. H42-2/67-23-2003 E). Ottawa: Health Canada; 2003
42 Goldberg N, Schneeweiss S, Kowal M, et al. Availability of comparative efficacy data at the time of drug approval in the United States. JAMA. 2011;305(17):1786–9. http://dx.doi.org/10.1001/jama.2011.539.
43 van Luijn J, Gribnau F, Leufkens H. Availability of comparative trials for the assessment of new medicines in the European Union at the moment of market authorization. Br J Clin Pharmacol. 2007;63(2):159–62. http://dx.doi.org/10.1111/j.1365-2125.2006.02812.x.
44 Garattini S, Bertelé V, Banzi R. Placebo? no thanks, it might be bad for me! Eur J Clin Pharmacol. 2013;69(3):711–14. http://dx.doi.org/10.1007/s00228-012-1383-6.
45 Health Products and Food Branch. Guidance for industry: good clinical practice: consolidated guideline ICH topic E6. Ottawa: Health Canada; 1997.
46 International Conference on Harmonisation of Technical Requirements for Registration of Pharmaceuticals for Human Use. ICH harmonised tripartite guideline: guideline for good clinical practice E6(R1) [Internet]. Geneva (Switzerland): ICH; c1996 [cited 2014 Sept 6]. Available from: http://www.ich.org/fileadmin/Public_Web_Site/ICH_Products/Guidelines/Efficacy/E6/E6_R1_Guideline.pdf.
47 Weijer C. Placebo trials and tribulations. CMAJ. 2002;166:603–4.
48 Hollobon J, Lipovenko D. Companies gamble money, but public also has stake. Globe and Mail. 1982 Oct 20; Sect. A:4.
49 Munro M. 'You failed to protect rights, safety and welfare' of boy. Vanc Sun. 2004 Feb 26; Sect. A:3

50 Lexchin J. Drug makers and drug regulators: too close for comfort. A study of the Canadian situation. Soc Sci Med. 1990;31(11):1257–63. http://dx.doi.org/10.1016/0277-9536(90)90133-D.
51 Canadian Press. Health Canada sets new clinical drug trial rules. Montreal: CTV.ca; 2006 [modified 2006 Oct 16, 2006; cited 2006 Dec 17]. Available from: http://www.ctvnews.ca/servlet/ArticleNews/print/CTVNews/20061016/h_canada_tr_061016/20061016/?hub=Health&subhub=PrintStory.
52 Health Canada. To clinical trial sponsors: requirements for tuberculosis screening of healthy volunteers in Phase I clinical trials involving immunosuppressant drugs or drugs with immunosuppressant properties (Contract No.: 06-116801-306). Ottawa: Health Canada; 2006 Jul 23.
53 Auditor General of Canada. 2000 December report of the Auditor General of Canada. Ottawa: Office of the Auditor General of Canada; 2000. Chapter 26, Health Canada – regulatory regime of biologics; p. 26-1–26-21.
54 Auditor General of Canada. Other audit observations: National Defence and Health Canada. Ottawa: Office of the Auditor General of Canada; 2000.
55 Health Products and Food Branch Inspectorate. Inspection strategy for clinical trials. Ottawa: Health Canada; 2002.
56 Shuchman M. Clinical trials regulation – how Canada compares. CMAJ. 2008;179(7):635–8. http://dx.doi.org/10.1503/cmaj.081271.
57 Auditor General of Canada. Report of the Auditor General of Canada. Ottawa: Office of the Auditor General of Canada; 2006. Chapter 8, allocating funds to regulatory programs – Health Canada.
58 Auditor General of Canada. Report of the Auditor General of Canada. Ottawa: Office of the Auditor General of Canada; 2011. Chapter 4, regulating pharmaceutical drugs – Health Canada.
59 Auditor General of Canada. Report of the Auditor General of Canada to the House of Commons. Ottawa: Office of the Auditor General of Canada; 2006. Chapter 8: allocating funds to regulatory programs – Health Canada.
60 Health Products and Food Branch. Summary report of the inspections of clinical trials conducted in 2003/2004 (Contract No.: 04-118942-280). Ottawa: Health Canada; 2004.
61 Health Canada. Update and response to OAG recommendations for the regulation of pharmaceutical drugs in fall 2011 [Internet]. Ottawa: Health Canada; c2013 [cited 2014 Sept 9]. Available from: http://www.hc-sc.gc.ca/ahc-asc/pubs/hpfb-dgpsa/oag-bvg-eng.php.
62 Health Products and Food Branch Inspectorate. Summary report of the inspections of clinical trials conducted under voluntary phase. Ottawa: Health Canada; 2003.

63 Health Products and Food Branch Inspectorate. Summary report of the inspections of clinical trials conducted in 2003/2004. Ottawa: Health Canada; 2004.

64 Health Products and Food Branch Inspectorate. Summary report of inspections of clinical trials conducted from April 2004 to March 2011. Ottawa: Health Canada; 2012.

65 McLean J, Bruser D. Drug-testing rules broken by Canadian researchers. Toronto Star. 2014 Sept 16; Sect A:1.

66 Kessler DA, Rose JL, Temple RJ, et al. Therapeutic-class wars – drug promotion in a competitive marketplace. N Engl J Med. 1994;331(20):1350–3. http://dx.doi.org/10.1056/NEJM199411173312007.

67 McQuaig L. MDs using Squibb drug in study receive computers for office use. Globe and Mail. 1988 Dec 15; Sect A:1.

68 Lurie P, Wolfe SM. Misleading data analyses in salmeterol (SMART) study. Lancet. 2005;366(9493):1261–2. http://dx.doi.org/10.1016/S0140-6736(05)67518-6.

69 Psaty BM, Kronmal RA. Reporting mortality findings in trials of rofecoxib for Alzheimer Disease or cognitive impairment: a case study based on documents from rofecoxib litigation. JAMA. 2008;299(15):1813–17. http://dx.doi.org/10.1001/jama.299.15.1813.

70 Preto CL. Pressures at the front lines: investigative sites and contract research organizations in Canadian clinical trials. Vancouver: University of British Columbia; 2014.

71 Davidoff F, DeAngelis CD, Drazen JM, et al. Sponsorship, authorship and accountability. CMAJ. 2001;165:786–7.

72 Kauffman M, Julien A. Scientists helped industry to push diet drug medical research: can we trust it? Hartford Courant. 2000 Apr 10; Sect A:1.

73 Singer N. Medical papers by ghostwriters pushed therapy. New York Times. 2009 Aug 5; Sect A:1.

74 Kondro W, Sibbald B. Drug company experts advised staff to withhold data about SSRI use in children. CMAJ. 2004;170(5):783. http://dx.doi.org/10.1503/cmaj.1040213.

75 Mathews AW, Martinez B. Warning signs: e-mails suggest Merck knew Vioxx's dangers at early stage as heart-risk evidence rose, officials played hardball; internal message: "dodge!" Wall Street Journal. 2004 Nov 1; Sect A:1.

76 Hirsch L. Randomized clinical trials: what gets published, and when? CMAJ. 2004;170:481–3.

77 Meier B. Merck backs U.S. database to track drug trials. New York Times. 2004 Jun 18; Sect. C:1.

78 Law M, Kawasumi Y, Morgan S. Despite law, fewer than one in eight completed studies of drugs and biologics are reported on time on clinicaltrials.gov. Health Aff. 2011;30(12):2338–45. http://dx.doi.org/10.1377/hlthaff.2011.0172.
79 House of Commons Standing Committee on Health. Opening the medicine cabinet: first report on health aspects of prescription drugs. Ottawa: House of Commons; 2004.
80 Health Canada. Clinical trials: registration and disclosure of information [Internet]. c2006 [cited 2006 Dec 21]. Available from: http://www.hc-sc.gc.ca/dhp-mps/prodpharma/proj/enreg-clini-info/2006-consult/index-eng.php.
81 External working group on the registration and disclosure of clinical trial information (EWG-CT). Final report: options for improving public access to information on clinical trials of health problems in Canada. Ottawa: Health Canada; 2006.
82 Health Canada, Drugs & Health Products. Clinical trials: registration and disclosure of information [Internet]. Ottawa: Health Canada; c2007 [modified 2013 Oct 17; cited 2007 Aug 13]. Available from: http://www.hc-sc.gc.ca/dhp-mps/prodpharma/proj/enreg-clini-info/index-eng.php.
83 Health Products and Food Branch. Blueprint for renewal II: modernizing Canada's regulatory system for health products and food. Ottawa: Health Canada; 2007.
84 Harper government launches clinical trials database – new initiatives provide guidance and education on clinical trials for Canadians [Internet]. Ottawa: Health Canada; c2013 [cited 2014 Sept 7]. Available from: http://news.gc.ca/web/article-en.do?nid=745809.
85 Shuchman M. Health Canada's new clinical trials database should be mandatory, says expert. CMAJ. 2013;185(11):946. http://dx.doi.org/10.1503/cmaj.109-4526.
86 Groves T. Mandatory disclosure of trial results for drugs and devices. BMJ. 2008;336(7637):170. http://dx.doi.org/10.1136/bmj.39469.465139.80.

3. Approving new drugs: Better or just more?

1 Pugsley LI. The administration and development of federal statutes on foods and drugs in Canada. Med Serv J Can. 1967;23(3):387–449. Medline:4861831
2 Health Canada. Final guidance document: Schedule A/section 3 to the Food and Drugs Act. : Health Canada; 2013 [cited 2014 Sept 8]. Available

from: http://www.hc-sc.gc.ca/dhp-mps/alt_formats/pdf/prodpharma/applic-demande/guide-ld/scha_guide_ld-eng.pdf.
3 The evolution of federal statutes on foods and drugs in Canada. Rx Bulletin. 1970;1(9):2–4.
4 Food and Drug Regulations, C.R.C., c. 870, (2014).
5 Darrow J. Pharmaceutical efficacy: the illusory legal standard. Wash Lee Law Rev. 2013;70:2073–136.
6 Hemminki E, Falkum E. Psychotropic drug registration in the Scandinavian countries: the role of clinical trials. Soc Sci Med Psychol Med Sociol. 1980;14A(6):547–59. Medline:7209629
7 Solomon K, Hart R. Pitfalls and prospects in clinical research on antianxiety drugs: benzodiazepines and placebo–a research review. J Clin Psychiatry. 1978;39(11):823–31. Medline:31354
8 Hughes F, editor. Compendium of pharmaceuticals and specialties (Canada). 3rd ed. Toronto: Canadian Pharmaceutical Association; c1967.
9 Greenblatt DJ, Shader RI, Abernethy DR. Drug therapy: current status of benzodiazepines [second of two parts]. N Engl J Med. 1983;309(7):410–16. Available from: http://dx.doi.org/10.1056/NEJM198308183090705. Medline:6135990
10 Medawar C. Power and dependence: Social audit on the safety of medicines. London: Social Audit; 1992.
11 Owen RT, Tyrer P. Benzodiazepine dependence. A review of the evidence. Drugs. 1983;25(4):385–98. http://dx.doi.org/10.2165/00003495-198325040-00003. Medline:6133736
12 Regush N. How a suspect arthritis drug evaded government checks. Montr Gaz. 1982. Oct 23;Sect. A:1, 6.
13 Auditor General of Canada. Report of the Auditor General of Canada. Ottawa: Office of the Auditor General of Canada; 1995. Chapter 4, Health Canada: management of the change initiative at Health Protection Branch.
14 KPMG Consulting LP. Report volume 1: review of the Therapeutic Products Programme cost recovery initiative. Ottawa: Health Canada; 2000 Jun 16.
15 Pharmaceutical submission and application review fees as of April 1, 2014 [Internet]. Ottawa: Health Canada; c2014 [cited 2014 Sept 8]. Available from: http://www.hc-sc.gc.ca/dhp-mps/finance/fees-frais/pharma-eng.php.
16 Health Canada's proposal to parliament for user fees and service standards for human drugs and medical devices programs [Internet]. Ottawa: Health Canada; c2010 [cited 2014 Sept 8]. Available from: http://www.hc-sc.gc.ca/dhp-mps/finance/costs-couts/fee-propo-frais-eng.php.
17 Evans R. Strained mercy: the economics of Canadian health care. Toronto: Butterworths; 1984.

18 Rx&D. Improving health through innovation: a new deal for Canadians. Ottawa: Rx&D; 2003.
19 Rx&D. Drug approval times: a question of access for Canadian patients to new and innovative therapies. Ottawa: Rx&D; 2004.
20 Towards a globally competitive research-based pharmaceutical sector. A submission to the steering group on the federal government's prosperity initiative. Ottawa: Pharmaceutical Manufacturers Association of Canada; 1992.
21 Lexchin J. Postmarket safety in Canada: are significant therapeutic advances and biologics less safe than other drugs? A cohort study. BMJ Open. 2014;4(2):e004289. http://dx.doi.org/10.1136/bmjopen-2013-004289. Medline:24549164
22 2009/10 report card for the Ontario Drug Benefit Program [Internet]. Toronto: Ontario Government; c2011 [cited 2013 Jun 29]. Available from: http://www.health.gov.on.ca/en/public/programs/drugs/publications/opdp/docs/odb_report_09.pdf.
23 Drugs Directorate. Drug product licensing. Ottawa: Health Canada; 1990.
24 Overstreet R, Aitken K, Berger J. Pre-market clearance of drug products: technical report no. 4, program evaluation study of the drug safety, quality and efficacy program, Health and Welfare Canada. Ottawa: Health and Welfare Canada; 1989.
25 Doern G. The Therapeutic Products Programme: from traditional science-based regulator to science-based risk-benefit manager? In: Reed E, Doern G, editors. Risky business: Canada's changing science-based policy and regulatory regime. Toronto: University of Toronto Press; 2000. p. 185–207.
26 Gagnon D. Working in partnerships: drug review for the future. Ottawa: Health and Welfare Canada; 1992.
27 Royal Commission of Inquiry on the Pharmaceutical Industry. Report of the commission of inquiry on the pharmaceutical industry. Ottawa: Supply and Services Canada; 1985.
28 Task Force on Program Review. Improved program delivery: health and sports. Ottawa: The Task Force; 1986.
29 Auditor General of Canada. Report to the House of Commons, fiscal year ended 31 March 1987. Ottawa: Office of the Auditor General of Canada; 1987.
30 Working Group on Drug Submission Review. Memorandum to the minister (the Stein report). Ottawa: Department of National Health and Welfare; 1987.
31 Drugs Directorate. Drug product licensing. Ottawa: Health and Welfare Canada; 1991.
32 Working Group on Backlog Assessment. Backlog assessment – final report. Ottawa: Drugs Directorate; 1994.

33 Michols D. The distinction between advertising and other activities: administrative update of January 12, 1996 policy. Ottawa: Health Products and Food Branch, Health Canada; 2005.
34 Lexchin J. Relationship between pharmaceutical company user fees and drug approvals in Canada and Australia: a hypothesis-generating study. Ann Pharmacother. 2006;40(12):2216–22. http://dx.doi.org/10.1345/aph.1H117. Medline:17132811
35 The Public Policy Forum. Improving Canada's regulatory process for therapeutic products. Ottawa: Public Policy Forum; 2003.
36 Health Canada. Cost recovery. Ottawa: Health Canada; 1998 September.
37 Department of Finance. Building the Canada we want – budget 2003: investing in Canada's health care system. Ottawa: Public Works and Government Services Canada; 2003 [cited 2004 Feb 15]. Available from: https://www.fin.gc.ca/budget03/pdf/bkheae.pdf.
38 Health Canada. Improving Canada's regulatory process for therapeutic products: building the action plan: multistakeholder consultation. Ottawa: Public Policy Forum; 2003 Nov 2–3.
39 Auditor General of Canada. Report of the Auditor General of Canada. Ottawa: Office of the Auditor General of Canada; 2006. Chapter 8, Allocating funds to regulatory programs – Health Canada.
40 Health Canada. Departmental performance report for the period ending March 31, 2007. Ottawa: Health Canada; 2007.
41 Bujar M, McAuslane, N. Centre for Innovation in Regulatory Science. The impact of the changing regulatory environment on the approval of new medicines across six major authorities 2004–2013. London; c2014 [cited 2015 February 17]. Available from: http://www.fdanews.com/ext/resources/files/01-15/01-14-2015-International-Drug-Approvals.pdf?1421272458.
42 Health Canada, Health Products and Food Branch. Guidance for industry: priority review of drug submissions. Ottawa: Health Canada; 2009.
43 Lexchin J. Health Canada's use of its priority review process for new drugs: a cohort study. BMJ Open. 2015;5(5):e006816. http://dx.doi.org/10.1136/bmjopen-2014-006816. Medline:25967989
44 Health Canada. Notice of compliance with conditions (NOC/c). Ottawa: Health Canada; 2002.
45 Health Canada. Clarification from Health Canada regarding the status of Iressa (gefitinib) in Canada [Internet]. Ottawa: Health Canada; c2005 [cited 2014 Oct 20]. Available from: http://www.hc-sc.gc.ca/dhp-mps/prodpharma/activit/fs-fi/fact_iressa-eng.php.
46 Thatcher N, Chang A, Parikh P, et al. Gefitinib plus best supportive care in previously treated patients with refractory advanced non-small-cell lung

cancer: results from a randomised, placebo-controlled, multicentre study (Iressa Survival Evaluation in Lung Cancer). Lancet. 2005;366(9496): 1527–37. http://dx.doi.org/10.1016/S0140-6736(05)67625-8. Medline:16257339

47 Kim ES, Hirsh V, Mok T, et al. Gefitinib versus docetaxel in previously treated non-small-cell lung cancer (INTEREST): a randomised phase III trial. Lancet. 2008;372(9652):1809–18. http://dx.doi.org/10.1016/S0140-6736(08)61758-4. Medline:19027483

48 Law MR. The characteristics and fulfillment of conditional prescription drug approvals in Canada. Health Policy. 2014;116(2-3):154–61. http://dx.doi.org/10.1016/j.healthpol.2014.03.003. Medline:24703857

49 Lexchin J. Notice of compliance with conditions: a policy in limbo. Healthc Policy. 2007;2(4):114–22. Medline:19305737

50 Davis C, Abraham J. Unhealthy pharmaceutical regulation: innovation, politics and promissory science. New York: Palgrave Macmillan; 2013. http://dx.doi.org/10.1057/9781137349477.

51 Health and Welfare Canada. Development of a national pharmaceutical strategy for Canada: terms of reference. 1992.

52 Ferguson J. Is drug policy pushing the limit? Globe and Mail. 1992 February 25; Sect. A:1,6.

53 Regush N. Objectivity is an issue when reviewers have ties to drug firms. Montr Gaz. 1992 Jun 6; Sect. B:1,2.

54 Auditor General of Canada. Report of the Auditor General of Canada. Chapter 4, Regulating pharmaceutical drugs – Health Canada. Ottawa: Office of the Auditor General of Canada; 2011.

55 Enhanced review capacity initiative - scientific expert database [Internet]. Ottawa: Health Canada; c2005 [cited 2014 Sept 9]. Available from: http://www.hc-sc.gc.ca/dhp-mps/prodpharma/activit/erci_iace/erci_iace_questions-eng.php.

56 Health Canada. Regulatory roadmap for health products and food [Internet]. Ottawa: Health Canada; c2012 [cited 2015 Feb 15]. Available from: http://www.hc-sc.gc.ca/ahc-asc/activit/strateg/mod/roadmap-feuillederoute/rm-fr-eng.php.

57 Kermode-Scott B. Canadian health ministry faces criticism for its secrecy. BMJ. 2004;328(7450):1222. http://dx.doi.org/10.1136/bmj.328.7450.1222-f.

58 Bruser D, McLean J, Mendleson R. Toronto doctor asks Health Canada about pregnancy drug, gets 212 pages of censored information. Toronto Star. 2015 April 24.

59 Crowe K. Health Canada requires doctor to sign confidentiality agreement to see drug data [Internet]. Toronto: CBC.ca; 2015 [updated 2015 Oct 14; cited 2015 Dec 29]. Available from: http://www.cbc.ca/news/health/health-canada-drug-confidentiality-data-1.3269107.
60 Herder M. Unlocking Health Canada's cache of trade secrets: mandatory disclosure of clinical trial results. CMAJ. 2012;184(2):194–9. http://dx.doi.org/10.1503/cmaj.110721. Medline:21876028
61 Hirsch L. Randomized clinical trials: what gets published, and when? CMAJ. 2004;170(4):481–3. Medline:14970095
62 US Food and Drug Administration. Drugs@FDA [Internet]. Washington (DC): US Department of Health & Human Services; c2014 [cited 2014 Sept 8]. Available from: http://www.accessdata.fda.gov/scripts/cder/drugsatfda/.
63 Schwartz LM, Woloshin S. Lost in transmission – FDA drug information that never reaches clinicians. N Engl J Med. 2009;361(18):1717–20. http://dx.doi.org/10.1056/NEJMp0907708. Medline:19846841
64 European public assessment reports [Internet]. London (England): European Medicines Agency; c2014 [cited 2014 Sept 8]. Available from: http://www.ema.europa.eu/ema/index.jsp?curl=pages/medicines/landing/epar_search.jsp&mid=WC0b01ac058001d124.
65 Steinbrook R. The European Medicines Agency and the brave new world of access to clinical trial data. JAMA Intern Med. 2013;173(5):373–4. http://dx.doi.org/10.1001/jamainternmed.2013.3842. Medline:23599919
66 Association Internationale de la Mutualité, Health Action International Europe, International Society of Drug Bulletins, Medicines in Europe Forum, Nordic Cochrane Centre. EMA's final policy on access to clinical data: proactive access to some data, but strings attached [Internet]. c2014 [cited 2014 October 22]. Available from: http://www.isdbweb.org/en/publications/view/ema-s-final-policy-on-access-to-clinical-data-proactive-access-to-some-data-but-strings-attached.
67 Vitry A, Lexchin J, Sasich L, et al. Provision of information on regulatory authorities' websites. Intern Med J. 2008;38(7):559–67. http://dx.doi.org/10.1111/j.1445-5994.2007.01588.x. Medline:18336542
68 Access to Information Act, R.S. 1985, c. A-1, (2003).
69 Health Products and Food Branch. Review of regulated products: policy on public input. Ottawa: Health Canada; 2007.
70 Health Canada. Health protective legislative renewal: detailed legislative proposal. Ottawa Health Canada; 2003.

71 Science Advisory Board Committee on the Drug Review Process. Report to Health Canada. Ottawa: Health Canada; 2000.

72 An Act to Amend the Food and Drugs Act and to Make Consequential Amendments to Other Acts, Bill C-51, 39th Parl., 2d Sess. (2008).

73 Wong W, Herder M. Trade secrets, transparency, and temporality [Internet]. Toronto: IP Osgoode; c2012 [cited 2014 Sept 9]. Available from: http://www.iposgoode.ca/2012/02/trade-secrets-transparency-and-temporality/.

74 Health Canada. Issue analysis summary: summary basis of decision – draft 7. Ottawa: Health Canada; 2004.

75 Habibi R, Lexchin J. Quality and quantity of information in summary basis of decision documents issued by Health Canada. PLoS One. 2014 Mar 20;9(3):e92038. Available from: http://dx.doi.org/10.1371/journal.pone.0092038. Medline:24651766

76 Lexchin J. New drugs with novel therapeutic characteristics. Have they been subject to randomized controlled trials? Can Fam Physician. 2002;48: 1487–92. Medline:12371307

77 Turner EH, Matthews AM, Linardatos E, et al. Selective publication of antidepressant trials and its influence on apparent efficacy. N Engl J Med. 2008;358(3):252–60. http://dx.doi.org/10.1056/NEJMsa065779. Medline:18199864

78 Health Canada. Frequently asked questions: summary basis of decision (SBD) project: phase II [Internet]. Ottawa: Health Canada; c2012 [updated 2012 Jun 29; cited 2014 Oct 19]. Available from: http://www.hc-sc.gc.ca/dhp-mps/prodpharma/sbd-smd/sbd_qa_smd_fq-eng.php.

79 Herder M, Gibson E, Graham J, et al. Regulating prescription drugs for patient safety: does Bill C-17 go far enough? CMAJ. 2014;186(8):E287–92. http://dx.doi.org/10.1503/cmaj.131850. Medline:24616135

80 Government of Canada. Harper government announces passage of Vanessa's Law – modernized laws for drugs and medical devices mark a new era in Canadian patient safety [Internet]. Ottawa: Government of Canada; c2014 [cited 2015 Feb 17]. Available from: http://news.gc.ca/web/article-en.do;jsessionid=eaa6c76f6abd3eb4126a1550dad40ba273cc45b8a8ba25c908c6bea7dd26f8da.e38RbhaLb3qNe38Maxj0?mthd=index&crtr.page=1&nid=900969.

81 An Act to Amend the Food and Drugs Act, Bill C-17, 1st reading, 41st Parl., 2d Sess. (2013).

82 International Working Group on Transparency and Accountability in Drug Regulation. Statement. Amsterdam: 1996.

83 McGarity TO, Shapiro SA. The trade secret status of health and safety testing information: reforming agency disclosure policies. Harv Law Rev. 1980;93(5):837–88. http://dx.doi.org/10.2307/1340420.

84 Health Canada. Consultation on the amendments to the Food and Drugs Act: guide to new authorities – what we heard [Internet]. Ottawa: Health Canada; c2015 [cited 2015 Aug 2]. Available from: http://www.hc-sc.gc.ca/dhp-mps/legislation/unsafedrugs-droguesdangereuses-heard-entendu-eng.php.

85 US Food and Drug Administration. Narrative by activity – human drugs program FY 2011 Congressional budget [Internet]. Silver Springs (MD): US Food and Drug Administration; c2010 [cited 2010 Dec 30]. Available from: http://www.fda.gov/downloads/AboutFDA/ReportsManualsForms/Reports/BudgetReports/UCM202321.pdf.

86 US Food and Drug Administration. Narrative by activity – biologics program FY 2011 Congressional budget [Internet]. Silver Springs (MD): US Food and Drug Administration; c2010 [cited 2010 Dec 30]. Available from: http://www.fda.gov/downloads/AboutFDA/ReportsManualsForms/Reports/BudgetReports/UCM205377.pdf.

87 Wiktorowicz M, Lexchin J, Moscou K, et al. Keeping an eye on prescription drugs: Keeping Canadians safe: active monitoring systems for drug safety and effectiveness in Canada and internationally. Toronto: Health Council of Canada; 2010.

88 European Medicines Agency. Funding [Internet]. Canary Wharf (England): European Medicines Agency; c2010 [cited 2010 Dec 30]. Available from: http://www.ema.europa.eu/ema/index.jsp?curl=pages/about_us/general/general_content_000130.jsp&murl=menus/about_us/about_us.jsp&mid=WC0b01ac0580029336.

89 Lexchin J, O'Donovan O. Prohibiting or "managing" conflict of interest? A review of policies and procedures in three European drug regulation agencies. Soc Sci Med. 2010;70(5):643–7. http://dx.doi.org/10.1016/j.socscimed.2009.09.002. Medline:19782458

90 Prescrire Editorial Staff. ICH: an exclusive club of drug regulatory agencies and drug companies imposing its rules on the rest of the world. Prescrire Int. 2010;19(108):183–6. Medline:20939460

91 Abraham J, Reed T. Trading risks for markets: the international harmonisation of pharmaceuticals regulation. Health Risk Soc. 2001;3(1):113–28. http://dx.doi.org/10.1080/713670172.

92 Therapeutic Products Programme, International Directorate. Therapeutic Products Programme's international strategy. Ottawa: Health Canada, Drugs and Health Products; 1999.

93 St-Pierre A. Industry consultation on international regulatory cooperation: preliminary results. Ottawa: International Policy Division, Bureau of Policy and Coordination, Health Canada; 1999.

94 Blackwell T. Canada mulls joint drug reviews with U.S. regulatory. National Post. 2006 Feb 28; Sect. A:1.

95 Expert Advisory Committee on Smart Regulation. Smart regulation: a regulatory strategy for Canada – report to the Government of Canada. Ottawa: External Advisory Committee on Smart Regulation; 2004.

96 Health Canada. Progressive licensing – mock framework exercises. Ottawa: Health Canada; 2007.

97 Buchholz K. Pharmaceutical risk communication at the point of care: an evaluation of Paxil® and Premplus® PILs: a report presented to the ICE drug policy futures program. 2006.

98 Sukkari SR, Sasich LD. Cisapride and patient information leaflets. CMAJ. 2001;164(9):1276–8, author reply 1278–9. Medline:11341134

99 Dickinson D, Raynor DK, Duman M. Patient information leaflets for medicines: using consumer testing to determine the most effective design. Patient Educ Couns. 2001;43(2):147–59. http://dx.doi.org/10.1016/S0738-3991(00)00156-7. Medline:11369148

100 Daemmrich AA. Pharmacopolitics: drug regulation in the United States and Germany. Chapel Hill: University of North Carolina Press; 2004.

4. Regulating promotion or licensing deception?

1 Gagnon M-A, Lexchin J. The cost of pushing pills: a new estimate of pharmaceutical promotion expenditures in the United States. PLoS Med. 2008;5(1):e1. http://dx.doi.org/10.1371/journal.pmed.0050001. Medline:18177202

2 Wittink D. Analysis of ROI for pharmaceutical promotion (ARPP) [Internet]. New Haven (CT): Yale School of Management; c2002 [cited 2015 Feb 18]. Available from: http://kurse.fh-regensburg.de/kurs_20/kursdateien/2010Analysis_of_ROI.pdf.

3 Angus Reid Group. Credibility and the marketing mix. Toronto: Angus Reid; 1991.

4 Chalkley P. Targeting accessible physicians. Canadian Pharmaceutical Marketing. 2009;(April):29–30.

5 Mintzes B, Lexchin J, Sutherland JM, et al. Pharmaceutical sales representatives and patient safety: a comparative prospective study of information quality in Canada, France and the United States. J Gen Intern Med. 2013;28(10):1368–75. http://dx.doi.org/10.1007/s11606-013-2411-7. Medline:23558775
6 Hodges B. Interactions with the pharmaceutical industry: experiences and attitudes of psychiatry residents, interns and clerks. CMAJ. 1995;153(5):553–9. Medline:7641153
7 Barfett J, Lanting B, Lee J, et al. Pharmaceutical marketing to medical students: the student perspective. McGill J Med. 2004;8:21–7.
8 Environics Research Group. Final report: adverse reaction reporting survey with health professionals. Toronto: Environics Research Group; 2007.
9 Spurling GK, Mansfield PR, Montgomery BD, et al. Information from pharmaceutical companies and the quality, quantity, and cost of physicians' prescribing: a systematic review. PLoS Med. 2010;7(10):e1000352. http://dx.doi.org/10.1371/journal.pmed.1000352. Medline:20976098
10 Food and Drugs Act, C.01.044, Stat. R.S.C., 1985, c. F-27 (1985).
11 Food and Drug Regulations, C.R.C., c. 870, (2014).
12 Health Products and Food Branch Inspectorate. Compliance and enforcement policy (POL-0001). Version 2. Ottawa: Health Canada; 2005.
13 Cocking C. The abuse of prescription drugs. Weekend Mag. 1977 Jun 18:16–9.
14 Lexchin J. The real pushers: a critical analysis of the Canadian drug industry. Vancouver: New Star Books; 1984.
15 Record of discussions: Canadian advertising preclearance agencies and Health Canada [Internet]. Ottawa: Health Canada; c2014 [cited 2014 Dec 7]. Available from: http://www.paab.ca/resources/pdfs/rod-2014.pdf.
16 Lexchin J, Kawachi I. Voluntary codes of pharmaceutical marketing: controlling promotion or licensing deception. In: Davis P, editor. Contested ground: public purpose and private interest in the regulation of prescription drugs. New York: Oxford University Press; 1996. p. 221–35.
17 Zetterqvist AV, Merlo J, Mulinari S. Complaints, complainants, and rulings regarding drug promotion in the United Kingdom and Sweden 2004–2012: a quantitative and qualitative study of pharmaceutical industry self-regulation. PLoS Med. 2015;12(2):e1001785. http://dx.doi.org/10.1371/journal.pmed.1001785. Medline:25689460
18 Director of Investigation and Research. Inquiry under section 2 of the Combines Investigation Act relating to the manufacture, distribution and sale of drugs: Hearing before the director of investigation and research, Combines Investigation Act. Ottawa: Department of Justice; 1961.

19 Parliament of Canada. Minutes of proceedings and evidence no. 5: Hearing before the House of Commons Special Committee on Drug Costs and Prices. June 23, 1966. Ottawa: Queen's Printer and Controller of Stationery; 1966.
20 Lang R. The politics of drugs: a comparative pressure-group study of the Canadian Pharmaceutical Manufacturers Association and the Association of the British Pharmaceutical Industry, 1930–1970. Westmead (England): Saxon House; 1974.
21 Rx&D. Code of Ethical Practices [Internet]. Ottawa: Canada's Research-Based Pharmaceutical Companies; c2013 [cited 2014 Sept 13]. Available from: https://www.cag-acg.org/images/about/2012_rxd_code_of_ethical_practices.pdf.
22 Lexchin J. The relationship between pharmaceutical regulation and inappropriate prescribing: the case of psychotropic drugs in Canada during the 1960s and early 1970s. Int J Risk Saf Med. 1998;11(1):49–59.
23 Raison A. The evolution of standards for pharmaceutical advertising in Canada. Pickering (ON): Pharmaceutical Advertising Advisory Board; 1989.
24 Pharmaceutical Advertising Advisory Board. Code of advertising acceptance [Internet]. Pickering (ON): PAAB; c2013 [cited 2014 Sept 13]. Available from: http://www.paab.ca/paab-code.htm.
25 Pharmaceutical Advertising Advisory Board. PAAB code of advertising acceptance. Pickering (ON): PAAB; 1986.
26 Kline S. Prescription drug advertising: communicating risk, benefit, and cost of pharmaceuticals. Proceedings of an invitational workshop; 1992 Feb 2–4; Vancouver: Canadian Public Health Association; c1992. p. 52–6.
27 Lexchin J. Canadian marketing codes: how well are they controlling pharmaceutical promotion? Int J Health Serv. 1994;24(1):91–104. http://dx.doi.org/10.2190/EKEP-D9JE-31A4-KTE5. Medline:8150569
28 Lexchin J. Enforcement of codes governing pharmaceutical promotion: what happens when companies breach advertising guidelines? CMAJ. 1997;156(3):351–6. Medline:9033415
29 Pharmaceutical Advertising Advisory Board. Newsletters [Internet]. Pickering (ON): PAAB; c2014 [cited 2014 Sept 13]. Available from: http://www.paab.ca/newsletters.htm.
30 Lexchin J, Holbrook A. Methodologic quality and relevance of references in pharmaceutical advertisements in a Canadian medical journal. CMAJ. 1994;151(1):47–54. Medline:8004560
31 Pharmaceutical Advertising Advisory Board. PAAB code of advertising acceptance. Pickering (ON): PAAB; 1997.
32 Sackett D, Haynes R, Guyatt G, et al. Clinical epidemiology: a basic science for clinical medicine. Boston: Little, Brown and Company; 1991.

33 Naylor CD, Chen E, Strauss B. Measured enthusiasm: does the method of reporting trial results alter perceptions of therapeutic effectiveness? Ann Intern Med. 1992;117(11):916–21. http://dx.doi.org/10.7326/0003-4819-117-11-916. Medline:1443954

34 Forrow L, Taylor WC, Arnold RM. Absolutely relative: how research results are summarized can affect treatment decisions. Am J Med. 1992;92(2):121–4. http://dx.doi.org/10.1016/0002-9343(92)90100-P. Medline:1543193

35 Bobbio M, Demichelis B, Giustetto G. Completeness of reporting trial results: effect on physicians' willingness to prescribe. Lancet. 1994;343(8907):1209–11. http://dx.doi.org/10.1016/S0140-6736(94)92407-4. Medline:7909875

36 Lexchin J. How patient outcomes are reported in drug advertisements. Can Fam Physician. 1999;45:1213–16. Medline:10349065

37 Svensson S, Menkes DB, Lexchin J. Surrogate outcomes in clinical trials: a cautionary tale. JAMA Intern Med. 2013;173(8):611–12. http://dx.doi.org/10.1001/jamainternmed.2013.3037. Medline:23529157

38 Chen DT, Wynia MK, Moloney RM, et al. U.S. physician knowledge of the FDA-approved indications and evidence base for commonly prescribed drugs: results of a national survey. Pharmacoepidemiol Drug Saf. 2009;18(11):1094–100. http://dx.doi.org/10.1002/pds.1825. Medline:19697444

39 Eguale T, Buckeridge DL, Winslade NE, et al. Drug, patient, and physician characteristics associated with off-label prescribing in primary care. Arch Intern Med. 2012;172(10):781–8. http://dx.doi.org/10.1001/archinternmed.2012.340. Medline:22507695

40 Health Products and Food Branch. Record of discussions – Canadian advertising preclearance agencies and Health Canada: April 5, 2012. Ottawa: Health Canada; 2012.

41 Othman N, Vitry A, Roughead EE. Quality of pharmaceutical advertisements in medical journals: a systematic review. PLoS One. 2009;4(7):e6350. http://dx.doi.org/10.1371/journal.pone.0006350. Medline:19623259

42 Parliament of Canada. Minutes of proceedings and evidence no. 4: Hearing before the House of Commons Special Committee on Drug Costs and Prices (June 16, 1966). Ottawa: Queen's Printer and Controller of Stationery; 1966).

43 Regush N. MDs not always expert on drugs they prescribe. Montr Gaz. 1982 Oct 26; Sect. A:1,8.

44 Summary publication – Drug symposium: drug information for the health care team; 1975, May 30–31; Montreal, Quebec.

45 Wipond R. Meet your doctor's generous friend. Focus online [Internet]. c2013 [2013 July/Aug; cited 2016 Mar 4]. Available from: http://focusonline.ca/?q=node/577.
46 Ross V. Between bliss and bedlam. Maclean's. 1980;38–40, 42.
47 Rx&D. Where we stand: detailing. Ottawa: Canada's Research-Based Pharmaceutical Companies; 2010. p. 2.
48 PMAC. Code of marketing practices. Ottawa: PMAC; 1991.
49 Murdoch L-A, Lum L. Timeliness of receipt of manufacturers' new product information. Can J Hosp Pharm. 1991;44(5):235–8. Medline:10115576
50 Toughill K. Rules for doctors at drug-firm seminars stir up controversy. Toronto Star. 1992 Apr 11; Sect. D:5.
51 Rx&D. Complaints 2008–2011 [Internet]. Ottawa: Canada's Research-Based Pharmaceutical Companies; c2013 [cited 2014 Sept 14]. Available from: http://innovativemedicines.ca/ethics/complaints/http://www.canadapharma.org/en/commitment-to-ethics/with-healthcare-professionals/complaints-2008-2011.
52 OxyContin Task Force. Final report. St. John's: Government of Newfoundland and Labrador; 2004.
53 Follert J, Mancini M, O'Meara J. Special report: wasted youth [Internet]; c2011 [updated 2011 Mar 31; cited 2011 May 22]. Available from: http://www.durhamregion.com/community-story/3514325-special-report-wasted-youth/.
54 Kitching C. Oxycodone becoming a drug of choice. Winnipeg Sun. [Internet]. 2010 Mar 1.
55 Dhalla IA, Mamdani MM, Sivilotti MLA, et al. Prescribing of opioid analgesics and related mortality before and after the introduction of long-acting oxycodone. CMAJ. 2009;181(12):891–6. http://dx.doi.org/10.1503/cmaj.090784. Medline:19969578
56 Advertisement for OxyContin. Can Fam Physician. 2000;46(2):328–9.
57 Persaud N. Questionable content of an industry-supported medical school lecture series: a case study. J Med Ethics. 2014;40(6):414–18. http://dx.doi.org/10.1136/medethics-2013-101343. Medline:23760579
58 Drugs Directorate. Renewal project D-18: advertising. Ottawa: Health Canada; 1994.
59 Alberta Breastfeeding Committee. Look what they're doing: monitoring code compliance in Alberta [Internet]. Edmonton: Alberta Breastfeeding Committee; [cited 2014 Sept 14]. Available from: http://www.infactcanada.ca/pdf/alberta-look-what-they-are-doing.pdf.
60 Therapeutic Products Programme. Advertising Standards Canada and the Therapeutic Products Programme's roles and consultation related to

advertising review and complaint adjudication. Ottawa: Health Canada; 2001.

61 Health Canada. Regulating advertising of health products [Internet]. c2011 [cited 2015 Dec 29]. Available from: http://www.hc-sc.gc.ca/dhp-mps/alt_formats/pdf/pubs/medeff/fs-if/2011-advert-publicite/2011-advert-publicite-eng.pdf.

62 Marketed Health Products Directorate. Notice of intent. Ottawa: Health Canada; 2006.

63 Advertising Standards Canada. Re: Advertising Standards Canada's response to Health Canada, August 16, 2006, consultation notice 06–118281–52 re draft attestation criteria for consumer advertising preclearance agencies. Toronto: Advertising Standards Canada; 2006.

64 Health Canada. List of Canadian advertising preclearance agencies [Internet]. Ottawa: Health Canada; c2012 [cited 2015 Dec 29]. Available from: http://www.hc-sc.gc.ca/dhp-mps/advert-publicit/preclear-preapprob/pca-apa_list-eng.php.

65 Health Products and Food Branch. Roundtable stakeholder consultation on section 2.21 (risk/safety information communication) of the consumer advertising guidelines for marketed health products (for nonprescription drugs including natural health products): roundtable report. Ottawa: Health Canada; 2006.

66 Health Products and Food Branch. Guidance document: consumer advertising guidelines for marketed health products (for nonprescription drugs including natural health products) [Internet]. Ottawa: Health Canada; c2006 [cited 2014 Sept 14]. Available from: http://www.hc-sc.gc.ca/dhp-mps/advert-publicit/pol/guide-ldir_consom_consum-eng.php.

67 Mintzes B. What are the public health implications? Direct-to-consumer advertising of prescription drugs in Canada. Toronto: Health Council of Canada; 2006.

68 Michols D. The distinction between advertising and other activities: administrative update of January 12, 1996 policy. Ottawa: Health Products and Food Branch, Health Canada; 2005.

69 Rowsell L. Advertising campaigns of branded and unbranded messages: policy statement [Internet]. Ottawa: Therapeutic Products Directorate, Health Canada; c2000 [cited 2012 Aug 19]. Available from: http://hc-sc.gc.ca/dhp-mps/advert-publicit/pol/advert-pub_camp-eng.php.

70 Mintzes B, Morgan S, Wright JM. Twelve years' experience with direct-to-consumer advertising of prescription drugs in Canada: a cautionary

tale. PLoS One. 2009;4(5):e5699. http://dx.doi.org/10.1371/journal.pone.0005699. Medline:19479084

71 Merck Frosst. Direct-to-consumer advertising of prescription pharmaceuticals: a Merck Frosst position paper on how to use comprehensive patient information to deliver improved, cost-effective health outcomes – submission to Health Canada's consultation on direct-to-consumer advertising of prescription drugs. Ottawa: Merck Frosst; 1996.

72 Rx&D. Advertising prescription medicines in Canada: why it makes sense. Ottawa: Rx&D; 2003.

73 Health Products and Food Branch. Guidance document: schedule A and section 3 to the Food and Drugs Act. Ottawa: Health Canada; c2013 [cited 2014 Sept 16]. Available from: http://www.hc-sc.gc.ca/dhp-mps/prodpharma/applic-demande/guide-ld/scha_guide_ld-eng.php.

74 Union des consommateurs and Women and Health Protection. External working group report on section 3 and schedule A: minority report [Internet]. Ottawa: Health Canada; 2003 [cited 2014 Sept 16]. Available from: http://www.hc-sc.gc.ca/dhp-mps/compli-conform/info-prod/drugs-drogues/sched-ann_a_min_rep-rap-eng.php.

75 Mintzes B. Advertising of prescription-only medicines to the public: does evidence of benefit counterbalance harm? Annu Rev Public Health. 2012;33(1):259–77. http://dx.doi.org/10.1146/annurev-publhealth-031811-124540. Medline:22429162

76 Lexchin J, Mintzes B. A compromise too far: a review of Canadian cases of direct-to-consumer advertising regulation. Int J Risk Saf Med. 2014;26(4):213–25. Medline:25420763

77 Aiello R. Health Canada not doing enough to discipline big pharma on false advertising: critics. Hill Times. 2015.

78 Health Canada. Health product advertising complaints [Internet]. Ottawa: Health Canada; c2015 [cited 2015 Dec 29]. Available from: http://www.hc-sc.gc.ca/dhp-mps/advert-publicit/complaint-plaintes/index-eng.php.

79 Law MR, Majumdar SR, Soumerai SB. Effect of illicit direct to consumer advertising on use of etanercept, mometasone, and tegaserod in Canada: controlled longitudinal study. BMJ. 2008;337(sep02 1):a1055. http://dx.doi.org/10.1136/bmj.a1055. Medline:18765444

80 Silversides A. Charter challenge of ban on direct-to-consumer advertising to be heard by Ontario court in mid-June. CMAJ. 2009;181(1-2):E5–6. http://dx.doi.org/10.1503/cmaj.091050. Medline:19581607

81 Almashat S, Wolfe S. Pharmaceutical criminal and civil penalties: an update [Internet]. Washington DC: Public Citizen; c2012 [cited 2014 Sept 16]. Available from: http://www.citizen.org/hrg2073.

82 Bruser D, McLean J, Bailey A. Dangers of off-label drug use kept secret. Toronto Star. 2014 Jun 26; Sect. A:1.

5. Health Canada and drug safety: How safe are we?

1 Lazarou J, Pomeranz BH, Corey PN. Incidence of adverse drug reactions in hospitalized patients: a meta-analysis of prospective studies. JAMA. 1998;279(15):1200–5. http://dx.doi.org/10.1001/jama.279.15.1200. Medline:9555760
2 Moore TJ, Cohen MR, Furberg CD. 2011 QuarterWatch: Quarter 4: FDA direct report rankings as risk index. p. 2–3.
3 Commission of the European Communities. Commission staff working document: impact assessment [Internet]. Brussels (Belgium): Commission of the European Communities; c2008 [cited 2014 Sept 17]. Available from: http://ec.europa.eu/health/files/pharmacos/pharmpack_12_2008/pharmacovigilance-ia-vol1_en.pdf.
4 Moore TJ, Cohen MR, Furberg CD. Serious adverse drug events reported to the Food and Drug Administration, 1998–2005. Arch Intern Med. 2007;167(16):1752–9. http://dx.doi.org/10.1001/archinte.167.16.1752. Medline:17846394
5 Lexchin J. Adverse drug reactions: review of the Canadian literature. Can Fam Physician. 1991;37:109–18. Medline:21234084
6 Baker GR, Norton PG, Flintoft V, et al. The Canadian Adverse Events Study: the incidence of adverse events among hospital patients in Canada. CMAJ. 2004;170(11):1678–86. http://dx.doi.org/10.1503/cmaj.1040498. Medline:15159366
7 Canadian Institute for Health Information. Hospital MIS statistics [Internet]. Ottawa: CIHI; c2014 [cited 2014 Sept 17]. Available from: https://www.cihi.ca/CIHI-ext-portal/internet/EN/Quick_Stats/quick+stats/quick_stats_main?xTopic=Spending&pageNumber=1&resultCount=10&filterTypeBy=undefined&filterTopicBy=14&autorefresh=1.
8 List of countries by traffic-related death rate: Wikipedia; 2014 [cited 2014 September 17]. Available from: https://en.wikipedia.org/wiki/List_of_countries_by_traffic-related_death_rate.
9 Lexchin J. How safe are new drugs? Market withdrawal of drugs approved in Canada between 1990 and 2009. Open Med. 2014;8(1):e14–19. Medline:25009681
10 Lexchin J. Drug withdrawals from the Canadian market for safety reasons, 1963-2004. CMAJ. 2005;172(6):765–7. http://dx.doi.org/10.1503/cmaj.045021. Medline:15767610

11 Rx&D. Code of ethical practices [Internet]. Ottawa: Canada's Research-Based Pharmaceutical Companies; c2013 [cited 2014 Sept 13]. Available from: https://www.cag-acg.org/images/about/2012_rxd_code_of_ethical_practices.pdf.

12 Health Canada. Health product vigilance framework [Internet]. Ottawa: Health Canada; c2012 [cited 2014 Sept 17]. Available from: http://www.hc-sc.gc.ca/dhp-mps/pubs/medeff/_fs-if/2012-hpvf-cvps/index-eng.php.

13 Hansson O. Inside Ciba-Geigy. Penang (Malaysia): International Organization of Consumers Unions; 1989.

14 Regush N. How a suspect arthritis drug evaded government checks. Montr Gaz. 1982 Oct 25; Sect. A:1,6.

15 Department of National Health and Welfare. Diethylstilbestrol and adenocarcinoma of the vagina. Rx Bulletin. 1971;2:158.

16 Facts about DES [Internet]. Montreal: DES Action Canada; [updated 1 Nov 2005; cited 2014 Nov 20]. Available from: http://www.descanada.ca/anglais/anglais.html.

17 Draft guidance document – triggers for issuance of risk communication documents for marketed health products for human use [Internet]. Ottawa: Health Canada; c2007 [cited 2013 Sept 26]. Available from: http://publications.gc.ca/collections/collection_2007/hc-sc/H164-48-2007E.pdf.

18 Marketed Health Products Directorate. How adverse reaction information on health products is used. Ottawa; 2004.

19 Turner C. Re: ADHD drugs suspected of hurting Canadian kids. Toronto Star. [Internet]. 2012 Sept 27.

20 Bruser D, Bailey A. ADHD drugs suspected of hurting Canadian kids. Toronto Star. [Internet]. 2012 Sept 26.

21 Villemure C. Health product safety board: progress update. Powerpoint presentation at Advisory Committee Meeting; 2005 Nov 24–25.

22 Health Products and Food Branch. Inaugural summary meeting report – Expert Advisory Committee on the Vigilance of Health Products, November 27–28, 2007 [Internet]. Ottawa: Health Canada; c2007 [cited 2014 Sept 17]. Available from: http://www.hc-sc.gc.ca/dhp-mps/medeff/advise-consult/eacvhp-ccevps/meet-reunion/nov-nov-07-eng.php.

23 Committee meeting summary reports [Internet]. Ottawa: Health Canada; c2012 [cited 2014 Sept 17]. Available from: http://www.hc-sc.gc.ca/dhp-mps/medeff/advise-consult/eacvhp-ccevps/meet-reunion/index-eng.php.

24 Expert Advisory Committee on the Vigilance of Health Products. In this topic [Internet]. Ottawa: Health Canada; c2012 [cited 2014 Sept 17].

Available from: http://www.hc-sc.gc.ca/dhp-mps/medeff/advise-consult/eacvhp-ccevps/index-eng.php.

25 Public Policy Forum. Improving Canada's regulatory process for therapeutic products: building the action plan: multi-stakeholder consultation. Ottawa: Public Policy Forum, 2003.

26 Auditor General of Canada. Report of the Auditor General of Canada to the House of Commons. Ottawa: Office of the Auditor General of Canada; 2006. Chapter 8, allocating funds to regulatory programs – Health Canada.

27 Lexchin J, Wiktorowicz M, Moscou K, et al. Provincial drug plan officials' views of the Canadian drug safety system. J Health Polit Policy Law. 2013;38(3):545–71. http://dx.doi.org/10.1215/03616878-2079514. Medline:23418364

28 Abraham J, Shepherd J. The therapeutic nightmare: the battle over the world's most controversial sleeping pill. Abingdon (England): Earthscan; 1999.

29 Health Protection Branch. Health Canada statement on triazolam (Halcion). Dear Doctor Bulletin. 1992; No. 39

30 Furberg CD, Psaty BM, Meyer JV. Nifedipine. Dose-related increase in mortality in patients with coronary heart disease. Circulation. 1995;92(5):1326–31. http://dx.doi.org/10.1161/01.CIR.92.5.1326. Medline:7648682

31 Health Protection Branch. Safety of calcium channel blockers in the treatment of patients with hypertension and coronary artery disease. Dear Doctor Bulletin. 1996; No. 44:1–5

32 Government of Canada. Ken Rubin v. Minister of Health; indexed as: Rubin v. Canada (Minister of Health). InfoSource Bulletin. 2003;26:96–9.

33 Risk Sciences International. Final report: review of Health Canada's actions in the recall of Alysena™ 28 [Internet]. Ottawa: RSI; c2013 [cited 2014 Sept 17]. Available from: http://www.hc-sc.gc.ca/ahc-asc/pubs/hpfb-dgpsa/2013-alysena-recall-rappel/index-eng.php.

34 Health Canada. Health Canada important safety information on Adderall XR™ (amphetamine salts) [Internet]. Ottawa: Health Canada; c2005 [updated Feb 9; cited 2009 Jan 4]. Available from:http://healthycanadians.gc.ca/recall-alert-rappel-avis/hc-sc/2005/14302a-eng.php.

35 Kondro W. Inconclusive evidence puts Adderall back on the market. CMAJ. 2005;173(8):858. http://dx.doi.org/10.1503/cmaj.051145. Medline:16217102

36 Zlomislic D. Risky acne drug Diane-35 underscores Health Canada's limitations. Toronto Star. [Internet]. 2013 Nov 9.

37 Wiktorowicz M, Lexchin J, Moscou K, et al. Keeping an eye on prescription drugs: Keeping Canadians safe: active monitoring systems for drug safety and effectiveness in Canada and internationally. Toronto: Health Council of Canada; 2010.
38 Lexchin J. New drugs and safety: what happened to new active substances approved in Canada between 1995 and 2010? Arch Intern Med. 2012;172(21):1680–1. http://dx.doi.org/10.1001/archinternmed.2012.4444. Medline:23044937
39 Lexchin J. Postmarket safety warnings for drugs approved in Canada under the Notice of Compliance with conditions policy. Br J Clin Pharmacol. 2015;79(5):847–59. Medline:25393960
40 Carpenter D, Zucker EJ, Avorn J. Drug-review deadlines and safety problems. N Engl J Med. 2008;358(13):1354–61. http://dx.doi.org/10.1056/NEJMsa0706341. Medline:18367738
41 Carpenter D. Drug-review deadlines and safety problems (author's reply). N Engl J Med. 2008;358(13):96–8.
42 Health Products and Food Branch. Cost recovery framework: official notice of fee proposal for human drugs and medical devices. Ottawa: Health Canada; 2007.
43 Auditor General of Canada. Report of the auditor general of Canada to the House of Commons. Ottawa: Office of the Auditor General of Canada; 2011. Chapter 4, regulating pharmaceutical drugs – Health Canada.
44 Decima Research Inc. Public opinion survey on key issues pertaining to post-market surveillance of marketed health products in Canada. Toronto: Decima Research; 2003.
45 Graham DJ, Drinkard CR, Shatin D, et al. Liver enzyme monitoring in patients treated with troglitazone. JAMA. 2001;286(7):831–3. http://dx.doi.org/10.1001/jama.286.7.831. Medline:11497537
46 Willy ME, Manda B, Shatin D, et al. A study of compliance with FDA recommendations for pemoline (Cylert). J Am Acad Child Adolesc Psychiatry. 2002;41(7):785–90. http://dx.doi.org/10.1097/00004583-200207000-00009. Medline:12108802
47 Valiyeva E, Herrmann N, Rochon PA, et al. Effect of regulatory warnings on antipsychotic prescription rates among elderly patients with dementia: a population-based time-series analysis. CMAJ. 2008;179(5):438–46. http://dx.doi.org/10.1503/cmaj.071540. Medline:18725616
48 Gomes T, Juurlink DN, Moore I, et al. The impact of federal warnings on publically funded desmopressin utilization among children in Ontario. J Pediatr Urol. 2012;8(3):249–53. http://dx.doi.org/10.1016/j.jpurol.2011.06.001. Medline:21767992

49 Council of Canadian Academies. Health product risk communication: is the message getting through? Ottawa: Council of Canadian Academies; 2015.
50 Berger J. Regulatory compliance – technical report no. 8: program evaluation study of the Drug Safety, Quality and Efficacy Program. Ottawa: Health and Welfare Canada; 1989.
51 Health Canada. Harper government moves to strengthen drug safety [Internet]. Ottawa: Health Canada; c2012 [cited 2014 Sept 19]. Available from: http://www.newswire.ca/news-releases/harper-government-moves-to-strengthen-drug-safety-511147101.html.
52 Health Products and Food Branch Inspectorate. Summary report of the drug good manufacturing practices (GMP) inspection program, April 1, 2006 to March 31, 2011. Ottawa: Health Canada; 2012.
53 Bruser D, McLean J. Canadians kept in dark about defective drugs. Toronto Star. [Internet]. 2014 Sept 11.
54 McLean J, Bruser D. 'Feeble' Health Canada can't block dodgy drug imports. Toronto Star. [Internet]. 2014 Sept 19.
55 McLean J, Bruser D. Canadian drug companies violating the law. Toronto Star. [Internet]. 2014 Nov 4.
56 Adverse reaction database [Internet] Ottawa: Health Canada; c2014 [cited 2014 Sept 19]. Available from: http://www.hc-sc.gc.ca/dhp-mps/medeff/databasdon/index-eng.php.
57 Auditor General of Canada. Report of the auditor general of Canada to the House of Commons. Ottawa: Office of the Auditor General of Canada; 2000. Chapter 26, Health Canada – regulatory regime of biologics.
58 Vitry A, Lexchin J, Sasich L, et al. Provision of information on regulatory authorities' websites. Intern Med J. 2008;38(7):559–67. http://dx.doi.org/10.1111/j.1445-5994.2007.01588.x. Medline:18336542
59 CBC News. Details on reports of adverse reactions connected with COX-2 inhibitors [Internet]. Toronto: CBC.ca; c2004 [cited 2014 September 20]. Available from: http://www.cbc.ca/news2/background/drugs/cox-2-adr.html.
60 Adverse reaction data on websites. Ottawa: Health Canada; 2004.
61 CBC News. In-depth: faint warning [Internet]. Toronto: CBC.ca; c2004 [cited 2014 Sept 20]. Available from: http://www.cbc.ca/news2/adr/media.html.
62 Health Products and Food Branch Inspectorate. Summary report of the post-market reporting compliance inspections conducted from September 1, 2005, to March 31, 2008 [Internet]. Ottawa: Health Canada; c2009 [cited 2014 Sept 20]. Available from: http://www.hc-sc.gc.ca/dhp-mps/compli-conform/gmp-bpf/docs/sum_rep_pmrc-rap_som_cedac_ltr-doc-eng.php.

63 McLean J. Dangers of off-label drug use kept secret. Toronto Star. [Internet]. 2014 Jun 26.
64 Eguale T, Buckeridge DL, Winslade NE, et al. Drug, patient, and physician characteristics associated with off-label prescribing in primary care. Arch Intern Med. 2012;172(10):781–8. http://dx.doi.org/10.1001/archinternmed.2012.340. Medline:22507695
65 NZPhvC. CARM [Internet]. Dunedin (NZ): New Zealand Pharmacovigilance Centre; c2014 [cited 2014 Sept 19]. Available from: https://nzphvc.otago.ac.nz/carm/.
66 Bruser D, McLean J. Health Canada brushes off reports of serious side effects. Toronto Star. [Internet]. 2012 October 29.
67 MedEffect Canada. Guidance document for industry – reporting adverse reactions to marketed health products. Ottawa: Ministry of Health; 2011.
68 Castle GH, Kelly B. Global harmonization is not all that global: divergent approaches in drug safety. Food Drug Law J. 2008;63(3):601–22. Medline:19031662
69 Health Council of Canada. A commentary on the national pharmaceuticals strategy: a prescription unfilled [Internet]. Toronto: Health Council; c2009 [cited 2014 Oct 14]. Available from: http://epe.lac-bac.gc.ca/100/200/301/hcc-ccs/commentary_ntl_pharmaceutical_strategy-e/H174-16-2009-2E.pdf.
70 Government of Canada. First minister's meeting on the future of health care 2004: A 10-year plan to strengthen health care [Internet]. Ottawa: Government of Canada; c2004 [cited 2014 Oct 14]. Available from: http://healthycanadians.gc.ca/health-system-systeme-sante/cards-cartes/collaboration/2004-meeting-racontre-eng.php.
71 Federal/Provincial/Territorial Ministerial Task Force. National pharmaceuticals strategy: progress report. Ottawa: Health Canada; 2006.
72 Collier R. Post-market drug surveillance projects developing slowly. CMAJ. 2010;182(1):E43. http://dx.doi.org/10.1503/cmaj.109-3103. Medline:19901045
73 Silversides A. Health Canada's investment in new post-market drug surveillance network a "pittance." CMAJ. 2008;179(5):412–13. http://dx.doi.org/10.1503/cmaj.081099. Medline:18635604
74 Ethinylestradiol + cyproterone. Good riddance. Prescrire Int. 2013;22(139):151.
75 Zlomislic D. Health Canada review of controversial acne drug kept secret. Toronto Star. [Internet]. 2013 Oct 19.
76 Zlomislic D. Drug safety reviews to be made public, health minister says. Toronto Star. [Internet]. 2013 Oct 24.

77 Regulatory transparency and openness [Internet]. Ottawa: Health Canada; c2014 [cited 2014 Sept 20]. Available from: http://www.hc-sc.gc.ca/home-accueil/rto-tor/index-eng.php.
78 Zlomislic D. Health Canada releases summary report of controversial drug Diane-35. Toronto Star. [Internet]. 2014 Apr 9.
79 Zlomislic D. Drugs reviews mostly stay secret. Toronto Star. [Internet]. 2014 Apr 3.
80 Health Products and Food Branch. Blueprint for renewal: transforming Canada's approach to regulating health products and food. Ottawa: Health Canada; 2006.
81 D.M.H. The 75th anniversary dinner. Food and Drug News. 1950;4(2): 21–3.
82 Weeks C, Galloway G. Ottawa gets tough on consumer safety: legislation would make it easier to pull potentially harmful products off the shelves and fast-track new drugs onto the market. Globe and Mail. 2008 Apr 8; Sect. A:1
83 An Act to Amend the Food and Drugs Act and to Make Consequential Amendments to Other Acts, Bill C-51, 39th Parl., 2d Sess. (2008).
84 Lundh A, Sismondo S, Lexchin J, et al. Industry sponsorship and research outcome. Cochrane Database Syst Rev. 2012;12(12):MR000033. Medline:23235689
85 Herder M, Gibson E, Graham J, et al. Regulating prescription drugs for patient safety: does Bill C-17 go far enough? CMAJ. 2014;186(8):E287–92. http://dx.doi.org/10.1503/cmaj.131850. Medline:24616135
86 An Act to Amend the Food and Drugs Act, Bill C-17, 1st reading, 41st Parl., 2d Sess. (2013).
87 Robinson W. Remarks before the House of Commons Standing Committee on Health on Bill C-17 [Internet]. Ottawa: Rx&D; c2014 [cited 2014 Sept 21]. Available from: http://sharing.canadapharma.org/CMFiles/Media%20Centre/Speeches%20and%20Presentations/20140612_Remarks_HESA_EN.pdf.
88 Rhines J, Robinson W. Standing Senate Committee on Social Affairs, Science and Technology, Bill C-17 [Internet]. Ottawa: Rx&D; c2014 [cited 2014 Oct 19]. Available from: http://sharing.canadapharma.org/CMFiles/Media%20Centre/Speeches%20and%20Presentations/20141001_Remarks_Rhines_Robinson_C-17_SOCI_EN_FINAL.pdf.
89 An Act to Amend the Food and Drugs Act, Bill C-17, 41st Parl., 2d Sess., passed 16 Jun 2014. (2014).
90 Standing Senate Committee on Social Affairs Science and Technology. Evidence [Internet]. Ottawa: Parliament of Canada; c2014 [updated 9 Oct

2014; cited 27 Oct 2014]. Available from: http://www.parl.gc.ca/content/sen/committee/412/SOCI/51634-E.HTM.

91 Hébert PC, Stanbrook MB, MacDonald N, et al. Can Health Canada protect Canadians from unsafe drugs? CMAJ. 2011;183(10):1125–6. http://dx.doi.org/10.1503/cmaj.110489. Medline:21502342

92 Maor M. Organizational reputations and the observability of public warnings in 10 pharmaceutical markets. Governance (Oxford). 2011;24(3):557–82. http://dx.doi.org/10.1111/j.1468-0491.2011.01536.x.

93 Eggertson L. Health Canada "passes the buck" on diabetes drug, researcher charges. CMAJ. 2011;183(2):E75–6. http://dx.doi.org/10.1503/cmaj.109-3762. Medline:21173068

94 Collier R. Scrutiny of Diane-35 due to potential dangers of off-label prescribing. CMAJ. 2013;185(5):E217–18. http://dx.doi.org/10.1503/cmaj.109-4414. Medline:23439622

95 Therapeutic Products Directorate. Business transformation progress report. Ottawa: Health Canada; 2004.

6. Is intellectual property a right?

1 Top 100 products based on Rx dollar value [Internet]. Toronto: Canadian Health Network; c2012 [cited 2014 Sept 29]. Available from: http://www.canadianhealthcarenetwork.ca/files/2012/03/Top-Rx-Drugs.pdf.

2 Parliament of Canada. Minutes of proceedings and evidence no. 4: Hearing before the House of Commons Special Committee on Drug Costs and Prices (16 June 1966). Ottawa: Queen's Printer and Controller of Stationery; 1966.

3 PMAC. Principles and code of marketing practice. Ottawa: PMAC; 1972.

4 Walkom T. Rae days: the rise and follies of the NDP. Toronto: Key Porter Books Limited; 1994.

5 Rx&D. S-17: a necessary first step to bring Canada's patent act to internationally competitive standards. A brief to the House of Commons Standing Committee on Industry, Science and Technology. Ottawa: Canada's Research-Based Pharmaceutical Companies; 2001.

6 Canadian Chamber of Commerce. Innovation for a better tomorrow: closing Canada's intellectual property gap in the pharmaceutical sector. Ottawa: Canadian Chamber of Commerce; 2011.

7 Paris V, Docteur E. Pharmaceutical pricing and reimbursement policies in Canada. Paris: OECD; 2006. http://dx.doi.org/10.1787/346071162287.

8 Patented Medicine Prices Review Board. Annual report 2013. Ottawa: PMPRB; 2014.

9 Lexchin J. Generics competition in the EU, US and Canada [Internet]. Amsterdam (Netherlands): Health Action International; 2012 [cited 2014 Sept 29]. Available from: http://www.politicsofmedicines.org/articles/generics-competition-in-the-eu-us-and-canada.
10 Hitchings AW, Baker EH, Khong TK. Making medicines evergreen. BMJ. 2012;345(nov29 3):e7941. http://dx.doi.org/10.1136/bmj.e7941. Medline:23197598
11 Svensson S, Mansfield PR. Escitalopram: superior to citalopram or a chiral chimera? Psychother Psychosom. 2004;73(1):10–16. http://dx.doi.org/10.1159/000074435. Medline:14665791
12 Scassa T. Patents for second medical indications and their potential impact on pharmacare in Canada. Health Law J. 2001;9:23–59. Medline:12141223
13 Hollis A. The anti-competitive effects of brand-controlled "pseudo-generics" in the Canadian pharmaceutical market. Can Public Policy. 2003;29(1):21–32. http://dx.doi.org/10.2307/3552486.
14 Hollis A. How do brands' "own generics" affect pharmaceutical prices? Rev Ind Organ. 2005;27(4):329–50. http://dx.doi.org/10.1007/s11151-005-5469-5.
15 Hemminki E, Hailey D, Koivusalo M. The courts – a challenge to health technology assessment. Science. 1999;285(5425):203–4. http://dx.doi.org/10.1126/science.285.5425.203. Medline:10428717
16 Shuchman M. Drug firm threatens suit over MD's product review Globe and Mail. 1999 Nov 17; Sect. A:1.
17 Talking points re: media reports – Dr. Holbrook and AstraZeneca [Internet]. Ottawa: Rx&D; c2002 [cited 2003 Mar 1]. Available from: https://web.archive.org/web/20020911190653/http://www.canadapharma.org/Media_Centre/Backgrounders/Holbrook99_e.html.
18 Restrictive Trade Practices Commission. Report concerning the manufacture, distribution and sale of drugs. Ottawa: Restrictive Trade Practices Commission; 1963.
19 Royal Commission on Health Services. Report. Ottawa: Queen's Printer and Controller of Stationery; 1964.
20 House of Commons of Canada. Second (final) report of the Special Committee of the House of Commons on Drug Costs and Prices. Ottawa: Queen's Printer and Controller of Stationery; 1967.
21 Canadian Generic Pharmaceutical Association. The Canadian generic market year 2013 [Internet]. Toronto: CGPA; c2014 [cited 2014 Sept 29]. Available from: http://www.canadiangenerics.ca/en/resources/market_trends.asp.

22 Shulman S, Richard B. The 1987 Canadian patent law amendments: revised pharmaceutical licensing provisions. Food Drug Cosmetic Law Journal. 1988;43:745–57.
23 Gorecki P. Regulating the price of prescription drugs in Canada: compulsory licensing, product selection and government reimbursement programmes. Ottawa: Economic Council of Canada; 1981.
24 Lang R. The politics of drugs: a comparative pressure-group study of the Canadian Pharmaceutical Manufacturers Association and the Association of the British Pharmaceutical Industry, 1930–1970. Westmead (England): Saxon House; 1974.
25 Reichman J, Hasenzahl C. Non-voluntary licensing of patented inventions: historical perspective, legal framework under TRIPS, and an overview of the practice in Canada and the USA (Issue paper no. 5). Geneva: UNCTAD-ICTSD; 2003.
26 Commission of Inquiry on the Pharmaceutical Industry. Report. Ottawa: Supply and Services Canada; 1985.
27 Sawatsky J, Cashore H. Inside dope. This Magazine; 1986 (September-October). p. 4–12.
28 McQuaig L. The quick and the dead. Toronto: Viking Press; 1991.
29 Andre, H. Notes for opening remarks to legislative committee on Bill C-22 by the Honourable Harvie Andre Minister of Consumer and Corporate Affairs Canada. Ottawa: Consumer and Corporate Affairs Canada; 1986.
30 Crane D. Drug bill concessions seem tied to trade talks. Toronto Star. 1986 Dec 7; Sect. B:1.
31 Howard R. MPs say Tories made deal on drug bill. Globe and Mail. 1987 Oct 16; Sect. A:13.
32 Auerbach S. US bowed to Canadian demands to change pact. Washington Post. 1987 Oct 17; Sect. G:2.
33 Lewington J. Drug-patent bill not enough to satisfy US on free trade. Globe and Mail. 1987 Aug 13; Sect. A:1.
34 McFetridge D. Intellectual property rights and the location of innovative activity: the Canadian experience with compulsory licensing of patented pharmaceuticals [Internet]. Ottawa: Carleton University; c1997 [cited 2014 Oct 3]. Available from: http://http-server.carleton.ca/~dmcfet/personal/NBER.PDF.
35 Lanjouw J, Jack W. Trading up: how much should poor countries pay to support pharmaceutical innovation. Washington (DC): Center for Global Development; c2004 [cited 2014 Sept 30]. Available from: http://www.cgdev.org/publication/trading-how-much-should-poor-countries-pay-support-pharmaceutical-innovation.

36 Drug patent law. Toronto: CBC Radio: The House; 1997 January 25.
37 Standing Committee on Industry of the House of Commons. Review of section 14 of the patent act amendment 1992 (chapter 2, statutes of Canada, 1993). Ottawa: Canada Communication Group; 1997.
38 MacKinnon M. WTO rejects patent law appeal. Globe and Mail. 2000 Sept 19; Sect. B:10.
39 Scoffield H. WTO upholds drug patent rule. Globe and Mail. 2000 Mar 18; Sect. B:3.
40 Canadian Drug Manufacturers Association. Battle to repeal automatic injunctions against generic drug approvals moves to the fall. CDMA Viewpoint. 2001;1:6.
41 Anderson M, Parent K. Timely access to generic drugs: issues for health policy in Canada. Kingston: Queen's University; 2001.
42 Lexchin J. Canada's patented medicine notice of compliance regulations: balancing the scales or tipping them? BMC Health Serv Res. 2011;11(1):64. http://dx.doi.org/10.1186/1472-6963-11-64. Medline:21435247
43 Faunce TA, Lexchin J. 'Linkage' pharmaceutical evergreening in Canada and Australia. Aust New Zealand Health Policy. 2007;4(1):8. http://dx.doi.org/10.1186/1743-8462-4-8. Medline:17543113
44 Government of Canada. Regulations amending the patented medicines (notice of compliance) regulations. Can Gaz, II. 2006;140(21):1503–25.
45 Rx&D. Protecting pharmaceutical innovation: an explanation of Canada's "linkage" regulations. Ottawa: Canada's Research-Based Pharmaceutical Companies; 2003.
46 CGPA. The patented medicines (notice of compliance) regulations. Toronto: Canadian Generic Pharmaceutical Association; 2003.
47 McGregor G. Industry committee votes 10–1 to hold review of NOC regulations. Ottawa Citizen. 2002 Jun 12; Sect. A:6.
48 McGregor G. Victory for big drug makers. MPs shelve review of policy that helps keep generic rivals off the market. Ottawa Citizen. 2003 Apr 1; Sect. A:1.
49 McGregor G. Generic drug makers argue patent laws stifle investment: "evergreening" quashes competition, boosts prices, Commons committee told. Ottawa Citizen. 2003 Jun 4; Sect. A:5.
50 McGregor G. Brand-name drugmakers urge status quo on patents: easing rules for cheaper products of competitors "violates trade obligations." Ottawa Citizen. 2003 Jun 5; Sect. A:5.
51 Jack I. Drug R&D at risk if rule changes, hearing told: brands v. generics. National Post. 2003 Jun 10; Sect. FP:4.

52 Grootendorst P, Bouchard R, Hollis A. Canada's laws on pharmaceutical intellectual property: the case for fundamental reform. CMAJ. 2012;184(5):543–9. http://dx.doi.org/10.1503/cmaj.110493. Medline:22065362
53 CGPA. Supreme court decision proves fed's gift to big pharma unnecessary. Toronto: Canadian Generic Pharmaceutical Association; 2006.
54 CPGA. Section 8 damages under pharmaceutical patent regulations [Internet]. Toronto: Canadian Generic Pharmaceutical Association; c2010 [cited 2010 Oct 30]. Available from: https://web.archive.org/web/20081115064850/http://www.canadiangenerics.ca/en/advocacy/section8_damages.asp.
55 Government of Canada. Regulations amending the patented medicines (notice of compliance) regulations. Can Gaz, II. 2008;142(13):1586–93.
56 Pharmaceutical Research and Manufacturers of America. Special 301 submission 2014. Washington (DC): USTR; 2014.
57 United States Trade Representative. 2010 Special 301 Report. Washington (DC): USTR; 2010.
58 Adamini S, Maarse H, Versluis E, et al. Policy making on data exclusivity in the European Union: from industrial interests to legal realities. J Health Polit Policy Law. 2009;34(6):979–1010. http://dx.doi.org/10.1215/03616878-2009-033. Medline:20018988
59 Grabowski H, Long G, Mortimer R. Data exclusivity for biologics. Nat Rev Drug Discov. 2011;10(1):15–16. http://dx.doi.org/10.1038/nrd3277. Medline:21193860
60 Pharmaceutical Research and Manufacturers of America. Special 301 submission 2003. Washington (DC): USTR; 2003.
61 Reichman J. The international legal status of undisclosed clinical trials data: from private to public goods? In: Roffe P, Tansey G, Vivas-Eugui D, editors. Negotiating health: intellectual property and access to medicines. London: Earthscan; 2006.
62 Food and Drug Regulations, C.R.C., c. 870, (2014).
63 Foreign Affairs Trade and Development Canada. The North American Free Trade Agreement (NAFTA) [Internet]. Ottawa: Government of Canada; c2014 [cited 2014 Oct 1]. Chapter 11, investment. Available from: http://www.international.gc.ca/trade-agreements-accords-commerciaux/topics-domaines/disp-diff/nafta.aspx?lang=eng.
64 Pavey B, Williams T. The North American free trade agreement [Internet]. Ottawa: Library of Parliament; c2003 [cited 2014 Oct 1]. Chapter 11. Available from: http://publications.gc.ca/collections/Collection-R/LoPBdP/EB-e/prb0254-e.pdf.

65 Sinclair S. NAFTA chapter 11 investor-state disputes to October 2010. Ottawa: Canadian Centre for Policy Alternatives; 2010.
66 Behsudi A. Eli Lilly sues Canada on drug patents [Internet]. Arlington, VA: Politico; c2013 [cited 2014 Oct 1]. Available from: http://www.politico.com/story/2013/09/eli-lilly-sues-canada-over-drug-patents-096743.
67 Stastna K. Eli Lilly files $500M NAFTA suit against Canada over drug patents [Internet]. Toronto: CBC.ca News; 2013 [updated Sept 13; cited 2014 Oct 1]. Available from: http://www.cbc.ca/news/business/eli-lilly-files-500m-nafta-suit-against-canada-over-drug-patents-1.1829854.
68 Gray J. Eli Lilly NAFTA challenge "without merit," Ottawa says. Globe and Mail. 2014 Jul 14; Sect. B:4
69 U.S. pharmaceutical corporation uses NAFTA foreign investor privileges regime to attack Canada's patent policy, demand $100 million for invalidation of a patent. Washington (DC): Public Citizen; 2013.
70 Panetta A. Canada reply to $500 million U.S. pharma suit: guesses don't make valid patents. Toronto Star. 2015 Feb 11; Sect. B:4.
71 Verbeeten D. CETA and changes to Canada's pharmaceutical regime: too much or not enough IP? Ottawa: Conference Board of Canada; 2014.
72 Bartucci S, Dawson L. Pills, patents & profits III – strong medicine: can free trade agreements cure Canada's pharmaceutical ills? Ottawa: Macdonald-Laurier Institute; 2013.
73 Manley J, Williams R. Enhancing trade by protecting intellectual property. National Post. 2011 Apr 14; Sect. A:16.
74 Scoffield H. Mulroney wades into EU free-trade talks, egging on brand-name pharma [Internet]. Toronto: Canadian Business; c2012 [cited 2014 Oct 1]. Available from: http://www.canadianbusiness.com/business-news/mulroney-wades-into-eu-free-trade-talks-egging-on-brand-name-pharma/.
75 Foreign Affairs Trade and Development Canada. Canada-European Union: Comprehensive Economic and Trade Agreement (CETA) [Internet]. Ottawa: Government of Canada; c2014 [cited 2015 Feb 22]. Available from: http://international.gc.ca/trade-agreements-accords-commerciaux/agr-acc/ceta-aecg/understanding-comprendre/brief-bref.aspx?lang=eng.
76 Sinclair S, Gagnon M-A, Lexchin J. Intellectual property rights: pharmaceuticals. In: Sinclair S, Trew S, Mertins-Kirkwood H, editors. Making sense of the CETA: an analysis of the final text of the Canada-European Union comprehensive economic and trade agreement. Ottawa: Canadian Centre for Policy Alternatives; 2014. p. 56–61.
77 Rx&D. Reality check: analysis of the CGPA's economic impact assessment of proposed pharmaceutical IP provisions. Ottawa: Rx&D; 2011.

78 Centre for Innovation in Regulatory Science. The impact of the changing regulatory environment on the approval of new medicines across six major authorities 2004–2013 [Internet]. London (England): Centre for Innovation in Regulatory Science; c2014 [cited 2015 Feb 17]. Available from: http://cirsci.org/publications/R&D%20Briefing%2055%20 16122014.pdf.
79 Shajarizadeh A, Hollis A. Delays in the submission of new drugs in Canada. CMAJ. 2015;187(1):E47–51
80 Lexchin J, Gagnon M-A. CETA and pharmaceuticals: impact of the trade agreement between Europe and Canada on the costs of prescription drugs. Global Health. 2014;10(1):30. http://dx.doi.org/10.1186/1744-8603-10-30. Medline:24885309
81 Secor-KPMG. Improving the health of Canadians: the contribution of the innovative pharmaceutical industry. Toronto: Secor-KPMG; 2012.
82 Industry Canada. Canada's pharmaceutical industry and prospects [Internet]. Ottawa: Industry Canada; c2013 [cited 2014 Oct 2]. Available from: http://www.ic.gc.ca/eic/site/lsg-pdsv.nsf/eng/hn01768.html.
83 Webster PC. CETA: a win for Canada or European pharma? CMAJ. 2014;186(15):E565–6. http://dx.doi.org/10.1503/cmaj.109-4904. Medline:25267767
84 Gagnon M-A, Gold R. Public financial support to the Canadian brand-name pharmaceutical sector: a cost-benefit analysis. Ottawa: Health Canada; 2011.
85 Gray J. Supreme Court backs Glaxo in transfer-pricing dispute. Globe and Mail. 2012 Oct 19; Sect. B:12
86 Morgan S, Gagnon M-A, Law M, Cunningham C, Kohler J. Pharmaceutical industry employment in Canada: levels, trends, and issues for consideration. Vancouver: Centre for Health Services and Policy Research; 2010.
87 Statistics Canada. Table 281-0024: Survey of Employment Payrolls and Hours (SEPH), employment by type of employee and detailed North American Industry Classification System (NAICS) [Internet]. Ottawa: Statistics Canada; c2014 [cited 2014 Oct 2]. Available from: http://www5.statcan.gc.ca/cansim/a05?lang=eng&id=2810024.
88 Bramley-Harker E, Lewis D, Farahnik J, et al. Key factors in attracting internationally mobile investments by the research-based pharmaceutical industry. London (England): NERA Economic Consulting; 2007.
89 Palmedo M. Do pharmaceutical firms invest more heavily in countries with data exclusivity? Currents. 2013;21:38–47. Available from: http://papers.ssrn.com/sol3/papers.cfm?abstract_id=2259797

90 Baker D, Chatani N. Promoting good ideas on drugs: are patents the best way? The relative efficiency of patent and public support for bio-medical research (briefing paper). Washington (DC): Center for Economic and Policy Research; 2002.
91 Blumenthal D, Campbell EG, Anderson MS, et al. Withholding research results in academic life science. Evidence from a national survey of faculty. JAMA. 1997;277(15):1224–8. http://dx.doi.org/10.1001/jama.1997.03540390054035. Medline:9103347
92 D'Cruz JR, Fleischmann G, Allison W. Response to the Fraser Institute's report: Canada's drug price paradox 2008. Toronto: Canadian Generic Pharmaceutical Association; 2008.
93 Coombe R, Turcotte J. Cultural, political, and social implications of intellectual property laws in an informational economy. In: UNESCO-EOLSS Joint Committee, editor. Culture, Civilization, and Human Society: Encyclopedia of life support systems (EOLSS). Paris (France): Eolss Publishers; 2012.
94 Expert Advisory Committee on Smart Regulation. Smart regulation: a regulatory strategy for Canada. Report to the Government of Canada. 2004.
95 Patterson RW. Whatever happened to the "America" in "corporate America"? [Internet]. New York: National Review; c2013 [cited 2016 Mar 1]. Available from: http://www.nationalreview.com/article/352429/whats-good-america-robert-w-patterson.

7. How revenue is generated: Prices, volume, mix, and overall spending

1 McDiarmid J. Hepatitis C cure available – but only if you can afford it. Toronto Star. [Internet]. 2014 Aug 4.
2 Verstraten K. Kalydeco: a "miracle drug," with a catch. Globe and Mail. [Internet]. 2014 Jun 20.
3 Blackwell T. World's most expensive drug – which costs up to $700,000 per year – too expensive, Canada says. National Post. 2015 Feb 3; Sect A:1.
4 Morgan SG, Daw JR. Canadian pharmacare: looking back, looking forward. Healthc Policy. 2012;8(1):14–23. Medline:23968600
5 Canada. Royal Commission on Health Services. Report. Ottawa: Queens' Printer; 1964.
6 Boothe K. Ideas and the limits on program expansion: the failure of nationwide pharmacare in Canada since 1944. Can J Polit Sci. 2013;46(02):419–53. http://dx.doi.org/10.1017/S000842391300022X.
7 Rosenthal E. The soaring cost of a simple breath. New York Times. [Internet]. 2013 Oct 12.

8 McKinnell H. A call to action: taking back healthcare for future generations. New York: McGraw Hill; 2005.
9 Mestre-Ferrandiz J, Sussex J, Towse A. The R&D cost of a new medicine. London (England): Office of Health Economics; 2012.
10 Bakan J. The corporation. London: Constable; 2004.
11 Rx&D. Letters to the editor [Internet]. Ottawa: Canada's Research-Based Pharmaceutical Companies; c2014 [updated 2014 Mar 10; cited 2014 Oct 6]. Available from: https://web.archive.org/web/20140428064228/http://www.canadapharma.org/editorletters.asp?a=view&id=68.
12 Patented Medicine Prices Review Board. Compendium of policies, guidelines and procedures – updated June 2014 [Internet]. Ottawa: PMPRB; c2014 [cited 2014 Oct 6]. Available from: http://www.pmprb-cepmb.gc.ca/view.asp?ccid=492.
13 Canadian Institute for Health Information. Drug expenditure in Canada, 1885 to 2012. Ottawa: CIHI; 2013.
14 OECD. Health at a glance 2013: OECD indicators. Paris (France): OECD; 2013.
15 Canadian Institute for Health Information. Drivers of prescription drug spending in Canada. Ottawa; CIHI; 2012.
16 Reid L. Testing patent laws. Financial Times. 1982 Oct 4. p. 14–15.
17 Parliament of Canada. Minutes of proceedings and evidence no. 4: Hearing before the House of Commons Special Committee on Drug Costs and Prices (16 June 1966). Ottawa: Queen's Printer and Controller of Stationery; 1966.
18 Rx&D. Saving lives – transforming care [Internet]. Ottawa: Canada's Research-Based Pharmaceutical Companies; c2013 [cited 2014 Sept 22]. Available from: http://sharing.canadapharma.org/CMFiles/Our%20Industry/Saving%20Lives%20-%20Transforming%20Care/20121022_Saving_Lives_high_res_Final_EN_Rev.pdf.
19 Lexchin J. Effect of generic drug competition on the price of prescription drugs in Ontario. CMAJ. 1993;148(1):35–8. Medline:8439888
20 PMAC. The pharmaceutical manufacturing industry. Ottawa: Pharmaceutical Manufacturers Association of Canada; 1973.
21 Brooke P. Resistant prices: a study of competitive strains in the antibiotic markets. New York: Council on Economic Priorities; 1975.
22 Advertisement for Anturan. Mod Med Can. 1982;37(Nov Suppl):214.
23 Crowe K. Drug companies using doctors, discount card to skirt generic substitutions: CBC.ca; 2015 [updated April 22; cited 2015 July 27]. Available from: http://www.cbc.ca/news/health/drug-companies-using-doctors-discount-cards-to-skirt-generic-substitutions-1.3042773.

24 Commission of Inquiry on the Pharmaceutical Industry. Report. Ottawa: Supply and Services Canada; 1985.
25 Svodoba M. Evaluation of the Patented Medicine Prices Review Board. Ottawa: Patented Medicine Prices Review Board; 2012.
26 Patented Medicine Prices Review Board. Annual report 2013. Ottawa: Patented Medicine Prices Review Board; 2014.
27 Decision on patent dedication. Patented Medicine Prices Review Board Bulletin. 1995 Oct;17.
28 Priest L. Canada: the staggering cost of survival with help of thalidomide. Globe and Mail. 2005 Aug 15; Sect. A:1.
29 PMPRB. Decision: PMPRB-07-DI-THALOMID [Internet]. Ottawa: PMPRB; c2008 [updated 2014 Jan 21; cited 2014 Oct 9]. Available from: http://www.pmprb-cepmb.gc.ca/CMFiles/Hearings%20and%20Decisions/Decisions%20and%20Orders/Board_Order_-_Statutory_Filings_-_Jan_21_0838JOP-1302008-6347.pdf.
30 North G, Newham C. Supreme Court of Canada finds Patented Medicine Prices Review Board has jurisdiction over price of Thalomid in Canada [Internet]. Toronto: Stikeman Elliott; c2011 [cited 2014 Oct 9]. Available from: http://www.canadiantechnologyiplaw.com/2011/01/articles/intellectual-property/patents-1/supreme-court-of-canada-finds-patented-medicine-prices-review-board-has-jurisdiction-over-price-of-thalomid-in-canada/print.html.
31 Gagnon M-A, Hébert G. The economic case for universal pharmacare: costs and benefits of publicly funded drug coverage for all Canadians. Ottawa: Canadian Centre for Policy Alternatives; 2010.
32 Gagnon M-A, Gold R. Public financial support to the Canadian brand-name pharmaceutical sector: a cost-benefit analysis. Ottawa: Health Canada; 2011.
33 Lexchin J. The effect of generic competition on the price of brand-name drugs. Health Policy. 2004;68(1):47–54. http://dx.doi.org/10.1016/j.healthpol.2003.07.007. Medline:15033552
34 Lexchin J. Do manufacturers of brand-name drugs engage in price competition? An analysis of introductory prices. CMAJ. 2006;174(8):1120–1. http://dx.doi.org/10.1503/cmaj.051687. Medline:16606961
35 Roberts EA, Herder M, Hollis A. Fair pricing of "old" orphan drugs: considerations for Canada's orphan drug policy. CMAJ. 2015;187(6):422–5. http://dx.doi.org/10.1503/cmaj.140308. Medline:25712953
36 Klass A. Report of the advisory committee on central drug purchasing and distribution. Winnipeg: Government of Manitoba; 1972.
37 Harper D. An open letter from Don Harper – no threat made by Dr. Wigle. Drug Merchandising. 1972;53(Sept):56, 74.

38 Cassels A. Paying for what works: BC's experience with the reference drug program as a model for rational policy making. Vancouver: Canadian Centre for Policy Alternatives; 2002.
39 PMAC launches campaign against reference-based pricing. PMAC News. 1995:1–2.
40 Reference pricing to stay in Canada. Scrip World News. 1996 Jun 18:14.
41 Rx&D. A vision for a healthier tomorrow: the pharma industry can pave the way to a stronger healthcare system and economy [Internet]. Ottawa: Canada's Research-Based Pharmaceutical Companies; c2010 [cited 2014 Oct 2]. Available from: http://www.chrisdaniels.ca/media/2007-Pharma-4.pdf.
42 Walkom T. Rae days: the rise and follies of the NDP. Toronto: Key Porter Books Limited; 1994.
43 Rx&D. Access to medicines: a critical health care issue. Ottawa: Canada's Research-Based Pharmaceutical Companies; nd.
44 CHPI. Comparing access to new drugs in Canada's federal and provincial public drug plans – Annual series: how good is your drug insurance? Toronto: Canadian Health Policy; 2014.
45 Pharmaceutical Industry Competitiveness Task Force. Competitiveness and performance indicators 2005 [Internet]. London (England): Association of the British Pharmaceutical Industry; c2006 [cited 2014 Sept 24]. Available from: http://www.abpi.org.uk/our-work/library/archive/Pages/competitiveness-task-force.aspx.
46 Crémieux P-Y, Meilleur M-C, Ouellette P, et al. Public and private pharmaceutical spending as determinants of health outcomes in Canada. Health Econ. 2005;14(2):107–16. http://dx.doi.org/10.1002/hec.922. Medline:15386658
47 Guindon GE, Contoyannis P. A second look at pharmaceutical spending as determinants of health outcomes in Canada. Health Econ. 2012;21(12):1477–95, discussion 1496–501. http://dx.doi.org/10.1002/hec.1415. Medline:18972325
48 Taylor C. The corporate response to rising health care costs. Ottawa: Conference Board of Canada; 1996.
49 Silversides A. Ontario's law curbing the cost of generic drugs sparks changes for pharmacies and other Canadian buyers. CMAJ. 2009;181(3-4):E43–5. http://dx.doi.org/10.1503/cmaj.091155. Medline:19652155
50 Government of Canada. Canadian generic drug sector study. Gatineau: Competition Bureau; 2007.
51 Stevenson H. An end to blank cheques: getting more value out of employer drug plans. Toronto: Reformulary Group; 2011.

52 Kratzer J, McGrail K, Strumpf E, et al. Cost-control mechanisms in Canadian private drug plans. Healthc Policy. 2013;9(1):35–43. Medline:23968672
53 Law MR, Kratzer J, Dhalla IA. The increasing inefficiency of private health insurance in Canada. CMAJ. 2014;186(12):E470–E474. http://dx.doi.org/10.1503/cmaj.130913. Medline:24664650
54 Standing Committee on Health of the House of Commons. Prescription drugs part 1 – common drug review: an F/P/T process. Ottawa: Communication Canada-Publishing; 2007.
55 Morgan SG, McMahon M, Mitton C, et al. Centralized drug review processes in Australia, Canada, New Zealand, and the United kingdom. Health Aff (Millwood). 2006;25(2):337–47. http://dx.doi.org/10.1377/hlthaff.25.2.337. Medline:16522575
56 Standing Committee on Health of the House of Commons . Evidence [Internet]. Ottawa: Parliament of Canada; c2007 [updated 2014 Apr 16; cited 2014 Oct 8]. Available from: http://www.parl.gc.ca/HousePublications/Publication.aspx?DocId=2833022&Language=E&Mode=1&Parl=39&Ses=1.
57 Lexchin J, Mintzes B. Medicine reimbursement recommendations in Canada, Australia, and Scotland. Am J Manag Care. 2008;14(9):581–8. Medline:18778173
58 Canadian Generic Pharmaceutical Association. The value of generic prescription medicines: are you taking full advantage [Internet]. Toronto: CGPA; c2013 [cited 2014 May 8]. Available from: http://www.canadiangenerics.ca/en/advocacy/docs/ValueofGenericPrescriptionMedicine2014.pdf
59 Morgan SG, Bassett KL, Wright JM, et al. "Breakthrough" drugs and growth in expenditure on prescription drugs in Canada. BMJ. 2005;331(7520):815–16. http://dx.doi.org/10.1136/bmj.38582.703866.AE. Medline:16141448
60 Zoutman DE, Ford BD, Bassili AR. A call for the regulation of prescription data mining. CMAJ. 2000;163(9):1146–8. Medline:11079059
61 Targeting doctors: the health data trade. Toronto: CBC News: Disclosure; 2002 March 5.
62 Mintzes B. Blurring the boundaries: new trends in drug promotion [Internet]. Amsterdam: HAI-Europe; c1998 [cited 2014 Oct 9]. Available from: https://web.archive.org/web/20140320210113/http://haiweb.org/pubs/blurring/blurring.intro.html.
63 Boyle T. New arthritis drug called "miracle" – eases painful side effects, maker claim. Toronto Star. 1999 Apr 16; Sect. A:1.
64 Pfizer. Making the connection™: the Heart and Stroke Foundation joins partnership to help Canadians control cholesterol. New York: Pfizer; 2014.

65 Lexchin J, Mintzes B. A compromise too far: a review of Canadian cases of direct-to-consumer advertising regulation. Int J Risk Saf Med. 2014;26(4):213–25. Medline:25420763

66 Rose C. Medical terrorism and the big lie [Internet]. Montreal: Panaceia or Hygeia; 2008 [cited 2014 Oct 9]. Available from: https://medicalmyths.wordpress.com/tag/canadian-lipid-nurse-network/.

67 Quick JD, Hogerzeil HV, Rägo L, et al. Ensuring ethical drug promotion--whose responsibility? Lancet. 2003;362(9385):747. http://dx.doi.org/10.1016/S0140-6736(03)14217-1. Medline:12957107

68 Diekmeyer P. DTC advertising battle heats up [Internet]. Dorval: Diekmeyer Report; c2002 [cited 2014 Oct 9]. Available from: http://www.peterdiekmeyer.com/020411.html.

69 Lougheed MD, Lemiere C, Ducharme FM, et al., and the Canadian Thoracic Society Asthma Clinical Assembly. Canadian Thoracic Society 2012 guideline update: diagnosis and management of asthma in preschoolers, children and adults. Can Respir J. 2012;19(2):127–64. Medline:22536582

70 Collier R. Clinical guideline writers often conflicted. CMAJ. 2011;183(3):E139–40. http://dx.doi.org/10.1503/cmaj.109-3757. Medline:21220450

71 Canadian Diabetes Association. Clinical practice guidelines [Internet]. Toronto: CDA; c2014 [cited 2014 Oct 9]. Available from: http://guidelines.diabetes.ca/disclaimer.

72 Neuman J, Korenstein D, Ross JS, et al. Prevalence of financial conflicts of interest among panel members producing clinical practice guidelines in Canada and United States: cross sectional study. BMJ. 2011;343:d5621. http://dx.doi.org/10.1136/bmj.d5621. Medline:21990257

73 Choudhry NK, Stelfox HT, Detsky AS. Relationships between authors of clinical practice guidelines and the pharmaceutical industry. JAMA. 2002;287(5):612–17. http://dx.doi.org/10.1001/jama.287.5.612. Medline:11829700

74 Cosgrove L, Bursztajn H, Erlich D, et al. Conflicts of interest and the quality of recommendations in clinical guidelines. J Eval Clin Pract. 2013;19(4):674–81. http://dx.doi.org/10.1111/jep.12016. Medline:23731207

75 Lacasse JR, Leo J. Ghostwriting at elite academic medical centers in the United States. PLoS Med. 2010;7(2):e1000230. http://dx.doi.org/10.1371/journal.pmed.1000230. Medline:20126384

76 McHenry L. On the origin of great ideas: science in the age of big pharma. Hastings Cent Rep. 2005;35(6):17–19. http://dx.doi.org/10.2307/3528561. Medline:16396201

77 Derfel A. McGill reprimands prof over ghostwriting scandal: failed to acknowledge DesignWrite's work. Montr Gaz. 2011; Sect. A:11
78 Johnson E. Inside the business of medical ghostwriting [broadcast]. Toronto: CBC Marketplace; c2003 Mar 25.
79 Shnier A, Lexchin J, Mintzes B, et al. Too few, too weak: conflict of interest policies at Canadian medical schools. PLoS One. 2013;8(7):e68633. http://dx.doi.org/10.1371/journal.pone.0068633. Medline:23861928
80 Government of Canada. A 10-year plan to strengthen health care [Internet]. Ottawa: Health Canada; c2004 [cited 2014 Oct 14]. Available from: http://healthycanadians.gc.ca/health-system-systeme-sante/cards-cartes/collaboration/2004-meeting-racontre-eng.php.
81 Health Council of Canada. A status report on the national pharmaceuticals strategy: a prescription unfilled Toronto: Health Council; 2009 [cited 2014 October 14]. Available from: http://www.healthcouncilcanada.ca/rpt_det.php?id=157.
82 Federal/Provincial/Territorial Ministerial Task Force. National pharmaceuticals strategy progress report. Ottawa: Health Canada; 2006.
83 Health Council of Canada. A commentary on the national pharmaceuticals strategy: a prescription unfilled [Internet]. Toronto: Health Council of Canada; c2009 [cited 2014 Oct 14]. Available from: http://epe.lac-bac.gc.ca/100/200/301/hcc-ccs/commentary_ntl_pharmaceutical_strategy-e/H174-16-2009-2E.pdf.
84 Standing Senate Committee on Social Affairs Science and Technology. Proceedings [Internet]. Ottawa: Parliament of Canada; c2011 [cited 2014 Oct 14]. Available from: http://www.parl.gc.ca/content/sen/committee/411/SOCI/08EVB-49206-E.HTM.
85 Pan-Canadian Pharmaceutical Alliance. Pan Canadian drugs negotiations report [Internet]. Ottawa: Council of the Federation; c2014 [cited 2015 Feb 24]. Available from: http://www.pmprovincesterritoires.ca/phocadownload/pcpa/pan_canadian_drugs_negotiations_report_march22_2014.pdf.
86 Canada's Premiers. Health care innovation working group [Internet]. Ottawa: Council of the Federation; c2014 [cited 2014 Oct 14]. Available from: http://www.canadaspremiers.ca/en/initiatives/128-health-care-innovation-working-group.
87 Canada's Premiers. The Pan-Canadian Pricing Alliance (PCPA): the "Goliath" of market access [Internet]. Ottawa: Council of the Federation; c2013 [cited 2014 Oct 14]. Available from: http://www.pmprovincesterritoires.ca/phocadownload/pcpa/pcpa-the_goliath_of_market_access_oct2013.pdf.

88 Smith J. Provinces target drug costs; faced with $10 billion tab, health ministers agree to negotiate with manufacturers for lower prices. Toronto Star. 2010 Sept 14; Sect. A1.
89 Rx&D. Rx&D reacts to Council of the Federation healthcare conclusions [Internet]. Ottawa: Canada's Research-Based Pharmaceutical Companies; c2013 [cited 2014 Oct 14]. Available from: https://web.archive.org/web/20130803033921/http://www.canadapharma.org/News.asp?a=view&id=66.
90 Demers V, Melo M, Jackevicius C, et al. Comparison of provincial prescription drug plans and the impact on patients' annual drug expenditures. CMAJ. 2008;178(4):405–9. http://dx.doi.org/10.1503/cmaj.070587. Medline:18268266
91 Law MR, Cheng L, Dhalla IA, et al. The effect of cost on adherence to prescription medications in Canada. CMAJ. 2012;184(3):297–302. http://dx.doi.org/10.1503/cmaj.111270. Medline:22249979

8. Who gets the value from research and development?

1 Parliament of Canada. Minutes of proceedings and evidence no. 4: Hearing before the House of Commons Special Committee on Drug Costs and Prices (16 June 1966). Ottawa: Queen's Printer and Controller of Stationery; 1966
2 Rx&D. Towards increasing research and development in Canada: a new innovative pharmaceutical strategy. Ottawa: Rx&D; 2004.
3 Rx&D. Saving lives – transforming care [Internet]. Ottawa: Canada's Research-Based Pharmaceutical Companies; c2013 [cited 2014 Sept 22]. Available from: http://sharing.canadapharma.org/our-industry/industry-facts/saving-lives—transforming-care
4 Aventis Pharma Inc. Submission presented to the federal government as part of Canada's innovation strategy. Laval: Aventis; 2003.
5 Rx&D. A vision for a healthier tomorrow. Ottawa: Rx&D; 2011.
6 Rx&D, Canadian Institutes of Health Research, Association of Canadian Academic Healthcare Organizations, Cameron Institute. Canadian clinical trial summit – starting the conversation [Internet]. Ottawa: ACAHO; c2011 [cited 2014 Sept 5]. Available from: http://www.healthcarecan.ca/wp-content/uploads/2014/07/Background-Document-Starting-the-Conversation.pdf.
7 Rx&D. Information guide. 2nd ed. Ottawa: Rx&D; c2003.
8 McKinlay JB, McKinlay SM. The questionable contribution of medical measures to the decline of mortality in the United States in the twentieth

century. Milbank Mem Fund Q Health Soc. 1977;55(3):405–28. http://dx.doi.org/10.2307/3349539. Medline:413067

9 Hollobon J, Lipovenko D. Coat-tail ride for "pirates" angers major drug firms. Globe and Mail. 1982 Oct 26;Sect. A:5.

10 Woods D. Antibusiness attitudes strangling drug research. Can Med Assoc J. 1982;127(7):559. Medline:20313795

11 Lexchin J. The real pushers: a critical analysis of the Canadian drug industry. Vancouver: New Star Books; 1984.

12 PMAC. The pharmaceutical industry and Ontario. Ottawa: PMAC; 1978.

13 Wigle WW. A pharmaceutical industry in Canada? Can Med Assoc J. 1967;97(22):1361. Medline:6061604

14 Guyatt G. Academic medicine and the pharmaceutical industry: a cautionary tale. CMAJ. 1994;150(6):951–3. Medline:8131127

15 DiMasi JA, Hansen RW, Grabowski HG. The price of innovation: new estimates of drug development costs. J Health Econ. 2003;22(2):151–85. http://dx.doi.org/10.1016/S0167-6296(02)00126-1. Medline:12606142

16 Secor-KPMG. Improving the health of Canadians: the contribution of the innovative pharmaceutical industry. Toronto: Secor-KPMG; 2012.

17 Tufts Center for the Study of Drug Development. Backgrounder: how the Tufts Center for the Study of Drug Development pegged the cost of a new drug at $2.6 billion [Internet]. Boston: Tufts; c2014 [cited 2015 Feb 24]. Available from: http://csdd.tufts.edu/files/uploads/cost_study_backgrounder.pdf.

18 Tufts Center for the Study of Drug Development. Financial disclosure [Internet]. Boston: Tufts; c2015 [cited 2015 Feb 24]. Available from: http://csdd.tufts.edu/about/financial_disclosure.

19 Light DW, Warburton RN. Extraordinary claims require extraordinary evidence. J Health Econ. 2005;24(5):1030–3, discussion 1034–53. http://dx.doi.org/10.1016/j.jhealeco.2005.07.001. Medline:16087260

20 DiMasi JA, Hansen RW, Grabowski HG. Extraordinary claims require extraordinary evidence [Reply]. J Health Econ. 2005;24(5):1034–44. http://dx.doi.org/10.1016/j.jhealeco.2005.07.002.

21 Light DW, Warburton RN. Setting the record straight in the reply by DiMasi, Hansen and Grabowski [Discussion]. J Health Econ. 2005;24(5):1045–8. http://dx.doi.org/10.1016/j.jhealeco.2005.07.003.

22 DiMasi JA, Hansen RW, Grabowski HG. Setting the record straight on setting the record straight: Response to the Light and Warburton rejoinder [Reply]. J Health Econ. 2004;24(5):1049–53. http://dx.doi.org/10.1016/j.jhealeco.2005.07.004.

23 Industry Canada. Canada's pharmaceutical industry and prospects. Ottawa: Industry Canada; 2013.
24 Commission of inquiry on the pharmaceutical industry. Report. Ottawa: Supply and Services Canada; 1985.
25 Gorecki P. Regulating the price of prescription drugs in Canada: compulsory licensing, product selection and government reimbursement programmes. Ottawa: Economic Council of Canada; 1981.
26 Gorecki PK, Henderson I. Compulsory patent licensing of drugs in Canada: a comment on the debate. Can Public Policy. 1981;7(4):559–68. http://dx.doi.org/10.2307/3549486.
27 Burstall M, Dunning J, Lake A. Multinational enterprises, governments and technologies – the pharmaceutical industry. Paris (France): OECD; 1981.
28 Palda K, Pazderka B. Background to a target: an international comparison of the Canadian pharmaceutical industry's R&D intensity (Research Report No. 71). Ottawa: Department of Industry, Trade and Commerce Canada; 1980.
29 Taylor P. Generics a bitter pill for big drug firms. Globe and Mail. 1983 Jul 16; Sect. B:1.
30 Pharmaceutical Industry Competitiveness Task Force. Competitiveness and performance indicators 2005 [Internet]. London (England): PICTF; c2006 [cited 2014 Sept 24]. Available from: http://www.abpi.org.uk/our-work/library/archive/Pages/competitiveness-task-force.aspx.
31 Toughill K. Drug firms to spend $93 million on research. Toronto Star. 1986 Nov 11; Sect. A:2.
32 Cote, M. Notes for remarks by the Honorable Michel Cote Minister of Consumer and Corporate Affairs. Ottawa: Parliament of Canada; 1986.
33 Andre, H. Notes for opening remarks to legislative committee on Bill C-22 by the Honourable Harvie Andre Minister of Consumer and Corporate Affairs Canada. Ottawa: Parliament of Canada; 1986.
34 Patented Medicine Prices Review Board. Annual report 2013. Ottawa: PMPRB; 2014.
35 Li S, Tomalin A. Patentees research and development expenditure in Canada. J Pharm Pharm Sci. 2002;5(1):5–11. Medline:12042113
36 McFetridge D. Intellectual property rights and the location of innovative activity: the Canadian experience with compulsory licensing of patented pharmaceuticals [Internet]. Ottawa: Carleton University; c1997 [cited 2014 Oct 3]. Available from: http://http-server.carleton.ca/~dmcfet/personal/NBER.PDF.
37 Taylor K. The impact of the pharmaceutical industry's clinical research programs on medical education, practice and researchers in Canada: a

discussion paper. Canadian pharmaceutical research and development: four short-term studies. Ottawa: Industry, Science & Technology Canada; 1991.
38 Statistics Canada. Industrial research and development: intentions, 1999–2014 (Report No. 88-202-X). Ottawa: Statistics Canada; 2015.
39 Grootendorst P, Matteo LD. The effect of pharmaceutical patent term length on research and development and drug expenditures in Canada. Healthc Policy. 2007;2(3):63–84. Medline:19305720
40 Pazderka B. The effect of pharmaceutical patent term length on R&D and drug expenditures in Canada. Healthc Policy. 2007;2(3):85–9. Medline:19305721
41 Schroeder H. Do patent terms impact domestic R&D spending in the pharmaceutical industry? Healthc Policy. 2007;2(3):90–4. Medline: 19305722
42 Koenig P, Macgarvie M. Regulatory policy and the location of bio-pharmaceutical foreign direct investment in Europe. J Health Econ. 2011;30(5):950–65. http://dx.doi.org/10.1016/j.jhealeco.2011.07.005. Medline:21899905
43 Government of Canada. Canada – your innovation partner in clinical trials (II). Ottawa: Industry Canada; 2009.
44 Government of Canada. Canada – your innovation partner in clinical trials [Internet]. Ottawa: Industry Canada; c2006 [cited 2014 Sept 5]. Available from: http://scimega.com/downloads/industry-reports/Canada_Innovation_Partner_Clinical-Trials.pdf.
45 Kermani F, Gittins R. Canada commits to R&D [Internet]. Bracknell (England): PharmiWeb; c2004 [cited 2006 Nov 22]. Available from: http://www.pharmiweb.com/features/feature.asp?ROW_ID=386.
46 Warda J. Measuring the attractiveness of R&D tax incentives: Canada and major industrial countries (Cat. No. 88F0006XIB-99010). Ottawa: Statistics Canada; 1999.
47 Warda J. Extending access to SR&ED tax credits: an international comparative analysis. Ottawa: Information Technology Association of Canada; 2003.
48 KPMG. Competitive alternatives – special report: focus on tax 2014 [Internet]. Toronto: KPMG; c2014 [cited 2014 Sept 24]. Available from: http://www.competitivealternatives.com/reports/2014_compalt_report_tax_en.pdf.
49 KPMG. Competitive alternatives – KPMG's guide to international business location costs [Internet]. Toronto: KPMG; c2014 [cited 2014 Sept 24]. Available from: http://www.competitivealternatives.com/reports/2014_compalt_execsum_en.pdf.

50 PriceWaterhouseCoopers. Rx&D companies: driving a better, stronger Canadian economy. Toronto: PriceWaterhouseCoopers; 2005.
51 Gagnon M-A, Gold R. Public financial support to the Canadian brand-name pharmaceutical sector: a cost-benefit analysis. Ottawa: Health Canada; 2011.
52 Taylor L. Quebec ends 15-year reimbursement for branded drugs. PharmaTimes Digital [Internet]. 2012 Nov 29 [cited 2014 Sept 29]. Available from: http://www.pharmatimes.com/Article/12-11-29/Quebec_ends_15-year_reimbursement_for_branded_drugs.aspx.
53 Therapeutics Initiative. Therapeutics Initiative: evidence based drug therapy [Internet]. Vancouver: Therapeutics Initiative; c2015 [cited 2015 Feb 17]. Available from: http://www.ti.ubc.ca.
54 Therapeutics Initiative. Celecoxib (Celebrex®) – is it a breakthrough drug? Therapeutics Letter. 1999 (31):1–2.
55 Silversides A. Highly lauded drug assessment program under attack. CMAJ. 2008;179(1):26–7. http://dx.doi.org/10.1503/cmaj.080845. Medline:18509096
56 Cousineau S. Pfizer to cut 300 Canadian jobs. Globe and Mail. 2012 Oct 28; Sect. B:3.
57 Canadian Press. Quebec Merck closure could mean "brain drain" [Internet]. Toronto: CBC News; c2010 [cited 2014 Sept 24]. Available from: http://www.cbc.ca/news/canada/montreal/quebec-merck-closure-could-mean-brain-drain-1.943253.
58 Marowits R. AstraZeneca closing Montreal R&D plant. Globe and Mail. 2012 Feb 2; Sect. B:7.
59 Silcoff S, Marotte B. Pharma giants slash jobs in Quebec. Globe and Mail. 2012 Jan 11; Sect. B:1.
60 Industry Canada. Canada's pharmaceutical industry and prospects [Internet]. Ottawa: Industry Canada; c2013 [cited 2014 Oct 2]. Available from: http://www.ic.gc.ca/eic/site/lsg-pdsv.nsf/eng/hn01768.html.
61 OECD. Science, technology and industry scoreboard 2005 [Internet]. Paris (France): OECD; c2005 [cited 2014 Sept 24]. Available from: http://www.oecd-ilibrary.org/science-and-technology/oecd-science-technology-and-industry-scoreboard-2005_sti_scoreboard-2005-en.
62 OECD. Science, technology and industry scoreboard 2009 [Internet]. Paris (France): OECD; c2009 [cited 2014 Sept 24]. Available from: http://www.oecd-ilibrary.org/science-and-technology/oecd-science-technology-and-industry-scoreboard-2009_sti_scoreboard-2009-en.
63 Kalant N, Shrier I. Research output of the Canadian pharmaceutical industry: where has all the R&D gone? Healthc Policy. 2006;1(4):21–34. Medline:19305677

64 Brydon R, Chesterley N, Dachis B, et al. Measuring innovation in Canada: the tale told by patent applications. Toronto: CD Howe Institute; 2014.
65 The Expert Panel on the State of Industrial R&D in Canada. The state of industrial R&D in Canada. Ottawa: Council of Canadian Academies; 2013.
66 Patented Medicine Prices Review Board. Patentee's guide to reporting – Form 3: licensees, revenues and expenditures [Internet]. Ottawa: PMPRB; c2012 [cited 2014 Sept 24]. Available from: http://www.pmprb-cepmb.gc.ca/view.asp?ccid=523#816.
67 KPMG. Summary of 2013 R&D spending and investments by Rx&D members. Toronto: KPMG; 2014.
68 Rx&D. Chronic under-reporting of investment works against Canada [Internet]. Ottawa: Canada's Research-Based Pharmaceutical Companies; c2014 [cited 2014 Sept 24]. Available from: http://sharing.canadapharma.org/News.asp?a=view&id=94.
69 Rx&D. PMPRB annual report a clear indication that Canada must move on global competitiveness [Internet]. Ottawa: Canada's Research-Based Pharmaceutical Companies; c2014 [cited 2014 Sept 24]. Available from: http://sharing.canadapharma.org/News.asp?a=view&id=96.
70 Gagnon M-A, Wolfe S. Mirror, mirror on the wall: Medicare Part D pays needlessly high brand-name drug prices compared with other OECD countries and with U.S. government programs. Ottawa: Carleton University; 2015.
71 Bramley-Harker E, Lewis D, Farahnik J, et al. Key factors in attracting internationally mobile investments by the research-based pharmaceutical industry. London (England): NERA Economic Consulting; 2007.
72 Expert Advisory Committee on Smart Regulation. Smart regulation: a regulatory strategy for Canada: Report to the Government of Canada. Ottawa: External Advisory Committee on Smart Regulation; 2004.
73 Health Products and Food Branch. Blueprint for renewal II: modernizing Canada's regulatory system for health products and food. Ottawa: Health Canada; 2007.
74 International Society of Drug Bulletins. ISDB declaration on therapeutic advance in the use of medicines. Paris (France): ISDB; 2001.
75 Kesselheim AS, Wang B, Avorn J. Defining "innovativeness" in drug development: a systematic review. Clin Pharmacol Ther. 2013;94(3):336–48. http://dx.doi.org/10.1038/clpt.2013.115. Medline:23722626
76 Yasuda SU, Woosley RL. The clinical value of FDA class C drugs approved from 1981 to 1988. Clin Pharmacol Ther. 1992;52(6):577–82. http://dx.doi.org/10.1038/clpt.1992.194. Medline:1458766

77 Lexchin J. Postmarket safety in Canada: are significant therapeutic advances and biologics less safe than other drugs? A cohort study. BMJ Open. 2014;4(2):e004289. http://dx.doi.org/10.1136/bmjopen-2013-004289. Medline:24549164

78 Prescrire Editorial Staff. New drugs and indications in 2013: little real progress but regulatory authorities take some positive steps. Prescrire Int. 2014;23(148):107–10. Medline:24860905

79 Medical Research Council of Canada. The Medical Research Council of Canada and the pharmaceutical patent legislation. Ottawa: Medical Research Council of Canada; 1987.

80 Baird PA. Funding medical and health-related research in the public interest. CMAJ. 1996;155(3):299–301. Medline:8705910

81 Matthews JH. Relationships between the academic community and the pharmaceutical industry: the legislative background and its effect on spending on medical research and development. Clin Invest Med. 1996;19(6):470–8. Medline:8959357

82 Berkowitz P. After slow start, project to channel drug company funds to universities builds steam. CMAJ. 1996;155(3):318–20. Medline:8705914

83 Kondro W. Canada's MRC and drug industry try to make amends. Lancet. 1996;347(9013):1478. http://dx.doi.org/10.1016/S0140-6736(96)91713-4.

84 Kondro W. Canadian MRC encourages private sector partnership. Lancet. 1995;346(8987):1417. http://dx.doi.org/10.1016/S0140-6736(95)92420-5.

85 Medical Research Council of Canada. Investing in Canada's health. A strategic plan for the Medical Research Council of Canada. Ottawa: Medical Research Council of Canada; 1992.

86 Friesen HG. The MRC: meeting the challenges of tomorrow. CMAJ. 1993;148(12):2127–8. Medline:8324685

87 Kraicer J. Response to the MRC's strategic plan. CMAJ. 1993;148(12):2137–9. Medline:8324687

88 Canadian Institutes of Health Research. Summary report of the interim evaluative study of the CIHR/Rx&D program [Internet]. Ottawa: CIHR; c2005 [cited 2014 Sept 26]. Available from: http://www.cihr-irsc.gc.ca/e/34742.html.

89 Bernstein A. Toward effective Canadian public-private partnerships in health research. CMAJ. 2003;168(3):288–9. Medline:12566334

90 Canadian Institutes of Health Research Act, Stat. S.C. 2000, c. 6 (2012).

91 Tyers M, Brown E, Andrews DW, et al. Problems with co-funding in Canada. Science. 2005;308(5730):1867. http://dx.doi.org/10.1126/science.308.5730.1867b. Medline:15976286

92 Canadian Institutes of Health Research. Health research roadmap: creating innovative research for better health and healthcare – CIHR's strategic plan 2009/10–2013/14 draft. Ottawa: CIHR; 2009.
93 Labonte R, Schrecker T. Open letter to Alain Beaudet, president CIHR. Ottawa: 2009 May 22.
94 Government of Canada. Mobilizing science and technology to Canada's advantage. Ottawa: Industry Canada; 2007.
95 Lewis S. Neoliberalism, conflict of interest, and the governance of health research in Canada. Open Med. 2010;4(1):e28–e30. Medline:21686290
96 Silversides A. Appointment of Pfizer executive to CIHR stirs controversy. CMAJ. 2009;181(11):E256–7. http://dx.doi.org/10.1503/cmaj.109-3085. Medline:19858244
97 Silversides A. Withdrawal of clinical trials policy by Canadian research institute is a "lost opportunity for increased transparency." BMJ. 2011;342(apr21 1):d2570. http://dx.doi.org/10.1136/bmj.d2570. Medline:21511787
98 Baylis F, Downie J. "Confusion worse confounded" [Rapid response]. BMJ. 2011;342:d2570. Available from: http://www.bmj.com/rapid-response/2011/11/03/confusion-worse-confounded-1.
99 Schafer A. Biomedical conflicts of interest: a defence of the sequestration thesis - learning from the cases of Nancy Olivieri and David Healy. Journal of Medical Ethics 2004;30:8–24.
100 Statistics Canada. Survey of intellectual property commercialization in the higher education sector. Ottawa; 2008.
101 Downie J, Herder M. Reflections on the commercialization of research conducted in public institutions in Canada. McGill J Law Health. 2007;1:23–44.
102. Stewart J. U of S adds research chair: pharmaceutical companies contribute to new position. Star Phoenix. 2009 Jun 16; Sect. A:3.
103 University of British Columbia Pharmaceutical Sciences. Professorship in sustainable health care established at UBC [Internet]. Vancouver: Faculty of Pharmaceutical Sciences; c2015 [cited 2015 Feb 24]. Available from: http://news.ubc.ca/2015/01/20/professorship-in-sustainable-health-care-established-at-ubc/.
104 Williams-Jones B, MacDonald C. Conflict of interest policies at Canadian universities: clarity and content. J Acad Ethics. 2008;6(1):79–90. http://dx.doi.org/10.1007/s10805-007-9052-6.
105 Lexchin J, Sekeres M, Gold J, et al. National evaluation of policies on individual financial conflicts of interest in Canadian academic health

science centers. J Gen Intern Med. 2008;23(11):1896–903. http://dx.doi.org/10.1007/s11606-008-0752-4. Medline:18716848

106 Rochon PA, Sekeres M, Lexchin J, et al. Institutional financial conflicts of interest policies at Canadian academic health science centres: a national survey. Open Med. 2010;4(3):e134–8. Medline:21687332

107 Rochon PA, Sekeres M, Hoey J, et al. Investigator experiences with financial conflicts of interest in clinical trials. Trials. 2011;12(1):9. http://dx.doi.org/10.1186/1745-6215-12-9. Medline:21226951

108 Shnier A, Lexchin J, Mintzes B, et al. Too few, too weak: conflict of interest policies at Canadian medical schools. PLoS One. 2013;8(7):e68633. http://dx.doi.org/10.1371/journal.pone.0068633. Medline:23861928

109 Blumenthal D, Gluck M, Louis KS, et al. University-industry research relationships in biotechnology: implications for the university. Science. 1986;232(4756):1361–6. http://dx.doi.org/10.1126/science.3715452. Medline:3715452

110 Blumenthal D, Campbell EG, Causino N, et al. Participation of life-science faculty in research relationships with industry. N Engl J Med. 1996;335(23):1734–9. http://dx.doi.org/10.1056/NEJM199612053352305. Medline:8929266

111 Zinner DE, Bolcic-Jankovic D, Clarridge B, et al. Participation of academic scientists in relationships with industry. Health Aff (Millwood). 2009;28(6):1814–25. http://dx.doi.org/10.1377/hlthaff.28.6.1814. Medline:19887423

112 Lewis S, Baird P, Evans RG, et al. Dancing with the porcupine: rules for governing the university-industry relationship. CMAJ. 2001;165(6):783–5. Medline:11584569

9. Canada, the pharmaceutical industry, and access to medicines in the Global South

1 Lu Y, Hernandez P, Abergunde D, et al. The world medicines situation 2011: medicine expenditure. Geneva (Switzerland): WHO; 2011.

2 Niëns LM, Cameron A, Van de Poel E, et al. Quantifying the impoverishing effects of purchasing medicines: a cross-country comparison of the affordability of medicines in the developing world. PLoS Med. 2010;7(8):e1000333. http://dx.doi.org/10.1371/journal.pmed.1000333. Medline:20824175

3 Cameron A, Ewen M, Ross-Degnan D, et al. Medicine prices, availability, and affordability in 36 developing and middle-income countries: a secondary

analysis. Lancet. 2009;373(9659):240–9. http://dx.doi.org/10.1016/S0140-6736(08)61762-6. Medline:19042012
4 Office of the High Commissioner for Human Rights. International covenant on economic, social and cultural rights. Geneva, Switzerland: OHCHR; 1966.
5 Blouin C, Foster J, Labonte R. Canada's foreign policy and health: toward policy coherence. In: Sanger M, Sinclair S, editors. Canadian health care reform in a globalizing world. Ottawa: Canadian Centre for Policy Alternatives; 2004. p. 93–182.
6 Commission on the Future of Health Care in Canada. Building on values: the future of health care in Canada – final report. Ottawa: Commission on the Future of Health Care in Canada; 2002.
7 Susser M. Health as a human right: an epidemiologist's perspective on the public health. Am J Public Health. 1993;83(3):418–26. http://dx.doi.org/10.2105/AJPH.83.3.418. Medline:8438984
8 't Hoen E. The global politics of pharmaceutical monopoly power: drug patents, access, innovation and the application of the WTO Doha Declaration on TRIPS and public health. Diement. Netherlands: AMB Publishers; 2009.
9 Lanjouw JO, Cockburn IM. New pills for poor people? Empirical evidence after GATT. World Dev. 2001;29(2):265–89. http://dx.doi.org/10.1016/S0305-750X(00)00099-1.
10 Campaign for Access to Essential Medicines. Untangling the web of antiretroviral price reductions. 13th ed. Geneva (Switzerland): Médecins Sans Frontières; 2010.
11 Campaign for Access to Essential Medicines. Untangling the web of antiretroviral price reductions. 14th ed. Geneva (Switzerland): Médecins Sans Frontières; 2011.
12 't Hoen E. TRIPS, pharmaceutical patents, and access to essential medicines: a long way from Seattle to Doha. Chic J Int Law. 2002;3(1):27–46. Medline:15709298
13 Government of Canada. Canadian initial sectoral/modal/horizontal negotiating proposals: General Agreement on Trade in Services [Internet]. Ottawa: Department of Foreign Affairs and International Trade. c2001 [cited 2013 Mar 3]. Available from: http://jmcti.org/2000round/build-in-agenda/service/S_CSS_W_046.pdf
14 World Trade Organization. Canada – patent protection of pharmaceutical products: report of the panel (WT/DS114/R). Geneva (Switzerland): WHO; 2000.

15 Pettigrew, P. Canada's objectives for the fourth WTO ministerial conference. Ottawa: Committee on Foreign Affairs and International Trade; 2001.
16 Department of Foreign Affairs and International Trade. WTO consultations Doha (Qatar) ministerial meeting: intellectual property rights – information paper. Ottawa: Department of Foreign Affairs and International Trade; 2001.
17 Foss K. Patent war looming over drug for anthrax decision asking manufacturer to infringe necessary for Canadians' safety, Rock says. Globe and Mail. 2001 Oct 19; Sect. A:1.
18 EU and US split over scope of TRIPS exceptions for public health [Internet]. Inside US Trade; c2002 [updated 2002 Mar 8; cited 2013 Jun 1]. Available from: https://web.archive.org/web/20040130145741/http://lists.essential.org/pipermail/ip-health/2002-March/002764.html.
19 Nolen S. Spearhead AIDS fight, UN envoy tells Canada. Globe and Mail. 2003 Sept 25; Sect. A:1.
20 Chase S, Fagan D. Drug companies balk at Ottawa's AIDS plan. Globe and Mail. 2003 Sept 27; Sect. A:1.
21 Rx&D. Partnership for developing countries. Ottawa: Rx&D; 2003.
22 Rx&D. Providing affordable medicines to patients in the developing world: a submission to the House of Commons Standing Committee on Industry, Science and Technology regarding Bill C-9. Ottawa: Rx&D; 2004.
23 Canadian HIV/AIDS Legal Network. Global access to medicines: will Canada meet the challenge? Supplementary submission to the Standing Committee on Industry, Science and Technology on Bill C-9, an act to amend the Patent Act and the Food and Drugs Act. Toronto: Canadian HIV/AIDS Legal Network; 2004.
24 Esmail LC, Kohler JC. The politics behind the implementation of the WTO Paragraph 6 Decision in Canada to increase global drug access. Global Health. 2012;8(1):7. http://dx.doi.org/10.1186/1744-8603-8-7. Medline:22472291
25 Chami G, Wasswa-Kintu S. Compulsory licensing of generic drugs remains mired in quagmires. CMAJ. 2011;183(11):E705–6. http://dx.doi.org/10.1503/cmaj.109-3898. Medline:21708968
26 Kohler JC, Lexchin J, Kuek V, et al. Canada's Access to Medicines Regime: promise or failure of humanitarian effort? Healthc Policy. 2010;5(3):40–8. Medline:21286267
27 Priest L. Pressure mounts to keep injection site. Globe and Mail. 2006 Aug 16; Sect. A:7.
28 Government of Canada. Report on the statutory review of sections 21.01 to 21.19 of the patent act. Ottawa: Industry Canada; 2007.

29 Galloway G. Tony Clement urges senators to block generic-drug legislation. Globe and Mail. [Internet]. 2011 Mar 24.
30 Canadian HIV/AIDS Legal Network, Grandmothers Advocacy Network. Fixing Canada's Access to Medicines Regime (CAMR): what you need to know about Bill C-398 [Internet]. Toronto: Canadian HIV/AIDS Legal Network; c2012 [cited 2013 Jun 3]. Available from: http://www.aidslaw.ca/site/fixing-canadas-access-to-medicines-regime-camr-what-you-need-to-know-about-bill-c-398/
31 Canadian HIV/AIDS Legal Network. Fixing Canada's access to medicines regime: Bill C-393 up for final vote in House of Commons in early March. Toronto: Canadian HIV/AIDS Legal Network; 2011.
32 Galloway G. Tories block bid to make cheaper medicines for poor nations. Globe and Mail. 2012 Nov 28; Sect. A:4.
33 Freudenberg N. Lethal but legal: corporations, consumption, and protecting public health. New York: Oxford University Press; 2014.
34 International Diabetes Federation. Diabetes and climate change report. Brussels (Belgium): International Diabetes Foundation; 2012.
35 World Health Organization. The world health report: 2003 – shaping the future. Geneva (Switzerland): World Health Organization; 2003.
36 Beaglehole R, Bonita R, Alleyne G, et al, and the Lancet NCD Action Group. UN High-Level Meeting on Non-Communicable Diseases: addressing four questions. Lancet. 2011;378(9789):449–55. http://dx.doi.org/10.1016/S0140-6736(11)60879-9. Medline:21665266
37 UN General Assembly. Political declaration of the high-level meeting of the general assembly on the prevention and control of non-communicable diseases (A/66/L.1) [Internet]. New York: United Nations; c2011 [cited 2013 Jun 3]. Available from: http://www.un.org/ga/search/view_doc.asp?symbol=A/66/L.1.
38 WHO IMPACT. Counterfeit medicines: an update on estimates [Internet]. Geneva (Switzerland): WHO; c2006 [cited 2013 Jun 3]. Available from: http://www.who.int/medicines/services/counterfeit/impact/TheNewEstimatesCounterfeit.pdf.
39 Attaran A, Barry D, Basheer S, et al. How to achieve international action on falsified and substandard medicines. BMJ. 2012;345(nov13 22):e7381. http://dx.doi.org/10.1136/bmj.e7381. Medline:23149211
40 Clift C. Combating counterfeit, falsified and substandard medicines: defining the way forward? London (England): Chatham House; 2010.
41 McManis CR. The proposed anti-counterfeiting trade agreement (ACTA): two tales of a treaty. Houst Law Rev. 2009;46:1235–56.

42 Health Action International. ACTA and access to medicines: a flawed process, flawed rationale and flawed agreement. Amsterdam (Netherlands): Health Action International – Europe; 2012.
43 Foreign Affairs and International Trade Canada. Anti-counterfeiting trade agreement (ACTA): ACTA and issues related to pharmaceuticals and counterfeit medicines [Internet]. Ottawa: Foreign Affairs and International Trade Canada; c2013 [cited 2013 Jun 10]. Available from: http://www.international.gc.ca/trade-agreements-accords-commerciaux/topics-domaines/ip-pi/consult-01.aspx?lang=eng.
44 Williams R. Letter to: Consultations and Liaison Division Anti-Counterfeiting Trade Agreement Foreign Affairs and International Trade Canada. Re: proposed anti-counterfeiting trade agreement; 2008.
45 Foreign Affairs and International Trade Canada. Canada signs historic anti-counterfeiting trade agreement [Internet]. Ottawa: Foreign Affairs and International Trade Canada; c2011 [cited 2013 Jun 10]. Available from: http://www.international.gc.ca/media_commerce/comm/news-communiques/2011/280.aspx?lang=eng.
46 European parliament rejection puts ACTA future in doubt [Internet]. Geneva (Switzerland): Intellectual Property Watch; c2012 [cited 2013 Jun 10]. Available from: http://www.ip-watch.org/2012/07/04/european-parliament-rejection-puts-acta-future-in-doubt/print/.
47 United Nations Conference on Trade and Development. The least developed countries report 2014 [Internet]. Geneva: UN; c2014 [cited 2016 Mar 14]. Available from: http://unctad.org/en/PublicationsLibrary/ldc2014_en.pdf.
48 Merso F. IP trends in African LDCs and the LDC TRIPS transition extension (Policy Brief No. 16). Geneva (Switzerland): ICTSD; 2013.
49 Global Commission on HIV and the Law. Risks, rights & health. New York: UNDP, HIV/AIDS Group; 2012.
50 Poorest nations held hostage by US/EU demands on TRIPS compliance TWN Info Service on Intellectual Property Issues [Internet]. Penang (Malaysia): Third World Network; c2013 [cited 2013 Jun 13]. Available from: http://www.twn.my/title2/intellectual_property/info.service/2013/ipr.info.130510.htm.
51 Abbott F. Technical note: the LDC TRIPS transition extension and the question of rollback (Policy Brief No. 15). Geneva (Switzerland): ICTSD; 2013.
52 South Centre welcomes WTO decision on LDCs and TRIPs [Internet]. Geneva (Switzerland): SouthNews; c2013 [cited 2013 Jun 13]. Available from: http://us5.campaign-archive1.com/?u=fa9cf38799136b5660f367ba6&id=f361a375e7.

53 The least developed get eight years more leeway on protecting intellectual property [Internet]. Geneva (Switzerland): World Trade Organization; 2013 [cited 2013 June 14]. Available from: https://www.wto.org/english/news_e/news13_e/trip_11jun13_e.htm.
54 EU welcomes TRIPS extension for LDCs [Internet]. Geneva (Switzerland): Permanent Mission of the European Union to the World Trade Organization; c2013 [cited 2013 Jun 18]. Available from: http://eeas.europa.eu/delegations/wto/press_corner/all_news/news/2013/eu_welcomes_trips_extension_for_ldcs_en.htm.
55 't Hoen E. Inside views: why the request by least developed countries for an extension of the transitional period for granting and enforcing medicines patents needs to be supported [Internet]. Geneva (Switzerland): Intellectual Property Watch; c2015 [cited 2015 Dec 29]. Available from: http://www.ip-watch.org/2015/02/27/why-the-request-by-least-developed-countries-for-an-extension-of-the-transitional-period-for-granting-and-enforcing-medicines-patents-needs-to-be-supported/.
56 Shashikant S. US stands in the way of LDCs' pharmaceutical transition period [Internet]. Washington (DC): American University Washington College of Law; c2015 [cited 2015 Dec 29]. Available from: http://infojustice.org/archives/35171.
57 Gulland A. Poor countries press for extension of exemption from drug patents. BMJ. 2015;351:h5605. http://dx.doi.org/10.1136/bmj.h5605. Medline:26486820
58 US, AU and CA try to block WTO LDC drug patent waiver because PhRMA's not happy enough with the TPP [Internet]. Washington (DC): Knowledge Ecology International; c2015 [updated 2015 Oct 12; cited 2015 Dec 29]. Available from: http://keionline.org/node/2337.
59 Shashikant S. Unconditional 17-year exemption from pharmaceuticals patents agreed [Internet]. Penang (Malaysia): Third World Network; c2015 [updated November 15; cited 2015 Dec 29]. Available from: http://www.twn.my/title2/wto.info/2015/ti151102.htm.
60 Government donors [Internet]. Geneva (Switzerland): The Global Fund to Fight AIDS, Tuberculosis and Malaria; c2013 [cited 2013 Jun 12]. Available from: http://www.theglobalfund.org/en/government/.
61 Moran M, Guzman J, Henderson K, et al. Neglected disease research and development: is the global financial crisis changing R&D? Sydney (Australia): Policy Cures; 2011.
62 Rx&D. Global compassion: improving access to medicines in the developing world [Internet]. Ottawa: Canada's Research-Based Pharmaceuticals Companies; c2013 [cited 2014 Oct 12]. Available from: http://

innovativemedicines.ca/wp-content/uploads/2015/05/RxD_2596_AccesstoMedicines_En_web.pdf.
63 Waning B, Kaplan W, King AC, et al. Global strategies to reduce the price of antiretroviral medicines: evidence from transactional databases. Bull World Health Organ. 2009;87(7):520–8. http://dx.doi.org/10.2471/BLT.08.058925. Medline:19649366
64 Walwyn D. Patents and profits: A disparity of manufacturing margins in the tenofovir value chain. Afr J AIDS Res. 2013;12(1):17–23. http://dx.doi.org/10.2989/16085906.2013.815407. Medline:25871307
65 SanJuan J, Malpani R. The price of joining the middle income country club: reduced access to medical innovation [Internet]. London (England): BMJ Blog; c2014 [cited 2014 Oct 13]. Available from: http://blogs.bmj.com/bmj/2014/10/10/judit-rius-sanjuan-and-rohit-malpani-the-price-of-joining-the-middle-income-country-club/.
66 "We didn't make this medicine for Indians … we made it for western patients who can afford it": pharmaceutical chief tries to stop India replicating its cancer treatment. DailyMailOnline [Internet]; c2014 [updated 2014 Jan 24; cited 2014 Oct 12]. Available from: http://www.dailymail.co.uk/news/article-2545360/Pharmaceutical-chief-tries-stop-India-replicating-cancer-treatment.html.
67 Lanjouw J, Jack W. Trading up: how much should poor countries pay to support pharmaceutical innovation? CGD Brief. 2004;4(3):1–8.
68 Commission on Intellectual Property Rights. Integrating intellectual property rights and development policy. London (England): Commission on Intellectual Property Rights; 2002.
69 Chirac P, Torreele E. Global framework on essential health R&D. Lancet. 2006;367(9522):1560–1. http://dx.doi.org/10.1016/S0140-6736(06)68672-8. Medline:16698397
70 Gabriel P, Goulding R, Morgan-Jonker C, et al. Fostering Canadian drug research and development for neglected tropical diseases. Open Med. 2010;4(2):e117– e122. Medline:21709722
71 Moran M, Ropars A-L, Guzman J, et al. The new landscape of neglected disease drug development. London: Wellcome Trust; 2005.
72 Jack A. Novartis chief in warning on cheap drugs. Financial Times. 2006 Sept 30. p. 8.
73 Park W. Intellectual property rights and international innovation. In: Mascus K, editor. Frontiers of economics and globalization. 1. Elsevier Science; 2007. p. 289–327.
74 Kyle MK, McGahan AM. Investments in pharmaceuticals before and after TRIPS. Rev Econ Stat. 2012;94(4):1157–72. http://dx.doi.org/10.1162/REST_a_00214.

75 Palmedo M. Do pharmaceutical firms invest more heavily in countries with data exclusivity? Currents. 2013;21:38–47. Available from: http://papers.ssrn.com/sol3/papers.cfm?abstract_id=2259797

76 Mendis S, Fukino K, Cameron A, et al. The availability and affordability of selected essential medicines for chronic diseases in six low- and middle-income countries. Bull World Health Organ. 2007;85(4):279–88. http://dx.doi.org/10.2471/BLT.06.033647. Medline:17546309

10. Courage, my friends; 'tis not too late to build a better world

1 Douglas-Coldwell Foundation. Support the DCF in promoting education and research in social democracy! [Internet]. Ottawa: Douglas-Coldwell Foundation; [cited 2016 Mar 14]. Available from: http://www.dcf.ca/index_en.htm.

2 Davis C, Abraham J. Unhealthy pharmaceutical regulation: innovation, politics and promissory science. New York: Palgrave Macmillan; 2013. http://dx.doi.org/10.1057/9781137349477.

3 Lang R. The politics of drugs: a comparative pressure-group study of the Canadian Pharmaceutical Manufacturers Association and the Association of the British Pharmaceutical Industry, 1930–1970. Westmead (England): Saxon House; 1974.

4 Friedman M. Capitalism and freedom. Chicago: University of Chicago Press; 1962.

5 Lessig L. Foreword: "Institutional corruption" defined. J Law Med Ethics. 2013;41(3):553–5. http://dx.doi.org/10.1111/jlme.12063. Medline:24088144

6 Avorn J. Paying for drug approvals–who's using whom? N Engl J Med. 2007;356(17):1697–700. http://dx.doi.org/10.1056/NEJMp078041. Medline:17435083

7 Department of Health and Human Services. Food and Drug Administration: fiscal year 2015 justification of estimates for appropriations committees. Silver Spring (MD): FDA; 2015.

8 Wiktorowicz M, Lexchin J, Moscou K, et al. Keeping an eye on prescription drugs ... keeping Canadians safe: active monitoring systems for drug safety and effectiveness in Canada and internationally. Toronto: Health Council of Canada; 2010.

9 World Health Organization. International standards for clinical trial registries [Internet]. Geneva (Switzerland): WHO Press; c2012 [cited 2014 Nov 8]. Available from: http://apps.who.int/iris/bitstream/10665/76705/1/9789241504294_eng.pdf?ua=1&ua=1.

10 World Health Organization. WHO statement on public disclosure of clinical trial results [Internet]. Geneva (Switzerland): WHO Press; c2014 [cited 2014 Nov 8]. Available from: http://www.who.int/ictrp/results/Draft_WHO_Statement_results_reporting_clinical_trials.pdf?ua=1.

11 Law MR, Kawasumi Y, Morgan SG. Despite law, fewer than one in eight completed studies of drugs and biologics are reported on time on ClinicalTrials.gov. Health Aff (Millwood). 2011;30(12):2338–45. http://dx.doi.org/10.1377/hlthaff.2011.0172. Medline:22147862

12 Wieseler B, Wolfram N, McGauran N, et al. Completeness of reporting of patient-relevant clinical trial outcomes: comparison of unpublished clinical study reports with publicly available data. PLoS Medicine. 2013;10:e1001526. http://dx.doi.org/10.1371/journal.pmed.1001526.

13 Schwartz LM, Woloshin S. Lost in transmission–FDA drug information that never reaches clinicians. N Engl J Med. 2009;361(18):1717–20. http://dx.doi.org/10.1056/NEJMp0907708. Medline:19846841

14 Woloshin S, Schwartz LM. Bringing the FDA's information to market. Arch Intern Med. 2009;169(21):1985–7. http://dx.doi.org/10.1001/archinternmed.2009.399. Medline:19933960

15 Barnett V. Drug hearings shouldn't be held in secret. Calg Her. 1986 Sept 11;Sect. A:8.

16 U.S. Department of Health and Human Services. Guidance for the public, FDA advisory committee members, and FDA staff: the open public hearing at FDA advisory committee meetings [Internet]. Silver Spring (MD): Food and Drug Administration; c2013 [cited 2014 Nov 8]. Available from: http://www.fda.gov/downloads/RegulatoryInformation/Guidances/UCM236144.pdf.

17 Wood AJ, Drazen JM, Greene MF. A sad day for science at the FDA. N Engl J Med. 2005;353(12):1197–9. http://dx.doi.org/10.1056/NEJMp058222. Medline:16141387

18 Pham-Kanter G. Revisiting financial conflicts of interest in FDA advisory committees. Milbank Q. 2014;92(3):446–70. http://dx.doi.org/10.1111/1468-0009.12073. Medline:25199895

19 O'Riordan M. "Mistakes" made: FDA acknowledges Lilly phoned to question Sanjay Kaul's inclusion on Prasugrel panel [Internet]. New York: Medscape cardiology; c2009 [cited 2015 Mar 3]. Available from: http://www.medscape.com/viewarticle/588550.

20 Lurie P, Almeida CM, Stine N, et al. Financial conflict of interest disclosure and voting patterns at Food and Drug Administration Drug Advisory Committee meetings. JAMA. 2006;295(16):1921–8. http://dx.doi.org/10.1001/jama.295.16.1921. Medline:16639051

21 Abraham J, Sheppard J. Democracy, technocracy, and the secret state of medicines control: expert and nonexpert perspectives. Sci Technol Human Values. 1997;22(2):139–67. http://dx.doi.org/10.1177/016224399702200201. Medline:11657435
22 National Institute for Health and Care Excellence. Citizens Council [Internet]. London (England): NICE; c2014 [cited 2014 Nov 18]. Available from: http://www.nice.org.uk/get-involved/citizens-council.
23 Garattini S, Bertele' V. Non-inferiority trials are unethical because they disregard patients' interests. Lancet. 2007;370(9602):1875–7. http://dx.doi.org/10.1016/S0140-6736(07)61604-3. Medline:17959239
24 Buurma H, Bodewitz H, Wieringa N, et al. Drug registration policy and therapeutic use of beta-blockers in The Netherlands and Norway. J Soc Adm Pharm. 1984;2:145–51.
25 Dukes MN, Lunde I. The regulatory control of non-steroidal anti-inflammatory agents. Eur J Clin Pharmacol. 1981;19(1):3–10. http://dx.doi.org/10.1007/BF00558371. Medline:7461020
26 Garattini S. Are me-too drugs justified? J Nephrol. 1997;10(6):283–94. Medline:9442441
27 Sorenson C, Naci H, Cylus J, et al. Evidence of comparative efficacy should have a formal role in European drug approvals. BMJ. 2011;343(sep06 1):d4849. http://dx.doi.org/10.1136/bmj.d4849. Medline:21896610
28 Overstreet R, Berger J, Maszczak W. Evaluation assessment study: drug safety, quality and efficacy. Volume II: evaluation approaches. Ottawa: Health and Welfare Canada; 1987.
29 Svensson S, Menkes DB, Lexchin J. Surrogate outcomes in clinical trials: a cautionary tale. JAMA Intern Med. 2013;173(8):611–12. http://dx.doi.org/10.1001/jamainternmed.2013.3037. Medline:23529157
30 Maynard A. Regulating the market for corruption in the pharmaceutical industry. 2001.
31 Schafer A. Biomedical conflicts of interest: a defence of the sequestration thesis – learning from the cases of Nancy Olivieri and David Healy. J Med Ethics. 2004;30:8–24. http://dx.doi.org/10.1136/jme.2003.005702.
32 Lewis TR, Reichman JH, So AD. The case for public funding and public oversight of clinical trials. Economists Voice. 2007;4(1):1–4. http://dx.doi.org/10.2202/1553-3832.1123.
33 Baker D. The benefits and savings from publicly funded clinical trials of prescription drugs. Int J Health Serv. 2008;38(4):731–50. http://dx.doi.org/10.2190/HS.38.4.i. Medline:19069290
34 ALLHAT Officers and Coordinators for the ALLHAT Collaborative Research Group. Major outcomes in high-risk hypertensive patients

randomized to angiotensin-converting enzyme inhibitor or calcium channel blocker vs diuretic: The antihypertensive and lipid-lowering treatment to prevent heart attack trial (ALLHAT). JAMA. 2002;288(23):2981–97. http://dx.doi.org/10.1001/jama.288.23.2981. Medline:12479763

35 Italian Medicines Agency (AIFA) Research & Development Working Group. Feasibility and challenges of independent research on drugs: the Italian medicines agency (AIFA) experience. Eur J Clin Invest. 2010;40(1):69–86. http://dx.doi.org/10.1111/j.1365-2362.2009.02226.x. Medline:20055898

36 Kiester M. DDMAC submissions [Internet]. Horsham (PA): Drug Information Association; c2011 [cited 2012 Jun 18]. Available from: https://web.archive.org/web/20120106035805/http://www.fda.gov/downloads/Drugs/DevelopmentApprovalProcess/FormsSubmissionRequirements/ElectronicSubmissions/UCM246563.pdf

37 Thaul S. Direct-to-consumer advertising of prescription drugs (R40590). Washington (DC): Congressional Research Service, Library of Congress; 2009.

38 Government Accounting Office. Prescription drugs: FDA's oversight of the promotion of drugs for off-label uses. Washington (DC): Government Accounting Office; 2008.

39 Roughead EE, Gilbert AL, Harvey KJ. Self-regulatory codes of conduct: are they effective in controlling pharmaceutical representatives' presentations to general medical practitioners? Int J Health Serv. 1998;28(2):269–79. http://dx.doi.org/10.2190/B81X-4A53-TY5M-C2HR. Medline:9595344

40 Othman N, Vitry A, Roughead EE. Quality of pharmaceutical advertisements in medical journals: a systematic review. PLoS One. 2009;4(7):e6350. http://dx.doi.org/10.1371/journal.pone.0006350. Medline:19623259

41 Ayres I, Braithwaite J. Responsive regulation. Transcending the deregulation debate. New York: Oxford University Press; 1992.

42 Lexchin J. Models for financing the regulation of pharmaceutical promotion. Global Health. 2012;8(1):24. http://dx.doi.org/10.1186/1744-8603-8-24. Medline:22784944

43 Gough S. Post-marketing surveillance: a UK/European perspective. Curr Med Res Opin. 2005;21(4):565–70. http://dx.doi.org/10.1185/030079905X41426. Medline:15899105

44 Medsafe: New Zealand Medicines and Medical Devices Safety Authority. New Zealand Regulatory Guidelines for Medicines. Volume 1: Guidance notes for applicants for consent to distribute new and changed medicines and related products [Internet]. (NZ): Ministry of Health; c2001 [cited 2008 February 19]. Fifth edition:[Available from: https://web.archive.

org/web/20061228182317/http://www.medsafe.govt.nz/Regulatory/Guideline/medicines.asp

45 Heeley E, Wilton LV, Shakir SAW. Automated signal generation in prescription-event monitoring. Drug Saf. 2002;25(6):423–32. http://dx.doi.org/10.2165/00002018-200225060-00006. Medline:12071779

46 Paterson M. Overview of novel drug plan and drug regulatory pharmacovigilance initiatives in the United States, United Kingdom, and select other jurisdictions. A background paper prepared for the Working Conference on Strengthening the Evaluation of Real World Drug Safety and Effectiveness; 2005 Sept 13–15; Toronto: Institute for Clinical Evaluative Sciences.

47 Key C, Layton D, Shakir SA. Results of a postal survey of the reasons for non-response by doctors in a Prescription Event Monitoring study of drug safety. Pharmacoepidemiol Drug Saf. 2002;11(2):143–8. http://dx.doi.org/10.1002/pds.690. Medline:11998539

48 Coulter DM. The New Zealand intensive medicines monitoring programme. Pharmacoepidemiol Drug Saf. 1998;7(2):79–90. http://dx.doi.org/10.1002/(SICI)1099-1557(199803/04)7:2<79::AID-PDS330>3.0.CO;2-1. Medline:15073731

49 Coulter DM. The New Zealand intensive medicines monitoring programme in pro-active safety surveillance. Pharmacoepidemiol Drug Saf. 2000;9(4):273–80. http://dx.doi.org/10.1002/1099-1557(200007/08)9:4<273::AID-PDS512>3.0.CO;2-T. Medline:19025828

50 Lexchin J. Involuntary medication: the possible effects of the Trans-Pacific Partnership on the cost and regulation of medicine in Canada. Ottawa: Canadian Centre for Policy Alternatives; 2016.

51 World Trade Organization. Compulsory licensing of pharmaceuticals and TRIPS [Internet]. Geneva (Switzerland); c2014 [cited 2014 Nov 11]. Available from: https://www.wto.org/english/tratop_e/trips_e/public_health_faq_e.htm.

52 World Trade Organization. Implementation of paragraph 6 of the Doha Declaration on the TRIPS Agreement and public health [Internet]. Geneva (Switzerland); c2003 [cited 2014 Nov 11]. Available from: http://www.who.int/medicines/areas/policy/WT_L_540_e.pdf?ua=1.

53 Attaran A. A modest but meaningful decision for Indian drug patents. Lancet. 2014;384(9942):477–9. http://dx.doi.org/10.1016/S0140-6736(13)60845-4. Medline:24976117

54 Husereau D, Jacobs P. Investigation and analysis of options to enhance Canada's patented medicine price ceiling regulatory regime. Edmonton: Institute of Health Economics; 2013.

55 Office of Fair Trading. Annexe D: global overview of the pharmaceutical industry [Internet]. London (England): OFT; c2007. Available from: http://www.med.mcgill.ca/epidemiology/courses/EPIB654/Summer2010/Pricing/oftd%20pharma.pdf
56 Patented Medicine Prices Review Board. Annual report 2013. Ottawa: PMPRB; 2014.
57 Pharmaceutical Management Agency. Purchasing medicines [Internet]. Wellington (NZ): PHARMAC; [cited 2014 Nov 12]. Available from: https://www.pharmac.govt.nz/assets/purchasing-medicines-information-sheet.pdf.
58 Pharmaceutical Management Agency. Annual review 2012. Wellington (NZ): PHARMAC; 2013.
59 Finkelstein S, Temin P. Reasonable Rx: solving the drug price crisis. Upper Saddle River: FT Press; 2008.
60 Chhina HK, Bhole VM, Goldsmith C, et al. Effectiveness of academic detailing to optimize medication prescribing behaviour of family physicians. J Pharm Pharm Sci. 2013;16(4):511–29. Medline:24210060
61 Jin M, Naumann T, Regier L, et al. A brief overview of academic detailing in Canada: Another role for pharmacists. Can Pharm J (Ott). 2012;145(3):142–146.e2. http://dx.doi.org/10.3821/145.3.cpj142. Medline:23509530
62 College of Physicians and Surgeons of Ontario. Jurisdictional research: prescription programs and information systems [Internet]. Toronto: CPSO; c2010 [cited 2014 Nov 13]. Available from: http://www.cpso.on.ca/uploadedfiles/policies/positions/jurisdictional_research.pdf.
63 O'Malley AS, Pham HH, Reschovsky JD. Predictors of the growing influence of clinical practice guidelines. J Gen Intern Med. 2007;22(6):742–8. http://dx.doi.org/10.1007/s11606-007-0155-y. Medline:17387556
64 Cosgrove L, Bursztajn H, Erlich D, et al. Conflicts of interest and the quality of recommendations in clinical guidelines. J Eval Clin Pract. 2013;19(4):674–81. http://dx.doi.org/10.1111/jep.12016. Medline:23731207
65 Agrawal S, Brennan N, Budetti P. The Sunshine Act–effects on physicians. N Engl J Med. 2013;368(22):2054–7. http://dx.doi.org/10.1056/NEJMp1303523. Medline:23718163
66 Wilson M. The Sunshine Act: commercial conflicts of interest and the limits of transparency. Open Med. 2014;8(1):e10–3. Medline:25009680
67 Office of Fair Trading. The pharmaceutical price regulation scheme: an OFT market study. London (England): OFT; 2007.
68 Bramley-Harker E, Lewis D, Farahnik J, et al. Key factors in attracting internationally mobile investments by the research-based pharmaceutical industry. London (England): NERA Economic Consulting; 2007.

69 Canadian Institutes of Health Research. CIHR internal assessment – report for the 2011 international review: long descriptions [Internet]. Ottawa: CIHR; c2011 [cited 2014 Nov 13]. Available from: http://www.cihr-irsc.gc.ca/e/44063.html.

70 National Institutes of Health. Mechanism detail – actual obligations FY 2000–FY 2011 [Internet]. Bethesda (MD): NIH; [cited 2014 Nov 13]. Available from: https://web.archive.org/web/20130215111157/http://officeofbudget.od.nih.gov/pdfs/FY13/spending list/Mechanism Detail for Total NIH FY 2000 - FY 2011.pdf.

71 Canadian Institutes of Health Research. Strategy for patient-oriented research: a discussion paper for a 10-year plan to change health care using the levers of research [Internet]. Ottawa: CIHR; c2010 [cited 2015 March 3]. Available from: http://www.cihr-irsc.gc.ca/e/41232.html.

72 Light D, Maturo A. Good pharma: the public-health model of the Mario Negri Institute. New York: Palgrave Macmillan; 2015. http://dx.doi.org/10.1057/9781137374332.

73 Moore, J. Canadian development aid no longer tied – just shackled to corporate mining interests [Internet]. Mining Watch; c2014 [cited 2014 Nov 23]. Available from: http://miningwatch.ca/blog/2014/3/27/canadian-development-aid-no-longer-tied-just-shackled-corporate-mining-interests.

74 Belluz J. Can asbestos be used "safely"? Maclean's [Internet]. c2011 [cited 2015 Mar 3]. Available from: http://www.macleans.ca/authors/julia-belluz/can-asbestos-be-used-safely/.

75 Hanington I. Canada's stand on desertification convention isolates us from the world [Internet]. Toronto: David Suzuki Foundation; c2013 [cited 2014 Nov 23]. Available from: http://www.davidsuzuki.org/blogs/panther-lounge/2013/03/canadas-stand-on-desertification-convention-isolates-us-from-the-world/.

76 Webster PC. Canada opposes harm reduction policies for drug users. CMAJ. 2014;186(4):256. http://dx.doi.org/10.1503/cmaj.109-4714. Medline:24491478

77 Bhushan A. Foreign aid and crises: examining 2012 aid data [Internet]. Ottawa: North-South Institute; c2013 [cited 2014 Nov 23]. Available from: http://www.nsi-ins.ca/wp-content/uploads/2013/05/2013-Foreign-Aid-and-Crises-Examining-2012-Aid-Data.pdf.

Index

Note: Page numbers with (t) refer to tables; numbers with (f) refer to figures; and numbers with (b) refer to boxes.

Printed and bound by CPI Group (UK) Ltd, Croydon, CR0 4YY
16/04/2025
14658338-0003